AF607981

GOODBYE *EROS*

Recasting Forms and Norms of Love in the Age of Cervantes

Goodbye *Eros*: Recasting Forms and Norms of Love in the Age of Cervantes

EDITED BY ANA MARÍA LAGUNA AND
JOHN BEUSTERIEN

UNIVERSITY OF TORONTO PRESS
Toronto Buffalo London

Toronto Buffalo London
utorontopress.com

ISBN 978-1-4875-0421-2 (cloth) ISBN 978-1-4875-1966-7 (PDF)
ISBN 978-1-4875-1967-4 (EPUB)

Library and Archives Canada Cataloguing in Publication

Title: Goodbye Eros : recasting forms and norms of love in the age of Cervantes / edited by Ana María Laguna and John Beusterien.
Names: Laguna, Ana María G., 1971– editor. | Beusterien, John, editor.
Series: Toronto Iberic ; 48.
Description: Series statement: Toronto Iberic ; 48 | Includes bibliographical references and index.
Identifiers: Canadiana (print) 20190223952 | Canadiana (ebook) 20190224010 | ISBN 9781487504212 (cloth) | ISBN 9781487519667 (PDF) | ISBN 9781487519674 (EPUB)
Subjects: LCSH: Spanish literature – Classical period, 1500–1700 – History and criticism. | LCSH: Love in literature.
Classification: LCC PQ6066 .G66 2020 | DDC 860.9/3543 – dc23

University of Toronto Press acknowledges the financial assistance to its publishing program of the Canada Council for the Arts and the Ontario Arts Council, an agency of the Government of Ontario.

Canada Council for the Arts
Conseil des Arts du Canada

Funded by the Government of Canada
Financé par le gouvernement du Canada
Canada

Contents

Illustrations

Acknowledgments

We would like to first and foremost thank Suzanne Rancourt for believing in this project early on and for guiding us so kindly and effectively through the publication process at University of Toronto Press. We immediately felt that this volume could not have had a better home than the Iberic series. Ms Rancourt's generous support allowed us to work with the inspiring collaborators of this volume. The talent, professionalism, and vision of this group have collectively inspired us to push traditional boundaries with the joyful irreverence that characterizes our field. Very rarely can one consider working through deadlines, deliveries, and revisions a delight, and yet, this has been our experience with each one of them during the long production that preceded this publication.

We are also deeply indebted to the editors that have so scrupulously helped us tighten up the final form of this collection: Katherine Aid and Audra Wolfe first, and Barbara Porter and Barbara Tessman, later, at University of Toronto Press. Their patience and understanding are unmatched.

Finally, we have been fortunate to have various sources of institutional support, which made this publication ultimately possible: the Rutgers University Research Council Program, the Chancellor Committee on Institutional Equity and Diversity Grant Program at Rutgers University at Camden, and the International Fund for the Cooperation and Promotion of Spanish Culture administered by Spain's Ministry of Culture. We are also deeply and loudly grateful to Guillermo Millán Meana from the University of Seville and the Study Abroad Program at the TTU Center in Seville for helping us write the index.

GOODBYE *EROS*

Recasting Forms and Norms of Love
in the Age of Cervantes

Introduction

Eros in the Age of Cervantes

JOHN BEUSTERIEN AND ANA MARÍA LAGUNA

Si tratáredes de amores, con dos onzas que sepáis de la lengua toscana, toparéis con León Hebreo que os hincha las medidas. Y si no queréis andaros por tierras estrañas, en vuestra casa tenéis a Fonseca, *Del amor de Dios,* donde se cifra todo lo que vos y el más ingenioso acertarea desear en tal materia.

(If you write about love, with the couple of ounces of Tuscan that you know, you'll run right into León Hebreo, who will inflate your metres. And if you don't care to travel into foreign lands, right at home you have Fonseca's *Del amor de Dios,* which summarizes everything that you or the most ingenious writer might wish to know about the subject.)

– Miguel de Cervantes, prologue, *Don Quijote* I[1]

In the prologue to Part I of *Don Quixote,* Cervantes has the "author" of the novel share his insecurities about writing with a mysterious visitor, a literary confidant who claims to be able to instantly remove the author's corrosive self-doubts, no matter their subject. On the question of love, as quoted in the epigraph above, he recommends a sturdy dose of two essential references: the influential philosopher Judah Leon Abravanel (also known as Leone Ebreo [ca. 1460–1535]) and, more surprisingly, the Spanish theologian Cristóbal de Fonseca (1550–1620), the relatively inconsequential author who translated Ebreo into Spanish. While the reference to Fonseca may be ironic, the evocation of Ebreo is telling, since his *Dialoghi d'amore* (*Dialogues of Love*) was an expected presence in any seventeenth-century author's library.[2] Ebreo's impressive synthesis of sacred and profane discourses of love provided a compass with which to navigate the dangerous waters of the "great sea" of love, as the subject was often described by humanists such as Sperone Speroni (1500–88) and Fernando de Herrera (1534–97).[3]

"The theme of love," Herrera had claimed, is "so spacious and abundant, so bountifully self-contained, that it cannot be fully grasped by a particular set of ingenious authors," not even by Petrarch, Bembo, or their classical predecessors (72). Although immersed in a blatent *translatio imperii* operation, Herrera compelled fellow Spaniards to seize the poetic opportunity presented to them by returning to and developing their own national models, equal to "the divine Italian verses" (las divinas rimas de Italia [73]) – a recommendation obviously disregarded by those who, like *Don Quixote*'s fictive author, continued to rely on Italian and European sources.[4] The poetic opportunity so happily identified by Herrera, however, might not have been as straightforward as he made it out to be. The fact that three of the greatest poets and poetic innovators of the age, both in and beyond Spain – Philip Sydney (1544–86), Gaspar Gil Polo (1520–91), and Luis de Góngora y Argote (1561–1627) – felt the need to build an overflowing love arcadia out of poetic shipwreck and to characterize their protagonists as tragic amorous castaways signals the perils involved in such literary exploration.[5]

Perhaps the quest for love was especially hazardous in the expanded referential world of the late 1500s, a world that, on the one hand, included new geographies, subjects, and sensibilities and that, on the other, was called on to reintegrate foundational classical authors such as Catullus (ca. 84–ca. 54 BCE) and Ovid (43 BCE–18 CE). Writers, including the distressed author of *Don Quixote*'s prologue, seemed painfully aware that no nationalistic or even encyclopaedic approach to the theme could allow them adequately to absorb, summarize, or even manage this ever-expanding field of literary references. Traditional lifelines such as Petrarchan and Neoplatonic paradigms of love were of little assistance, since they were nearly completely spent and had begun to show clear signs of inadequacy and exhaustion.[6]

Within such an overwhelming and disconcerting literary landscape, the casual possibility that opens this introduction – "If you write about love ..." – actually advances an urgent and climactic concern: how to approach, treat, or formulate a master metaphor such as love. This volume provides multiple and multifaceted answers to this central question as it explores how Golden Age letters rose to the challenge of revamping, recreating, and reflecting on the foundational amatory forms and norms that flourished or languished on the Spanish literary scene.

Contributors to this volume have paid special attention to how the enlarged societal, literary, and spatial conditions at the beginning of the seventeenth century translated into expanded ideas of desire that voiced new identities and subjectivities (in terms of race, ethnicity, religion, and even with regard to human and non-human categories), which in turn transformed the literary moulds that produced them in canonical and non-canonical writers alike. In tracing the fascinating literary expansion and rearrangement that resulted in the forging of new discursive paths and the reconfiguration of old formulaic venues, this volume documents the shifts that the theme of love experienced in the Spain of the 1500s and 1600s as that theme mutated into an array of motifs. Some of those shifts would become transformative drives for the genres that subsumed them, such as the displacement of "other" by "self" that, in pastoral fiction, indicated a consequential turn in the development of the genre; the conversion of love into jealousy that marked new directions in lyric and dramatic production; and the switch from *eros* to *eris* that defined epic experimentation.

This book delves into the deep and far-reaching implications of such genre-defining displacements in the works of authors such as Miguel de Cervantes (1547–1616), Diego Hurtado de Mendoza (1503–75), Francisco de Quevedo (1580–1645), Luis de Góngora (1561–1627), Lope de Vega (1562–1635), and the little-known playwright Francisco de la Torre y Sevil (1625–81). Rather than concerning themselves with conventional ideas of love, these authors explored issues only tangentially related to that sentiment, such as the thorny question of self-love, always troubling in women (chapter 1); the vindication of female agency, even when it leads to adultery (chapter 2); the urge to transition from *caritas* to *agape* (chapter 3); the attempt to reconcile affect with reason (chapter 4); the rejection of societal rationales that cancel out or severely constrain the individual's ability to love and live freely (chapter 5); women's affection for their animal companions (chapter 6); the censure of a Morisca's deviant sexuality, which becomes imposed on a whole body politic (that is, Moriscos) (chapter 7); the dismantling of a racialized logic that hypersexualizes black-skinned subjects while neutralizing the sexuality of black Madonnas as worshipped icons (chapter 8); the ability to write an epic, heroic story that is not erotic (chapter 9); the replacement of *eros* with *eris* in the epic narratives of the 1600s (chapter 10); and the political consequences of romanticizing the unstable erotic and heroic paradigms of a classic like *Don Quixote* (chapter 11).

More broadly, the volume divides the eleven chapters into four parts, reflecting how Spanish authors reframe the optics of love. The authors studied in this volume innovate the treatment of genre and gender (part 1); show the role of reason in love's configuration (part 2); blur normative sexualities (part 3); and recast heroic, epic, and chivalric literary moulds (part 4). Taking their cue from Cervantes's fictional author, who jokes around about the hackneyed literary mould of *eros*, Cervantes and his contemporaries look far beyond Fonseca and Ebreo. In exploring how new perspectives on gender, genre, and sexual norms emerge, the volume also takes note of social upheavals that radically altered the love literary landscape, like clashes with the Ottomans in the Mediterranean, the expulsion of the Moriscos, and the presence of Afro-Iberians. The chapters in this book, then, attest to the displacement of the theme of love as literary epicentre and trace the fascinating rearrangement process that occus when the centre no longer holds.

~

If there is one idea widely shared by the disparate authors of the far-ranging Golden Age tradition, it is that love, despite its various premises and promises, produced an unsatisfying emotional state. Largely responsible for this negative outlook were medieval treaties such as Ibn Hazm's *The Ring of the Dove* (ca. 1022) and Andreas Capellanus's *De amore* (1185) – inspired by Ovid's *Ars amatoria* and *Remedia amoris* – and Petrarch's foundational *Canzionere* (1366), which had re-energized the expression of love all over Europe at the expense of associating it with a consuming desire on the male lover's part and a muted and disempowered female beloved.[7] The success of the courtly and Petrarchan paradigms remained constant on the peninsula thanks to the multiple editions and reprints of Castillo's *Cancionero general* (1511) in its various – elite and popular – versions and formats.[8] Not even the Neoplatonic prospect of elevating the lover's soul through the divine contemplation of his beloved's beauty – advocated by Marsilio Ficino (1433–99) and continued with Ebreo – could minimize the sting of Petrarchan anguish, objectification, and dissatisfaction at the heart of prevailing views of love.

In Spain, as Alfonso Rey has explained, the intertwining of Petrarchan and Neoplatonic influences in the Golden Age, rather than appeasing Petrarchan woes, resulted in the weakening of a Neoplatonic doctrine. Incapable of producing a well-defined ideology of love, Neoplatonism in the Iberian Peninsula translated into a series of stereotyped and disconnected *topoi* that identified love with "the motor for the world, spiritual elevation, the absent lover, images engraved on the soul, the light of eyes, and other similar themes" (152). Such thematic motifs would emphasize not only the (male) lover's distressed longing for the (female) beloved but also the fragmentary constructedness of the sentiment, two dimensions that only accelerated the unavoidable exhaustion of the amatory formulae that was starting to be felt all over Europe.

In England, the attentive John Donne (1572–1631) despised love as a "triple fool" and conceived of Petrarchism as "whining poetry."[9] In Spain, the powerful Cervantes indicted the "chimeric" poets – who spent their days "whining about war or singing about love" (llorando guerras o cantando amores) – even more graphically by allegorically wrecking their ship as they attempt to sail to Parnassus, and by turning these poets into floating pumpkins (5: 184–249). The irreverent Spanish troupe that surrounds Cervantes – writers such as Herrera and poets such as Góngora and Quevedo – would seal the fate of the Petrarchan cliché by crippling it mercilessly, using hyperbole, parody, subversion, and all the other means afforded by baroque expression.[10]

While love is hyperbolically referred to in Quevedo as a disjointed string of antithetical but simultaneous attributes and propositions ("child and God, paradise and abysm, peace and war," and so on; Smith 102),[11] the beloved is eulogized in Góngora with attributes both exquisite and mundane, as he compares the beauty and grace of her features to a Petrarchan ideal ("Mientras por competir con tu cabello"), the walls of a building ("De pura honestidad, templo sagrado"), and the demeanor of a peacock ("pavón de Venus" [Dent-Young xvii]). Time and again, John Dent-Yong notes, we witness incredibly gifted poets such as Góngora produce "love sonnets [that] show little feeling," as each poet utilizes instead "all the literary conventions of his time, from pastoral and chivalresque fiction to the popular ballads," as poetic tools and discourses waiting, "like Everest," to be "conquered" (xvii). It is the force and severity with which these poets aim to climb that mountain and make a personal mark on the tradition that ultimately erodes so gravely the tradition's greatest referent, *eros*.[12] In viewing this theme – love – as a poetic discourse to surpass (Góngora) or deconstruct (Quevedo), these two giants are emblematically representative of how a poetic tradition drove itself away from the genre that had largely developed it.[13] As Steven Rupp concludes, "[t]he poets of the Spanish Baroque write of love for women, but the true object of their devotion is the lyric tradition. The female figures of their poetry – Floralba, Celalba, Claris, Lisis – mark their allegiance to [or competition with] such poetic predecessors as Propertius, Ovid, Horace, and Petrarch" (215). In light of such formal evolution and thematic displacement, we could thus extend to the entire Spanish baroque the paradox traditionally reserved for Quevedo that, while others might have loved more sincerely, few had done it so eloquently (Gaylord 236).

Although such eloquent elaborations have been amply documented in Spanish baroque poetry, they have been less explored in other genres, even though they deeply affected all literary moulds and sensibilities.

Poets, playwrights, and novelists of all sorts demonstrate in the same unequivocal fashion how the Spanish Golden Age tells a distinct "love story," a story in transition, full of fractures and uncertainties, where emotions such as jealousy and hubris – hardly loving or amorous – are often alluded to and grouped under a loose rubric of *eros* (Torres ix). By invoking love as an ambiguous emotion that could just as easily be characterized as lust or jealousy, Spanish writers demonstrate how, despite Ebreos's positive spin, a tainted view of the sentiment was taking a strong hold in their tradition.

The defining relationship between jealousy and love that would later be exploited in the *comedias*, was, then, also established in the Spanish lyric tradition. "Who is the parent (jealous) and who the child (love)?" wonders Kathleen Jeffs, as she documents that the inability to decide "which comes first in a chicken-or-egg debate of primogeniture is a commonplace in the Golden Age" (50). One of the earliest possible hints for this difficult genealogy comes from the father, if not of love, of the Golden Age poetic expression of the sentiment, Garcilaso de la Vega. It was Garcilaso who, as Mary Barnard reminds us, first broke the "fragile balance advocated by Petrarchan love lyric between physical beauty and chastity" (73), and he, too, cemented the inherent relationship between love, envy, and jealousy. In sonnet 31, for instance, Garcilaso states that jealousy is the emotion that guards and nurtures love, even though it ends up killing the lover.[14] Such confident vindication of jealousy as *eros*'s most fatal manifestation sets a new stage in Spanish baroque poetry, a stage on which the anguished Petrarchan lover not only renounces emotional peace and sexual satisfaction but also a life free of the poisonous reach of jealousy.

Rather than considering these thematic kernels, love and jealousy, as two subjects that evolve out of the discursive amatory tradition of the age, traditional criticism approached the frequent appearance of these themes as a straightforward illustration of the "natural" Spanish obsession with these issues.[15] "The Spanish honor code has remained an obsession within the Spanish literary tradition for centuries," writes Tracie Amend, even arguing that "this particularly *Iberian obsession ... remained notably entrenched in the Spanish consciousness* after the first production of Calderón's tragedies" (6; emphasis added). Significantly, literary and anthropological research of the past three decades has largely deconstructed the enduring historical generalizations that took honour plays as realistic depictions of the Spanish "consciousness." For one thing, criminal and civil records provide a picture quite different from the rigid, blood-thirsty prescriptions of wife-murdering plays by Calderón de la Barca (1600–80), Tirso de Molina (1579–1648), and

Lope de Vega. Records indicate that honour-related crimes were rare in seventeenth-century Spanish communities and that the public reputations of both men and women did not rely so exclusively on their sexual behaviour.[16] As Matthew Stroud points out, a Spanish audience "would have probably deemed the actions of the husbands in these plays to be unusual, extreme and probably archaic, and for that reason would have no doubt found them to be most engaging as dramatic plots" (93). Contrary to what is depicted on stage, women, according to historical records, found little trouble in taking into their own hands the defence of their reputation or that of their family members – including their husbands – not hesitating to resort to discursive or physical violence in order to defend it. "Castilians" of both genders, Scott Taylor observes, invoked "honor whenever interpersonal problems arose" (9), and not only in contexts of romance or passion.

Critical misconceptions (and stereotypes) about the presumed Spanish obsession with honour prevented whole generations of scholars from accurately assessing the thematic evolution of the fundamental *topos* of love in Spanish baroque theatre. Roberto González Echevarría contextualizes this progression by explaining how Calderón de la Barca and Tirso de Molina, two successors of the greatest dramatic innovator, Lope de Vega, early on identified love *and* honour as the dramatic themes of Lope's success and astutely understood that, in order to maximize the dramatic function of these subjects decades later, they needed to pitch these two elements *against* one another. This dramatic twist would then generate a renewed theatrical success that Lope would attempt to reappropriate in late plays such as *Punishment without Revenge* (*Castigo sin venganza*, 1631):

> In Lope's theater they [love and honor] were, of course, also in conflict, but love and honor provided solutions as well as clashes, and their validity as mainsprings for action is rarely questioned. In Tirso, the inherent evils of love are displayed to the fullest by Don Juan ... In Calderón honor appears as a destructive force that was at odds with the most elementary Christian tenets. Together, these two annihilating passions produce some of Calderón's most chilling tragedies ... In *El castigo sin venganza*, Lope sets out to go further than Tirso and Calderón, to flee into the deepest source of the tragic contradictions that his successors have found in his dramatic formula. (González Echevarría 67)

The emergence of plays concerned with honour is thus linked to an evolution of the theme of love and its performative ability to incorporate other interests of Spanish audiences, such as unsolvable marital conflicts, the emergence of women in the public spheres of society, and the sceptical mindset that had started to distrust the illusory power of the senses. Thus, while "[f]or a century, scholars have tried to determine what was so special about Spanish society and culture that it could produce the honor plays of Lope and Calderón" (Taylor 232), the only thing that turned out to be so special was the critical ability to make a small number of *comedias* representative of an entire massive theatrical production, and to isolate the question of honour from the amatory exploits that had originally produced it.[17]

The exorbitant critical emphasis on wife-murdering dramas also displaced attention from other genres, such as romance, that, in and beyond Spain, had a long history of reflecting on love-related matters such as jealousy and revenge. As George Mariscal reminds us, romance provides a formidable insight into the emotional reactions of a protagonist who is forced to experience multiple trials "from victory to defeat, from splendor to hardship" (163) in a debilitating solitude where the passionate longing for his lady often translates into violent jealous outbursts. The sentimental prose romance, which appeared in Spanish between 1440 and 1550, and amalgamated a series of generic traditions – from epistles, allegories, glosses, and visions – produced hybrid inquisitions and demonstrations into the emotional disturbances of love. As E. Michael Gerli writes, this sentimental corpus produced "a deliberate subversive, at times humorously ironic, confrontation between newly fashioned texts and their orthodox models" (xv).

In a continuation of the genre fusing found in the Spanish sentimental prose romance, novelists such as Cervantes demonstrate the evolution of morally ambiguous narratives in exploring jealousy-obsessed protagonists, which also reflect the influence of Italian models such as Ludovico Ariosto (1474–1533) and Torquato Tasso (1544–95).[18] In this volume, Mercedes Alcalá Galán demonstrates how the deluded lover of canto 28 of *Orlando furioso* (1532), for example, shows strong parallels with Cervantes's parodic interlude *The Jealous Old Man* (*El viejo celoso*, 1615), which, in turn, elicits a similar treatment of the subject in María de Zayas's comic novel *Forewarned but Not Forearmed* (*El prevenido engañado*, 1647).[19] Romance might have opened interiority to those authors interested in exploring a deviation of love such as jealousy, just like the stage seems to have provided a site for the negotiation or exploitation of the shifting fantasies regarding love, sex, and desire that collided in Spanish literature at the beginning of the seventeenth century (Rose 138–40).

We close this brief summary on the evolution of the *topos* by acknowledging the attention that recent scholarship is paying to how discourses of love articulate emerging ideas of otherness.[20] The debate over female autonomy – which had started to disrupt the most formulaic ideas of love – and the proper place of these female subjects in society echoed corresponding reflections on ethnicity and race. The disparate views of the role that gender, ethnicity, race, religion, and sexual orientation – among other factors – play in "what is now termed the intersectionality of identity," often contradictory and ideologically charged, naturally converge in approaches to *eros* (Williamsen 188); it is therefore easy to agree with Isabel Torres that discourses of love in this context connote "an authoritative and authorizing epistemology: a coercive ideological apparatus behind which a range of other narratives can find cover, one of the most effective smokescreens available to the politics of cultural production" (ix).[21] However, the studies collected in this volume reveal not only the workings of this smokescreen but also the many ways in which it is challenged. After all, as one of our contributors, Adrienne Martín, has argued in a fundamental study on the matter, "[r]ather than being exempla of sin and repentance," Spanish works often "reflect the existence of a complex set of surprisingly tolerant attitudes towards the literary representation of sexuality and eroticism in early modern Spain" (171).

~

In uniting the stunning findings of often surprising texts, *Goodbye Eros* takes a deep look at how Golden Age moral, ideological, scientific, and literary discourses intersected in their challenges to and reformulations of the trope of love. The first section of this volume, titled "Ambiguous Optics: Reframing Perception, Gender Subjectivity, and Genre Convention," attests how, regardless of whether or not they had a Renaissance – as Joan Kelly famously wondered forty years ago – women of the early modern age "were not uniformly oppressed, contained, and restrained within the home and convent during the sixteenth and seventeenth centuries," as literary representations can easily make us believe (Quintero 12).

In the Spanish context, the work of Mary Elizabeth Perry, Melveena McKendrick, Paul Julian Smith, Anne Cruz, Maria Cristina Quintero, Adrienne Martín, Marina Brownlee, Teresa Soufas, Georgina Dopico Black, and Lisa Vollendorf, among others, has confirmed the fact that living conditions of female subjects were not consistent with the harsh restrictions prescribed by moralists such as Fray Luis de León (1527–91), Juan Luis Vives (1493–1540), and Gaspar de Astete (1537–1601). On the contrary, the moral and conduct treatises that so rigidly defined female boundaries seemed to have appeared as a "defensive response to the increasingly visible activity on the part of women" (Quintero 12). Women were not only freer than we had assumed but also more diverse than expected: whether secular, religious, noble, or humble, women of the Spanish Golden Age contributed to the period's enormous cultural production "in ways that are still being determined" (Baranda and Cruz 2).

Spanish *comedias* – a genre once considered the rigid and straightforward cultural channel of Habsburg political authority, and the illustration, in wife-murder plays, of the supposed total lack of female agency in Spanish society – provide a striking indication of women's participation in this literary culture. The work of female playwrights such as María de Zayas, Ana Caro, Leonor de la Cueva, and Feliciana Enríquez de Guzmán "serve to question textual, social, and political authority, particularly as exercised within a patriarchal framework" (Williamsen 188). Even when these female-authored plays "portray women as objects of desire, they do it in different ways that pose challenges to established paradigms" (Williamsen 190). While a play's historical exemplarity remains ambiguous and can be endlessly argued, the mere presence of female subjects on and off the stage, cross-dressed or not, already contradicts official prescriptions of silence and enclosure more explicitly than other narrative or poetic genres.

Other established literary moulds were equally impacted by female authors, including Oliva de Sabuco (1562–1622), Cristobalina Fernández de Alarcón (1576–1646), and Mariana de Carvajal y Saavedra (1620–70), to name only a few. Even works written by men – especially by sensitive authors such as Diego de San Pedro, Gaspar Gil Polo, and Cervantes – manifest how the emergence of strong female protagonists in various narratives happily disrupts essential conventional expectations. Even in an idealized world like the pastoral, so dependent on alienating Petrarchan paradigms, female characters of the late 1500s "possess the experience and intellect equal to that of male shepherds; they play active roles equal to those male characters, desiring as well as being desired" (Pérez and Ihrie 157). The infamous "unattainability" of the Petrarchan beloved materializes in a female apathy or rejection of amatory schemes that conveys a "decision made by the woman herself" (Luhman 49). The two chapters included in "Ambiguous Optics" examine the deeper changes that this enhanced female presence, discourse, and subjectivity have infused into the definition of genres such as the sentimental romance, pastoral fiction, and dramatic interlude.

Chapter 1 explores the story of the captivating shepherdess Marcela, the protagonist of the first pastoral episode of *Don Quixote*, Part I, which has traditionally been considered either a quintessential Cervantine cry for female independence or, alternatively, an illustration of the destructive, narcissistic female spirit that nurtures a desire for such independence. Joan Cammarata and Ana María Laguna explore how the critical fascination with the character of Marcela has created a mystique that has hindered a full understanding of the self-love for which she ultimately advocates. While critics have attacked her as egoistic, not even theologians such as Saint Augustine and Saint Thomas could categorically censure *amor sui* – they considered it a virtuous sentiment so long as it did not interfere with the love of God. Marcela's pastoral of the self – her insistence on reaching emotional (and perhaps erotic) self-fulfilment in solitude – defines a striking innovation of the pastoral genre in that, through the new, ambiguous literary territory of self-love, Cervantes expands the amatory limits of the conventional arcadia genre. This chapter reminds us that, in putting to rest Grisóstomo's remains, Cervantes buries the classic pastoral convention that had made love a poisonous, rather than a fulfilling, emotional expectation. By showing the societal difficulty in acknowledging individual satisfaction, Cervantes nonetheless keeps vibrantly alive the *topos* of amatory and emotional conflict characteristic of pastoral fiction.

Chapter 2 explores Cervantes's debts to Ariosto's *Orlando furioso* (1532) through textual and visual allusion by focusing on two Cervantine works, *The Impertinent Curious Man* (*El curioso impertinente*, 1605) – the interpolated novel in *Don Quixote*, Part I – and the dramatic interlude *The Jealous Old Man* (*El viejo celoso*). Mercedes Alcalá Galán explains how Cervantes's critique of male jealousy and his vindication of female agency – even when it translates into adultery – closely follows Ariosto's classic. Both Ariosto and Cervantes examine the decriminalization of female adultery and the delegitimization of male jealousy. They also both illustrate the myth of women's lasciviousness, only to dismantle the moral and social attributions built around it by providing a specific context – full of extenuating circumstances – where this behaviour is either explicated or exculpated altogether. Rather than representing female infidelity as indicative of women's flawed nature, they present adultery as the natural consequence of limiting or unjust circumstances, such as the uneven marriage of an old man and a young woman. The jealousy of the husbands, so central to the plots of the three works studied here, is presented as completely unrelated to love, intimately associated instead with hypocrisy and misogyny, and responsible for the grave and inexcusable sexual offences committed by the male protagonists. In establishing similar realms of visual allusion in both authors, the chapter underlines how Cervantes and Ariosto shared an unusual perspective that affirms female freedom while exposing the self-defeating expectations of patriarchal structures.

The second cluster of the volume, titled "Reasoning the Unreasonable: Toward a Rationale of Love," explores the impact of emerging epistemologies of perception, reason, and emotion on prevailing views of love. The proto-scientific dimension of the Spanish Golden Age is gaining increasing critical currency, and the work of baroque authors such as Baltasar Gracián (1601–58), Antonio López de la Vega (1586–1655), and Francisco Gutiérrez de los Ríos (1644–1721) is now deemed fundamental for understanding the redefinition of the "value system inherited from the Renaissance" (Robbins 143). According to Jeremy Robbins, the Spanish "intellectual foundations of an empiricist epistemology" made Iberia one of the most receptive societies to John Locke's (1632–1704) logical positivism (ibid.).

In chapter 3, Eric Graf documents how the spread of geometry "offered early modern writers nothing less than an entire system of representation to rival that of language, whereby all bodies, places, and ideas, no matter how distinct, might be rendered conceptually equivalent to one another" (Turner 6). Graf identifies how the influential Euclidean mathematical metaphor of the isosceles triangle theorem ("angles opposite the two sides of an isosceles triangle are equal") structures the work of both El Greco and Cervantes, literally and figuratively. The chapter connects the triangular logic of Euclid's *Elements*, also known as the *pons asinorum* (bridge of asses) or *fuga* (flight), with the figural disposition of El Greco's painting *Flight into Egypt* as it depicts the bridge of moral and intellectual progress toward the light and love of reason. A similar trajectory can be found in Cervantes's fiction, especially in the underlying triangulation of desire that defines so many love stories of both parts of *Don Quixote* – such as that of Anselmo, Lotario, and Camila in *The Impertinent Curious Man*, the same work discussed in this volume by Mercedes Alcalá Galán. Graf shows how the structural disposition of these episodes reinforces the triangular structure of the novel as a whole, since elements like the interpolated novel of *The Impertinent Curious Man* appear as a third fictional element bridging two separate scenarios.

For Graf, the triangulation of Cervantes's and El Greco's works echoes a Platonic view of the universe, as established in *Timaeus*, where triangles are associated with both the universe's most pressing problems and their most logical solutions. Similarly, the amatory triangular universe of writers such as Cervantes and artists such as El Greco advocates for a measured return to reason, since *eros* can turn too easily into narcissism and rivalry. It is thus this urge to substitute *eros* for *agape* (the rational version of love) that, for Graf, articulates many of Cervantes's and El Greco's works and defines their views of love in all its racial, moral, and gendered dimensions.

In chapter 4, Eli Cohen analyses Cervantes's exemplary novel "The Little Gypsy Girl" (La gitanilla), where rationality is unexpectedly associated with two distinct marginal subjects: women and gypsies. According to Cohen, the novel's protagonist, Preciosa, is characterized by a denial of emotion as a valid form of response to events and experiences of all sorts. Such repudiation of *eros* directly ties to the superiority of reason. Various elements of the novel evolve in a plot that at first sight appears to be a highly conventional love story – one that would posit a mutually exclusive relationship between reason and affect – but ends up recognizing the striking mutuality of cognition and emotion, as proclaimed by Juan Vives and Huarte de San Juan. By having a female character reaffirm the interplay between emotional and rational processes, Cervantes revamps the traditional concept of love coined by misogynist expectations and Petrarchan ideals that tie women to silence. Preciosa's convincing discourse and "clear thinking" is presented as a productive alternative to the limiting effects on women's agency of traditional domestic and amatory paradigms. The consummate rhetorical skills of this protagonist, rather than isolating her like Marcela, allow her to move her audience to the ends and emotions that she seeks to induce: empathy (Corregidor), trust (Cristina), and even a safer and calmer form of love (Andrés). In considering the implications of the phenomenological view of affect in the novel, Cohen signals the correspondence between Cervantes's view of the emotion and current cognitive theories, as they both emphasize the ethical effect that emotions like love can have on readers and society. In replacing the static ideals of Petrarchan and Neoplatonic conventions for the dynamic, ethical understanding of affect, Cohen reveals one of the Cervantes's most optimistic views of the sentiment.

Spanish letters are not without their share of lovelorn characters. Broadening further the way in which Cervantes takes a pioneering approach to rational love, in chapter 5, Jesús Maestro explains how Cervantes transfers the state of the lovesick character into the creation of the anomic character. Maestro uses "anomie," the condition by which an individual loses all sense of moral selfhood, to understand some of Cervantes's more perplexing characters. Like "baroque," "anomie" is a twentieth-century term. It originated in reference to highly industrialized societies where the loss of a sense of self is linked to the alienating conditions of the industrialized environment.[22] Moreover, the concept also has ample valence in the Renaissance, where it indicates the mismatch between social and individual ethical standards that produces a disorienting, personal loss of reality and self-identity. In Cervantine studies, the anomic perspective is particularly useful for understanding how love causes the breakdown of iconic Cervantine characters such as Tomás Rodaja, Grisóstomo, Cardenio, and even Don Quixote. In his chapter, Maestro shows how anomie functions quite differently in Cervantes's last novel, *The Trials of Persiles and Sigismunda* (*Persiles y Sigismunda*, 1616), where the breakdown of its protagonists is not caused by love but results from their aim to achieve freedom. Anomic characters in *The Trials of Persiles and Sigismunda*, such as Rutilio, Clodio, Renato, Cenotia, and Soldino, thus oppose societal or religious prerogatives in their attempt to live and love freely, even as they suffer the consequences – almost total social uprootedness – for doing so.

Where the second cluster of essays in the volume examines aspects of reason that permeate love, the third section, "Kissing between the Lines: Blurring Racial and Sexual Norms," looks to how non-normative sexualities inform early modern Spanish literature. Each of the essays in this section points to a radical literary reconstruction of socially sanctioned norms and notions of sexual deviation. Each chapter illuminates a recalibration of *eros*: Adrienne Martín examines women and dogs in poetry; Christina Lee examines the case of a Moorish woman and a Christian youth in prose; and John Beusterien examines a black African man and a white woman in drama.

The editors of this volume, Ana Laguna and John Beusterien, have published studies on how cultural status and pictorial representation of dogs illuminate the complexity of human sympathy for animals, and how writers such as Cervantes unsettle humankind's self-fashioning in the Renaissance.[23] Further developing on critical perspectives toward canines in the Spanish context, and also building upon her own landmark scholarship on "erotic philology," Adrienne Martín in chapter 6, "Sexy Beasts: Women and Lapdogs in Baroque Satirical Verse," examines satirical verse to show the impact of how an animal studies approach can elucidate the role of Spanish literature in twisting love tropes.

Martín's chapter begins by showing the profound depth of human attachment to companion animals, most especially dogs, by noting the ubiquitousness of pet cemeteries across time and place in the West. She explains how mental, emotional, and moral obligations toward dogs had expanded in the early modern period in material culture, philosophy, hunting treatises, and other literary forms, especially poetry. Martín's essay focuses on Spanish satirical poetry in which women invited toy dogs into the enigmatic, intimate, and secluded space of their home. The Spanish poetry that Martín studies does not communicate women's affective relationships with dogs, but instead only the sexual aspects of that relationship. Martín illuminates how male writers use dogs to construct notions of women's aberrant sexuality, which contrast with the asexual depiction of their own relationship with dogs (for example, those depicted as sporting companions in hunting manuals). The male may eulogize his best friend, but then, displacing the canine's closeness to his heart, he demeans the female's love of her small dog in tropes of satiric bestiality. Martín evaluates works by Diego Hurtado de Mendoza, Francisco de Quevedo, and Luis de Góngora, as well as an anonymous poet – works that have received scanty critical attention. Ultimately, she presents a feminist reading of poetry of the Golden Age that satirically celebrates new emotional connections (between human and dogs), as exemplified by poets such as Góngora, who was able to transform a crude patriarchal cliché (a dog licking a woman's genitals) into a remarkable poetic accomplishment.

If Martín's critical approach illuminates a new poetic appreciation of animals, the next contribution, by Christina Lee, connects to Martín's essay by demonstrating how the literary renovation of a genre often challenges prevailing sexual norms. In Spanish Golden Age literature and society, many voices had labelled religious outsiders such as Moriscos as "dogs," witches, or a combination of the two (witches were supposedly able to turn into or give birth to dogs). Lee shows how Cervantes borrows on the common denigrating literary Morisca trope in the story of Cenotia's seducing a young Christian man. But Cervantes, as he does with Preciosa in "The Little Gypsy Girl," brilliantly uses literary invention to craft a radically new character and mindset. Using the veneer of a literary cliché, Cervantes deftly creates a character that offers a counterpoint to Spain's official strategy that rejects Moriscos from the Spanish body politic. Echoing the historical-social reality of abandoned Morisco children, Cenotia's obsessive erotic fascination with the adolescent Antonio reveals Cervantes's empathy for the lingering personal trauma of this Morisca that ultimately prompts a broader sympathy for the entire Morisco problem.

Lee's contribution also connects back to chapter 5 by Jesús Maestro, as both examine *The Trials of Persiles and Sigismunda* and both assess Cervantes's creation of the character Cenotia. While Christina Lee's chapter, "Sexual Deviance and Morisco Marginality in Cervantes's *The Trials of Persiles and Sigismunda*," reads Cenotia as a counterpoint to the Morisco expulsion, Maestro examines the same character within the social-cultural dynamics of anomic behaviour, one that allows her to oppose prevailing social norms by loving freely. Although Lee looks to a specific socio-cultural context (the expulsion), and Maestro focuses on a generalized behaviour (anomie), both contributors reach a similar conclusion, which declares this character, Cenotia, as a key element in Cervantes's reshaping of the trope of *eros* in his last prose masterpiece.

At a time when debates about biological difference, religious affiliation, origin, and humoral composition, attempted to define and regulate ethnic otherness, "nowhere is the ideological conjuncture of love and empire more noticeable than in the period's penchant for cross-racial couples" (Nocentelli 116). Pairings like Cenotia and the Christian boy who is the object of her love abound in the novels of Cervantes and the plays of Lope de Vega. While the reception, fate, and authorial intent of cross-racial relationships varies enormously among works and writers, their presence testifies to the fact that "between the late sixteenth century and the mid-seventeenth, interracial desire became something of a fixture both on the stage and on the page, oftentimes, at the center of stories casting expansion in overtly erotic terms" (ibid.). Whereas interracial couples like Lope de Vega's protagonists of the play *The Reproved Gallant* (*El galán escarmentado*, 1598) tend to end in death, couples in Cervantine fiction, such as Zoraida and Ruy Pérez, or Ana Félix and her Christian admirer, have more promising prospects, as they are even presented as "individuals whose integration into Spanish society seems desirable," although their optimism might be "naïve," given that "they do not seem to fully understand the prejudices they face" (Childers 178).

In this regard, some Golden Age *comedias* provide a formidable representational platform for the exploration of prevailing racial tensions. In chapter 8, John Beusterien examines Francisco de la Torre y Sevil's play *The Confession with the Devil* (*La confesión con el demonio*). He examines how the question of differences in religion and skin colour fuses in a drama that contains a black Madonna icon. In this play, the woman and the man who preys upon her are both Christians, but one is black and other is white. Beusterien's chapter examines blackness in a modern racial sense because the play depicts both a black Madonna icon and a black-white sexual relationship that results in a pregnancy, which the white mother aborts.

Beusterien's analysis illuminates the particular anxieties prompted by Afro-Iberians in their unique connection to Christianity. *The Confession with the Devil* includes characters such as Francesca, the sister of the vehement anti-Semite Vicente Ferrer, and Tucapel, a black character who converts to Christianity but ends up burning in purgatory's flames. The play also includes an image of Tucapel eating his aborted son, a child who appears on stage in blackface. As part of its *telenovela*-like melodramatic themes, Torre's play visits the conventional question of *eros* with regard to male-female sexuality and religious worship, particularly with respect to the Virgin Mary. Beusterien points out how the dark Madonna icon in the play evokes how people constructed and projected gendered and racial norms in religious artefacts. Rather than refashioning the conventions of *eros*, Torre's play reinforces troubling amorous conventions that subjugate women and, moreover, include race in that subjectification. This chapter, however, recognizes the implicit connection between drama and conventional erotic norms, especially those based on race, a recognition that opens a door for the reappraisal of those conventions and for dismantling the racialized logic that hypersexualizes black people.

The final cluster of chapters, "Recasting Epic and Heroic Moulds," examines three significant changes to the forms and norms of epic convention in the age of Cervantes. In chapter 9, Diana de Armas Wilson examines the life story of a Calabrian convert to Islam and provides a brief biography that demonstrates the significance of his supreme love, the Mediterranean Sea. Wilson details the story of Uludj Ali, the commander of the Ottoman fleet in Lepanto and one of the most emblematic representatives of the Ottoman's hyper-heroic and anti-erotic ideal. Both dimensions – *eros* and a heroic *ethos* – were actively present in the Ottoman's world, which had incorporated not only "long tradition[s] of the spiritualization of love" in its literature, but also chivalric ideals in its military organization (Andrews and Kalpakli 17). However, whereas Western fictional representations of chivalry required from the knight two essential skills, "martial prowess and amorous excellence," that were "inextricably intertwined" (Cavallaro 122), Eastern literature emphasized the religious nature of the knight's mission, detaching any personal amorous ambitions from his conquering aims.[24]

Uludj Ali embodies the powerful sense of purpose enabled by cohesion with – and brotherly affection for – his fellow warriors, since in a society like his, whose political body was fully dedicated to military conquest, a fighter distinguished himself not for the sake of an amorous reward but by his military effectiveness and his bond with fellow combatants (Wittek 60). In contrast to an entire Western tradition that appraised almost "more-than-human" knights for their ability "to perform their duties as fighters and lovers" (Cavallaro 122), this chapter describes Uludj Ali as an illustration of the practical Ottoman *ethos* whose rank-effacing love prioritized male unity and allowed "ordinary" men of every origin and military branch to attain exceptional success. As de Armas concludes, the only love in Uludj Ali's story is that of the Mediterranean – or, as Ottomans called it, the White Sea.

Because it examines a poem that celebrates military victory, with no apparent focus on romantic love, chapter 10 provides a fitting continuation of de Armas's description of Uludj Ali's story. Here, Jason

McCloskey examines Lope de Vega's *Jerusalem Conquered* (*Jerusalén conquistada*), a heroic poem that clearly sets out to compete in literary stature with Torquato Tasso's *Gerusalemme liberate* (1581). Lope's patriotic poem narrates the heroic (and fictional) Spanish efforts in the crusades (in which Spain never participated) in an effort to emulate Tasso's homage to Italian courage. The crashing defeat of the Spanish troops in Lope's poem, however, and the telling absence of the two quintessential epic elements – *eros* and some form of military *ethos* – have forced innumerable generations of readers and critics to question what kind of epic is at stake in Lope's puzzling poem.

By asking us to consider a different genre, Aristotle's tragedy rather than heroic romance, as a poetic framework, McCloskey uncovers an unexpected thematic and structural coherence in Lope's poetic exercise. Suddenly, Lope's indulgent description of the Spanish inability to regain Jerusalem from Muslim hands – a topic not so welcomed by his contemporaries – is explained by the ekphrasis of paintings on the walls that detail the causes of the tragedy. These visual descriptions show the reader the workings of *eris* among the Spanish military forces, depicting them as a military ruled by inner frictions, disobedience, and gratuitous violence. In showing, ekphrastically, how *eris* has unravelled the Christian Spanish troops from within, Lope points to the disappearance of a heroic ethos in the Spanish faction. The *eris* that drives the poem from beginning to end exposes a troubling vacuum at the heart of a national epic also deprived of any erotic subtexts. Lope's tragedy acquires a critical dimension by inviting his readers to cathartically reflect on the unheroic performance of a mythical Spanish army.

The final chapter in this volume turns from a study of Lope's loveless poem to Don Quixote, often considered one of the most iconic and devoted lovers of Spanish literature. Ana María Laguna examines the heroic and erotic permutations that have articulated the understanding of Cervantes's novel in the late nineteenth and twentieth centuries. She compares two strikingly different critical responses – those of the Generation of 1898 and the Generation of 1927 – to the central question of whether it is love, or the figure of the beloved, that ultimately motivates Cervantes's chivalric hero to undertake his quest. Whereas the first, the Generation of 1898, heavily philosophical, nationalistic, and political, privileged the novel's heroic dimension by equating the protagonist's ultimate aim with a desire for glory, justice, or destiny – rather than love – the latter, the Generation of 1927, textually bound, and highly sensitive to Cervantes's literary inclinations, sought to recover the sentimental dimension of the novel by reassessing Cervantes's relationship with *eros* and its entire literary tradition. In pointing to the clash between these two schools, or generations, Laguna's chapter contests the critical assessment provided by Anthony Close's seminal *The Romantic Approach to Don Quixote* (1978) more than forty years ago. The recovery of a Spanish Cervantine criticism far more complex than Close made it out to be illuminates, moreover, the extent to which the interpretation of a supposedly purely literary subject, such as love, reflects a society's inner struggles and values, and advances even its most troubling political developments.

To a certain degree, Laguna's description of the reception of Cervantes in criticism through the trope of love is paradigmatic for the volume as a whole. Demonstrating a textual attentiveness similar to the Generation of '27, the authors in this volume study early modern Spain's literature in a sophisticated and sensitive way, faithful to the enriching critical methodology of close reading. Yet, echoing the Generation of '98 reading of the novel in terms of nationalism, by assessing the amorous literary balloon that has lost its air, the contributors also prove to be in tune with new subjectivities that emerged in the Spanish early modern period.

After all, in the opening of *Don Quixote,* Cervantes nods to proto-Spanish nationalism in a satiric way, by suggesting that an author who wants to write about love can find everything necessary in Fonseca's *Del amor de Dios,* the inconsequential text not written in Italian, but found "right at home" in Spain and written in Spanish. The following chapters show that the trope of love in the work of Cervantes and his contemporaries is not as simple and one-sided as Cervantes's fictional author leads the reader to believe when he writes that Fonseca "summarizes everything that you or the most ingenious writer might wish to know about the subject." In taking on the subtle and critical provocation from *Don Quixote*'s prologue, this book demonstrates that writing about love in the Spanish Golden Age was a tremendously complicated exercise that required a similarly colossal – if artificial – suffering on the author's part. Since reading and examining the resulting literary artefacts that formed part of that effort produces unstoppable delight, we hope that our volume contributes to the ever-lasting enjoyment that the reading of these works affords.

NOTES

1 The Spanish is taken from the edition edited by Luis Murillo (Cervantes, "Prólogo," *El ingenioso hildalgo Don Quijote,* I: 56–7); the English is from the translation by Edith Grossman (Cervantes, "Prologue," *Don Quixote,* I: 7). All subsequent quotes from the novel are from these editions. All other translations, unless otherwise indicated, are our own.

2 The *Dialoghi* offered an impressive synthesis of sacred and profane discourses of love that reconciled the most influential classic and contemporary views on the emotion. See Alfonso Rey, "Erotic Neoplatonism," in *The Last Days of Humanism*, 151–61.
3 See Sperone Speroni's sea comparison, in "Apologia dei dialogi," 698. Reinier Leushuis opens his monograph on the theme of love with a commentary on this quote: see *Speaking of Love*, 1. Herrera's comment is from his edition of *Obras de Garcilasso de la Vega*, 72.
4 Ignacio Navarrete evaluates this process, and Herrera's role in it, in his chapter "Herrera and the Return to Style," in *Orphans of Petrarch*, 126–89.
5 See Laguna's "Shipwrecked Na(rra)tion," where she notes that Sidney's *Countess of Pembroke's Arcadia* (1593; Harmondsworth: Penguin, 1977, 66) begins with "a sight full of piteous strangeness: a ship, or rather the carcase of the ship, or rather some few bones of the carcase hulling there, part broken, part burned, part drowned"; Góngora does the same, characterizing his protagonist, in the very first stanza of his *Soledades* (1613), as a "naúfrago y desdeñado" (castaway, disdained lover) who has been "vomitado" (vomited up) by the Ocean (22–3). Before both poets had depicted their protagonists in this fashion, Gil Polo Gaspar had already portrayed this conventional state in the *Diana enamorada* (1564), which opens with a male siren, "Sireno," impossibly "tormented" by love, and a female protagonist, Diana, who confesses to having "navigated the stormy waters of the sea of love, and safely arrived in the harbor of inner peace" (pasé en el mar de amor peligrosas agonías y tormentas, y ahora estoy gozando del seguro y sosegado puerto [5]).
6 See Anthony Mortimer, *Petrarch's* Canzionere *in the English Renaissance*, 26, and Armando Maggi, *In the Company of Demons*, 161. In his study *Post-Petrarchism*, Roland Green reminds us that "Petrarchism is neither static nor one sort of thing," since it constitutes "a highly adaptable complex" that "seems under a compulsion to change all the time but remains recognizably the same" (3).
7 About Ibn Hazm's influence in Spain, José Luis Gómez Martínez summarizes the controversy between Américo Castro and García Gómez, *Américo Castro y el origen de los españoles*, 179–80. For Ovid as a foundation for the convention of courtly love, see John Parry's "Introduction" to Capellanus's *The Art of Courtly Love*, 2–27. The "male egotism" characteristic of this poetry is explored by critics such as Bruce Woodcock, "'Anxious to Amuse,'" and Leah Middlebrook, *Imperial Lyric*, especially in the chapter "Juan Boscán Courtirizes Song," 59–102.
8 See Hart, *Cervantes and Ariosto*, 83. Petrarchism, and its idea of unrequited love, has been seen as an essential theory of power though its imperialist logic, since, for critics such as Roland Green, Leah Middlebrook, and Carmen Nocentelli, this love paradigm ultimately entails a gender-based

hierarchy of agency and expression that produced troubling applications in colonial contexts.

9 Donne's allusion is explored by Woodcock, "'Anxious to Amuse,'" 51–2.

10 Mortimer astutely observes that "Petrarchan manner could only survive by detaching it from Petrarchan experience" – that is, by using a formulaic expression with radically different purpose (*Petrarch's* Canzionere, 26).

11 As seen, for example, in Quevedo's poem "Este es el niño Amor, éste es tu abismo," in Espina, *Quevedo*, 141. Julián Olivares believes that in sonnets like "Solo sin vos y mi dolor presente," Quevedo consciously describes his "failure" as a courtly lover (121), as he hyperbolically conveys an amorous "exaggeration of suffering to the point of ludicrousness," reinforcing the idea that the "real source of his [the poet's] agony is his vexing awareness that he has been reduced by an absurd convention to a situation worse than that of the *fin amant*" (*Love Poetry*, 121).

12 Ignacio Navarrete, for example, has described how the "violent anti-petrarchism" of Quevedo's poetry "transgresses the rules of *sprezzatura* and *decorum*, and soils the genre of Castiglione, Boscán, and Garcilaso" (236). While Góngora's envious eye had "tested the [Petrarchan] system as far as it would go," but without intending "to destroy it," Quevedo, on the other hand, "by merging Petrarchism and the burlesque he tosses out one of the few vehicles for establishing one's legitimacy as a lover and as a poet" (*Orphans of Petrarch*, 238).

13 In their conscious engagement and competition with a previous literary tradition, courtly poets such as Góngora or Quevedo often subordinate the theme to the occasion. While both of them compete with previous models, Góngora attempts to surpass them and integrate them, whereas Quevedo uses his moral deconstruction of Petrarch to invalidate all of those previous readings (Navarrete, *Orphans of Petrarch*, 239).

14 Garcilaso's sonnet 31 reads:

Dentro de mi alma fue de mí engendrado
un dulce amor, y de mi sentimiento
tan aprobado fue su nacimiento
como de un solo hijo deseado.
Mas luego de él nació quien ha estragado
del todo el amoroso pensamiento:
que en áspero rigor y en gran tormento
los primeros deleites ha tornado.
¡Oh crudo nieto, que das vida al padre,
y matas al agüelo! ¿Por qué creces
tan desconforme a aquel de que has nacido?
¡Oh, celoso temor! ¿a quién pareces?
¡Que aun la envidia, tu propia y fiera madre,

se espanta en ver el monstruo que ha parido!

A gentle love was fathered once by me / within my soul, and my affections smiled / upon his birth so unreservedly / that he was like a longed-for only child. / But then he fathered one who is the blight / of all my loving thoughts and expectations, / and who has turned my earlier delight / into tormented, bitter tribulations. / O hard and heartless grandson! You restore / your father's life and strike his father dead! / Why are you so unlike your genitor? / And whom do you take after, jealous dread? / For even cruel envy's struck with awe / When she beholds the monster that she's bred.

Rutherford, *The Spanish Golden Age Sonnet*, 60–1.

15 In *Honor and Violence in Golden Age Spain*, Scott Taylor argues that "[a] new generation of anthropologists asserts that the earlier focus on [Spain and] sexual behavior, supposedly the key to honor and shame in the Mediterranean, may say more about the anxieties of anthropologists that it does about the subjects" (6).

16 Melvena Mackedrick provides detailed commentary on the rare and documented "crímene de pasión" in a large city like Valencia in her study *Identities in Crisis*, 3–38. More recently, Scott Taylor has shown how complex was the idea of honour in this society, which resulted not only from sexual-related matters; "for men," Taylor explains, "defending the sexual reputation of their women was important, but male honor included much else, including competence in one's trade or office, the management of one's credit and debit relationships, and one's performance in the aggressive competitive play that composed much of male sociability" (*Honor and Violence*, 9). The case for women was actually similar, since a woman's good name was defined not only by her marital fidelity and sexual purity; good behaviour in this terrain, although obviously important, needed to match her creditworthiness as a highly determinant element for her public reputation (ibid., 156).

17 Thankfully, the quintessential importance of these *comedias* has also been recently revised, as scholars such as Jody Campbell show how even honour plays are "far more ambiguous" than traditional literary criticism has made them out to be, and did not even constitute a genre – honour plays, or wife-murdering drama – prior to the nineteenth century (*Monarchy, Political Culture, and Drama in Seventeenth-Century Madrid*, 15). It is thus not surprising to attest that honour plays that conform to the most extreme prerogatives of the honour code constitute a minuscule number of dramas and do not represent the massive dramatic production of the period. See also Stroud, "The Wife-Murder Plays"; Taylor, *Honor and Violence*; and González Echevarría, *Celestina's Brood*.

18 See, for example, Adrienne Martin's chapter on eros and the *novella*, "Eros and Art of Cuckoldry," in *An Erotic Philology of Golden Age Spain*, 169–202.

19 Alcalá Galán's detailed study of these similarities can be found in chapter 2 of the present volume.
20 The view of love referred to here was articulated by Luhman, Bloch, and Munk. When considering a more political perspective for the study of these themes – love and desire – a play like *Burlador de Sevilla* by Tirso de Molina, a drama that could be read simply as an illustration of "raw male aggression and female victimization" or as a "domestic allegory of colonization" can become a manifestation of the clash between two forms of desire of two different forms of societies, a capitalist one (where subjects are organized around the idea of social class) and a feudal one (still built around the idea of genealogical kingship or caste), see Cascardi, *Ideologies of History in the Spanish Golden Age* , 171–3.
21 Torres's view of love is in line with that of Roland Green, who sees it as a discourse that is not only "interpersonal but political and imperial" (Torres, *Love Poetry in the Spanish Golden Age,* 1).
22 Critics use the concept to refer to classic literature and thought. See Ineke Sluiter and Ralph Rosen, *Free Speech in Classical Antiquity,* 140.
23 See Beusterien's *Canines in Cervantes and Velázquez,* and Laguna's "Through the Bonfires of Petrarchism."
24 In the Ottoman and Islamic world, chivalric brotherhoods (known as *futuwwa*) comprised "unmarried young men bound together by oaths of fidelity, special costume, and a shared allegiance to chivalric virtues."Meri and Bacharach, eds, *Medieval Islamic Civilization,* 1: 153.

REFERENCES

Amend, Tracie. *The Adulteress on the Spanish Stage: Gender and Modernity in 19th Century Romantic Drama.* Jefferson, NC: McFarland, 2015.

Andrews, Walter G., and Mehmet Kalpakli. *The Age of Beloveds: Love and the Beloved in Early-Modern Ottoman and European Culture and Society.* Durham, NC: Duke University Press, 2005.

Astete, Gaspar de. *Doctrina cristiana y documentos de crianza.* Valladolid, 1599.

Baranda, Nieves, and Anne Cruz, eds. *The Routledge Research Companion to Early Modern Spanish Women Writers.* New York: Routledge, 2018.

Barnard, Mary. *Garcilaso de la Vega and the Material Culture of Renaissance Europe.* Toronto: University of Toronto Press, 2014.

Beusterien, John. *Canines in Cervantes and Velázquez: An Animal Studies Reading of Early Modern Spain.* Aldershot, UK: Ashgate, 2013.

Bloch, Howard. *Medieval Misogyny and the Invention of Western Romantic Love.* Chicago: University of Chicago Press, 1991.

Brownlee, Marina. *The Cultural Labyrinth of María de Zayas.* Philadelphia: University of Pennsylvania Press, 2000.

Campbell, Jody. *Monarchy, Political Culture, and Drama in Seventeenth-Century Madrid: Theater of Negotiation.* New York: Routledge, 2006.
Capellanus, Andreas. *The Art of Courtly Love.* Edited by John Parry. New York: Columbia University Press, 1960.
Cascardi, Anthony. *Ideologies of History in the Spanish Golden Age.* University Park: Pennsylvania State University, 2010.
Castillo, Hernando del. *Cancionero general.* Valencia: Cristóbal Koffman, 1511.
Cavallaro, Dani. *The Chivalric Romance and the Essence of Fiction.* Jefferson, NC: McFarland, 2015.
Cervantes Saavedra, Miguel de. *Don Quixote.* Translated by Edith Grossman. New York: Harper Collins, 2003.
– *El ingenioso hidalgo don Quijote de la Mancha.* Edited by Luis Murillo. Madrid: Castalia, 1978.
– *Novelas ejemplares.* Edited by Juan Bautista Avalle-Arce. Madrid: Castalia, 1987.
– *Poesías Completas.* Vol. 1, *Viaje del Parnaso and Adjunta al Parnaso.* Edited by Vicente Gaos. Madrid: Castalia, 1973.
Childers, William. *Transatlantic Cervantes.* Toronto: University of Toronto Press, 2006.
Dent-Young, John, ed., *Selected Poems of Luis de Góngora: A Bilingual Edition.* Chicago: University of Chicago Press, 2016.
Donne, John. *The Songs and Sonnets of John Donne.* Edited by Theodore Redpath. Cambridge, MA: Harvard University Press, 2009.
Dopico Black, Georgina. *Perfect Wives, Other Women: Adultery and Inquisition in Early Modern Spain.* Durham, NC: Duke University Press, 2001.
Espina, Antonio. *Quevedo, estudio y antología.* Madrid: Bibliográfica española, 1962.
Fonseca, Cristóbal de. *Tratado del amor de Dios.* Salamanca: Guillermo Foquel, 1592.
Gaspar, Gil Polo. *Diana enamorada.* Valencia: Joan Mey, 1564.
Gaylord, Mary. "The Making of Baroque Poetry." In *The Cambridge History of Spanish Literature*, edited by David T. Gies, 222–37. Cambridge: Cambridge University Press, 2005.
Gerli, Michael E. "Introduction." In *Studies on the Spanish Sentimental Romance, 1440–1550: Redefining a Genre*, edited by Joseph J. Gwara and E. Michael Gerli, xiii–xvii. London: Tamesis, 1997.
Gómez Martínez, José Luis. *Américo Castro y el origen de los españoles: Historia de una polémica.* Madrid: Gredos, 1975.
Góngora y Argote, Luis de. *Soledades.* 1613. Reprint. Madrid: Imprenta Real, 1636.
González Echevarría, Roberto. *Celestina's Brood: Continuities of the Baroque in Spanish and Latin American Literature.* Durham, NC: Duke University Press, 1993.

Green, Roland. *Post-Petrarchism: Origins and Innovations of the Western Lyric Sequence*. Princeton, NJ: Princeton University Press, 2014.
Hart, Thomas. *Cervantes and Ariosto: Renewing Fiction*. Princeton, NJ: Princeton University Press, 1989.
Hazm, Ibn. *El anillo de la paloma*. Reprint. Madrid: Alianza Editorial, 2012.
Hebreo, León. *Dialogues of Love*. Edited by Bacich Cosmos and Rosella Pescatori. Toronto: University of Toronto Press, 2009.
Herrera, Fernando de, ed. *Obras de Garcilasso de la Vega con anotaciones*. Seville: Alonso de Barrera, 1580.
Jeffs, Kathleen. *Staging the Spanish Golden Age: Translation and Performance*. Oxford: Oxford University Press 2018.
Jones, Frederic J. *Structure Petrarch Canzoniere*. Cambridge, UK: D.S. Brewer, 1995.
Kelly, Joan. "Did Women Have a Renaissance?" In *Women, History, and Theory: The Essays of Joan Kelly*. 19–50. Chicago: University of Chicago Press, 1987.
Laguna, Ana María. "Shipwrecked Na(rra)tion in Cervantes." *Hispanic Review* 87, no. 2 (2019): 183–207.
– "Through the Bonfires of Petrarchism: Flemish Aesthetics in 'El Coloquio de los perros.'" *Hispanic Review* 75, no. 1 (2007): 23–45.
León, Fray Luis. *La perfecta casada*. 1583. Reprint. Madrid: Espasa Calpe, 1980.
Leushuis, Reinier. *Speaking of Love: The Love Dialogue in Italian and French Renaissance Literature*. Leiden, NL: Brill, 2017.
Luhman, Niklas. *The Codification of Intimacy*. Palo Alto, CA: Stanford University Press, 1982.
Maggi, Armando. *In the Company of Demons: Unnatural Beings, Love, and Identity*. Chicago: University of Chicago Press, 2008.
Mariscal, George. *Contradictory Subjects: Quevedo, Cervantes, and Seventeenth-century Spanish Culture*. Ithaca, NY: Cornell University Press, 1991.
Marsilio Ficino. *Commentaries on Plato*. Edited and translated by Michael J.B. Allen Cambridge, MA: Harvard University Press, 2008.
Martín, Adrienne. *An Erotic Philology of Golden Age Spain*. Nashville, TN: Vanderbilt University Press, 2008.
McKendrick, Melveena. *Identities in Crisis: Essays on Honour, Gender and Women in the Comedia*. Volume 77. Kassel, DE: Reichenberger, 2002.
Meri, Joseph W., and Jere L. Bacharach. *Medieval Islamic Civilization: An Encyclopedia*. Vol. 1, *A–K Index*. New York and London: Routledge, 2006.
Middlebrook, Leah. *Imperial Lyric: New Poetry and New Subjects in Early Modern Spain*. University Park: Pennsylvania State University, 2009.
Mortimer, Anthony. *Petrarch's* Canzionere *in the English Renaissance*. Amsterdam: Rodopi, 2005.
Munk, Victor C. *Romantic Love and Sexual Behavior: Perspectives from the Social Sciences*. Westport, CT: Greenwood, 1998.

Navarrete, Ignacio. *Orphans of Petrarch: Poetry and Theory in the Spanish Renaissance*. Los Angeles: Center for Medieval and Renaissance Studies, 1994.
Nocentelli, Carmen. *Empires of Love: Europe, Asia, and the Making of Early Modern Identity*. Philadelphia: University of Pennsylvania Press, 2014.
Olivares, Julián. *The Love Poetry of Francisco de Quevedo*. Cambridge: Cambridge University Press, 1983.
Pérez, Janet, and Maureen Ihrie, *The Feminist Encyclopedia of Spanish Literature: A–M*. Greenwood, CT: Westport, 2002.
Perry, Mary Elizabeth. *Gender and Disorder in Early Modern Seville*. Princeton, NJ: Princeton University Press, 1991.
Petrarch. *Canzionere*. 1366. Reprint. Edited by Marco Santagata. Milan: Mondadori, 1996.
Quintero, María Cristina. *Gendering the Crown in the Spanish Baroque* Comedia. Aldershot, UK: Ashagte, 2016.
Rey, Alfonso. *The Last Days of Humanism: A Reappraisal of Quevedo's Thought*. Leeds, UK: Modern Humanities Research Association and Routledge, 2015.
Robbins, Jeremy. *Arts of Perception: The Epistemological Mentality of the Spanish Baroque*. Abingdon-on-Thames, UK: Routledge, 2007.
Rose, Mary Beth. *The Expense of the Spirit: Love and Sexuality in English Renaissance Drama*. Ithaca, NY: Cornell University Press, 1991.
Rupp, Stephen. "Love." In *Lexikon of the Hispanic Baroque: Transatlantic Exchange and Transformation*, edited by Evonne Levy and Kenneth Mills, 213–15. Austin: University of Texas Press, 2014.
Rutherford, John, ed. *The Spanish Golden Age Sonnet*. Cardiff: University of Wales Press, 2016.
Sauter, Michael. "Love of Geometry: The Rise of Euclidism in the Early Modern World, 1450–1850." In *Kinship, Community, and Self: Essays in Honor of David Warren Sabean*, edited by Jason Coy, Benjamin Marschke, and Jared Poley, 185–201. New York and Oxford: Berghahn, 2014.
Sluiter, Ineke, and Ralph Rosen. *Free Speech in Classical Antiquity*. Leiden, NL: Brill, 2004.
Smith, Julian. *The Body Hispanic: Gender and Sexuality in Spanish and Spanish American Literature*. Oxford: Clarendon Press, 1992.
Soufas, Teresa. *Dramas of Distinction: Plays by Golden Age Women*. Lexington: University Press of Kentucky, 1997.
Speroni, Sperone. "Apologia dei dialogi." In *Trattatisti del Cinquecento*, edited by Mario Pozzi. Milan and Naples: Ricciardi, 1978.
Stroud, Mathew. "The Wife-Murder Plays." In *A Companion to Early Modern Hispanic Theater*, edited by Hilaire Kallendorf, 91–103. Leiden, NL: Brill, 2014.
Sydney, Philip. *Countess of Pembroke's Arcadia*. Harmondsworth, UK: Penguin, 1977.

Taylor, Scott. "Honor." In *Transatlantic Exchange and Transformation,* edited by Evonne Levy and Kenneth Mills, 156–58. Austin: University of Texas Press, 2014.

– *Honor and Violence in Golden Age Spain.* New Haven, CT: Yale University Press, 2008.

Torres, Isabel. *Love Poetry in the Spanish Golden Age: Eros, Eris, and Empire.* Woodbridge, UK: Tamesis, 2013.

Turner, Henry. *The English Renaissance Stage: Geometry, Poetics, and the Practical Spatial Arts, 1580–1630.* Oxford: Oxford University Press, 1991.

Vives, Juan Luis. *De institutione feminae christianae,* 1523. Reprint. Leiden, NL: Brill, 2012.

Vollendorf, Lisa. *Reclaiming the Body.* Chapel Hill: University of North Carolina Press, 2001.

Williamsen, Amy. "Women Playwrights." In *The Routledge Research Companion to Early Modern Spanish Women Writers.* Edited by Nieves Baranda and Anne J. Cruz, 187–202. New York: Routledge, 2018.

Wittek, Paul. *Rise of the Ottoman Empire.* Royal Society, 1938. Reprint, New York and London: Routledge, 2012.

Woodcock, Bruce. "'Anxious to Amuse': Metaphysical Poetry and the Discourse of Renaissance Masculinity." In *Writing and the English Renaissance,* edited by William Zunder and Suzane Trill, 51–68. London: Longman, 1996.

PART I

Ambiguous Optics: Reframing Perception, Gender Subjectivity, and Genre Convention

Chapter One

Egocentricity versus Persuasion: *Eros, Logos,* and *Pathos* in Cervantes's Marcela and Grisóstomo Episode

JOAN CAMMARATA AND ANA MARÍA LAGUNA

In chapters 11–14 of Part I of his *Don Quixote,* Cervantes introduces in an arcadian *locus amoenus* the unrequited love story of two self-styled shepherds, Grisóstomo and Marcela. The reader soon learns that the departed Grisóstomo aims to honour his love for Marcela even after death: he instructs his fellow shepherds to bury him at the very spot where Marcela's beauty had first caught his gaze, illustrating, with this gesture, the classical and courtly notion that love enters a lover's soul through the eyes. On the other hand, Marcela, much as the title character of Cervantes's 1585 pastoral novel *La Galatea,* is described early on as a virtuous young woman who inspires love in many suitors but who rejects them all to remain self-sufficient. From its very start, the episode in *Don Quixote* emblematizes the amorous conflict characteristic of pastoral fiction, a genre that Cervantes seemed to have been intimately attached to from his first work, *La Galatea,* Part I, to his promised but never completed last novel, *La Galatea,* Part II.[1]

In Cervantes's lifelong commitment to the pastoral, critics have seen a belief in the possibilities of a genre particularly suited to the exploration of "the sentiments of love and the discussion of its psychology, ethics, and metaphysics" (Close, "Miguel de Cervantes," 205). Not coincidentally, love, a quintessential element in this kind of romance, is also so prevalent in Cervantes's writings that it has been at times considered "a shaping form of [his] fiction" (González Echevarría xviii).[2] Stressing the association between the pastoral context and Cervantes's fondness for this topic, numerous scholars have argued that Cervantes, "an inveterate commentator on love in all its forms" (Thompson 272), seems to have forged his personal – and arguably negative – view of the emotion precisely in the bucolic stories that regularly depict it as volatile and unsatisfying desire.

Eros, in Cervantes, is often described in pessimistic terms; Lenio, a shepherd in *La Galatea*, for instance, characterizes it as a "perturbation" (pertubación del alma [IV: 420]) caused by physical urges – "love is nothing but lust" (el amor no es otra cosa que el deseo [IV: 420]) – and responsible for poisonous effects – "Oh, bitter sweetness, oh poisonous medicine for lovers's malady! Oh unhappy joy!" (¡Oh venenosa medicina de los amantes no sanos; ¡oh, triste alegría! [IV: 427]).[3] While critics such as Ruth El Saffar, Javier Herrero, and John Weiger have attributed this negative perspective to Cervantes's personal views of the emotion,[4] others, like Anthony Close, consider it a default mechanism extracted from pastoral convention and applied systematically – after writing *La Galatea* – to all his "subsequent romantic fiction" ("Miguel de Cervantes," 205).[5] Regardless of the reasons for this unfavourable treatment or understanding of the emotion, echoes of Lenio's indictment can be found throughout the entirety of Cervantine works.[6] Time and again, some of Cervantes's most iconic lovers, from Quixote to Cardenio, Grisóstomo, Anselmo, and Lotario, embody or exemplify a negative – even "pestilent" (amorosa pestilencia) – outlook on the sentiment.[7]

At first sight, Marcela's rejection of love for the sake of "a celibate *vita solitaria*" appears to illustrate plainly this anti-erotic pastoral bias (Close, *Quixote*, 34). However, a careful analysis of her discourse indicates a redirection rather than a total rejection of her desire: "[W]hen he [Grisóstomo] revealed to me the virtue of his desire," she reminds us, "I told him that *mine was* to *live perpetually alone* and *have the earth enjoy the fruit of my seclusion and the spoils of my beauty*" (*Don Quixote* I.14: 100; emphasis added) (cuando me descubrió la bondad de su intención, le dije yo que *la mía* era vivir en perpetua soledad y de que *sola la tierra gozase el fruto de mi recogimiento y los despojos de mi hermosura* [*Ingenioso hidalgo* I.14: 187; emphasis added]). With this statement, the shepherdess vindicates the uniqueness of a personal desire ("mine") that is to be experienced and enjoyed in absolute privacy and seclusion. The intent to live in nature while enjoying complete independence has traditionally been considered essentially narcissistic and egotistic; yet, by defending her aim to reach emotional and perhaps erotic self-fulfilment in such solitude, Marcela is strikingly expanding the amatory limits of a conventional arcadia to the ambiguous and unexplored territory of self-love. By exploring this expansion – in all its literary, ethical, and rhetoric dimensions – this chapter aims to determine to what extent Marcela's self-contained position permits her to escape the crippling effects of traditional eroticism or compels her to surrender to another

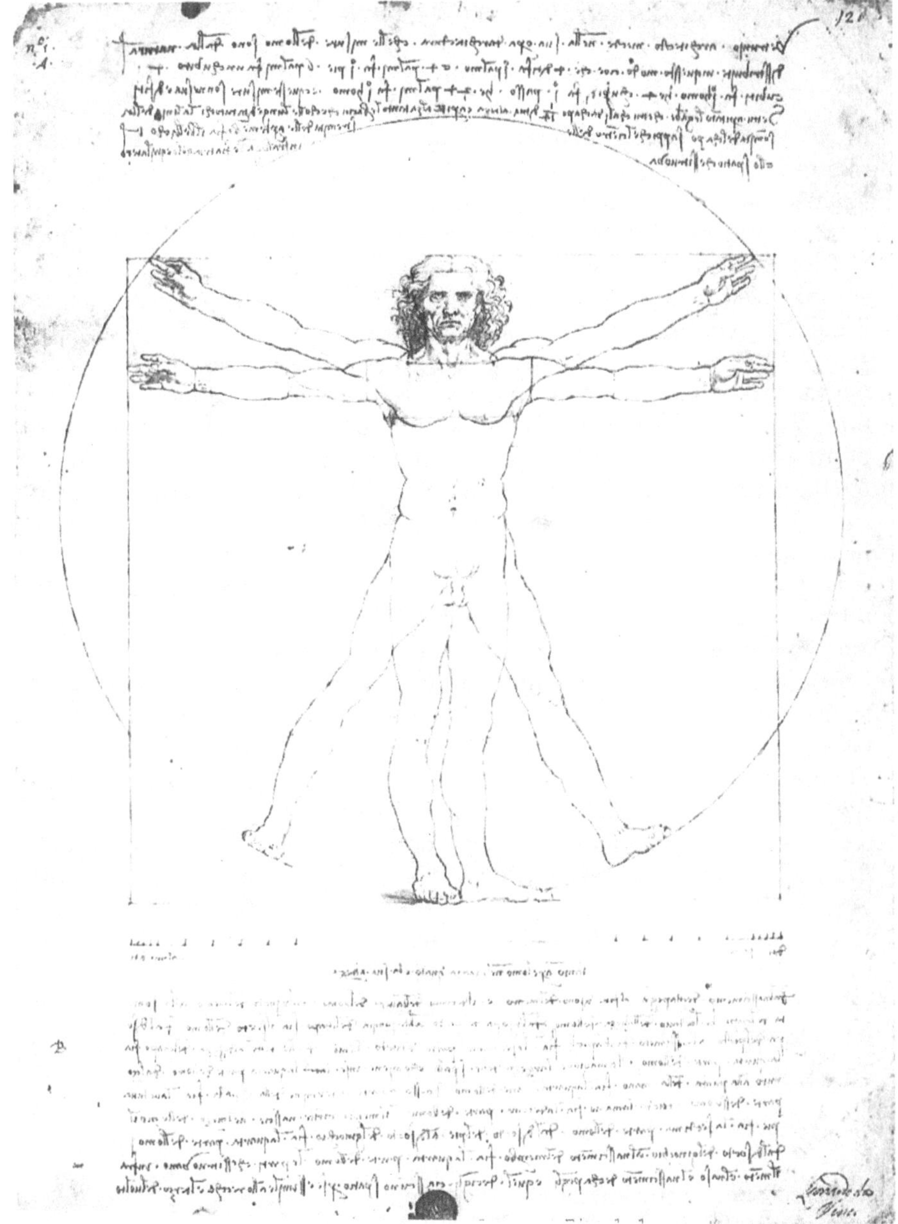

Fig. 1.1. Leonardo da Vinci's *Vitruvian Man*.
Source: Wikimedia Commons.

form of potentially damaging appetite, the "third mode of (self)desire," or self-love.

The early modern idea of the self as a space of love and desire – a topic often neglected in early modern scholarship, despite its centrality in the culture – constituted a poetic and moral domain much more ambiguous than generally assumed. Our contemporary preconceptions against self-love, which often equate it with a corrosive form of egotism, do not correspond with the elevated regard for human autonomy and self-realization that sustained the Renaissance and that was iconically summarized in Leonardo da Vinci's *Vitruvian Man* (fig. 1.1) (Brown 62; Reid 35). Even theologically or morally speaking, the concept of *amor sui* could not be bluntly disqualified given Christ's twofold love command: "You shall love your neighbor as yourself" (O'Donovan 1). The notion is supported by the fact that the most reputed moral references of the Golden Age, Saint Augustine and Saint Thomas, wisely refused to characterize this affection as inherently "sinful," deeming it instead as a virtuous and "well-ordered" sentiment as long as it did not exclude or compete with God's love.[8]

Regardless of its official moral neutrality, however, Marcela's self-reference has been traditionally and hyperbolically characterized as egoistic, "arrogant," "callous," "narcissistic," and "self-absorbed" (González Echevarría 86).[9] Not surprisingly, feminist criticism has strongly rebuked such judgments, considering them "gender-inflicted interpretative prisons" (Jehenson 16) predicated on dated and gender-prejudiced grounds. Thanks to the feminist lens, Marcela, rather than being considered "a wily and chatty female" (hembra ... ladina y habladora), is celebrated today as a "superb, equal, hence 'impossible' subject" (Jehenson, 16, 30), the embodiment of freedom (Rosales 320), and one of Cervantes's most "fascinating female characters" (Vollendorf 38). Profoundly misunderstood before, widely admired now, this unique character and the mystique surrounding her may have hindered our ability to do what this essay ultimately intends to accomplish: to understand the impact that her frustrated, self-erotic tale has on Cervantes's idea of love and on his sweeping innovation of the pastoral form.

Toward a New, Self-contained Arcadia

Renato Poggioli, immune to Marcela's charm, was one of the first critics to censure the shepherdess's *ethos* while still recognizing the striking narrative shift that, with her, Cervantes introduces in Spanish letters. For Poggioli, Marcela's interlude incorporates in the Spanish pastoral – decades earlier than in other European traditions – the notion of a "pastoral of the self," a narrative correction forged in the specific literary conditions of the moment:

> [O]ne could say that the task of European seventeenth-century literature was to liberate the pastoral from the excessive and exclusive concern with passion and sex that had shaped the bucolic vision of the Italians. The writers of that age succeed in doing so by taking up its neglected variants, such as the pastorals of melancholy and solitude, which they developed in either contact or contrast to the Italian example and then by creating a novel variant, such as *the pastoral of self,* which in the end transcended all previous traditions of the genre. ("The Pastoral," 686; emphasis added)

According to Poggioli, Marcela illustrated the particular conflict between the pastoral of love (and sex) and the "pastoral of the self" (or self-fulfilment), which resulted in the victory of the latter. Cervantes rejected love for the sake of an individual affirmation that was even more provocative when voiced by a female character. Nevertheless, the Italian critic considers Marcela's "*excessive* concern with selfhood" as an attitude that almost inevitably ends "in self-love" ("The Pastoral," 693; emphasis added), understanding by this term not the "well-ordered" affection praised by Saint Thomas but the tainted self-concern with which Cicero criticized those uniquely preoccupied with themselves (Cicero V.37).[10]

However, new developments in this "pastoral of the self" notion, have questioned some of Poggioli's critique of this fictional form. The increasingly stronger self-awareness of pastoral protagonists is now regarded as an intentional strategy used by Renaissance authors to infuse into such characters a deeper and more defined individuality. After all, the plights of love – the essential pastoral obsession – are almost always about another person, and, given that characters consume almost all their energies in praising their beloved or lamenting his or her absence and indifference, these protagonists are generally left with little time or interest to reflect on themselves.[11] Critics such as Sue Starke and Judith Haber believe that pastoral protagonists manifest not only a considerable lack of self-awareness but also a striking absence of personal configuration in the narrative, and that this lack of personal development creates an endemic descriptive deficit in the genre. For these critics, pastoral fiction often compensates for such deficit through constant extrapolations of the protagonists's emotional states onto their natural surroundings, as if these landscape projections had the capacity to allow us to gain a better understanding of their undeveloped psychology. In other words, it is because of the absence of distinct self-descriptions in the pastoral that landscapes appear so often and so heavily humanized, since these natural descriptions act as ontological extensions of the generic characters that inhabit them (Haber 112).

It is easy to see this poetic principle at work in Marcela's episode, as her suitors are described by Pedro – one of Grisóstomo's fellow shepherds – as an undefined collective:

> And if you spent one day here, Señor, you'd hear these mountains and valleys echoing with the lamentations of the disappointed men who follow her. Not very far from here is a place where there are almost two dozen tall beech trees, and there's not one that doesn't have the name of Marcela carved and written on the its smooth bark, and at the top of some there's a crown carved into the tree, as if the lover were saying even more clearly that Marcela wears and deserves the crown more than any other human beauty. (*Don Quixote* I.12: 85)

> (Y si aquí estuviéseis, señor, algún día, veríades resonar estas sierras y estos valles con los lamentos de los desengañados que la siguen. No está muy lejos de aquí un sitio donde hay casi dos docenas de altas hayas, y no hay ninguna que en su lisa corteza no tenga grabado y escrito el nombre de Marcela, y encima de alguna una corona grabada en el mesmo árbol, como si más claramente dijera su amante que Marcela la lleva y la merece de toda la hermosura humana. [*Ingenioso hidalgo* I.12: 166])

Rather than acting as a witness to or a mediator of these suitors' desire, nature – the valleys and the beech trees – appears as a metonymical substitution for all such human subjects, as an indivisible experiential continuum at odds with any individual differentiation.

The attitude seems peculiarly intensive to Cervantes, even when using motifs – like that of carving the name of one's beloved in a tree – that are not new or unique to him. While the visually evocative episode is found in numerous classic authors, from Virgil to Ovid and Propertius, and was widely revived in Renaissance paintings and letters (with Sannazaro, Boiardo, and Ariosto) (see fig. 1.2), men and natural elements do retain their ontological distinction in all instances.[12]

The peculiar Cervantine assimilation of pastoral protagonists into their natural environments applies to female characters as well. Diana de Armas points out, for example, how the intriguing character Feliciana de la Voz from *The Trials of Persiles and Sigismunda* (1616) – a pregnant woman who, like Marcela, chooses to embark on a "crude pastoral" adventure – is described by an aged shepherd – a rustic clown who sees no difference at all "between a woman and a cow giving birth" (del parto de una mujer que del de una res) – as enclosed and nurtured within a "pregnant tree" (200).

Fig. 1.2. "Roland déracine les arbres," L. Ariosto, *Orlando furioso* (Venice: Giolito, 1542).

Marcela, at first, seems to be affected by a similarly unglamorous confusion as she is depicted by the rustic Pedro as no less than poison to the fields: "And by living this way, she does more harm in this land than the plague" (*Don Quixote* I.12: 85) (Y con esta manera de condición hace más daño a esta tierra que si por ella pasara la pestilencia [*Ingenioso hidalgo* I.12: 166]). However, when she is given the chance to describe herself, she proudly affirms her independence and individuality through an intimate communion with nature: "*I* was born free, and in order to live free I chose the solitude of the countryside. The trees of these mountains are *my* companions, the clear water of these streams *my* mirrors; *I* communicate *my* thoughts and *my* beauty to the trees and to the waters" (*Don Quixote* I.14: 99, emphasis added) (*Yo* nací libre, y para poder vivir libre escogí la soledad de los campos. Los árboles destas montañas son *mi* compañía, las claras aguas destos arroyos *mis* espejos; con los árboles y con las aguas comunico *mis* pensamientos y hermosura [*Ingenioso hidalgo* I.14: 186]). In this case, Marcela's self-definition, discursively emphasized by the repetitive usage of the first-person subject "I" is clear: rather than being assimilated to them, she uses fields, mountains, and streams as supportive companions of *her* ("my") independence. The strategy not only humanizes but also sexualizes such natural elements, which now appear characterized as the only parties allowed to share and enjoy her presence and beauty. In doing so, as Starke points out, Marcela uses "the language of eroticism to argue for her right to freedom from it" (12). Furthermore, by characterizing nature as her chosen lover, the shepherdess creates out of this idyllic *locus amoenus* an unbeatable romantic rival to Grisóstomo, since nature offers "an improvement over what mortal man has to offer" (Starke 11). In establishing an intimate connection with a form of nature that embraces her individuality while also affirming nature ontologically and erotically, Marcela reinforces her choice of desire and eliminates societal obligations and moral threats to her honour. She, nonetheless, opens herself up to the charges of narcissism and egotism that surround this form of affection, placing her on the uncharted – and easily condemnable – moral ground of self-love.

Cervantes's Arcadia and the Perils of Self-love

Poggioli's brilliant recognition of the shift from a "pastoral of love" to a "pastoral of self" in seventeenth-century fiction assumes the substitution of one thematic element (love) for another (self); what he did not, or could not, specify, however, was the moral quality of each one of those elements (that is, "love" and "selfhood"). Was Poggioli thinking of an egotistical form of self-awareness (Marcela's, in this case) that tragically replaces a pure and selfless kind of love (Grisóstomo's)? But what if Grisóstomo's affection for Marcela was not that innocent and Marcela's self-regard not that reprehensible? Could Poggioli's hypothesis accurately apply or describe the ambiguous intents and sentiments that usually characterize Cervantes's protagonists?

Ironically, in an arcadia populated by protagonists like Grisóstomo, Marcela, Don Quixote, Cardenio, and Feliciana de la Voz, the "pastoral of love" might not be that different from the "pastoral of the self," since, there, all protagonists seem to follow Richard Rubenstein's suggestion that "the genesis of human love" *is* "self-centered desire" (44). David Quint has explored how it is, in fact, a purely egoistic motivation that inspires a good number of Cervantine lovers, from Cardenio to Anselmo and Lotario, including Grisóstomo, Tomás Rodaja, and Fernando (24–5). To him, all such *inamorati* follow the lead of the most narcissistic lover of all, Quixote (24). All of these male protagonists approach love as a solution to at least two self-centred aims: the affirmation of their superiority as lovers – proven in the defeat of all the rivals they encounter – and the satisfaction of the various self-serving romantic fantasies that set them off in their journeys (Quint 24; Poggioli, "The Pastoral," 693).[13]

Current theorists agree with Rubenstein and Quint on the inherent selfishness of romantic love. Karl Barth, a Swiss theologian, for example, claims that "the man who loves erotically is not really thinking of the other but of himself ... as an expected increase and gain for his own existence, as an acquisition, a booty, prey, to be used in the pursuance of some purpose" (746). In literature, this particularly self-obsessed view of love, although not exclusive to the pastoral, seems to make the genre particularly prone to it. It might not be a coincidence, as Quint also reminds us, that all the Cervantine lovers that love so similarly – Cardenio, Grisóstomo, Quixote, and the like – become, sooner or later, wrapped in pastoral and Petrarchan convention: "Cardenio writes an accusatory sonnet to Luscinda, giving her the name of Phyllis ... Anselmo encourages Lotario to write sonnets to Camila, addressing her as Cloris ... Grisóstomo literally reenacts the role of the lovelorn pastoral swain" (Quint 24). After all, the pastoral lifts from its protagonists all other sets of social circumstances and obligations, leaving them completely exposed to their affective obsessions, which are often self-centred.

The Rhetoric of Self-love

It is hardly surprising then that, in this self-oriented landscape, Marcela appears as a character no less self-centred than her male counterparts – even though she is by far the one most aggressively criticized for it. While her refusal to accede to Grisóstomo's importuning can hardly be called selfish, her strong defiance about accommodating social and erotic mandates has been characterized, in the best-case scenario, as a "selfish idealism" (González del Valle and Baena; González Echevarría) and, worse, as an obsessive "denial of the Christian command of love, as well as that of the pastoral one" (Poggioli, "The Pastoral," 693). Nevertheless, critics have not fully explained what this "selfish idealism" entails or how the mandates of Christian and pastoral love – apparently so divergent, one being chaste while the other is at least ambiguously erotic – could apply to the character.[14] Marcela's refusal of Grisostómo's courtly and Petrarchan amorous obligations can simply be considered a blunt rejection of these poetic codes, two literary and symbolic systems of reference that were under constant "attack at the beginning of the 1600s" (Iventosch 70).[15]

Part of the scrutiny and revision of these courtly and Petrarchan references had been imposed by the Neoplatonic masterminds Marsilio Ficino and Leone Ebreo, who had critically revisited the bucolic "highly stylized ... preoccupation with the nature of love and suffering" inherited from these two love paradigms (Gerli 188). Love, Gies reminds us, is still the centre that pastoral novels like *Diana* revolve around, but now it is a centre severely scrutinized, where different shades, natures, and intents start to emerge and become recognized. "True love" thus becomes identified as "chaste and pure and moved by virtue" and "[f]alse love, on the other hand, springs from the appetites and pursues physical satisfaction" (Gies 189).

Marcela adds a new essential dimension to this definition of "true love" by advocating that it must also "be voluntary, not forced" (*Don Quixote* I.14: 99) (el verdadero amor ... ha de ser voluntario y no forzoso [*Ingenioso hidalgo* I.14: 186]). Other critical distinctions about the sentiment, such as the difference between love and infatuation or obsession, are equally evident in Marcela's speech, as she reminds her audience that it was Grisóstomo's impatience and ill desire, not her cruelty, that had killed him: "I have given no hope to Grisóstomo or to any other man regarding those desires, it is correct to say that his obstinacy, not my cruelty, is what killed him" (*Don Quixote* I.14: 99) (no habiendo yo dado alguna [esperanza] a Grisóstomo ni a ningún otro, bien puede decirse que le mató su porfía no mi crueldad [*Ingenioso hidalgo* I:14: 187]).

The idea is repeated numerous times:

> [Grisóstomo] persisted though I discouraged him; he despaired though I did not despise him: tell me now if it is reasonable to blame me for his grief! ... Let it be understood from this day forth that if anyone dies because of me, he does not die of jealousy or misfortune, because he who loves no one cannot make anyone jealous, and discouragement should not be taken from disdain ... Impatience and rash desire killed Grisóstomo. (*Don Quixote* I.14: 100)

> ([Grisóstomo] [p]orfió desengañado, desesperó sin ser aborrecido; ¡mirad ahora si será razón que de su pena se me dé a mí la culpa! ... entiéndase de aquí en adelante, que si alguno por mí muere, no muere de celoso ni desdichado, porque quien a nadie quiere, a ninguno debe dar celos, que los desengaños no se han de tomar a cuenta de desdenes ... a Grisóstomo mató su impaciencia y arrojado deseo. [*Ingenioso hidalgo* I.14: 187])

The first cause that Marcela argues to defend her lack of responsibility for Grisostómo's death is the lack of real love that characterized her suitor, since it was impatience and lack of self-control, rather than love, that killed him. Furthermore, her refusal to accept any responsibility for Grisóstomo's death indicates the lack of moral or poetic legitimacy that courtly love's most basic structure – the assumed cruelty of the beloved, and the prescribed suffering of the male lover – seemed to have in 1605. Her dismissal of Grisóstomo's poem also conveys the dismantling of the "grandiose edifice of Petrarchism" (Iventosch 70) that had used poetry to reward and justify the absurdity of unrequited male love (Rupp 15).

Yet, the charges of narcissism, self-righteousness, and even misanthropy that surround her rejection of these courtly and Petrarchan assumptions mounted. Poggioli, particularly, believes that it was her unjustifiable self-centeredness, rather than empathy, that made her appear at Grisóstomo's funeral:

> [N]o other detail proves this [degeneration of self-love] as eloquently as the fact that Marcela attends Grisóstomo's funeral merely because it is also her trial. If she comes, it is not to pay tribute of pity at the grave of a dead friend, but to use that grave as a tribune from which to plead the cause of the self ... Not unlike the devotees of *Eros*, she treats her far less carnal but no less profane passion as if it were a form of sacred love. (Poggioli, "The Pastoral," 693)

Marcela's intervention at Grisóstomo's funeral does indeed denote a self-interested purpose at odds with an empathic reaction toward his death; however, the incompatibility between these two positions (self-centredness and empathy) does not exclusively apply to the shepherdess, as the full scene demonstrates.

A lack of sympathy toward Marcela from her audience – and from subsequent critics writing in various periods – might prevent her speech from doing what it was originally designed to do: persuade all funeral attendees of her innocence. As a consummate rhetorician, she knows that, in order to persuade a particular audience, the orator must influence emotions or *pathos*.[16] A similar recommendation had been given by all masterful rhetoricians, from Aristotle to Quintilian, as the former reminds us: "[w]hen the facts and their importance are clearly understood, you must excite your hearer's emotions" (*Rhetoric* 19.3). The shepherdess, however, soon abandons this emotional appeal to construct a much more rational *oratio* that seems even juridical in its style. Through an obvious *interrogatio* (interrogative mode), she engages her listeners through clever rhetorical questioning: "For if his impatience and rash desire killed Grisóstomo, why should my virtuous behavior and reserve be blamed? If I preserve my purity in the company of trees, why should a man want me to lose it if he wants me to keep it in the company of men?" [*Don Quixote* I.14: 100] (Que si a Grisóstomo mató su impaciencia y arrojado deseo, ¿por qué se ha de culpar mi honesto proceder y recato? Si yo conservo mi limpieza con la compañía de los árboles, ¿por qué ha de querer que la pierda el que quiere que la tenga con los hombres? [*Ingenioso hidalgo* I.14: 187]).

Her exquisite defence, founded in reason (*logos*) does not strike an emotional connection with her audience, making her overtly rational *expositio* clash with the emotional contagion produced by the reading of Grisóstomo's "Song of Despair" moments earlier. The recitation of Grisóstomo's poem had produced, among his funeral attendees, a visceral understanding of his love and pain that had triggered a general and empathetic response in its audience, predisposing it – even more strongly – against Marcela.[17]

With its adverse reaction against the shepherdess, the crowd demonstrates a paradoxical and "unsympathetic" side of empathy, one that allows individuals or collectives to strongly side with one particular cause or position while not applying the same understanding to another. The surprising dimension of this emotion demonstrates that, contrary to expectations, as Douglas Hollan explains, sympathy does not always unify individuals: "Although we often think of empathy as a feeling, understanding, or disposition that enables people to build bridges among themselves, we must remember that one person's bridge is another person's boundary. Flows of empathy may facilitate in-group cohesiveness and identity, but at the same time, clearly demarcate boundaries between in-group and out-group and reinforce social hierarchies of various kinds" (83). A possible reason for this surprising side effect is the fact that an individual is likely to react with less compassion when a person observed in pain has previously been perceived as having fault in his or her own pain (Singer et al. 467). This emotional response has been reaffirmed by Fritz Breithaupt, who concurs that "it seems reasonable to speculate that someone who observes the mishap of another may have less empathy if he also attributes the 'fault' of the mishap to the other" (86).[18] An audience, then, is very unlikely to show any empathy to a party whom it believes has inflicted pain or damage onto himself or herself, or onto another person.

In Marcela's episode, this causal argument works on both sides of the spectrum: while Marcela attributes causal fault to Grisóstomo, and shows little empathy for his suffering and demise, the funeral attendees, attributing moral fault to Marcela, refuse to show any understanding for her position.[19] Thus, although there is a mutual lack of empathy, the absence of an emotional, compassionate understanding is more detrimental to Marcela, whose perceived detachment reinforces the perception of being cruel and cold.

Standing outside of this emotional dialectic, Don Quixote unilaterally exonerates Marcela in a judicial tone and terminology close to the one she employed:

> Let no person, whatever his circumstance or condition, dare to follow the beautiful Marcela, lest he fall victim to my fury and outrage. She has

> shown with clear and sufficient reasons that she bears little or no blame in the death of Grisóstomo, and she has also shown how far she is from acquiescing to the desires of any who love her, and therefore it is just that rather than being followed and persecuted, she should be honored and esteemed by all good people in the world, for she has shown herself to be the only woman in it who lives with so virtuous a desire. (*Don Quixote* I.14: 101)

> (Ninguna persona, de cualquier estado y condición que sea, se atreve a seguir a la hermosa Marcela, so pena de caer en la furiosa indignación mía. Ella ha mostrado con claras y suficientes razones la poca o ninguna culpa que ha tenido en la muerte de Grisóstomo, y cuán ajena vive de condescender con los deseos de ninguno de sus amantes, a cuya causa es justo que, en lugar de ser seguida y perseguida, sea honrada y estimada de todos los buenos del mundo, pues muestra que en él es sola la que con tan honesta intención vive. [*Ingenioso hidalgo* I.14: 188])

Quixote's triumphant recognition of Marcela's "virtuous desire," the desire of self-fulfilment, has no effect on the shepherdess, who had already returned to her arcadia, without expecting permission to do so, perhaps aware that a negative verdict has already been issued in the pastoral court of opinion.

Marcela's episode shows how, ultimately, the pastoral of the self cannot escape Cervantes's pervading irony; here, a valiant woman exposes the delusion and narcissism of Petrarchan and patriarchal love, but, in doing so, she demonstrates herself to be no less self-centred than her male counterparts (Starke 14). Marcela is partially successful in creating a pastoral of the self, one that might provide her with self-satisfaction, even though it may also grant her an almost complete seclusion from society – as Quixote points out when he certifies that she is "to be alone" (es sola). The new arcadian space – or fiction – that she creates might be less affected by the exhausting and agonizing demands of Petrarchan or courtly love conventions, but it continues to be plagued by damaging emotional and rational unrest, misjudgment, and confusion. In locating this deep-reaching poetic tension in a burial context, Cervantes lays to rest, with Grisóstomo's remains, the classic pastoral convention that had made love an unavoidable self-inflicted torment (and even atonement). Nonetheless, by recognizing the discord and exclusion that result from a unilateral rejection of true, self-effacing love, he creates the vacuum necessary for the writing of a new pastoral chapter, one cleansed from worn-out conventional expectations and renewed in the inexhaustible springs of bucolic romance.

NOTES

1 In the prologue to the second part of *Don Quixote*, Cervantes pronounced, "I forgot to tell you to expect the *Persiles*, which I am finishing now, and the second part of *Galatea*" (*Don Quixote* 458) (Olvídaseme de decirte que esperes el *Persiles*, que ya estoy acabando, y la segunda parte de la *Galatea* [*Ingenioso hidalgo* 26]). All citations from Cervantes's *Don Quijote* are taken from Luis Murillo's Spanish edition and from Edith Grossman's English translation.
2 Diana de Armas had similarly identified the expression of desire as a very "recurrent question" that articulates Cervantes's "entire literary project" (*Allegories of Love*, 92).
3 This long description of love is voiced by the character Lenio, who is, in John Weiger's opinion, Cervantes's clear *alter ego* (*The Substance of Cervantes*, 120).
4 It has often been suggested that Cervantes's negative views of love reflect a personal position; see, for example, El Saffar, *Novel to Romance*, 18, and Weiger, *Substance*, 120. Javier Herrero, on the other hand, agrees with Close; see "Arcadia's Inferno," 289.
5 Herrero evaluates the negative aspects of love presented in the pastoral genre. He observes that a different and happy ending for Grisóstomo would be marriage to Marcela: "True love for Cervantes, as for the Christian humanists who were his masters, is the one which brings man joy of living and acceptance of this world; it is not the heretical emotion which pushes him to self-destruction and torture. As the novels that are closely linked with the Grisóstomo-Marcela episode show (the interpolated stories of Cardenio-Luscinda and Fernando-Dorotea), true love, for Cervantes, as for Erasmus, ends in marriage" ("Arcadia's Inferno," 293).
6 See Cervantes's exemplary novel "La ilustre fregona," in *Novelas ejemplares*, 59.
7 There are, of course, more positive love stories in Cervantes, some of them even ending in marriage. Wedlock is often the goal of some of Cervantes's happiest lovers (Persiles and Sigismunda, Fernando and Dorotea, Basilio and Quiteria), even in circumstances as questionable as those of *La fuerza de la sangre*'s protagonists, Leocadia and Rodolfo. For critics such as Marsha Collins and, before her, Batallón or Herrero, marriage is, in all imperfections, the place where love is more often presented as an emotionally and sexually satisfying experience, a reminiscence of the influence that humanists such as Erasmus had on Cervantes (Collins, *Imagining Arcadia in Renaissance Romance*, 166). Others remain suspicious of the sincerity of the happiness of this ending (see Sullivan, *Grotesque Purgatory*, 53), considering Cervantes's usage of conventional wedlock as an artificial, irresolute

solution to what is perhaps the most essential ethical conflict of Golden Age literature: legitimacy of premarital or extramarital sex (Close, "Miguel de Cervantes," 205). Diana de Armas reminds us of the need to avoid generalizations of Cervantes's view of love, marriage, or carnal desire (*cupiditas*), since each of these erotic elements tends to be framed very differently by the existing forms of fiction; thus, while we could not say that courtly love or chivalric fiction "promoted" the institution of marriage, since love in these contexts usually signifies "first and foremost, sexual gratification for privileged people," Greek romance, on the other hand, regards love as "first and foremost marital fidelity for ordinary people" (de Armas, *Allegories of Love,* 15); Greek love stories are thus usually "organized as the trials of the protagonist's unflinching mutual fidelity, despite innumerable temptations, to a love whose goal is marriage, either attained ... [or] restored" (ibid., 15).

8 In Saint Thomas Aquinas's "Causes of Sin," he states: "a man desires a fitting good for himself [which] is right and natural; but inordinate self-love leads to contempt for God which Augustine reckons to sin" (*The Passions*, 537). Saint Augustine's views are more conflicting; although he appears to neatly differentiate human and divine love when he claims that there are "[t]wo different kinds of love [that] have given origin to two cities, a heavenly city and an earthy one," and that "[s]elf love, even unto contempt of God, gave origin to the earthy one; love of God, even unto contempt of self, gave origin to the heavenly one" (*The City of God against the Pagan* 14:28). He also considers both kinds of affection as mutually constitutive, as he states that "there is no way in which God could be loved without the lover loving himself as well" (O'Donovan, *The Problem of Self-love,* 37); for more on this paradoxical duality, see O'Donovan. Most of Saint Thomas's and Saint Augustine's views of love are based on classical thinking. It is worth noting that secular thinkers such as Plotinus, Plato, and Aristotle think positively of the virtue, and that it is Cicero who most often warns readers (and, centuries later, moral humanists and scholastics) to disassociate a constructive self-love from "the taint" and dangers "of pure self-interest" (*On Ends* 5.37). For the application and understanding of these theological and philosophical outlooks in the Spanish Golden Age, see Robbins, *Arts of Perception*.

9 Scholars are critical of Marcela's disposition, with assessments ranging from uncharitable and insensitive to self-serving and demonic; see McGaha "The Sources and Meaning," 69; Poggioli, *The Oaten Flute*, 174; Hart and Rendall, "Rhetoric and Persuasion," 292; Bandera, *Mimesis conflictiva*, 95; Sieber, "Society and the Pastoral Vision," 191; and Herrero, "Arcadia's Inferno," 296. Other critics defend Marcela's expectation of

the freedom of choice to live her life as she wishes: see Macht de Vera, "Indagación en los personajes de Cervantes," 7; Wiltrout, "Las mujeres del *Quijote*," 169; Chambers, "Structure and the Search for Truth," 314; Iventosch, "Cervantes and Courtly Love," 71; Mackey, "Rhetoric and Characterization in *Don Quijote*," 61; Dudley, "Don Quijote as Magus," 362; and Munich, "Notorious Signs," 245.

10 See also note 8.

11 See Starke, *The Heroines of English Pastoral Romance*, 130. A different subject is the self-awareness of the pastoral genre, as Alpers describes it: "self-consciously acknowledging its fictions while maintaining the pretense of reality, has been a pastoral capacity since its Alexandrian beginnings" (*What Is Pastoral?*, 362).

12 Lee claims that, despite its popularity in classical lyric, the motif had been largely forgotten until Ariosto reclaimed it in canto 19 of his *Orlando furioso*, where he is original in depicting an idyllic scene that is joyous and blissful as both Angelica and Medoro together happily link their names on trees (*Writing on Trees*, 30). For an updated history of the image, see Leah Knight's dedicated chapter, "Writing Green: Inscribing Early Modern Trees," in *Reading Green*, 81–109.

13 See also González Echevarría, *Love and the Law in Cervantes*, 88–93. Poggioli does recognize the inherent "hedonism" of the male erotic idyll at the heart of bucolic love ("The Pastoral," 692).

14 As Jean Harvey explains, "[e]mpathy, understood as a kind of opening to another is incompatible with being arrogant, scornful, or self-centered" (*Civilized Oppression*, 47).

15 Besides Iventosch ("Cervantes and Courtly Love"), this is noted by many Cervantists such as Witrout ("Las mujeres del *Quijote*," 169), El Saffar ("In Marcela's Case," 158), Nadeau (*The Women of the Prologue*, 104), and Bayliss (*The Discourse of Courtly Love*, 138).

16 Mancing has referred to Marcela's long eloquent speech as "an elegant defence of her proto-feminist philosophy above love and agency ... which is perhaps the single most impressive rhetorical display in the entire novel" (*Cervantes's* Don Quixote, 126). Mackey, and Hart and Rendall have analysed the rhetorical techniques used in the Marcela-Grisóstomo episode. Mackey concludes, "Cervantes' intimate knowledge of rhetorical precepts, the ease with which he uses the classical figures of thought and language, are apparent in every line" ("Rhetoric and Characterization," 51).

17 Aristotle observes that "emotions are pity, indignation, anger, hatred, envy, emulation, pugnacity" (*Art of Rhetoric* 19.3). Empathy is not identified as such, since the word "empathy" was introduced into English in the early twentieth century from its linguistic roots in the Greek *empatheia* (from

em- "in" + *pathos* "feeling"). In the classical world, empathy is usually identified with pity. Pity is not only endorsed by rhetorical manuals for simply creating an emotional/irrational connection with an audience but also for entailing a sophisticated thought structure that facilitates reasoning and deliberation (Boler, "The Risks of Empathy," 257); see also Martha Nussbaum, *Upheavals of Thought*.

18 Breithaupt's study on empathy, "A Three-Person Model of Empathy," addresses how a group elects to provide support to a given side during a confrontation.

19 González Echeverría has explained why this scene – as well as the whole episode – resembles a trial: "The conflict, involving injury, restitution, possible revenge, accusations, defense, judgment, and release from culpability, unfolds and is resolved in a decidedly judicial manner" (*Love and the Law,* 79), and there is the body of evidence, the corpse of Grisóstomo, for all to view.

REFERENCES

Alpers, Paul. *What Is Pastoral?* Chicago: University of Chicago Press, 1980.

Aquinas, Saint Thomas. *The Passions: Basic Writings*. Edited by Anton C. Pegis. Vol. 2. New York: Random House, 1945.

Aristotle. *Art of Rhetoric,* Translated by J.H. Freese. Cambridge, MA: Harvard University Press, 1926.

Augustine, Saint. *The City of God against the Pagan*. Edited by R.W. Dyson. Cambridge: Cambridge University Press, 1998.

Bandera, Cesáreo. *Mimesis conflictiva*. Madrid: Gredos, 1975.

Barth, Karl. *Church Dogmatics* IV. Translated by G.W. Bromiley. Edinburgh: T. & T. Clark, 1961.

Bataillon, Marcel. "Cervantes y el matrimonio cristiano." In *Varia lección de Clásicos Españoles,* edited by José Pérez Riesco, 238–55. Madrid: Gredos, 1964.

Bayliss, Robert. E. *The Discourse of Courtly Love in Seventeenth-Century Spanish Theater.* Lewisburg, PA: Bucknell University Press, 2009.

Boler, Megan. "The Risks of Empathy: Interrogating Multiculturalism's Gaze." *Cultural Studies* 11 (May 1997): 253–73.

Breithaupt, Fritz. "A Three-Person Model of Empathy." *Emotion Review* 4, no. 1 (2012): 84–91.

Brown, Alison. *The Renaissance*. Abingdon-on-Thames, UK: Routledge, 1998.

Cervantes Saavedra, Miguel de. *Don Quixote.* Translated by Edith Grossman. New York: Harper Collins, 2003.

– *El ingenioso hidalgo don Quijote de la Mancha.* Edited by Luis Murillo. Madrid: Castalia, 1978.

– *La Galatea*. Edited by Francisco López and Maria Teresa López García Berdoy. Madrid: Cátedra, 1999.
– *Novelas ejemplares*. Edited by Juan Bautista Avalle-Arce. Madrid: Castalia, 1987.
Chambers, Leland H. "Structure and the Search for Truth in the *Quijote*: Notes toward a Comprehensive View." *Hispanic Review* 35, no. 4 (Winter 1967): 309–26.
Cicero, Marcus T. *On Ends (De Finibus Bonorum et Malorum)*. Translated by H. Rackman. Cambridge, MA: Loeb Classical Library, 1914.
Close, Anthony. *Don Quixote*. Cambridge: Cambridge University Press, 1990.
– "Miguel de Cervantes." In *The Cambridge History of Spanish Literature*, edited by David T. Gies, 201–21. Cambridge: Cambridge University Press, 2004.
Collins, Marsha S. *Imagining Arcadia in Renaissance Romance*. Abingdon-on-Thames, UK: Routledge, 2016.
de Armas, Diana. *Allegories of Love: Cervantes's* Persiles and Sigismunda. Oxford: Oxford University Press, 1991.
Dudley, Edward. "Don Quijote as Magus: The Rhetoric of Interpolation." *Bulletin of Hispanic Studies* 49 (1972): 355–68.
El Saffar, Ruth. "In Marcela's Case." In *Quixotic Desire*, edited by Ruth El Saffar and Diana de Armas Wilson, 157–78. Ithaca, NY: Cornell University Press, 1993.
– *Novel to Romance: A Study of Cervantes's* Novelas ejemplares. Baltimore, MD: Johns Hopkins University Press, 1974.
Gerli, Michael E. "The Antecedents of the Novel in Sixteenth-Century Spain." In *The Cambridge History of Spanish Literature*, edited by David T. Gies, 178–200. Cambridge: Cambridge University Press, 2004.
Gies, David T., ed. *The Cambridge History of Spanish Literature*. Cambridge: Cambridge University Press, 2004.
González del Valle, Luis, and Julio Baena, eds. *Critical Essays on the Literatures of Spain and Spanish-America*. Boulder, CO: Society of Spanish and Spanish American Studies, 1999.
González Echevarría, Roberto. *Love and the Law in Cervantes*. New Haven, CT: Yale University Press, 2005.
Haber, Judith. *Pastoral and the Poetics of Self-Contradiction: Theocritus to Marvell*. Cambridge: Cambridge University Press, 1995.
Hart, Thomas R., and Steven Rendall. "Rhetoric and Persuasion in Marcela's Address to the Shepherds." *Hispanic Review* 46, no. 3 (Summer 1978): 287–98.
Harvey, Jean. *Civilized Oppression and Moral Relations*. New York: Palgrave, 2015.
Herrero, Javier. "Arcadia's Inferno: Cervantes's Attack on Pastoral." *Bulletin of Hispanic Studies* 55 (1978): 289–99.
Hollan, Douglas. "The Definition and Morality of Empathy." *Emotion Review* 4, no. 1 (January 2012): 83–83.

Iventosch, Herman. "Cervantes and Courtly Love: The Grisóstomo-Marcela Episode of *Don Quixote*." *PMLA* 89, no.1 (January 1974): 64–76.

Jehenson, Yvonne. "The Pastoral Episode in Cervantes's *Don Quijote*: Marcela Once Again." *Cervantes* 10, no. 2 (1990): 15–35.

Knight, Leah. *Reading Green in Early Modern England*. Abingdon-on-Thames, UK: Routledge, 2014.

Lee, Rensselaer W. *Writing on Trees: Ariosto into Art*. Princeton, NJ: Princeton University Press, 1977.

Macht de Vera, Elvira. "Indagación en los personajes de Cervantes: Marcela o la libertad." *Explicación de Textos Literarios* 13–15 (1984–5): 3–17.

Mackey, Mary. "Rhetoric and Characterization in *Don Quijote*." *Hispanic Review* 42, no. 1 (Winter 1974): 51–66.

Mancing, Howard. *Cervantes's* Don Quixote: *A Reference Guide*. Westport, CT: Greenwood Press, 2006.

McGaha, Michael K. "The Sources and Meaning of the Grisóstomo-Marcela Episode." *Anales cervantinos* 16 (1977): 33–69.

Munich, Adrienne. "Notorious Signs, Feminist Criticism and Literary Traditions." In *Making a Difference: Feminist Literary Criticism*, edited by Gayle Green and Coppelia Kahn, 238–59. Abingdon-on-Thames, UK: Routledge, 2005.

Nadeau, Carolyn. *The Women of the Prologue: Imitation, Myth, and Magic in* Don Quijote I. Lewisburg, PA: Bucknell University Press, 2002.

Nussbaum, Martha. *Upheavals of Thought: The Intelligence of Emotions*. Cambridge: Cambridge University Press, 2001.

O'Donovan, Oliver. *The Problem of Self-Love in St. Augustine*. New Haven, CT: Yale University Press, 1980.

Poggioli, Renato. *The Oaten Flute: Essays on Pastoral Poetry and the Pastoral Ideal*. Cambridge: Harvard University Press, 1975.

– "The Pastoral of the Self." *Daedalus* 88, no. 4 (1959): 686–99.

Quint, David. *Cervantes's Novel of Modern Times: A New Reading of* Don Quixote. Princeton, NJ: Princeton University Press, 2003.

Reid, Robert Lanier. "The Problem of Self-Love in Shakespeare's Tragedies and in Renaissance Reformation Theology." In *The Protestant and Catholic Poetics of* Julius Cesar, Macbeth *and* Hamlet, edited by Beatrice Batson, 35–56. Waco, TX: Baylor University Press, 2006.

Robbins, Jeremy. *Arts of Perception: The Epistemological Mentality of the Spanish Baroque*. Abingdon-on-Thames, UK: Routledge, 2007.

Rosales, Luis. *Cervantes y la libertad*. Vol. 2. Madrid: Ediciones Cultura Hispánica, 1985.

Rubenstein, Richard L. *Morality and Eros*. New York: McGraw-Hill, 1970.

Rupp, Stephen. "True Pastoral in *Don Quixote*." *Renaissance and Reformation* 16, no. 3 (1993): 5–17.

Sieber, Harry. "Society and the Pastoral Vision in the Marcela-Grisóstomo Episode of *Don Quijote*." In *Estudios literarios de hispanistas norteamericanos dedicados a Helmut Hatzfeld con motivo de su 80 aniversario*, edited by Josep M. Solá-Solé, Alessandro Crisafulli, and Bruno Damiani, 185–96. Barcelona: Hispam, 1974.

Singer, T., et al. "Empathetic Neural Responses Are Modulated by the Perceived Fairness of Others." *Nature* 439 (2006): 466–9.

Starke, Sue. *The Heroines of English Pastoral Romance*. Cambridge, UK: D.S. Brewer, 2007.

Sullivan, Henry. *Grotesque Purgatory*. University Park: Pennsylvania State University Press, 1996.

Thompson, Colin. "Eutrapelia and Exemplarity in the *Novelas ejemplares*." In *A Companion to Cervantes's* Novelas Ejemplares, edited by Stephen Boyd, 261–302. Rochester, NY: Boydell and Brewer, 2005.

Vollendorf, Lisa. *Reclaiming the Body*. Chapel Hill: University of North Carolina Press, 2001.

Weiger, John. *The Substance of Cervantes*. Cambridge: Cambridge University Press, 1998.

Wiltrout, Ann. "Las mujeres del *Quijote*." *Anales cervantinos* 12 (1973): 167–72.

Chapter Two

The Deceived Gaze: Visual Fantasy, Art, and Feminine Adultery in Cervantes's Reading of Ariosto

MERCEDES ALCALÁ GALÁN

In this chapter, I explore the various links that Cervantes established with Ariosto's *Orlando furioso* in two texts that deal with the theme of feminine adultery: the interpolated *Impertinent Curious Man* (*Novela del curioso impertinente*) in *Don Quixote*, Part I, chapters 33–5, and the interlude *The Jealous Old Man* (*El viejo celoso*). Besides developing a direct intertextual relationship between his texts and aspects of cantos 43 and 28 of *Orlando furioso*, Cervantes, as we will see, also draws on Ariosto by reworking certain visual techniques and iconographic references. Most importantly, both writers share a vision of feminine adultery that enquires into the roots of misogyny and relativizes adultery by locating transgressions of expected feminine conduct within a new ethical perspective.

The *Impertinent Curious Man* and the Deceived Gaze

Innumerable studies have explored the influence of *Orlando furioso* on Cervantes, especially with respect to *Don Quixote*.[1] Perhaps the most commented upon passages in this regard are those of Don Quixote's penitence in Sierra Morena and, above all, the intercalated novel *The Impertinent Curious Man* with its theme of jealousy, its direct allusion to canto 43, and the episode of the chalice from which Rinaldo wisely refuses to drink. In this essay, I will turn from *Don Quixote* so as to look into visual codes that configure the interlude *The Jealous Old Man*. In order to set up this exploration, I shall first approach the concept of visual fantasy that Cervantes takes from Ariosto and develops in the passage of *The Impertinent Curious Man* in which Camila dramatizes a tragic defence of her chastity. Camila's performance is configured in accordance with the widely known suicide of Lucretia, pictorial illustrations of which were ubiquitous in the early modern European world, including Spain. Camila (with the help of Lotario and Leonela) acts out Lucretia's suicide, playing the part of the chaste wife who stabs herself with a dagger for having her honour blemished by a suitor, in this case, through Lotario's amorous requests. The scene is organized with Camila knowing all the while that her husband, Anselmo, is covertly watching. The inspiration for this act in Lucrecia's famous immolation cannot be overstated, since the *Curioso* explicitly cites her – Lucretia – as the model deliberately chosen by Camila:

> "You may go, Leonela my friend, certain that I shall not," responded Camila, "because although in your opinion it is rash and foolish to defend my honor, I shall not go as far as that Lucretia who, they say, killed herself even though she had done no wrong, and without first killing the one responsible for her misfortune. I shall die, if I must; but I have to take my revenge and exact satisfaction from the man who has brought me to this place to weep over the insolence of his actions, for which I am blameless." (*Don Quixote* I.34: 299–300)

> (Ve segura, Leonela amiga, que no haré – respondió Camila –, porque ya que sea atrevida y simple, a tu parecer, en volver por mi honra, no lo he de ser tanto como aquella Lucrecia de quien dicen que se mató sin haber cometido error alguno y sin haber muerto primero a quien tuvo la causa de su desgracia. Yo moriré, si muero, pero ha de ser vengada y satisfecha del que me ha dado ocasión de venir a este lugar a llorar sus atrevimientos, nacidos tan sin culpa mía. [*Don Quijote* I.34: 408])[2]

In this passage, Cervantes plays with and complicates narrative techniques that involve the visual, not only in the supposedly clandestine gaze of Anselmo, but also through the theatricalization of the popular visual motif of Lucretia's suicide. The multitude of pictorial versions of her death, not only in the renowned rendition of important painters but in affordable woodcut printed cards or *estampas*, had turned this Roman legend into the icon of female chastity that supposedly defined the value of women. Frederick de Armas believes that Cervantes had referenced this icon before: "Raphael's *Lucretia* was also a preferred model of the knight errant, as well as Camila in *The Impertinent Curious Man*. Here we have a theatrical scene conceived, acted and directed by Camila in order that the spectator (Anselmo) accept her fidelity" (la *Lucrecia* de Rafael es también el modelo preferido del caballero andante, también lo es de Camila en la novela del "Curioso impertinente." Aquí tenemos una escena de teatro, concebida, actuada y dirigida por Camila para que el espectador [Anselmo] acepte su fidelidad) ("Pinturas de Lucrecia," 114–15).

In considering how a simple artistic representation encapsulates an entire literary scene as climactic as Camila's performance, we should remember the enormous weight of artistic iconography in Spanish society. Javier Portús Pérez and Jesusa Vega have attributed the popularity of such iconography to the ability of most households to possess quality *estampas* of secular themes that, by popular demand, reproduced the paintings of famous artists such as Titian, Raphael, Marten de Vos, and Federico Zuccaro (169).[3] The widespread awareness of iconographic elements such as those depicting Lucretia's suicide, then, may explain an inherent interconnection between artistic and literary works and motifs of Golden Age culture. This may explain the extremely important interconnection between the plastic arts and literature in an era in which the dissemination and knowledge of works of art was not accessible to the wider public through original paintings (although a more restricted audience did have some access to certain collections). It is thus necessary to consider the important and little-studied role of the *estampa* of non-religious themes in the dissemination of the plastic arts. Portús points to the common literary device whereby, in many early modern works, especially plays, there is an abundant presence of artworks, which explains why "these works reveal an iconography constituted as a reflection of the plot of the dramatic work" (169).

In the case of Cervantes, the use of these works of art whose significance is evident for his readers allows him to go deeper into the theme and exhibit an admirable economy of technique: the artistic background makes it unnecessary to construe fundamental aspects of the work that are already present via the amplifying power of artistic connotation. There is also a *trompe-l'œil* at work in *The Impertinent Curious Man*, because the true drama of Anselmo's deception is developed offstage. While Anselmo is hiding behind tapestries, he changes his opinion about Camilla thanks to her farce. Here I see a major parallel with the palace created by Argìa in *Orlando furioso*, which serves as a trap for her husband, who, incidentally, is also called Anselmo. As opposed to the husband Anselmo who hides to see an orchestrated performance in Cervantes, Ariosto has the wife, Argìa, be the one who hides and sees the truth. In Cervantes, the husband believes himself to be the one setting a trap for Camila, assuming that he is spying on her without her knowing, yet Camila, knowing that Anselmo observes her, is able to disarm the theatrical moment. Camila's whole act, then, was designed to satisfy Anselmo's gaze, but, rather than satisfying his gaze with the truth, Camila succeeds in tricking him by exploiting his jealous assumptions. Cervantes thus gives us theatre in reverse, in which truth and lies are mutually reflected in a sophisticated play of mirrors that would be impossible without a careful use of ekphrastic techniques and a narrative that explores the possibilities of the visual.

The historical character of Lucretia is not the visual or pictorial reference that allows Camila to succeed in her theatrical scheme. As Frederick de Armas has rightly pointed out, *The Impertinent Curious Man* contains visual references to Danae as well: "The Cervantine text prepares the reader to understand the impact of the myth of Danae, which in turn conceals an entire series of readings and visual elements that enrich the text. The visual hides behind fleeting allusions to paintings and statues, but is always present in the gazes, in how each of the three characters observes the others" ("El mito de Dánae," 151).[4] In fact, Cervantes conjures up a pictorial imagination that reinforces the emphasis on the gaze as an epistemological means that ends up being a trap for the senses. The entire *Curioso impertinente* is a sort of invisible museum that subtly evokes artistic representations that in turn nuance and enter into dialogue with the conflict formulated in the plot. The theme of the deceived gaze in the case of Cervantes is amplified owing to the intertextual framework in which literary texts are interwoven with plastic representations.

In canto 43 of *Orlando furioso*, after the oft-cited episode of the chalice to which the *Curioso impertinente* refers, we are told how Argìa eludes the punishment of her husband. Like the Cervantine Camila, Argìa has deceived her husband with a handsome youth, Adonio, in exchange for a magic lapdog (none other than the metamorphosed fairy Manto), which, when it shakes itself, casts off every kind of incalculable riches. When Anselmo finds out about her infidelity, he looks for her with the intention of killing her, but in an isolated place a fabulous palace appears before him, created by the fairy Manto as an illusion for his eyes. In the doorway there is a beggar, characterized in Ariosto's text as repulsively ugly – besides being described as an Ethiopian, a Moor, and black – who says he's the owner of the palace and then invites Anselmo to visit it. During the visit the beggar proposes to Anselmo to have sex with him in exchange for the palace. Anselmo acquiesces and is caught in the act by Argìa, who has been observing the scene from a hiding spot. In this terrible bind, Anselmo can only pardon his wife on condition that both of them forget their affronts (524–5).

These passages from Ariosto and Cervantes offer points of contact: first, the feminine trap that uses a visual fantasy – a palace on the part of Argìa and the personification of Lucrecia represented in art on the part of Camila – and, second, the hidden gaze, voyeurism. We should also notice that Cervantes's Anselmo, significantly, hides behind tapestries that serve as a blank iconographic surface on which could be inscribed, through transference of meaning, the image of Lucretia with the dagger in her hand so often represented in the art of that era. Cervantes's text marks this tension between being hidden by tapestries, which protect him from others' gazes, and the surprising passivity of Anselmo, whose urge to watch prevents him from reacting to save his friend and wife. In two different moments we see how he *listens* and *contemplates*, as if he were in a state of hypnosis, his life turned into a spectacle in which the metaphor of the fourth wall almost becomes a physical reality. Steven Hutchinson explains precisely the uncontrollable fascination that Anselmo experiences when faced with his artistic (theatrical and plastic) fantasies thanks to their mise-en-scène by Camila, Leonela, and Lotario:

> Anselmo experiences emotions not as a participant but as a spectator. He has become one of *us*, who admire artistically convincing performances, who want to know, imagine, see and feel through art. Although he *can* intervene, why would he ruin such a sublime piece of work? ... His wife and great friend are on the other side of the curtain, transformed into spectacle, into illusion ... [And] perhaps this is exactly what he wants: to see his surroundings as an illusion, and to "deliciously" enjoy as a witness the emotions that the spectacle excites. He demonstrates not a will to truth, but a will to non-truth. ("Anselmo y sus adicciones," 134–5)

Indeed, this "moral paralysis" that prevents him from breaking the spell of the spectacle he believes he has created through the traps laid for Camila captures the essence of this enigmatic character whose motivation is not jealousy, nor a sublimated homoerotic interest in Lotario, nor a morbid curiosity, as has been argued countless times. Anselmo manipulates life and turns it into a reflection of his desires and fantasies. Unlike many others, including Don Quixote, Anselmo does not try to turn fiction into life; on the contrary, his obsession is to turn life into a representation of the imagination, into a fiction, as though he were an artist. The perversion lies in the fact that Anselmo, without being an artist, is absorbed in the spectacle in which his fantasies come alive through the theatricalization of the painting of Lucretia protagonized by Camila: "Anselmo *listened* to all of this, and each word Camila said changed his thoughts, but when he realized that she had determined to kill Lotario, he wanted to come out and show himself and prevent her from doing so; he was held back, however, by *his desire to see* the outcome of so gallant and virtuous a resolve" (I.34: 299; my emphasis) (Todo esto *escuchaba* Anselmo, y a cada palabra que Camila decía se le mudaban los pensamientos; mas cuando entendió que estaba resuelta en matar a Lotario, quiso salir y descubrirse, porque tal cosa no se hiciese, pero detúvole *el deseo de ver* en qué paraba tanta gallardía y honesta resolución (I.34: 407; my emphasis). His "desire to see" – without intervening – is such that he contemplates how Camila stabs herself with a dagger as she feigns committing suicide (with Anselmo not knowing the wound will turn out to be superficial):

> Anselmo *watched it all*, concealed behind the tapestries where he had hidden; *he was astonished* by everything, and it seemed to him that what he had *seen and heard* was enough to allay the greatest suspicions, and he would have liked to forego the proofs that would come with Lotario's arrival, fearing some dreadful mishap. He was about to show himself and come out of hiding to embrace and reassure his wife, but he stopped when he *saw* Leonela return, leading Lotario by the hand. (I.34: 301; my emphasis)
>
> (*Todo lo miraba* Anselmo, cubierto detrás de unos tapices donde se había escondido, y de todo se *admiraba,* y ya le parecía que lo que había *visto y oído* era bastante satisfación para mayores sospechas y ya quisiera que la prueba de venir Lotario faltara, temeroso de algún mal repentino suceso. Y estando ya para manifestarse y salir, para abrazar y desengañar a su esposa, se detuvo porque *vio* que Leonela volvía con Lotario de la mano. [I.34: 409; my emphasis])

This example from the *The Impertinent Curious Man* shows how Cervantes establishes a rich literary relationship with the *Furioso* that goes beyond the theme of jealousy. *The Impertinent Curious Man* puts into play a visual rhetoric in which artistic quotations are interlaced with a narrative use of the gaze that, in turn, becomes a poetic technique that helps to compose the text. It is also important to emphasize that both Cervantes and Ariosto consider feminine adultery not as an absolute evil without relation to the marital context, but as conduct freely enacted that must be understood in comparison with the attitude of the husband. In the *Curioso,* Anselmo is seen as a husband who deserves neither the love nor fidelity of Camila, who decides of her own accord to give herself over to Lotario, to whom she is completely faithful until the end. Camila decides for herself and escapes the trial that her husband imposes on her without any moral right, willfully falling into the trap he has laid for her and concealing the reality through an appearance of virtue.

The scene in which Camila personifies the chaste Lucretia, before an Anselmo who believes he is watching without being seen summarizes and exemplifies the play of gazes and feignings that underpin the entire plot of the *Curioso*. Camila ends up directing this madness of ruses and illusions designed by Anselmo, not only by deliberately falling into the trap laid for her chastity but also by tricking the hunter into thinking that his prey has not fallen:

> Anselmo had been very attentive as he *heard and watched* the performance of the tragedy of the death of his honor, which had been performed with such unusual and convincing effects by the actors that they seemed to have been *transformed into the very truth that they were feigning* ... And so Anselmo was the most deliciously deceived man in the world: he himself led into his house the man who was the ruination of his name, believing he had been the instrument of his glory. (I.34: 304–5; my emphasis; translation modified)

> (Atentísimo había estado Anselmo a *escuchar y a ver* representar la tragedia de la muerte de su honra, la cual con tan estraños y eficaces afectos la representaron los personajes della, que pareció que se habían *transformado en la mesma verdad de lo que fingían* ... Con esto quedó Anselmo el hombre más sabrosamente engañado que pudo haber en el mundo: él mismo llevaba por la mano a su casa, creyendo que llevaba el instrumento de su gloria, toda la perdición de su fama. [I.34: 414; my emphasis])

In the case of Ariosto, the dénouement is very clear: Argìa betrays the jealous Anselmo with a handsome, generous, and devoted lover. In order to equalize the transgression of feminine adultery in an era in which masculine infidelity was the norm and bore no burden of social wrongdoing, Ariosto, as we've seen, has the jealous and righteous husband, a judge no less, give himself over for wealth to an old, "ugly, foul-smelling" black man, all of which implied, in that period, an act as degraded as his wife's transgression. Significantly, Ariosto goes to great lengths to level the behaviour of both parties and seek a resolution by which the husband has to pardon his wife because he has as much or more to hide.[5]

The Jealous Old Man: The Deceived Gaze Once Again

The interlude of *The Jealous Old Man* also reveals both the emphasis on visual techniques and the relativization of feminine culpability. Critics have traditionally linked this interlude to canto 28 of the *Furioso*, from which Cervantes takes the theme of a woman's deceiving her husband in his very presence. Moreover, the influence of the *Furioso* is obvious with the appearance of four of its characters in a tapestry of painted leather, a *guadamecí*. Cervantes's interlude of *The Jealous Old Man* follows Ariosto in the treatment of jealousy and acknowledges the source of its inspiration by means of a reverse ekphrasis that evokes, through the figures of this tapestry, Rodomonte, a character of the *Furioso* who would have his own life outside the book and would be a paradigm of jealousy, misfortune, and ineptitude in love.

The tapestry in *The Jealous Old Man* presents us with four characters from the *Furioso* who belong to the group of infidels: Rodomonte, Mandricardo, Ruggiero, and Gradasso. It is no surprise that Rodomonte stands out among them and has his face covered by his cape, which significantly distinguishes him from the others. Rodomonte, for his part, would have an important presence in early modern literature as an embodiment of jealousy, as, for example, in plays by Lope de Vega and Rojas Zorrilla, which both bear the title *The Jealousy of Rodamonte* (*Los celos de Rodamonte*).[6] As Carmen Marín Pina has pointed out, the term *rodomontade* was used as a synonym for brazen stupidity after the character was transformed from chivalric hero into a comical and braggart character (479). As she explains, it is very curious that, outside of the expected anti-Spanish circles in Italy and Spain, Rodomonte is linked with the figure of the boasting soldier, and that this would lead to the creation of a minor literary genre formed by a French and Italian group of satirical works that incorporate anecdotes of bragging Spanish soldiers. These works were inaugurated by Pierre de Bourdeille, Sieur de Brantôme, at the end of the sixteenth century, with his *Rodomontades Espaignolles*, opening the way for a good number of works also titled *Rodomontades*, published at the beginning of the seventeenth century (487–9).

Interestingly, Cervantes, by way of that visual quotation, strongly links his interlude to the *Furioso*, establishing an iconographic connection that not only figures importantly in the poetics of *The Jealous Old Man*, but also creates an intertextual web of correspondences between the two works. The technique of the tapestry that operates as an iconographic association between the two texts extends throughout Cervantes's interlude to resonate between characters and suggest reminiscences of the *Furioso* in the construction of the characters of Cañizares, the old husband, and Lorenza, the young wife. Cervantes can get away with the extreme economy of literary resources that he employs in this piece because the *Furioso* itself is a kind of imaginary background tapestry that clarifies, deepens, and sketches the themes of jealousy, misogyny, deception, and feminine agency. Most important in Cervantes's text is not what is seen but what is *not* seen, and also what is *imagined*, which, as I'll discuss further on, depicts the invisible.

What Cervantes does with *The Jealous Old Man* – as well as with the *Impertinent Curious Man*, although in another way – is defend feminine freedom by dismantling the concept of the wife's adultery as an absolute and totalizing crime that is presented as something isolated from the context in which it is produced. Besides the visual citations that relate the text of *The Jealous Old Man* with the *Furioso*, there is a much more essential point of contact between both visions of feminine adultery – namely, the relativization of feminine blame always contextualized by masculine behaviour, which produces the same attitude that we've seen in the *Curioso*. The Cervantine vision of feminine adultery is distinctively original in comparison to the treatment that tends to be given to this theme in the literature of his epoch. As Américo Castro rightly affirms, "Cervantes never presented a [feminine] adultery which he does not fundamentally approve or excuse" (242). Cervantes's adulteresses are always presented in a context in which this grave offence is not excused or pardoned but rather in which the emphasis on the notion of blame is removed and completely deactivated. Rather, the text enquires into the legitimacy of masculine jealousy, lack of love, the treatment of wives on the part of husbands, and, above all, the right of women to feel their own emotions and to live according to the impulse of their own sensuality. Feminine sexuality, especially in a text like *The Jealous Old Man*, is framed within a context of the natural, leaving aside the idea of behavioural deviation or concupiscent vice according to the marital, social, or religious norm, which, in turn, applies to the deceived husband, who ends up being portrayed as a morally inadequate being who also exudes, at the very least, a problematic sexuality. This is completely unexpected and unusual in the literature of this period, and presents an ideological opening that can only be characterized as revolutionary. As Hutchinson observes, referring to baroque literature, "in the most serious genres, adultery tends to be considered an absolute evil, a transgression of moral norms so severe that it is not questioned or analysed in context. Adultery is thus bluntly condemned, and the social norm is implicitly sanctioned" ("Norma social," 196).

In the interlude *The Jealous Old Man*, given its minor and burlesque genre, Cervantes is able to develop very far indeed the theme of the adulteress. As Marcial Rubio Árquez observes, the true theme of this interlude is not a hackneyed and traditional vision of the old man and the girl, abundantly broaching the same old misogyny inherent in the development of this cliché, but is, on the contrary, a defence of the freedom of feminine love (106). Although I by no means disagree with this reading that connects with canto 28 of the *Furioso*, I believe that Cervantes goes beyond this and suggests a more turbid situation than that of the unsatisfied young wife. It is obliquely suggested to us that the girl is trapped in a marriage that is not so innocuous as it seems. As will be recalled, the development of the story of *The Jealous Old Man* is quite crude, and is surprising for the directness of the actions and affirmations of the characters that do not justify her sexual desire through love or some romantic varnish.

The Genealogy of Misogyny: From the *Thousand and One Nights* to the *Furioso*

Before examining the Cervantine interlude, I would like to delve into the textual genealogy of its Ariostesque source. Canto 28 of the *Furioso* presents the same theme as *The Jealous Old Man*: on the one hand, it develops the topic of the wife's infidelity before the very eyes of the husband, who is unable not to be deceived, but, on the other, it questions the logic of jealousy and of deception, and, after presenting us with a scandalous example of feminine infidelity, both works ultimately use this example as an exercise of affirmation of the value of the woman. There is a very interesting datum with regard to the genealogy of this Cervantine source. According to María Jesús Rubiera, the *Furioso*'s source is taken from the *Thousand and One Nights*, still unpublished in Europe at the time, although some of its episodes were quite widely known in different versions before the publication of the collection of stories. Rubiera affirms that the collection's place of origin is very uncertain, although it appears to be India. Its first known source was Persian, and that source was translated and adapted into Arabic at the end of the eighth century (160). A complicated textual history followed, with diverse adaptations and modifications until the first-known written version in Arabic in the fourteenth century – which would be followed by others with important variants – was composed during the period of the Syrio-Egyptian dynasty of the Mamluks (1250–1517). Not until some undetermined moment of this period would the story that serves as the collection's cornice be significantly modified (160).[7]

In the primitive version, the king kills a wife every night, quite simply driven by his cruelty and misogynist scorn until, as we know, Shahrazad entertains him by telling him stories each night. Thus, in the earliest versions, no cause is given for this cruel punishment of the king's successive wives. It was probably in a medieval Arabic version that, for the first time, the king's cruelty was linked to feminine infidelity.[8] As Rubiera notes, in the primitive version, we have a cruel king who is appeased by Shahrazad's talent: this is an epic in which the villain is the king while the heroine who saves the community from such barbarity is a woman whose weapon is the word. However, the later version featuring the adulterous wives is more adjusted to the marked patriarchal character of Arab society, since it represents the women as guilty and the king as just. Shahrazad thus saves herself but does not represent or redeem women, to whom she is a brilliant and rare exception for her intelligence and virtue (165).

Canto 28 of the *Furioso* begins with a version of the frame-tale of the *Thousand and One Nights* and is, precisely, that narrative link, lacking in the primitive tale, that refers to women's immoral tendency toward infidelity.[9] Curiously, although some of the tales in the *Thousand and One Nights* were transmitted independently in Europe, this narrative motif appears for the second time in Europe in the *Furioso* (the first time it appears is in a story of Giovanni Sercambi in 1374), but, as Luis Bernabé shows, its source is unknown, since the story differs markedly from that of Sercambi (101–9). What Ariosto borrows from the *Thousand and One Nights* is the episode in which a king begins a journey to visit his brother but, shortly after leaving, returns to his palace because he has forgotten a jewel he was going to take as a present. He finds his wife with a black slave and kills them both. He proceeds with his journey but loses his health and colour. When his brother, the other king, notices that he recovers his healthy appearance one day and asks him why, he finds himself obliged to confess that he has seen his brother's wife, the queen, committing adultery, just as his own wife did, and that this has consoled him. Devastated, both kings go hunting and come upon a fearful genie or *efrit* who is sleeping and is attended by a very beautiful captive woman. The frightened kings try to hide, but the lovely young woman compels them to have sex with her under the threat of awakening the genie and being punished. When the erotic encounter is over, the woman asks them for their rings as a souvenir, and, to their surprise, they see that the captive has a collection of 560 rings, which correspond to the same number of lovers. The lass explains to them: "This *efrit* carried me off on my wedding night, put me in the box, placed the box in the chest, attached seven padlocks to it and dragged it to the bottom of the sea below the dashing waves. Little did he know that when a woman desires something, nothing can stop her" (Smithers 109).

The adaptation in the *Furioso* tells us how a knight and a king, both of them extremely handsome and valiant, are deceived by their spouses (and, as in the original story, the first of them loses his health and good looks until he discovers that the king, being more powerful, has had the same misfortune). Disenchanted, they travel the world, easily seducing whichever married women they choose. Fed up with feminine infidelity, they come up with a solution: they will share a young woman who, having two men, will thus satisfy her intrinsic need to be unfaithful. One night, a former suitor of the chosen woman slips into the bed that the three of them share, sneaking in at her feet and getting on top of her, and they make love all night long, despite their doing so between the two friends. In the morning, she confesses her infidelity, and both of the men realize that it is impossible to avoid feminine deception even when they're in a woman's presence.

Ariosto uses this story, which condemns all women and, in effect, justifies misogynist thinking, to identify and later ridicule Rodomonte's view of women. The story is told at an inn so as to please the jealous Rodomonte, who is resentful toward all women after having been abandoned by Doralice. Yet the episode ends in a surprising way, despite the displeasure of Rodomonte, who won't accept anyone speaking well of women, with the wise words of an elderly man who undoes this myth of feminine adultery as something extraneous to a husband's responsibility and behaviour:

> Now tell me: is there one among you who has kept faith with his wife, or denies ever going after another man's wife, given the opportunity, and even giving her presents? Do you believe you'll find one such man in all the world? Who says yes lies, who believes it is a fool. You, have you ever found a woman soliciting you? – and I don't mean street walkers.
>
> Do you know any man who would not leave his wife, however beautiful she was, to follow another woman, if he had hopes of a quick and easy conquest? And what would he do if a woman or young girl paid court to him or offered him presents? To please some woman I believe that every one of us would forfeit our own skins.
>
> The women who have left their husbands, more often than not they've had good cause: they find their men tired of them at home and gone out eager for other men's wives. But men, when they love, ought to wish their love returned, to receive in measure as they give ...
>
> Unchastity is the worst vice that can be imputed to women, and not to the whole sex at that. But in this respect who has a worse record than we do? Not a single chaste man is to be found. And we have all the greater cause to blush, considering that swearing, theft, fraud, usury, murder, and worse, if worse there be, is rare except among men. (canto 28, 79–83)

Ariosto's strategy here resembles Cervantes's approach: he lays out a scandalous story that, a priori, justifies jealousy and misogynistic rancour for the purpose of using that same story as a mocking portrait of the jealous man, emphasizing the absurdity of his view of women. Thus Ariosto, like Cervantes, after this story that corroborates the madness of masculine jealousy, stresses the responsibility of men in the conduct of women and looks for an equilibrium and equivalence between the responsibilities and obligations of husbands and wives by, surprisingly, comparing masculine to feminine adultery and insisting that, although a few women are unfaithful, women are nonetheless morally superior to men, who therefore have no right to vilify them.[10] Ariosto dismantles and invalidates the initial story with the words of this man who personifies a wise *auctoritas* and who, with his eloquence, convinces the reader, and the other characters who hear him, while provoking the ire of the irrational and ridiculed Rodomonte.

As we will see, *The Jealous Old Man* highlights the theme taken from Ariosto of the deception on the part of the wife in the presence of her own husband, which, as already said, comes framed by an interesting iconographic citation or inverse ekphrasis. Most interesting in this Cervantine text is the relativization of adultery as maximum transgression, contextualizing it within an unjust and abusive marital relationship in which the husband's impotence is the least of his wife's woes, as the text will suggest to us.

The Jealous Old Man: "Tricks Played on the Eyes Are the Devil's Work"

The plot of *The Jealous Old Man* begins *in medias res* with a conversation between an unhappily married young woman, Lorenza, and a go-between neighbour, Ortigosa, in the presence of Cristinica, the niece of Lorenza's old husband, Cañizares, a woman who is close to Lorenza's age and lives with the couple. Ortigosa promises Lorenza to bring her a handsome lad and put him in her bedroom, despite the jealous precautions of her husband. Lorenza explains that she can never go out or speak to anyone and that her husband has the keys to the seven doors that lead to the bedroom. Ortigosa tells her not to worry because she'll manage to bring her a lover so that she can enjoy love "even if the old man has more eyes than Argos and sees more than a fortune-teller" (204).[11] Cristinica, too, imposes conditions for this reified lad: "Mire, señora Ortigosa, tráyanosle galán, limpio, desenvuelto, un poco atrevido, y, sobre todo, mozo" (205).[12] Given Lorenza's difficulty in communicating with the external world, the neighbour foregoes all semblance of courtship and arranges a first rendezvous in which a sexual encounter is consummated without any attempt whatsoever at camouflaging the purely physical nature of this tryst. Expounding on the extremes of jealousy that her husband reaches, Lorenza tells how he rejected an excellent tapestry with human figures that was a good price and bought a more expensive one of landscapes so as not to have the figures of men in his house. This will turn out to be an important detail. When Lorenza complains about the seven doors, Cristinica tells her to look for the master key in Canizares's undergarments. Alluding to the old man's impotence, Lorenza declares: "No lo creas, sobrina; que yo duermo con él, y jamás le he visto ni sentido que tenga llave alguna" (206).[13]

Meanwhile, the old Cañizares tells a friend that he hasn't lived peacefully since he married. The dialogue is significant because the friend says to him that a young wife needs to enjoy the full fruits of marriage: "Y con razón se puede tener ese temor; porque las mujeres querrían gozar enteros los frutos del matrimonio" (210).[14] Cañizares replies in an ambiguous and surprising way: "La mía los goza doblados" (210).[15] Besides being an admission of the old man's impotence, evident when the friend responds that that is exactly the problem – "Ahí está el daño, señor compadre" (210)[16] – I believe the ambiguous and polysemic term *doblados* (folded) may also be read as "twisted." For the time being, Cañizares is unconcerned about his impotence – so graphically expressed by the term *doblado* – because he is assured of Lorenza's ignorance and innocence in bedroom matters: "Es más simple Lorencica que una paloma, y hasta ahora no entiende nada de esas filaterías" (210).[17] Nonetheless, as we'll see, Lorenza's raciness and determination have little to do with innocence and inexperience. Besides, when referring to her sexual desires, she expresses herself crudely and directly at the same time, as she makes her resentment known.

Later on, the neighbour Ortigosa comes to the house and wants to sell Cañizares a tapestry, saying she needs the money. Represented in it are four armed, infidel characters, among whom Rodomonte (with his face covered) stands out and provokes special displeasure in Cañizares. The old man can't accept the tapestry because it shows painted men, but he doesn't notice that it's all a trap on the part of the neighbour and that Lorenza's lover comes in behind it and goes with her into the bedroom. The intertextual play with the *Furioso* becomes evident with the tapestry that Ortigosa wants to sell the old man and that serves as a curtain behind which the lover hides and enters the house. Cañizares pays the neighbour so that she'll leave, but emphatically refuses the tapestry because the figure of Rodomonte perturbs him: "¡Oh qué lindo Rodamonte! ¿Y qué quiere el señor rebozadito en mi casa? Aun si se supiese que tan amigo soy yo de estas cosas y destos rebocitos, espantarse ía" (213).[18] On the other hand, whereas Cañizares gets annoyed at seeing Rodomonte painted as though he were a rival, he is incapable of seeing in him a certain reflection of himself. In the *Furioso*, Rodomonte, besides being jealous, is the most inept and unfortunate of all lovers: first Doralice abandons him in favour of Mandricardo, and later, he falls in love with Isabel, who escapes from his lascivious desires and chooses death instead. Rodomonte, drunk and trusting what Isabel tells him, unwittingly beheads her with his sword. Through her death, Isabel escapes his pursuit of her and ends up victorious by dying free.

Besides the tapestry, there are several references to painting in Cervantes's interlude. For the old man, any plastic representation of a human being provokes his displeasure – "ella no sabe mi condición ni cuan enemigo soy de aquestas pinturas" (213)[19] – whereas, for Cristinica and Lorenza, painting is related to erotic fantasy, to the freedom of desire. Cristinica, for example, requests a *frailecico* (little friar) for her enjoyment, to which Ortigosa is amenable: "Yo se lo traeré a la niña pintado";[20] to which Cristinica responds, "¡Que no lo quiero pintado, sino vivo, vivo, chiquito, como unas perlas!" (208),[21] and Lorenza says of her young lover that his "cara es como la de un ángel pintado" (216).[22]

When the young lover sneaks into the house, passing behind the tapestry, Lorenza encloses herself in the bedroom. Locking the door, she feigns being annoyed at her husband and starts to speak in the most scandalous way the details of her sexual relations with her lover, at the same time as she complains of how her husband has kept her deceived until now. After Lorenza presumably consummates the sexual relation with the young lover, she says, infuriated, "Ahora echo de ver quién eres, viejo maldito, que hasta aquí he vivido engañada contigo" (216),[23] and shamelessly points out the youth and beauty of her lover by referring to a beard that is not exactly on his face: "Lavar quiero a un galán las pocas barbas que tiene con una bacía llena de agua de ángeles, porque su cara es como la de un ángel pintado" (216).[24] Cañizares thinks these are jokes, and when Lorenza finally opens the door she throws the basin of water into his eyes and runs to dry him, allowing the lover to escape without being seen. With his eyes wet, the old man significantly exclaims: "Al diablo se dan las burlas que se arremeten a los ojos" (216).[25] This deception of the gaze of Cañizares, who is unwittingly present at his wife's adultery, brings us to canto 28 of the *Furioso* and to the theme of feminine adultery in the very presence of the husband.[26]

By means of the tapestry that links the text with the *Furioso*, relationships are established between the characters and those of Ariosto. The evocation of the *Furioso* establishes a rich texture of meanings and connotations that allow for a series of associations between the characters who, despite having been cursorily sketched out, possess a depth understood by the public thanks to the fact that they reflect characters and other plots well known at that time. The identification between Lorenza and Angelica is patent: like Angelica, Lorenza is able to make herself invisible, not with a magic ring but behind the door that gives her immunity, and behind which she tells of what can't be seen. Moreover, the relationship between Lorenza and the impotent old man bears some resemblance to that of Angelica and the hermit, as the old husband possesses her against her will and deceives her by enclosing and isolating her to try to preserve her dovish innocence. This infantilization and intended suppression of his young wife's natural instincts is similar to what the hermit tries to do with Angelica. Ultimately both Cañizares and the hermit fall short of the desires of each of these women, and their attempted control over them fails. As Ita Mac Carthy observes, "The decrepit old hermit drugs Angelica so he can rape her but his infirm body ('il corpo infermo') and disused libido are as ineffectual as the faltering leaps of an incapacitated steed. No matter how much the metaphorical rider spurs on his lazy nag ('pigro rozzon') it can do no more than raise its head ('non può far che tenga la testa alta'), until the defeated rider falls asleep, exhausted" (54).

In effect, Cañizares's jealousy conceals the simulacrum of marriage, an incapacity, a lack, a fraud. The material gifts, the clothing and jewels, turn the child-spouse into a doll to be dressed and adorned, thus exerting a control and an effect over her body that acts as a substitute for sexual possession. It is not strange, then, that Lorenza complains about her clothing and jewels and accuses Cañizares of having deprived her also of the pleasure so typical of women of that epoch of dressing up, and tells him that she would pardon him so many presents if, in exchange, he didn't have her so penned up and didn't do to her other things never seen in matters of decency ("otras cosas no vistas en materia de recato"). What is this text saying to us?

> [Q]ue me sobran las joyas, y me ponen en confusión las diferencias de colores de mis muchos vestidos; *hasta eso no tengo que desear*, que Dios le dé salud a Cañizares; más vestida me tiene que un palmito, y con más joyas que la vedriera de un platero rico. No me clavara él las ventanas, cerrara las puertas, visitara a todas horas de la casa ... que a trueco de que no hiciera esto *y otras cosas no vistas en materia de recato*, yo le perdonaría sus dádivas y mercedes. (205–6)[27]

Cañizares's naive malice, believing that supporting his wife as an ignorant child protects him, recalls María de Zayas's *El prevenido, engañado*, in which Fadrique prevents his wife from knowing anything about "la vida de los casados" (married life), unwittingly making possible the infidelity of his wife, who innocently gives herself over to another man, as everyone can see, because she understands nothing of the intimacy of marriage or the rules of decorum. Although *The Jealous Old Man* also ends in disaster for the husband, it is by no means because of an excessive ignorance on the part of Lorenza. The Cervantine interlude formulates a situation that goes beyond the joke of the husband's impotence and the ignorance of the young wife. The robust comic nature of the work, whose story derives from literary tradition, does not completely hide the intuition that not everything is so simple and jocose in this grotesque equation of the old man and the girl.[28] For example, a sentence in the interlude is nothing less than disturbing. In an earlier moment Lorenza tells Cristinica that Cañizares loves her well, to which Cristinica, irate, replies: "¿Deja por eso de ser viejo? Cuanto más, que yo he oído decir que siempre los viejos son amigos de niñas" (208).[29] What does this imply? We know that Cañizares is impotent but that he also takes a strange pleasure in having his girl-wife enclosed; he wants to prolong her childhood indefinitely and lavishes her with jewels and clothing as if she were a captive doll. Furthermore, he has his niece waiting on him as an adolescent servant every night all night long to take care of his maladies. It would appear that Cañizares's deficient sexuality is compensated for by the possession and confinement of two girls, if we include poor Cristinica, on both of whom he imposes the exclusiveness of his gaze, since they can't be seen by anyone else. Not allowing them to see anyone, whether alive or painted, betrays a desire to control the thoughts and fantasies of Lorenza and his niece, and contravenes the common custom of girls being able to look at the street through the latticework, since what was especially important for their honour was not to be seen.

What's more, as has often been observed, Lorenza is very different from Leonora, the innocent protagonist of Cervantes's exemplary novel *El celoso extremeño* (*The Jealous Extremaduran*), whom the duenna[30] tries to corrupt and the young gallant Loaysa tries to seduce after he uses his wiles to get into the almost impregnable house, although the child-spouse remains naive and innocent, particularly in the definitive 1613 version. Lorenza knows what she wants and does what she can to have it. She says she can't speak to anyone, but the text makes it clear that this is not the first time she speaks to her neighbour, and we witness a conversation that seems to be the last of a series in which the sexual relief of the young *malcasada* (ill-married woman) is arranged. She also says that there are seven doors between the outside and her bedroom, yet the young lover easily sneaks into her chamber. There are simply too many hyperboles and imprecisions in a story that goes beyond the cliché of the jealous old impotent man and the innocent child-wife. Besides, it is extremely revealing that the young lover has no name or agency or role in this act of sexual remediation in which all seduction, temptation, human interest, romanticism, or semblance of falling in love is brutally omitted. In this, Cervantes's text is callously clear: the lover is reified, he is compared to a green *jinjo* tree (a bright, beautiful plant), his wealth and generosity are of no interest to Lorenza (breaking with the tradition of seduction by way of gifts), and all she asks for is that he be young, handsome, and ready to carry out his sexual duty. In this text, Cañizares's rival, the feared masculine lover, is no more than an object desired by Lorenza and provided by the neighbour, inverting the equation of the masculine as seducer and the feminine as seduced. Lorenza's lover disappears behind the tapestry and comes and goes according to the will of the women who have brought him into existence in that forbidden domain where they order and command, despite the many hidden keys guarded by the naive Cañizares. Nor should we fail to notice the freedom and frankness with which Lorenza speaks about sex, as, for example, when she says that all of her flesh trembles while she is with her lover (216), which would be unseemly for a girl ignorant of the pleasures of sensuality.

Yet what seems most significant to me when figuring out what is really happening in that house is Lorenza's (and also Cristinica's) disproportionate rancour, resentment, and repulsion toward the husband who has her enjoy doubled ("doblados"), or maybe twisted, the fruits of marriage. This diverges widely from the dove's innocence that he attributes to her and can't be explained merely by the old Cañizares's lack of attention to bedroom matters. As I've said, we don't know what happens in that house, nor does it matter, because in this interlude so loaded with references to sight and to painting, what's most important is what's *not* seen. Lorenza's reaction should be calibrated as an escape from, and vengeance against, something that is inscribed in many ways in a text full of references to an enigmatic and disturbing intimacy that shows itself behind the comic façade of the work. In this way, we can better understand Lorenza's scornful taunt: "Ahora echo de ver quién eres, viejo maldito, que hasta aquí he vivido engañada contigo" (216).

With the tapestry of the characters of the *Orlando*, Cervantes presents us with an inverse ekphrasis that visually describes a literary text via evocation. In the tapestry there is a front side and a back side, and the deception is made possible thanks to that game of appearances and confusions. On the other hand, the old man is a sort of Rodomonte, clumsy, jealous, misogynistic, and unfortunate in love; in a certain way, the painting that hides the deception is a sort of mirror that reflects the protagonist and reveals the truth. This theme of the deceived gaze not only applies to the plot but also transcends the text and extends to the reader, to whom enough clues have been given about the tapestry and its deceitful reverse side to look for the meaning of the text in what is not seen, in the daily life of the marriage of Lorenza and Cañizares.[31]

A Sequence of Tapestries: Visual Memory and Collective Imagination

It was not fortuitous that Cervantes chose Ariosto as author of the camouflaged tapestry that serves as a backdrop to the entire interlude. Like Cervantes, Ariosto was able to colonize the collective imagination of the men and women of his time and, as is the case with Don Quixote and Sancho, the feats and actions of his characters were not only known but also imagined and visualized before illustrations and *estampas* circulated, giving form and body to these beings made of words. It is often mistakenly believed that graphic illustrations facilitated characters' exit from the book that contained them and enabled them to inhabit the imagination of readers. I believe, on the contrary, that texts with such visual power as the *Furioso* or *Don Quixote* could be imagined by readers long before being iconographically represented. On the other hand, the evocatively visual character of the *Furioso* leads some critics to speak of the work as a textual tapestry.[32] Louis Pérez, for instance, speaks of the notion of tapestry as inherent in Ariosto's literary conception: "Ariosto's epic abounds in tapestry references; he was attracted in part by their wealth of detail. The pictorial design caught his eye – the design enhanced by the thread which was traceable and interwoven in many color combinations and rhythmical patterns" (291). From the veiled visual tapestry of the *Furioso* that reveals itself in the depths of *Don Quixote* emerges a flux of resonances that establish a dialogue with the bare and embryonic Cervantine interlude. Thanks to this, *The Jealous Old Man* exhibits an enormous density of meanings organized into a complex play of connotations and innuendos that are reinforced by a relentless and precise use of ellipses and elusions.

If we observe carefully, besides the great metaphorical tapestry of the *Furioso* that operates from a distant backdrop, there is a sequence of three tapestries in *The Jealous Old Man*, ordered in a kind of crescendo with regard to their importance: (1) the one that the old man rejects in the marketplace because the painted figures perturb him (and which prepares the terrain for the next ones); (2) the one with Ariosto's characters, which establishes the text's filiation with the *Furioso* and brings to the foreground the figure of Rodomonte as a reflection and nemesis of Cañizares; and (3) the most important one, with which the work reaches its climax, a third canvas, which is not one, but whose surface functions as a plane on which the imagination of the old man is projected according to Lorenza's narrative in a brilliantly erotic and destabilizing ekphrasis. I am referring here to the door behind which Lorenza encloses herself with her lover and behind which the young woman narrates the pleasurable details of her sexual encounter.[33] This is a verbal tapestry or, more accurately, an eroticized tapestry in motion, a "motion picture" in which Cervantes resorts to the evocative capacity of the discourse to turn into a sequence of mental images.

Cervantes is a writer who in his literary creation has systematically explored the visual potential of language and who understandably draws from the *Furioso*, one of the books that has most clearly been "seen" by generations of readers (and by "second-hand readers" who know of this work through what others say about it). Lorenza's simultaneous verbalization of her love encounter recalls the happy honeymoon of Angelica and Medoro, with their bliss and erotic energy. This episode understandably was immensely popular in Spanish letters of the sixteenth century and is even commented upon in the episode of the penitence of Sierra Morena in *Don Quixote*. Significantly, the niece Cristinica is present with the old man at the scandalous transmission of the happy amorous feats of the two young lovers, and she encourages him to punish and tear Lorenza to pieces, saying "Despedácela, tío" (216).[34] Curiously, Cañizares responds that all he wants to tear to pieces is the door, not his wife: "No la despedazaré yo a ella, sino a la puerta que la encubre" (216),[35] since, undoubtedly, the images that Lorenza's narrative tells about are inscribed on the door.

As we have seen, in this interlude, as in the *Curioso*, there is a symbiosis between the theatrical and plastic art, and we see the fantasy of the conversion of the literary into art. Cervantes leads us to forget that his art is always an art of words on the pages of texts. Nonetheless, he plays with the artistic imagination of his readers who certainly would have the images of Lucrecia archived in their memory, along with those of the *Orlando* that circulated not only in paintings but also in engravings and picture cards at a lesser price. It is clear that the potential public of the interludes, like the readers of the *Curioso*, were endowed with a visual memory capable of identifying these characters even without naming them, since only Rodomonte is named in the dialogue of *The Jealous Old Man*. A reliable proof of this is that Cervantes indicates who all four of the characters are only in a stage direction: "Entra Ortigosa, y trae un guadamecí, y en las pieles de las cuatro esquinas han de venir pintados Rodamonte, Mandricardo, Rugero y Gradaso: y Rodamonte venga pintado como arrebozado" (212).[36] This makes clear that the public would immediately recognize these characters of the *Furioso*, three of whom Cervantes never mentions by name.

Above all, with this inverse ekphrasis that recreates in a literary text the supposed plastic representations of another literary text, Cervantes establishes an intertextual connection with Ariosto's text, reinforcing the theme of jealousy and "the trick that invades the eyes." The tapestry is also an object whose duplicity expresses in plastic and visual form the conflict that this text expresses: on the one hand, Rodomonte is perceived as a threat for Cañizares at the same time as Rodomonte, with his jealousy and ineptitude, is a mirror of Cañizares. The tapestry covers the deception at the same time as it announces it, serving as the front and reverse side of the same reality. The figures of painted men, so vexing to the old husband, are inoffensive in one way, and yet they enable Lorenza's lover to penetrate the house, invading the closed space of the inaccessible body of the wife and of the inviolable house. Ultimately, the comic terror that the jealous old man professed toward the paintings had its justification.

As we have seen in this chapter, Cervantes dedicates to Ariosto a varied and complex literary homage that goes beyond the indirect citation of any passage. Besides reworking in both the *Curioso* and *The Jealous Old Man* the theme of feminine adultery – exploring and questioning the misogynistic focus that indicts the woman as absolute culprit without taking into account her right to listen to her desires and to decide her actions – Cervantes undertakes a reconnaissance of the poetic pathways inaugurated by Ariosto, investigating from different angles the theme of the *engaño a los ojos* or the deceived gaze.[37]

NOTES

1 Among many others, critics including Thomas Hart, Bruce Wardropper, Marina Brownlee, Maxime Chevalier, Eduardo Urbina, Frederick de Armas, Anne Cruz, Georges Güntert, Marcial Rubio Árquez, and David Quint, have taken up this theme.

2 I have used Edith Grossman's translation for *Don Quixote*, and Guido Waldman's for *Orlando furioso*. I have also consulted Dawn Smith's translation of Cervantes's *Eight Interludes* for *El viejo celoso*. Otherwise, translations are mine.

3 Javier Portús Pérez and Jesusa Vega (*La estampa religiosa en el Antiguo Régimen*), point out an example in Lope de Vega's *La viuda valenciana* (*The Valencian Widow*), a play in which Valerio, disguised as a producer of *estampas*, shows his beloved Leonarda an *estampa* of Titian's *Venus and Adonis*:

[Valerio, dressed as a card [*estampa*] merchant]
VALERIO: Come buy my fine cards [*estampas*]!
. . . .
LEONARDA: Show them to me, what's on this one?
VALERIO: Titian's *Adonis*, no less
the artist with a divine hand

and a wondrous brush.
[Valerio, en hábito de mercader con estampas]
¡A la rica estampa fina!
. . . .
LEONARDA: Mostrá, ¿qué es este papel?
VALERIO: El *Adonis* del Tiziano,
que tuvo divina mano
y peregrino pincel. (430)

Portús Pérez and Vega have documented the important role that these artistic artefacts played in the dissemination of pictorial referents in Golden Age society, which is often illustrated casually – as in the previous example – in its theatre. The abundant presence and/or reference that paintings acquire in Spanish drama reveals for him the fact that "iconography constituted a substantial element of the plot of many dramatic works" (169).

4 Frederick de Armas identifies three differentiated acts in Camila's performance that he relates to Terentius's the Eunuch ("El mito de Dánae," 152). He also traces the influences both literary and pictorial that are present in Cervantes's text.

5 Here we see how *Orlando*'s text repeatedly insists on that idea of the equivalence of faults and, as a result, on the pardoning of feminine transgression:

All this while, his wife Argìa had been hidden close by; as soon as she saw him fall, she leapt out and cried "Aha! a fine thing for a man reputed a learned Doctor to do!" Caught out in the depth of depravity, he was struck speechless and blushed, as you may imagine ... "If you thought I deserved to die, know this: you deserve a hundred deaths! / Now although I can dispose of you here at will, such is my power, I do not mean to exact a worse vengeance for your misdeed. Let us give and receive equally, husband: as I pardon you, so do you pardon me. / Let us make peace and concord, every past error forgotten. May I never, in word or deed, remind you of your lapse, nor you of mine." (Canto 43, 140–3, [525])

6 In his introduction to the works of Lope de Vega, Marcelino Menéndez y Pelayo observes, with reference to the *comedia* of Lope: "The materials could not have been better, but their accumulation suffocated the dramatist. This *comedia* is one of the worst and most monstrous of its genre. Only the style and versification of some passages deserve praise, with a noteworthy abundance of tercets, and the ease with which Lope adapts them to dramatic dialogue, of which they seem so inappropriate" (cxxi). The work by the same title of Rojas Zorrilla is likewise nonsensical although, curiously, it approaches to some extent the Cervantine and Ariostesque idea of deception before one's own eyes. In this *comedia*, Doralice deceives with

various ruses the jealous Rodomonte so as to escape with Mandricardo. Rodamonte is a jealous character who always ends up being deceived.

7 As Luis Bernabé clearly explains, the work we know as the *Thousand and One Nights* was a text in continuous transformation at least until the eighteenth century. According to Bernabé, the first translation from Arabic to a European language is that of Antoine Galland, published between 1704 and 1713. The text that Galland used was the oldest written version we know, dating from the fourteenth century. It was, of course, a text derived from the Indian and later Persian tradition, crossing over to Arabic in the eighth century following the practice of translating and incorporating into the Arab heritage works originating from great ancient cultures (93–4).

8 As Bernabé writes, in the medieval period "it is not known exactly when the frame-story was incorporated into Arab culture over and above the Indo-Persian tradition that had been translated during the thriving new empire, but this frame did indeed establish itself as of that period as the beginning and leitmotif of the collection of stories" (101).

9 Margherita Spampinato Beretta analyses with precision the intertextual relations between canto 28 of the *Furioso* and the frame tale of the *Thousand and One Nights*.

10 On the treatment of misogyny and philogyny in Ariosto, see the study by Annalisa Izzo.

11 As Cervantes's text describes it:

> El mozo es como un jinjo verde; quiere bien, sabe callar y agradecer lo que por él se hace; y pues los celos y el recato del viejo no nos dan lugar a demandas ni a respuestas, resolución y buen ánimo: que, por la orden que hemos dado, yo le pondré al galán en su aposento de vuestra merced y le sacaré, si bien tuviese el viejo más ojos que Argos, y viese más que un zahorí (204).

> The lad's like a green bush, he's a good lover and knows how to keep quiet and show his gratitude for favors received. Since the old man's jealousy and precautions leave us no room for planning it more, we must proceed with courage and determination. By our agreement, I'll bring the gallant to your room and take him away later, even if the old man has more eyes than Argos and sees more than a fortune-teller.

12 "See here, Mistress Ortigosa, bring us a young man who's gallant, clean, spirited, a touch bold, and above all, young!"

13 "Don't you believe it, niece, because I sleep with him, and I've never seen or felt his having any key at all."

14 "You're right to be afraid, because wives would like to enjoy the full fruits of marriage."

15 "Mine enjoys them doubled."

16 "That's precisely the trouble, my friend."

17 "Little Lorenza is more innocent than a dove, and so far she understands nothing of that sort of talk."

18 "Oh what a lovely Rodamonte! What's that little fellow in a cloak doing in my house? If he knew how little I care for disguises and that kind of thing, he'd make himself scarce."

19 "[S]he [Ortigosa] doesn't know my condition, nor how I loathe these paintings."

20 "I'll bring him to you painted."

21 "I don't want him painted, but alive, alive and little, like luscious pearls!"

22 "[H]is face is like a painted angel." Enrique Martínez López carries out a detailed analysis of the *double entendres* and erotic connotations of many expressions in the interlude, such as those cited above. José Ramón Fernández de Cano deals with this more briefly in an article on the same topic.

23 "Now I see you for what you are, wretched old man. Until now my life with you has been a sham!"

24 "I want to wash the sparse beard of my young lover with a basin of angels' water, because his face is like a painted angel."

25 "Tricks played on the eyes are the devil's work."

26 Charles Presberg sees Cañizares as author, scriptwriter, director and actor of the *comedia* of his marriage, imposing on Lorenza her role as actress until she performs her own *comedia,* although, according to Presberg, she cedes to Ortigosa the control and authorship of her theatrical work.

27 "I am laden with jewels and quite overwhelmed by all the colors of my many dresses. Cañizares took away the pleasure of dressing up. He keeps me dressed up with more jewels than you'll see in a silversmith's shop. If he didn't nail up the windows on me, lock the doors, patrol the house at all hours ... in exchange for his not doing all this *and other things never seen in regard to decency*, I'd gladly forego his gifts and favors."

28 Eduardo Urbina believes that the text brings us close to the notion of incest. Although I agree that there is something that puts us ill at ease, I don't believe it can be identified as incest. Cervantes simply makes it clear that there is something disquieting that we can't know in the marital intimacy of Lorenza and Cañizares.

29 "Is he any less old because of that? Besides, I've heard that old men always dote on young girls."

30 In Spanish, *dueña*. In her translation of *Don Quixote*, Edith Grossman notes that a "duenna was an older woman of good family, usually a widow, in the service of a noblewomen" (658n).

31 Anne Cruz traces an interesting connection between the unfinished *comedia* "El engaño a los ojos," which Cervantes promises in his prologue to the *Ocho comedias y ocho entremeses nunca representados* (*Eight Comedias and Eight*

Interludes Never Performed), and the notion of deception and visuality explored in his *Entremeses* (*Interludes*), especially *El viejo celoso* (122–3).

32 In an apt simile, Clorinda Donato characterizes the *Furioso* as a rhetorical tapestry.

33 Enrique Martínez López briefly refers to a verbal tapestry of Lorenza (350), an image that Carmela Mattza in turn takes up.

34 "Uncle, tear her to pieces!"

35 "I won't tear her to pieces but rather the door that hides her."

36 "Ortigosa enters carrying a leather tapestry, and in the four corners the figures of Rodamonte, Mandricardo, Rugero and Gradaso are painted; and Rodamonte is depicted as covered with his cape."

37 As noted, this refers to a *comedia* promised by Cervantes in the prologue of his *Ocho comedias y ocho entremeses* published in 1615. For a more detailed study see Mercedes Alcalá Galán (197–203).

REFERENCES

Alcalá Galán, Mercedes. *Escritura desatada: Poéticas de la representación en Cervantes*. Madrid: Centro de Estudios Cervantinos, 2009.

Ariosto, Ludovico. *Orlando Furioso*. Translated by Guido Waldman. New York: Oxford University Press, 1983.

Bernabé Pons, Luis. "La transmisión de los cuentos de las *Mil y una noches* (a través de Nápoles) a España." In *Napoli Viceregno Spagnolo. Una capitale della cultura alle origini dell'Europa Moderna (sec. XVI–XVII)*, edited by Monika Bosse and André Stoll, 93–109. Naples: Vivarium, 2001.

Brownlee, Marina Scordilis. "Cervantes as Reader of Ariosto." In *Romance: Generic Transformation from Chrétien de Troyes to Cervantes*, edited by Kevin Brownlee and Marina Scordilis Brownlee, 220–37. Hanover, NH: University Press of New England, 1985.

Castro, Américo. *El pensamiento de Cervantes*. Barcelona: Crítica, 1987.

Cervantes Saavedra, Miguel de. *Don Quijote de la Mancha*. Edited by Francisco Rico. 2nd ed. Barcelona: Crítica, 1998.

– *Don Quixote*. Translated by Edith Grossman. New York: HarperCollins, 2003.

– *Eight Interludes*. Translated and edited by Dawn L. Smith. London: J.M. Dent, 1996.

– *Entremeses*. Edited by Eugenio Asensio. Madrid: Castalia, 1970

– *Novelas ejemplares*. Edited by Harry Sieber. 2 vols. Madrid: Cátedra, 1980.

Chevalier, Maxime. *L'Arioste en Espagne (1530–1650): Recherches sur l'influence du "Roland Furieux."* Bordeaux: Institut d'Études Ibériques et Ibéro-Américaines de l'Université de Bordeaux, 1966.

Cruz, Anne J. "Deceit, Desire, and the Limits of Subversion in Cervantes's *Interludes.*" *Cervantes: Bulletin of the Cervantes Society of America* 14, no. 2 (1994): 119–36.

de Armas, Frederick A. "El mito de Dánae en *El curioso impertinente*: Terencio, Tiziano y Cervantes." *Anales cervantinos* 42 (2010): 147–62.

– "Pinturas de Lucrecia en el *Quijote:* Tiziano, Rafael y Lope de Vega." *Anuario de Estudios Cervantinos* 1 (2004): 109–19.

Donato, Clorinda. "The Rhetorical Tapestry: A Model for Perspective Reality in *Orlando Furioso* and *Don Quijote.*" *Comitatus: Journal of Medieval and Renaisance Studies* 17, no. 1 (1986): 12–21.

Fernández de Cano, José Ramón. "El vocabulario erótico cervantino: Algunas 'calas al aire' en el entremés de *El viejo celoso.*" *Cervantes: Bulletin of the Cervantes Society of America* 12, no. 2 (1992): 105–16.

Güntert, Georges. "Ariosto en el *Quijote*: Replanteamiento de una cuestión." In *Actas del XII Congreso de la Asociación Internacional de Hispanistas*, edited by Trevor Dadson, Dirk Flitter, and Patricia Odber de Baubeta, 271–83. Birmingham, UK: University of Birmingham Press, 1998.

Hart, Thomas R. *Cervantes and Ariosto: Renewing Fiction*. Princeton, NJ: Princeton University Press, 2014.

Hutchinson, Steven. "Anselmo y sus adicciones." In *El "Quijote" desde América*, edited by Gustavo Illades and James Iffland, 119–38. Puebla/Mexico City: Benemérita Universidad Autónoma de Puebla / El Colegio de México, 2006.

– "Norma social y ética privada: El adulterio femenino en Cervantes." *Anales Cervantinos* 47 (2010): 193–207.

Ife, B. "Cervantes, Herodotus and the Eternal Triangle: Another Look at the Sources of *El curioso impertinente.*" *Bulletin of Hispanic Studies* 82, no. 5 (2005): 671–82.

Izzo, Annalisa. "Misoginia e filoginia nell'*Orlando Furioso.*" *Croniques Italiennes* 22, no. 1 (2012): 1–24.

Kenworthy, Patricia. "The Character of Lorenza and the Moral of Cervantes' *El viejo celoso.*" *Bulletin of the Comediantes* 31, no. 2 (1979): 103–8.

Mac Carthy, Ita. *Women and Making of Poetry in Ariosto's "Orlando furioso."* Leicester, UK: Troubador, 2007.

Marín Pina, Carmen. "De Rodamonte a las rodomontadas: La conversión de un héroe carolingio en género bufo." In *Amadís de Gaula, quinientos años después: Estudios en homenaje a Juan Manuel Cacho Blecua*, edited by José Manuel Lucía, 471–502. Alcalá de Henares, ES: Centro de Estudios Cervantinos, 2008.

Martínez López, Enrique. "Erotismo y ejemplaridad en *El viejo celoso* de Cervantes." In *Erotismo en las letras hispánicas: Aspectos, modos y fronteras*, edited by Luce López Baralt and Francisco Márquez Villanueva, 335–85. Mexico City: Colegio de México, 1995.

Mattza, Carmela. "Écfrasis discursiva y metateatro: Rodamonte en el entremés del *Viejo celoso*." *Pictavia aurea: Actas del IX Congreso de la AISO*, edited by Alain Bègue and Emma Herrán Alonso, 973–80. Toulouse: Presses Universitaires du Mirail, 2013.

Menéndez y Pelayo, Marcelino. "Introducción a las obras de Lope de Vega." In *Obras de Lope de Vega: Crónicas y leyendas dramáticas de España*, 13: xiii–cxlviii. Madrid: Real Academia Española, 1902.

Pérez, Louis C. "The Theme of the Tapestry in Ariosto and Cervantes." *Revista de Estudios Hispánicos* 7, no. 2 (1973): 289–98.

Portús Pérez, Javier, and Jesusa Vega. *La estampa religiosa en la España del Antiguo Régimen*. Madrid: Fundación Universitaria Española, 1999.

Presberg, Charles D. "Making a Liar of Truth: The 'Play' of Society, Fiction and Deceit in Cervantes's *El viejo celoso*." *Revista de Estudios Hispánicos* 33, no. 2 (1999): 265–84.

Quint, David. "Narrative Interlace and Narrative Genres in *Don Quijote* and the *Orlando Furioso*." *Modern Language Quarterly* 58, no. 3 (1997): 241–68.

Rubiera Mata, María Jesús. "Los ojos de Chehrezada." *Revista del Instituto Egipcio de Estudios Islámicos en Madrid* 35 (2003): 159–71.

Rubio Árquez, Marcial. "Cervantes, *El viejo celoso*: Ariosto." *Theatralia: Revista de Poética del Teatro* 16 (2014): 95–107.

Sieber, Harry. "On Juan Huarte de San Juan and Anselmo's *locura* in *El curioso impertinente*." *Revista Hispánica Moderna* 36, nos. 1–2 (1970): 1–8.

Smithers, Leonard, *The Book of the Thousand Nights and a Night*. 12 vols. Translated by R.F. Burton. London: Nichols and Soho Square, 1894.

Spampinato Beretta, Margherita. "La cornice narrativa delle *Mille e una notte* ed il canto XXVIII dell'*Orlando Furioso*." *Medioevo romanzo e orientale: Il viaggio dei testi. III Colloquio Internazionale*, edited by Antonio Pioletti and Francesca Rizzo Nervo, 229–49. Soveria Mannelli, IT: Rubbettino, 1999.

Urbina, Eduardo. "Hacia *El viejo celoso* de Cervantes." *Nueva Revista de Filología Hispánica* 38, no. 2 (1990): 733–42.

Vega, Lope de. *La viuda valenciana*, edited by Teresa Ferrer. Madrid: Castalia, 2001.

Wardropper, Bruce W. "Ambiguity in *El viejo celoso*." *Cervantes: Bulletin of the Cervantes Society of America* 1, no. 1 (1981): 19–28.

Zayas y Sotomayor, María de. "*El prevenido engañado*": *Novelas amorosas y ejemplares*, edited by Julián Olivares, 295–342. Madrid: Cátedra, 2010.

PART II

Reasoning the Unreasonable: Toward a Rationale of Love

Chapter Three

El Greco's and Cervantes's Euclidean Theologies

ERIC CLIFFORD GRAF

> ... a lust of the mind, that by a perseverance of delight in the continual and indefatigable generation of knowledge, exceedeth the short vehemence of any carnal pleasure.
>
> – Thomas Hobbes, *Leviathan* 1.6

Modern viewers are ill equipped to decipher the philosophical problems represented by El Greco's *The Flight to Egypt* (*La huida a Egipto*, ca. 1570; fig. 3.1). A Renaissance Christian visualization of Neoplatonism, the painting marries theological mystery and mathematical truth: the biblical story of the escape of Joseph, Mary, and Jesus from Bethlehem to Egypt; and Euclid's geometrical proposition that the base angles of an isosceles triangle are equal, known in Latin as *pons asinorum*, or "bridge of asses." The specific passages cited by El Greco are the following:

> Now when they had departed, behold, an angel of the Lord appeared to Joseph in a dream, saying, "Arise, take the young Child and His mother, flee to Egypt, and stay there until I bring you word; for Herod will seek the young Child to destroy Him." When he arose, he took the young Child and His mother by night and departed for Egypt, and was there until the death of Herod, that it might be fulfilled which was spoken by the Lord through the prophet, saying, "Out of Egypt I called My Son." (Matthew 2.13–15)

> In any isosceles triangle, if the equal sides be produced, the external angles at the base are equal, and the internal angles at the base are also equal. (*Elements* I.5)

El Greco's allusion to the Bible being obvious, of greater interest is his insinuation of Euclidean geometry, which educated sixteenth-century

Fig. 3.1. El Greco's *The Flight to Egypt*.
Source: Wikimedia Commons.

viewers would have recognized. As striking as El Greco's painting is Oliver Byrne's colour-coded version of *Elements* I.5 in his London edition of 1847 (fig. 3.2). As compelling in its own day was Rodrigo Zamorano's version in his Seville edition of 1576 (fig. 3.3). Zamorano's translation of history's greatest mathematical work had no rival in Spanish until the early nineteenth century.

The Flight to Egypt echoes *Elements* I.5 in three ways: 1) the bridge over which Joseph leads his family; 2) the animal's back upon which Mary and Jesus are seated; and 3) the triangle implied by the golden thread running from the ass's noseband to Joseph's right hand and then dropping in a plumb-line toward the earth. Joseph's vertical staff alludes to, and can substitute for, this plumb-line. Readers familiar with *Elements* I.12 will recognize that, if Joseph's plumb-line is viewed in relation to the bridge, a straight line can be drawn from the ass's noseband perpendicular to the plumb-line, forming a right triangle. So we should specify that, as would any successful student of classical geometry, El Greco refers to Euclid's *pons asinorum* as the first major step in a series of proofs leading up to the epic Pythagorean theorem of *Elements* I.47 (see figs. 3.4 and 3.5).

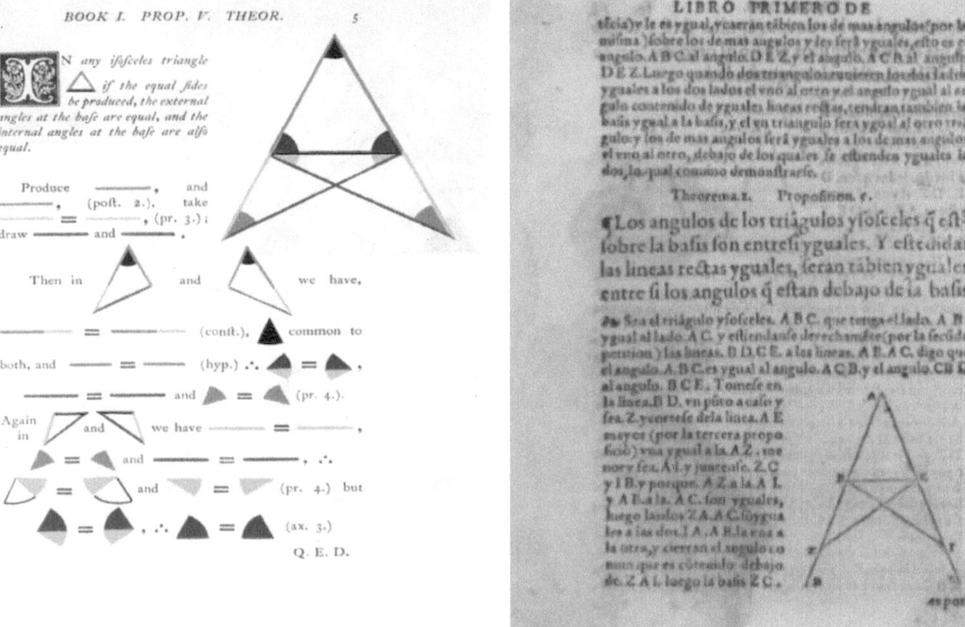
BOOK I. PROP. V. THEOR. 5

IN any isosceles triangle if the equal sides be produced, the external angles at the base are equal, and the internal angles at the base are also equal.

LIBRO PRIMERO DE

Theorema.2. Proposicion.5.

¶Los angulos de los triãgulos ysosceles q̃ estã sobre la basis son entresi yguales. Y estendidas las lineas rectas yguales, seran tãbien yguales entre si los angulos q̃ estan debajo de la basis

Figs. 3.2 and 3.3. Euclid's *Elements* I.5.
Source: Euclid, *Elements*; *Los seis libros*.

Why *Elements* I.5 is called *pons asinorum* is somewhat disputed. The first explanation is that aspects of the proof's diagram resemble bridges and the head of an ass. The second, more popular, explanation, found as early as Christopher Clavius's commentary of 1574, is that the fifth proof is the first major stumbling block in Euclid's masterpiece (Heilbron 84). Requiring more abstract thinking and recollection, and following a less intuitive sequence of steps, the proof effectively assesses the willpower and mental abilities of its students, turning back the stubborn and the witless. In *The Flight to Egypt*, El Greco's odd positioning of the head and ears of the ass visually suggests the proof's famous diagram. More literally, it directs our attention to the bridge within the painting and also highlights the animal's notorious obstinacy.

Similarly, as early as the fourteenth century French philosopher Jean Buridan – indeed, perhaps as far back as the twelfth-century Andalusian Arab philosopher Averroes – *pons asinorum*, both as a bridge and a test of deductive reasoning, is a metaphor for the middle term, or minor premise, which is key when evaluating the validity of a syllogism (West and Thompson 86–8). A syllogism is a tripartite logical figure, as in the

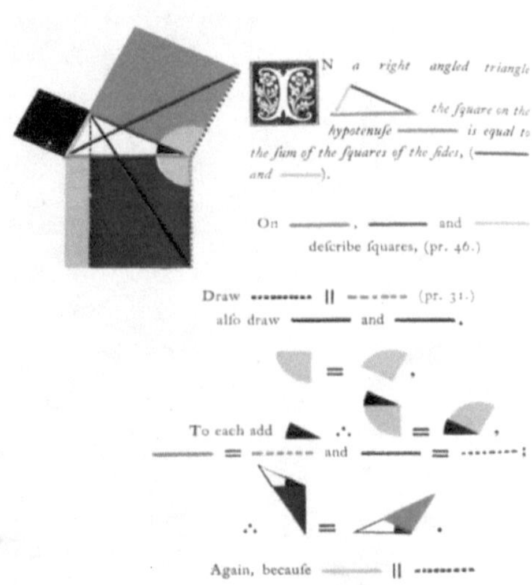

LIBRO PRIMERO DE

¶En los triangulos rectangulos el quadrado que es hecho de el lado q̃ esta opuesto al angulo recto es ygual a los dos quadrados q̃ son hechos de los lados q̃ cõtienen el angulo recto,

Sea el triangulo rectãgulo. A B C. q̃ tenga recto el angulo B A C. digo que el quadrado q̃ es hecho del lado. B C. es ygual a los quadrados q̃ se hazen de B A. y de. A C. Describase, por la. 46. dela. B C. el quadrado. B D C E, y por la misma, de la B A. y dela, A C. los quadrados. A B Z I. A C K T. y por el pũto A. tirese. A L. parallela cõ la. B D. C E, por la proposiciõ. 31, y por la. 1. peticiõ tirẽse A D. C Z. y porq̃ los ãgulos. B A C. B A I son rectos. Luego tiradas dos lineas rectas. A C. A I. desde vna linea recta. A B. y desde vn pũcto en ella. A. no hacia vnas mismas ptes hacẽ de vna y otra pte ãgulos yguales a dos rectos, por la. 14. ppoficiõ) luego ẽ derecho esta la. A C. dla. A I y por esto tãbiẽ B A esta ẽ derecho de. A T y por q̃ el angulo. D B C. es ygual al angulo. Z B A. porq̃ cada vno dellos es recto: põgase comũ el angulo A B C. Luego todo D B A es ygual a todo el angulo Z B C. y porq̃ las dos. A B. B D. son yguales a las dos B Z. B C. la vna a la otra, y el ãgulo. D B A es ygual al angulo. Z B C. luego la basis. A D, por la. 4. pposiciõ, es ygual a la basis. Z C. y el triangulo. A B D. al triangulo. Z B C. es tãbien ygual. Y el parallelogramo. BL, por la. 41, es doblo del triangulo. A B D por

Figs. 3.4 and 3.5. Euclid's *Elements* I.47.
Source: Byrne and Zamorano editions.

standard formula inspired by Aristotle: "All men are mortal; Socrates is a man; therefore Socrates is mortal" (see Dante, *Paradiso* 13.97–102).

Thirteenth-century English scholastic philosopher Roger Bacon cites another tradition that refers to *Elements* I.5 as *elefuga,* which he says combines the Greek *elegia,* or "misery," and the Latin *fuga,* or "flight" (6.22). Bacon's more fanciful etymology signifies "flight of the wretches" because pupils were typically freed from studying Euclid upon reaching his fifth proof. This tradition inspired fourteenth-century English poet Geoffrey Chaucer. In *Troilus and Criseyde,* Criseyde's uncle, Pindarus, expands the scope of Bacon's metaphor by describing *Elements* I.47 as "flemyng of wrenches" or "banishment of wretches" (3.135: 933), because schoolboys prove unwilling or unable to learn it. El Greco's *The Flight to Egypt* advances a theological take on Bacon's and Chaucer's notion of *Elements* I.5 as a pedagogical desideratum. Here, the humbled Holy Family flees the persecution of Herod. Do we understand? As Euclid's modern editor Thomas Heath points out, a better etymology of *elefuga* than Bacon's starts with the Greek *eleos,* meaning "pity (or the object of pity)" (*Thirteen* 416). As we approach an esoteric reading of the *pons asinorum,* it's worth noting that Proclus, late classical antiquity's most systematic Neoplatonic philosopher, was a sophisticated commentator on Euclid, even producing his own simplified version of *Elements* I.5.

According to Francisco Pacheco's first-hand testimony, El Greco's painterly skills included something cerebral: "he was a great philosopher" (fue gran filósofo [537]). To summarize *The Flight to Egypt*: Euclid's geometry, Plato's philosophy, and Christianity's theology reveal the same logical fabric of the universe. It's a triple trajectory of enlightenment. With *Genesis*'s trees of life and knowledge in the background, we are urged across the bridge of moral and intellectual progress toward the light of love and reason emanating from above and beyond Joseph. Simultaneously, constitutive triads from Euclid's *Elements* and Christian doctrine (e.g., El Greco's *La Trinidad*) focus our attention back onto what should be the objects of our pity: the Virgin Mary, the Christ child, and ourselves or others in the form of a reluctant donkey still stuck in an ambulatory cave of ignorance.

Don Quixote, Bridges, and Asses

References to geometry and mathematical calculations abound in *Don Quijote*. I argue that, with regard to the significance of Cervantes's novel as a whole, these are neither arbitrary nor minor allusions. Explaining the science of chivalry to Don Lorenzo, Don Quixote says the following: "he must know mathematics, because at every step he will have need of them" (*Don Quixote* II.18: 570) (ha de saber las matemáticas, porque a cada paso se le ofrecerá tener necesidad dellas [*Don Quijote* II.18: 774]). Later in the same chapter, in his parting advice to Don Lorenzo, Don Quixote expressly cites the so-called Pythagorean "Y," which posits life as a forking path: "you need do nothing else but leave the narrow path of poetry and follow the even narrower of knight errantry" (*Don Quixote* II.18: 575) (no tiene que hacer otra cosa sino dejar a una parte la senda de la poesía, algo estrecha, y tomar la estrechísima de la andante caballeria [*Don Quijote* II.18: 780]). Note how Cervantes deploys math and geometry to fuse together the significance of creative writing and chivalry. As another example, consider the narrator's friend's assertion in the first prologue that geometry is unnecessary for understanding the novel: "geometrical measurements are of no importance to them" (*Don Quixote* I. Prologue: 8) (ni le son de importancia las medidas geométricas [*Don Quijote* I. Prologue: 17]). Now consider Don Quixote's affirmation at the beginning of Part II that certain bones unearthed in Sicily indicate that giants did indeed exist –"geometry proves this truth beyond any doubt" (*Don Quixote* II.1: 467) (que la geometría saca esta verdad de duda [*Don Quijote* II.1: 637]). Note how the first references to geometry in both parts of the novel are suggestively contradictory. Which is it? Is geometry pointless? Or does it point to the truth in a world plagued by doubt? Similarly, in his very first adventure, Don Quixote comically miscalculates the back salary that Juan Haldudo owes to the shepherd boy Andrés, whom he is whipping: "He said wages for nine months, at seven *reales* a month. Don Quixote calculated the sum and found that it amounted to seventy-three *reales*" (*Don Quixote* I.4: 36) (al cual preguntó Don Quijote que cuánto le debía su amo. Él dijo que nueve meses, a siete reales cada mes. Hizo la cuenta don Quijote y halló que montaban setenta y tres reales [*Don Quijote* I.4: 64]). By contrast, at the end of Part II, illiterate Sancho's calculation of how much his master will pay him for his 3,300 lashes is nothing short of miraculous:

> and we come to the three thousand and three hundred [lashes], which at a *cuartillo* each, and I won't do it for less even if the whole world orders me to, comes to three thousand and three hundred *cuartillos*, and those three thousand come to fifteen hundred half-*reales*, which make for seven hundred and fifty reales; and those three hundred come to one hundred and fifty half-*reales*, which make for seventy-five *reales*, which together with the seven hundred and fifty make for a total of eight hundred and twenty-five *reales*. (Don Quixote II.71: 920)

> (vengamos a los tres mil y trecientos, que a cuartillo cada uno, que no llevaré menos si todo el mundo me lo mandase, montan tres mil y trecientos

> cuartillos, que son los tres mil, mil y quinientos medios reales, que hacen setecientos y cincuenta reales; y los trecientos hacen ciento y cincuenta medios reales, que vienen a hacer setenta y cinco reales, que juntándose a los setecientos y cincuenta son por todos ochocientos y veinte y cinco reales. [*Don Quijote* II.71: 1199–1200])

Again, there is authorial purpose here. The novel traces an enlightening circle: the ignorant enslavement of Andrés is ultimately undone by the sophisticated employment contract between our hidalgo and his squire. And enlightenment requires reason and calculation.

Cervantes's most explicit allusion to Euclid's *Elements* in *Don Quijote* is a direct quotation of the "third common notion" – also known as the "subtraction property of equality"– found roughly three-fifths of the way through Part I, at the beginning of the interpolated tale *The Curious Impertinent*. Here Lotario explains to his virtually identical friend, Anselmo, that the latter's request that he seduce his new wife Camila exhibits flawed logic:

> It seems to me, my dear Anselmo, that your mind is now in the state in which the Moors have theirs, for they cannot be made to understand the error of their sect with commentaries from Holy Scripture, or arguments that depend on rational understanding or are founded on articles of faith; instead, they must be presented with palpable, comprehensible, intelligible, demonstrable, indubitable examples, with mathematical proofs that cannot be denied, as when ones says, "If, from two equal parts, we remove equal parts, those parts that remain are also equal"; if they do not understand the words, as in fact they do not, then it must be shown to them with one's hands, and placed before their eyes, yet even after all this, no one can persuade them of the truths of our holy religion. (*Don Quixote* I.33: 277)

> (Paréceme, ¡oh Anselmo!, que tienes tú ahora el ingenio como el que siempre tienen los moros, a los cuales no se les puede dar a entender el error de su secta con las acotaciones de la Santa Escritura, ni con razones que consistan en especulación del entendimiento, ni que vayan fundadas en artículos de fe, sino que les han de traer ejemplos palpables, fáciles, intelegibles, demonstrativos, indubitables, con demostraciones matemáticas que no se pueden negar, como cuando dicen: "Si de dos partes iguales quitamos partes iguales, las que quedan también son iguales"; y cuando esto no entiendan de palabra, como en efeto no lo entienden, háseles de mostrar con las manos y ponérselo delante de los ojos, y aun con todo esto no basta nadie con ellos a persuadirles las verdades de nuestra sacra religión. [*Don Quijote* I.33: 381–2])

Euclid's third common notion is part of Cervantes's systematic allusion to the *pons asinorum* in *Don Quijote*. First, the proof requires subtracting equal angles, a more abstract idea than subtracting line segments or bounded areas, and so a comprehensive grasp of the third common notion is essential to success with *Elements* I.5. Second, in *The Curious Impertinent* Cervantes deploys the third common notion in the creation of an isosceles love triangle drawn about Camila via equal vectors of desire produced by Anselmo and Lotario. The narrator describes the latter duo as "such good friends that they were known by everyone as *the two friends*" (tan amigos, que, por excelencia y antonomasia, de todos los que los conocían "los dos amigos" eran llamados), adding two touches of mathematical precision: "all of which was sufficient cause for both of them to feel a mutual, reciprocal friendship" (todo lo cual era bastante causa a que los dos con recíproca amistad se correspondiesen) and "in this fashion their desires were so attuned that no clock had ever been conceived to run so well" (*Don Quixote* I.33: 272) (desta manera andaban tan a una sus voluntades, que no había concertado reloj que así lo anduviese [*Don Quijote* I.33: 372, 375–6]). Third, regarding the overarching structure of *Don Quijote*, this interpolated isosceles love triangle is a textual bridge between the labyrinthian triangles of the Sierra Morena lovers – Cardenio, Luscinda, Fernando, Dorotea – and the final dyad of *La historia del cautivo*, which ends with the flight of Ruy Pérez de Viedma and Zoraida-María, the latter atop an ass. Fourth, *The Curious Impertinent* is analogous to the story of Eros and Psyche, which spans Books 4, 5, and 7 of Apuleius's late classical picaresque novel the *Metamorphoses*, also known via Augustine as *Asinus aureus*, or *The Golden Ass*. The mad knight's asinine interruption of the triangular tragedy of *The Impertinent Curious Man* in chapter 35 represents *Don Quijote*'s most overt link to Apuleius, serving as a short, multifaceted textual bridge within a larger one.

But Cervantes does more than quote Euclid's third common notion as the basis of an interpolated isosceles love triangle, locate this triangle among a larger sequence of love triangles, and inscribe these in a series of textual bridges and allusions to *The Golden Ass*. In the preamble to *The Curious Impertinent*, during the theoretical debate between the priest and the innkeeper, Cervantes also refers to an actual, historically important bridge. Opposite the extravagant novels of chivalry cherished by the innkeeper, the priest cites a two-part text he considers more worthwhile: *Historia del Gran Capitán Gonzalo Hernández de Córdoba, con la vida de Diego García de Paredes*. He elaborates: "Diego García de Paredes was a distinguished nobleman, a native of the city of Trujillo, in Extremadura, a very courageous soldier, and so strong that with one finger he could stop a millwheel as it turned; standing with a broadsword at the entrance to a bridge, he brought an immense army to a halt and would not permit it to cross" (*Don Quixote* I.33: 269)

Fig. 3.6. Christopher Roelofs's *Battle of Garigliano*. Courtesy of artist.

(este Diego García de Paredes fue un principal caballero, natural de la ciudad de Trujillo, en Estremadura, valentísimo soldado, y de tantas fuerzas naturales, que detenía con un dedo una rueda de molino en la mitad de su furia, y, puesto con un montante en la entrada de una puente, detuvo a todo un innumerable ejército, que no pasase por ella [*Don Quijote* I.32: 371–2]). With this last detail, Cervantes turns our attention to the bridge at the Battle of Garigliano (29 December 1503; see fig. 3.6), at which the Spanish defeated the French north of Naples toward the end of the Second Italian War (1499–1504).

The Battle of Garigliano's bridge unleashes another web of textual bridges. First, it's an overt intertextual link to the *Historia del Gran Capitán*. Second, the priest specifically directs us to the life of García de Paredes, a subjoined extension that first appeared in the Alcalá edition of 1584. Third, the reference forms a prefatory intratextual arc toward *The Curious Impertinent*. Fourth, since *The Curious Impertinent* occurs in Florence, both interpolation and preface map a broad geographical, military, and cultural conduit between Spain and Italy. Fifth, the Battle of Garigliano lays the groundwork for a returning intratextual link at the ensuing tale's end, where Camila's and Lotario's final fates are tied to the Battle of Cerignola (28 April 1503), the Great Captain's other victory in the same Second Italian War:

> It was said that although a widow, she did not wish to leave the convent, much less take vows to be a nun; then, a few days later, the news reached her that Lotario had died in the battle between Monsieur de Lautrec and the Great Captain Gonzalo Fernández de Córdoba, which had just taken place in the kingdom of Naples, where Anselmo's friend, repentant too late, had fled; when Camila learned this, she took her vows, and not long afterward her life ended with a pitiless embrace of sorrow and melancholy. This was the end met by the three born of such rash beginnings. (*Don Quixote* I.35: 312)
>
> (Dícese que, aunque se vio viuda, no quiso salir del monesterio, ni menos hacer profesión de monja, hasta que no de allí a muchos días le vinieron nuevas que Lotario había muerto en una batalla que en aquel tiempo dio monsiur de Lautrec al Gran Capitán Gonzalo Fernández de Córdoba en el reino de Nápoles, donde había ido a parar el tarde arrepentido amigo; lo cual sabido por Camila, hizo profesión y acabó en breves días la vida a las rigurosas manos de tristezas y melancolías. Este fue el fin que tuvieron todos, nacido de un tan desatinado principio. [*Don Quijote* I.35: 423])

The Great Captain's Italian victories framing *Curious Impertinent* also symbolically reinforce the trajectory that it already represents between the chaotic passions of the Sierra Morena and Pérez de Viedma's calm veneration of Zoraida-María in *La historia del cautivo*. This is because Pérez de Viedma will turn out to be a captain who travels to Italy via Andalucía. And Cervantes's reference to the Battle of Garigliano makes for yet another intratextual bridge. In the penultimate chapter of *Don Quijote*, Part I, Eugenio describes his rival, the blustering soldier/seducer Vicente de la Roca, by way of a final gesture toward García de Paredes: "There was no land anywhere in the world that he had not seen, and no battle in which he had not fought; he had killed as many Moors as live in Morocco and Tunis and had engaged in more single combats than Gante and Luna, Diego García de Paredes, and another thousand men he named, and from all of them he had emerged victorious, without shedding a single drop of blood" (*Don Quixote* I.51: 435) (No había tierra en todo el orbe que no hubiese visto, ni batalla donde no se hubiese hallado: había muerto más moros que tiene Marruecos y Túnez, y entrado en más singulares desafíos, según él decía, que Gante y Luna, Diego García de Paredes y otros mil que nombraba, y de todos había salido con vitoria; sin que le hubiesen derramado una sola gota de sangre [*Don Quijote* 1.51: 578]).

One way to understand the significance of all of these bridges is that they are leading us precisely toward a contemplation of the essence of Don Quixote's identity. I would argue that it's no accident that our hero's single explicit reference to his ancestor Gutierre Quijada – "from which I am descended directly through the male line" (de cuya alcurnia yo deciendo por línea recta de varón) – comes in the context of his reference to "the jousts of Suero de Quiñones at the Pass" (*Don Quixote* I.49: 426) (las justas de Suero de Quiñones, del Paso [*Don Quijote* I.49: 566–7]). Suero de Quiñones's defence of the Órbigo Bridge on the Camino de Santiago in 1434 was, according to editor Francisco Rico, the most well-known chivalric feat from the fifteenth century and was very popular in the age of Cervantes (*Don Quijote* I.49: 567n56). For his part, Suero de Quiñones was later killed by none other than Gutierre Quijada. In other words, here Cervantes's satire of Spanish chivalry's feeble grasp on reality boils down to Don Quixote's nostalgia for his ancestor's victory over the defender of a bridge.

More indications that Cervantes wove a protracted allusion to Euclid's *pons asinorum* into *Don Quijote* are found in his numerous insinuations of the second term. If two real bridges and several multipronged textual bridges accompany his quotation of the *Elements*, so too do asses. I have written much about Apuleius's *The Golden Ass* as Cervantes's classical model for *Don Quijote*.[1] Cervantes's reliance on Apuleius's picaresque means that asses signal symbolic transformations. For example, in *Don Quijote*, Part I, the disappearance of Sancho's ass in chapters 23 and 25, followed by its return in chapters 30 and 46, frames and connects the conception and dissolution of the Micomicón subplot. Thus, Cervantes articulates his Apuleian criticism of Spanish imperialism and colonialism, the latter delineated most acutely by Sancho's dark plan to get rich by selling the black African citizens of Micomicón into slavery via one side of the triangular trade route, no less, between Iberia, Africa, and the New World. The critical zenith occurs when the squire stumbles on his brutal idea, and it's no accident that this is the only moment when he's happy in the absence of his ass. As everyone else mounts up to exit the Sierra Morena, Sancho gets upset, since "he was left to go on foot, feeling again the loss of his gray, which he needed so much now" (quedándose a pie, donde de nuevo se le renovó la pérdida del rucio, con la falta que entonces le hacía). But then he recalls that he will soon be King of Micomicón:

> What difference does it make to me if my vassals are blacks? All I have to do is put them on a ship and bring them to Spain, where I can sell them,

> and I'll be paid for them in cash, and with that money I'll be able to buy some title or office and live on that for the rest of my life ... By God, I'll sell them all, large or small, it's all the same to me, and no matter how black they are, I'll turn them white and yellow. Bring them on, then, I'm no fool!
>
> This made him so eager and happy that he forgot about his sorrow at having to walk. (*Don Quixote* I.29: 245)
>
> (– ¿Qué se me da a mí que mis vasallos sean negros? ¿Habrá más que cargar con ellos y traerlos a España, donde los podré vender y adonde me los pagarán de contado, de cuyo dinero podré comprar algún título o algún oficio con que vivir descansado todos los días de mi vida? ... Par Dios que los he de volar, chico con grande, o como pudiere, y que, por negros que sean, los he de volver blancos o amarillos. ¡Llegaos, que me mamo el dedo!
>
> Con esto andaba tan solícito y tan contento, que se le olvidaba la pesadumbre de caminar a pie. [*Don Quijote* I.29: 339–40])

By the same token, nearing the end of Part I, there arrives a redemptive ass – like that of El Greco's *The Flight to Egypt* – in the form of the animal mounted by Zoraida-María in chapters 37 and 41. Finding the bridge, and then the ass, are part and parcel of Cervantes's art of the novel. Parallel to Zoraida-María's biblical ass, the animal symbolically attaches to a series of male characters undergoing transformations. At the end of *La historia del cautivo*, the freed slave Pérez de Viedma briefly transports Zoraida-María in asinine fashion – "I carried her on my shoulders" (alguna vez la puse sobre mis hombros) – before spending cash to smooth the way: "I bought this animal that she is riding" (*Don Quixote* I.41: 366) (compré este animal en que ella viene [*Don Quijote* I.41: 489–90]). Next, Maritornes uses the halter of Sancho's mysterious ass to tie our knightly hidalgo's hand to a post in the inn's hayloft (1.43–4: 507–12; see fig. 3.1). Finally, Don Luis transforms from a shadowy "mozo de mulas" into the future husband of Doña Clara (I.42: 500–18). In the first edition of *Don Quijote*, this all occurs simultaneously and in conjunction with another odd textual bridge: chapter 42 jumps to 44, with no indication of 43. It also coincides with the slow re-emergence of Sancho's missing grey donkey (*rucio*), which begins its return via a series of metonymical allusions to its "aparejos," "cabestro," and "albarda" (I.42: 499, I.43: 507, I.45: 518; see also Flores). Note that Sancho's ass makes its final appearance in the same "caballeriza" from which Don Luis was heard singing the night before disguised as a "mozo de mulas"; and that Sancho, too, undergoes a major metamorphosis by surrendering his claim to the Kingdom of Micomicón.

An analogous combination of Euclid and Apuleius structures *Don Quijote*, Part II, where key geometrical allusions echo the quotation of Euclid's third common notion. Prior to their duel, the bachelor Corchuelo scoffs at the licentiate's antiquated idea that math is the basis for the art of fencing: "Dismount, and use your changes of posture, your circles, your angles, and your science; I expect to make you see stars at midday with my crude, modern skills" (*Don Quixote* II.19: 580) (Apeaos y usad de vuestro compás de pies, de vuestros círculos y vuestros ángulos y ciencia, que yo espero de haceros ver estrellas a medio día con mi destreza moderna y zafia [*Don Quijote* II.19: 787]). When Corchuelo hurls his foil away in frustration, the narrator signals the calculation of angles and distances involved in the more modern art of artillery: "in fury, anger, and rage the bachelor seized his foil by the hilt and threw it into the air with so much force that one of the peasants, who was a notary, went to retrieve it and subsequently testified that it had flown almost three-quarters of a league" (*Don Quixote* II.19: 581) (de despecho, cólera y rabia asió la espada por la empuñadura y arrojóla por el aire con tanta fuerza, que uno de los labradores asistentes, que era escribano, que fue por ella, dio después por testimonio que la alongó de sí casi tres cuartos de legua [*Don Quijote* II.19: 788–9]). Afterward, the victorious licentiate praises fencing using the same Euclidean language that has just been mocked by Corchuelo: "For the rest of their journey the licentiate told them about the excellencies of the sword, with so many demonstrations and figures and mathematical proofs that all of them were well-informed regarding the virtues of the science" (*Don Quixote* II.19: 581) (En lo que faltaba del camino, les fue contando el licenciado las excelencias de la espada, con tantas razones demostrativas y con tantas figuras y demostraciones matemáticas, que todos quedaron enterados de la bondad de la ciencia [*Don Quijote* II.19: 789]. These two Salamancan students reprise the isosceles rivalry epitomized in Part I by Anselmo and Lotario. Later in Part II, Cervantes restates the idea that triangles are the basis of conflict via his description of Countess Trifaldi's odd dress:

> Her train, or skirt, or whatever it is called, ended in three points, which were held up by the hands of three pages, also dressed in mourning, making an attractive mathematical figure with the three acute angles formed by the three points, leading everyone who saw the acutely pointed skirt to conclude that this was why she was called *The Countess Trifaldi*, as if we had said *The Countess of the Three Skirts*; and this, says Benengeli, was true, for her real name was *The Countess Lobuna*, because there were many wolves in her county, and if there had been foxes instead of wolves, she

would have been called *The Countess Zorruna*, because it was the custom in those parts for nobles to take their titles from the thing or things that are most abundant on their lands; but this countess, to favor the novelty of her skirt, abandoned *Lobuna* and adopted *Trifaldi*. (*Don Quixote* II.38: 704–5)

(La cola o falda, o como llamarla quisieren, era de tres puntas, las cuales se sustentaban en las manos de tres pajes asimesmo vestidos de luto, haciendo una vistosa y matemática figura con aquellos tres ángulos acutos que las tres puntas formaban; por lo cual cayeron todos los que la falda puntiaguda miraron que por ella se debía llamar la condesa Trifaldi, como si dijésemos la condesa "de las Tres Faldas," y así dice Benengeli que fue verdad, y que de su propio apellido se llamó la condesa Lobuna, a causa que se criaban en su condado muchos lobos, y que si como eran lobos fueran zorras, la llamaran la condesa Zorruna, por ser costumbre en aquellas partes tomar los señores la denominación de sus nombres de la cosa o cosas en que más sus estados abundan; empero esta condesa, por favorecer la novedad de su falda, dejó el Lobuna y tomó el Trifaldi. [*Don Quijote* II.38: 939])

Conflict among human beings is not the only issue that Cervantes associates with triangles. Desire, or attraction to other human beings, is also at issue. In *Mensonge romantique et vérité romanesque* (1961), translated into English as *Deceit, Desire and the Novel*, anthropologist René Girard coined the term "mimetic desire," whereby the erotic drive attains a metaphysical quality, because it's modelled by a rival who desires the same object. Embracing French novelist Marcel Proust's idea of "psychological laws," Girard indicates Don Quixote's imitation of Amadís of Gaul's love for Oriana as a prime example of his triangulated theory. Earlier still, Sigmund Freud made much of the Oedipal complex and the primal horde's murder of the alpha, finding male rivalry over females expressed in all sorts of myths, fantasies, and sexualities.[2]

It is easy to understand why Cervantes's novel leads to Freudian and Girardian thinking. Problematic love triangles are the elemental stuff according to which *Don Quijote* operates: Marcela, Grisóstomo, and Guillermo; Luscinda, Fernando, and Cardenio; Princess Micomicona, the "mal gigante," and Don Quijote; Angélica, Roland, and Medoro; Camila, Anselmo, and Lotario; Zoraida, Agi Morato, and Ruy Pérez de Viedma; Clara, Juan Pérez de Viedma, and Luis; Leandra, Eugenio, and Vicente; Belerma, Merlín, and Durandarte; Melisendra, Marsilio de Sansueña, and Gaiferos; Quiteria, Camacho, and Basilio; Antonomasia, Mambruno, and Don Clavijo; Ana Félix, Ricote, and Gregorio; Dulcinea, Merlín, and Don Quijote; and many more.

Freud and Girard intuit something universal about desire that helps us understand El Greco and Cervantes. Triangles are problems to be overcome by maturation, understanding, and peace. Renaissance Neoplatonism lets us be more specific. Painter and writer combine three traditions – the Bible's Christian ass, Euclid's *pons asinorum,* and Apuleius's metamorphosical ass – to indicate a trajectory away from ignorant, narcissistic possessiveness toward reasoned self-sacrifice and enlightenment. We can sort this process as lust or appetite (Greek *eros,* Latin *libido* or *curiositas*) changing itself by means of logic or reason (Greek *logos,* Latin *ratio*) into the social values of respect or charity (Greek *agape,* Latin *caritas*), which results in *eirene* peace (Greek *eirene,* Latin *pax*). Christian theology signals the divine word as *logos* and the ultimate moral lesson of Christ as *caritas.* Augustine's *Confessions* takes narcissistic *libido* as the starting point.

The role of the ass in this process is found in Matthew 2.13–15, or John 12.15: "Fear not, daughter of Zion; behold, your king is coming, sitting on an ass's colt." The ass symbolizes Christ's pacifying humility as opposed to the triumphant parades of warriors on stallions. Echoing this, first-century writers such as Tacitus produced caricatures of Christians worshipping asses. One Gnostic sect identified Christ as the Egyptian ass-headed god Typhon-Seth (Mathews 23–53). In Euclid's *Elements,* we witness the human capacity for pure reason, the *pons asinorum* being its first major step. Euclid's logic inspired Plato's *Timaeus,* in which triangles are the basic building blocks of the universe. Plato plots further arcs toward enlightenment in the *Symposium,* where *eros* provides the initial spark that sends the philosopher after spiritual insight, and *The Republic,* where the cave allegory models the philosopher's escape from the dark ignorance of material existence into the divine light of metaphysical truth. Apuleius, the greatest Neoplatonist of late antiquity, charts a trajectory from *curiositas* to *caritas* in *The Golden Ass,* which greatly influenced Augustine. After an erotic encounter, Lucius transforms into an ass; upon renouncing his carnal self, he metamorphoses back into a man. Apuleius signals the same via specific goddesses: Lucius lusts after the carnal beauties Diana and Venus and then prostrates himself before the celestial mother Isis. The interpolated allegory of the marriage of Eros (Love) and Psyche (Soul) repeats the lesson: desire draws the penitent spirit toward immortality. *The Golden Ass* channels an Ovidian tradition of metamorphosis and a plethora of Platonic concepts, but some as yet unidentified ancient formulation of Euclid's *Elements* I.5 as *pons asinorum* would also coincide with its overarching metaphor. Finally, we note Apuleius's reference to the Christian ass in the tale "The Royal Virgin Fleeing Captivity on Ass-back" (144), a clear sign of the syncretism at the heart of late classical Platonism.

Whether or not we embrace the "psychological laws" of modern theorists such as Freud and Girard, the logical Neoplatonic trajectory from *eros* to *agape* clarifies El Greco's paintings and Cervantes's narratives. Painter and writer produce artistic palliatives for the illogical dangers of *eros*. While *eros* is the spark of philosophy leading to the harmony of *agape* and *eirene*, it can also go bad, leading to narcissism and rivalry (i.e., *thanatos* [death] and *polemus* [conflict]). Fleeing *eros* toward *agape* is tantamount to fleeing egotism, jealousy, envy, enmity, and war. Herod's tyrannical cruelty looms as context for *The Flight to Egypt*, just as the Second Italian War and the struggle against Islam do for *The Curious Impertinent* and *La historia del cautivo*. Throughout *Don Quijote*, our hero's mad adventurousness parallels the suicidal possessiveness of Grisóstomo, the insane curiosity of Anselmo, the treacherous aggression of Fernando, and the angry misogyny of Eugenio. Reasonable alternatives then appear, coinciding with Don Quijote's return home in a cage: the Sierra Morena lovers work things out; the exemplary Don Pedro de Aguilar settles down "safe, rich, and married, with three children" (I.39: 341) (bueno y rico, casado y con tres hijos [I.39: 459]; and Clara and Luis are destined to marry. The same Christian resolution of *The Flight to Egypt* structures *Don Quixote* when the Holy Family arrives at the inn in the guise of Pérez de Viedma and Zoraida-María (see fig. 3.7; see also Gerli and Murillo).

The Geometry of Feminism, Moriscos, and Race

In the rest of this chapter, I argue that Cervantes and El Greco highlight three additional aspects of Renaissance Christian Neoplatonism's mathematical vision of the triumph of *eirene* over *polemus*. First, the painter and the novelist advocate an early modern form of feminism. Second, they attend to the ethnic clash between Old Christians and Moriscos. Third, they contest the new notion of skin colour as a marker of racial inferiority. I'll deal with these one at a time, although, as we shall see, they overlap.

As a rule in *Don Quijote*, men cause problems and women posit solutions (see Dudley; Herrero, "Beheading" and "Sierra Morena"). Cardenio's vision of male desire sums up this dynamic: "love in young men is, for the most part, nothing but appetite, which, having pleasure as its ultimate goal, ends when that goal is achieved" (*Don Quixote* I.24: 186–7) (el amor en los mozos por la mayor parte no lo es, sino apetito, el cual, como tiene por último fin el deleite, en llegando a alcanzarle se acaba [*Don Quijote* I.24: 266]). Dorotea assesses Fernando's passion the same way: "his lascivious appetite becoming even more inflamed, for that is the name I wish to give the desire he revealed to me" (*Don

Fig. 3.7. Christopher Roelofs's *The Flight to Spain*. Courtesy of artist.

Quixote I.24: 232) (su lascivo apetito, que este nombre quiero dar a la voluntad que me mostraba [*Don Quijote* I.28: 324]). One after another, Marcela, Luscinda, Dorotea, Camila, Zoraida, Clara, Quiteria, the Duchess, Trifaldi, Ana Félix, and, in the most extreme case, Claudia Jerónima offer counterweights to men's baser instincts. Marcela proclaims an overarching lesson: "Yo nací libre" (I.14.154; see El Saffar). Luscinda's victory over Fernando's lust occurs when, noticing his hand moving toward his sword, she talks him out of attacking his rival. In overt proximity to Euclid, Camila's role in *The Curious Impertinent* turns a woman's right to choose her mate into the moral fulcrum of Part I. Likewise, in Part II, prior to the geometrical fencing match between the students of Salamanca, Sancho locates the tipping point of female desire: "I wouldn't dare put the point of a pin between a woman's yes and no, because it wouldn't fit" (*Don Quixote* II.19: 579) (entre el *sí* y el *no* de la mujer no me atrevería yo a poner una punta de alfiler, porque no cabría [*Don Quijote* II.19: 786]). Like the duel, Sancho's phrase anticipates the love triangle among Quiteria, Camacho, and Basilio, which nearly causes a war between the bands of the opposing suitors. Yet reason prevails, and Quiteria's desire to marry Basilio is accepted by all.

The Sierra Morena between Castile and Andalucía as the site of triangular conflicts in *Don Quijote*, Part I, and the clash between Camacho's and Basilio's clans over Quiteria in Part II reveal problematic *eros* as the source of larger conflicts. The idea that competitive desire leads to wars among ethnicities and civilizations informs Mediterranean myths from Helen of Troy in ancient Greece to La Cava in early medieval Spain. In late sixteenth-century Iberia, the epic struggle between Christianity and Islam extended the fifteenth-century Reconquista. On an international level, El Greco's and Cervantes's careers coincided with the fights against the Turkish Empire and the Barbary States. A general stalemate took hold after the conquest of Granada in 1492 and the Battle of Lepanto in 1571. At the local level, this conflict centred on the Morisco question in southern Spain. If they converted to Christianity, hundreds of thousands of people of Moorish ancestry avoided expulsion in 1502 and so remained a vital part of the cultures and economies of Andalucía, Valencia, and Aragon until 1609. Urban Moriscos tended to embrace Christianity; rural Moriscos often continued to practise Islam. A series of Morisco uprisings marked the second half of the sixteenth century. The bloodiest was the Alpujarras Rebellion (1568–71), after which the Habsburgs enforced relocation and assimilation. What to do about the Moriscos was by far the major domestic issue of the next forty years. Old Christians and hardliners such as Archbishop Juan de Ribera advocated expulsion and even slavery. Humanists and scholastics such as Diego Hurtado de Mendoza pleaded for reason and tolerance. Hardliners won, and the final expulsion took place between 1609 and 1614, with regions like Valencia and Aragon losing on the order of 33 and 20 per cent, respectively, of their total populations (Lynch 45). Until 1609, then, the demographic context for artists such as El Greco and Cervantes was a countryside riddled with increasing pockets of Moriscos as opposed to the diminishing communities of their Old Christian rivals. The problem affected regions like Castile, where many Moriscos were relocated after the Alpujarras War, although it was most intense to the south and east (fig. 3.8).

Don Quijote negotiates the Morisco problem in both of its parts, published before and after the expulsion, respectively. Cervantes emphasizes a fundamental irony: even though our hidalgo thinks of himself and Dulcinea as pure Christians, the Moorish presence in Iberia for nearly 800 years makes this impossible, especially in frontier zones like La Mancha and Aragon. Don Quixote's madness alludes to this impossibility from the beginning. After Toledan merchants thrash him, Don Quixote returns home atop his neighbour Pedro Alonso's ass, at which point our confused hero identifies himself as the "moro Abendarráez" and Dulcinea as his Mooress lover: "esta hermosa Jarifa que he dicho es ahora la linda Dulcinea del Toboso" (*Don Quijote* I.5: 73). At the second

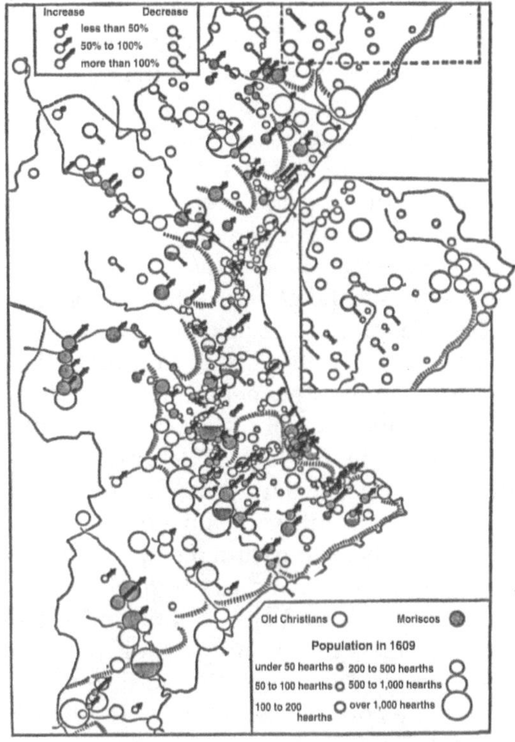

Fig. 3.8. Population changes in Valencia between 1565 and 1609.
Source: Fernand Braudel, *The Mediterranean and the Mediterranean World in the Age of Philip II*, vol. 2 (New York: Harper, 1949), 784.

inn, Don Quijote falls in love with Maritornes, who for her part attempts a sexual encounter with a relative of the original Moorish author Cide Mahamete Benengeli (*Don Quijote* I.16: 171). Our hidalgo's ethnic identity crisis climaxes in chapters 25 and 26 of Part I. At first, he admits that Dulcinea is actually a Morisca; then he reverts to his obsession with Christian purity by rejecting the idea. After telling Sancho that he knows Dulcinea is really Aldonza Lorenzo, the knight wavers between Amadís of Gaul and Roland as models. Then he recalls the love triangle formed by Roland, Angélica, and the Moor Medoro, and realizes that he can't identify with Roland because, unlike Angélica, Aldonza Lorenzo "has not in all her days seen a single Moor" (*Don Quixote* I.26: 205) (no ha visto en todos los días de su vida moro alguno [*Don Quijote* I.26: 291]). The irony derives from the fact that El Toboso was populated by Moriscos and that our hero's love object is unlikely to be an

Old Christian. When the Holy Family arrives at the inn in the form of Pérez de Viedma and Zoraida-María, we see that, in 1605, Cervantes favoured intermarriage and miscegenation in lieu of expulsion.

Sancho, who constantly brags about his Old Christian heritage, learns the same lesson. In Part II, Sancho's hypocrisy is most acute regarding the Morisco family of Ricote and his daughter Ana Félix, who have been expelled from Spain and are seeking to return. Ricote's name alludes to a valley in Murcia populated by loyal Moriscos. Following his governorship of Barataria, Sancho quaffs the wine and wolfs down the caviar of his friend and neighbour while refusing to assist him in the recovery of his treasure. In the next scene, Sancho and his ass fall into a cave. It's poetic justice for his crude support of the expulsion. The cave also references the celebrated metaphor of Plato's *Republic*: instead of escaping into the divine light of reason, Sancho remains in the cave of ignorance. Later, reprising the roles of Pérez de Viedma and Zoraida-María, Ana Félix and her Christian lover Gregorio provide a counter-narrative to Sancho's ethnocentrism. Don Antonio Moreno even offers to represent Ricote's family in court and plead for their readmission into Spanish society. In other words, and as the work of Francisco Márquez Villanueva ("El morisco"), Luce López Baralt, and Frederick de Armas implies, Cervantes opposed the looming expulsion in 1605, and, as late as 1615, he envisioned a more pragmatic and flexible policy.[3]

It is vital to see that a confluence of political, religious, and cultural concerns gave birth to an early modern feminist agenda, which, for its part, is the essence of Cervantes's ongoing case for miscegenation and intermarriage.[4] The illogical undertakings and madness of Spaniards and Christians such as Don Quijote, Grisóstomo, Cardenio, Anselmo, Fernando, and Eugenio yield before female *eros*, to which no male *eros* has any absolute claim. As critics such as Edward Dudley, Javier Herrero, and Diana de Armas Wilson have pointed out, the love sickness of the Sierra Morena is reduced to its triangular essence in *The Curious Impertinent*, after which male excesses are cured, restrained, and caged.

But this civilizing trajectory towards *agape* does not end here. Early modern feminism reforms European men, but there remains the cultural chasm represented by Islam. Historian Bernard Lewis puts it succinctly: "Western civilization was richer for women's presence; Muslim civilization, poorer by their absence" (24). Christianity's Virgin birth has always been most unacceptable to Islam, which can be seen throughout the *Koran*. El Greco and Cervantes repackage this metaphysical myth as *logos* and *caritas*, and then leverage it along the religious fault lines of the Mediterranean and southern Spain. El Greco's *The Flight to Egypt* and Cervantes's Pérez de Viedma and Zoraida-María are examples of worldly morality and ethics, of basic respect for women's amorous choices in life. In other words, the true miracle of the Virgin birth is not the birth *per se* but, rather, a man's willingness to love and respect a woman regardless. Thus, Lotario accuses his friend Anselmo, who obsesses over Camila's sexual purity, of reasoning like a Moor. The climactic problem of Part I of *Don Quijote* is Zoraida's despicable father, Agi Morato, in *La historia del cautivo*. His rejection of his daughter's *eros* makes him akin to Herod. Zoraida tells Pérez de Viedma that if her father discovers her plan to marry a Christian and flee to Spain, "he will throw me in a well and cover me over with stones" (*Don Quixote* I.40: 347) (me echará luego en un pozo y me cubrirá de piedras [*Don Quijote* I.40: 467]). When she gazes at Pérez de Viedma as Spanish women implore her to remove her veil and in public, he urges her to do so, and in Arabic, no less. And she's adamant about her new name: "¡No, no *Zoraida*: *María, María*!" (*Don Quijote* I.37: 441). Similarly, in Part II, Ricote's acceptance of his daughter Ana Félix's love for Gregorio is what makes him redeemable as a Morisco with Christian values.

How does all this relate to Euclid? Think of it this way: male *eros*'s potential for *polemus* in general and the Morisco question in particular are the *pons asinorum* that must be bridged via the logic of respect for women, intermarriage, and miscegenation. Taking a broader perspective on *Don Quijote*, the Italian bridge that frames the Euclidean isosceles triangle of *The Curious Impertinent* presages the cultural bridge between Christians and Moors achieved by Pérez de Viedma and Zoraida-María. Sancho's ass provides parallel support for the Euclidean metaphor by disappearing during Don Quijote's ethnic identity crisis and reappearing upon its symbolic resolution. Pedro Alonso's ass does likewise, as does that of Zoraida-María.

We find another version of the *pons asinorum* in *Don Quijote*, Part II. To see this, we must grasp how Sancho's governorship of Barataria relates to the Morisco question and then relate these to another important bridge as well as the perpetual ass theme. The social context is again conflict in general and an absurd civil war in particular. In "The Braying Episode" of chapters 25 and 27, knight and squire are caught between two towns that claim superiority at making donkey calls. Later, echoing Don Quixote's worry that Clavileño's belly might contain soldiers, the mock invasion of Barataria in chapter 53 is a metaphor for the Moriscos as a fifth column of the Islamic enemy. Prior to the invasion, Governor Sancho undergoes a final test based on the thought experiment known as "Buridan's ass." An early source of *pons asinorum* as a metaphor for the middle term of a syllogism, Buridan was also credited with the dilemma of a hungry ass who starves to death because he is unable to decide between two equal bales of hay.

In chapter 51, Cervantes creates an ingenious version of this paradox. Sancho must decide a case involving a law that requires travellers to state their intentions before crossing a bridge. If they lie, they are put to death. The paradox arises when a traveller states his intention to cross the bridge in order to get killed. Sancho chooses mercy over the law and orders that the traveller be allowed to cross. This exemplifies a legal principle: "In dubio, pro reo," or "Innocent until proven guilty." The social irony here is twofold. First, Sancho solves the legal paradox, but his government fails to resolve the true Bridge of Asses – that is, the Morisco question. The invasion still happens in chapter 53, and Sancho still exploits the exiled Ricote in chapter 54 and then falls with his ass into a political cave in chapter 55. Second, given Sancho's excessive preoccupation with his mysterious ass, and given that he must undergo 3,300 lashes in order to free Dulcinea from enchantment, Cervantes figures Sancho himself as the ultimate symbolic ass of Part II. In other words, the merciful moral of "in dubio, pro reo," by which our governor-ass resolves the paradox of the bridge, is precisely the answer to the social *pons asinorum* that is the Morisco question.

Once we see *Elements* I.5 as a structural metaphor for both parts of *Don Quijote*, we must reconsider the other famously nicknamed proof in Book I of Euclid's masterpiece. The Pythagorean theorem of *Elements* I.47 (fig. 3.5) has two epithets: "the Windmill," as per the obtuse triangles crossing at the diagram's centre (CBZ and ABD in Zamorano's edition); and "Dulcarnon," from the Arabic *ḏū al-qarnayn*, meaning "the two-horned one," as per the two squares protruding from the top of the right triangle (see Chaucer 3.134–5). We must now consider the possibility that the most popular symbol of Cervantes's great novel forms yet another aspect of an extended allusion to the entirety of book one of Euclid's *Elements* (see fig. 3.9; see also Caro Baroja; Fajardo-Acosta). We must also consider that said symbol has transcultural implications. Note that, before the priest refers to the bridge at the Battle of Garigliano, his intratextual reference to Diego García de Paredes also recalls the windmill of chapter 8: "with one finger he could stop a millwheel as it turned" (I.32: 269) (detenía con un dedo una rueda de molino en la mitad de su furia [I.32: 372]). Note also that, after the windmill episode, Don Quixote imitates Diego Pérez de Vargas y Machuca, a hero against the Moors; and, further, that the narrative break between chapters 8 and 9 leads the narrator to seek out the lost Arabic manuscript, which, for its part, is translated for him by a Morisco in Toledo. In other words, Cervantes's windmill also signals the Pythagorean "Dulcarnon" as a

Fig. 3.9. Gustave Doré, *Don Quixote Fights the Windmill.*
Source: Wikipedia Commons.

cultural and linguistic bridge in Southern Spain (Graf, "*Don Quijote* and Islam"). Tilting at windmills strikes modern readers as romantic and positive; but heroic zeal is problematic when it tilts against reason and logic by demonizing others.

In the late sixteenth century, southern Europe witnessed the beginnings of another social problem: a form of racism based on skin colour instead of bloodline. There are two reasons for this: the darkening of relatively more Moorish populations living at the margins of southern Europe in places like Italy and Spain; and the rise of the transatlantic trade in black African slaves pioneered by Portugal, which was annexed by Spain in 1580. In cities like Seville and Valencia, the latter phenomenon resulted in significant black African populations condemned to the same inferior social status as the Moriscos. Cervantes overtly criticizes this new type of racism in Part I of *Don Quijote* via Sancho's horrific Micomicón fantasy, which we detailed above as our author's critique of the evil leg of the triangular trade route between Europe, Africa, and the New World.

Cervantes criticizes this new type of racism yet again in Part II via Don Quixote's angry comparison of the fate of old soldiers to that of freed black slaves: "it is not right that they be treated the way blacks are treated who are emancipated and freed when they are old and can no longer serve, and are thrown out of the house and called free men, making them slaves to hunger" (*Don Quixote* II.24: 619) (no es bien que se haga con ellos lo que suelen hacer los que ahorran y dan libertad a sus negros cuando ya son viejos y no pueden servir, y echándolos de casa con título de libres los hacen esclavos de la hambre [*Don Quijote* II.24: 835]). More subtle and ironic indications of the pigmentary theme appear in Sancho's "rucio": the description of Pérez de Viedma with "his face rather dark" (I.37: 326) (algo moreno de rostro [*Don Quijote* I.37: 439]); the racist and misogynistic fugitive "black-, white-, and gray-spotted nanny goat" (I.37: 432) (toda la piel manchada de negro, blanco y pardo [*Don Quijote* I.50: 574; see also Márquez Villanueva, "La cabra *manchada*"]); and the effigy of the Virgin Mary, whose face is covered by a black mourning veil, carried by the penitents whom Don Quixote attacks in the final scene of Part I (*Don Quijote* 1.52: 585). The *pons asinorum* of the Morisco question is also that of race. Cervantes holds that enslaving, exiling, and mistreating a fellow human being because she speaks Arabic or dresses like a Morisca is as ignorant and repugnant as doing so because she has darker skin.

Throughout his career, El Greco advanced the same idea in spectacular fashion. Like *The Flight to Egypt*, his *Healing of the Blind Man* (*La curación del ciego*, ca. 1570 (fig. 3.10) incorporates Euclidean geometry into an allegory for progress toward *eirene* and away from *thanatos* and *polemus*. The architectural remains of the Baths of Diocletian in Rome locate ancient tyrannical violence at the painting's vanishing point, but parallel lines leave that point behind, rescuing us with expansive triangles, dimensionality, and depth. As Christ cures a blind man to the left, *agape* occupies the centre foreground in the form of the positive *eros* of a clearly biracial couple. The figures to the right – reminiscent of Socrates, Plato, Aristotle, and both biblical Josephs – emphasize the solutions of reason, charity, and miscegenation by gesticulating at both pairings with astonished admiration. Note the wildly multicolored coat worn by the figure at the painting's right margin and the turban behind Christ's right shoulder. El Greco's famous hallucinogenic colour schemes celebrate a multiracial Mediterranean utopia as the culmination of all the horrific violence of ancient history.

Two more intersections of race and geometry in Cervantes and El Greco merit attention. First, Cervantes's exemplary novels "The Deceitful Marriage" ("El casamiento engañoso") and "The Colloquy of the Dogs"

Fig. 3.10 El Greco's *Healing of the Blind Man*.
Source: Wikipedia Commons.

("El coloquio de los perros") form a two-part picaresque written around the same time as *Don Quixote*, Part I. The Apuleian and Quixotic problem of *curiositas*, or unrestrained *eros*, haunts both the soldier Campuzano and the dog Berganza. Campuzano deceives a prostitute and gets syphilis and madness in return. For his part, Berganza lives out the poetic justice of remaining a dog, because he fails to fulfil the prophecy that he will metamorphose back into a man upon displaying humility and helping the wretched (see Virgil 6.853 and Matthew 23.12). Instead, Berganza reciprocates the kindness of an old witch by exposing her to a mob, and he mauls a black African slave who, as she passed him in the night, had fed him better than his own master: "for the black woman was in love with a black man, also belonging to the house" (la negra de la casa estaba enamorada de un negro, asimismo esclavo de la casa [*Coloquio* 313]). In other words, Berganza embraces *polemus* and enforces a kind of *eros interruptus* on the most wretched victims of Spanish colonialism. "The Colloquy of the Dogs" is Cervantes's pessimistic inversion of El Greco's *Healing of the Blind Man*. Berganza remains blind to his own capacity for evil. Significantly, El Greco painted another version of *Healing of the Blind Man* in which a dog takes the place of the biracial couple.

At the conclusion of "The Colloquy of the Dogs," Berganza reports a conversation among four *arbitristas*, crackpot utopian patients in the same hospital as Campuzano. One of these men is a mathematician frustrated by his efforts to find the ultimate fixed point and square the circle:

For two and twenty years I have been in pursuit of the fixed point; here I miss it, there I get sight of it again, and just when it seems that I am down upon it so that it can by no means escape me, I find myself on a sudden so far away from it that I am utterly amazed. It is just the same with the quadrature of the circle. I have been within such a hair's breadth of it, that I cannot conceive how it is that I have not got it in my pocket. Thus, I suffer a torment like that of Tantalus, who starves with fruits all round him, and burns with thirst with water at his lip. At one moment I seem to grasp the truth, at another it is far away from me; and, like another Sisyphus, I begin again to climb the hill which I have just rolled down, along with all the mass of my labours.

(Veinte y dos años ha que ando tras hallar el punto fijo, y aquí lo dejo, y allí lo tomo, y, pareciéndome que ya lo he hallado y que no se me puede escapar en ninguna manera, cuando no me cato, me hallo tan lejos del, que me admiro; lo mismo me acaece con la cuadratura del círculo, que he llegado tan al remate de hallarla, que no sé ni puedo pensar cómo no la tengo ya en la faldriquera; y así, es mi pena semejable á las de Tántalo, que está cerca del fruto, y muere de hambre; y propincuo al agua y perece de sed. Por momentos pienso dar en la coyuntura de la verdad, y por minutos me hallo tan lejos della, que vuelvo á subir el monte que acabé de bajar, con el canto de mi trabajo á cuestas, como otro nuevo Sísifo. [*Coloquio* 360])

Editor Agustín G. de Amezúa y Mayo shares the following anecdote about the quest to square the circle that so obsessed Europeans until the modern age, when it was recognized as an impossibility. One night, while in his native city of Valencia, the Neoplatonic mathematician Jaime Falcó (1522–94; fig. 3.11) thought he had solved one of classical antiquity's most vexing geometrical problems. He ran through the city's plazas shouting a tragically false eureka in Latin: "Falco has squared the circle that no one has squared!" (*Coloquio* 689n347). So Cervantes caps his most cynical and satirical text with another Euclidean metaphor: the quest by history's greatest novelist to smooth race relations in southern Spain is tantamount to Falcó's quest for mathematical glory (see fig. 3.8). At the end of "The Colloquy of the Dogs," Campuzano stays insane and Berganza cannot be a man because both fail at charity and reason, the only ways to square the circle of human conflict.

El Greco's greatest meditation on race, *Saint Martin and the Beggar* (*San Martín y el mendigo*, ca. 1597–9; fig. 3.12), deploys the same geometrical metaphor centred on the Morisco question. This ingenious painting is history's first racialized version of Saint Martin's defining act of charity. A simple anachronism reworks the myth into an encounter

Fig. 3.11. José de Ribalta's *Jaime Juan Falcó y Segura*.
Source: Museo de Bellas Artes de Valencia.

between a Hapsburg and a Morisco outside Toledo (see *Don Quijote* I.9). Overwhelming the foreground, we have the moral tipping point. With his sword at the ready, is Martin going to kill the impertinent beggar? No, we know the saint moves to cut his cape and share it with the man, who will appear to him as Christ in that night's dream. But do we? Racial contrasts swarm the painting: the two-toned clouds, the men's skin colours, the saint's armour versus his collar and cuffs, the horse's legs and black hooves next to the beggar's legs with a white bandage, and the horse's coat covered by black trappings, most notably the enormous cross of its breastcollar. The motion of Martin's sword, the beggar's right forefinger, the horse's raised left hoof, and the strange arcing shadow of its right leg, all draw our attention to an odd device in the distance of the painting's lower right-hand corner: the ever-out-of-reach squared circle. It's a more hopeful version of race relations in southern Spain than Cervantes's "The Colloquy of the Dogs," but the metaphor and the mechanics are identical. Some viewers will see; others will not.

Fig. 3.12. El Greco's *Saint Martin and the Beggar*. Source: Wikipedia Commons.

Conclusion

To sum up, El Greco and Cervantes plot an intellectual ethos of *agape* that evolves out of *eros*, moving away from the latter's concomitant problems of madness, jealousy, misogyny, racism, enmity, tyranny, and war. Their greatest paintings and novels do this by equating theology and geometry, a major theoretical aspect of Neoplatonism. El Greco's *The Flight to Egypt* and *Healing of the Blind Man* envision *logos* (*ratio*) as creating a Mediterranean utopia, which emerges as the discovery and application of Euclidean reasoning in Euclidean space: the *pons asinorum* of the Virgin birth and the vanishing point, parallel lines, and triangles of Christian *caritas* leave Herod and Diocletian behind. The endpoints of this movement are social harmony and *eirene*, achieved by overcoming racism and aggression, as in *Saint Martin and the Beggar*, with its squaring of the circle of the Spanish Morisco question visible in the distance. For his part, much like Chaucer, Cervantes recombines the third common notion, the Bridge of Asses, the Windmill, and a range of triangles, weaving them into the symbolic moral landscape of *Don Quijote*. Less inclined toward hagiography than El Greco, Cervantes foregrounds the harsh realism of the picaresque, meditating more on the corruption of *eros* and *curiositas* (i.e., lust, appetite, and so on). In "The Deceitful Marriage" and "The Colloquy of the Dogs," the syphilis of Campuzano and the cruelty of Berganza are two sides of the same carnal coin, and Cervantes ultimately withholds those positive aspects of the picaresque still found in *Don Quixote*, such as sexual maturation and social integration. Nevertheless, like El Greco, Cervantes signals Christian *caritas* as a moral endpoint and the discovery and resolution of Euclidean proofs as metaphors for overcoming conflict between Christians and Moriscos. Neither should the iconographic tendencies of El Greco obscure his own grasp of ignorance, narcissism, and tyranny as original problems. The blind donkey of *The Flight to Egypt* and the contextual allusions to Herod and Diocletian in *Healing of the Blind Man* and *Saint Martin and the Beggar* are tantamount to Cervantes's host of sick, mad lovers and abusive fathers. In other words, painter and novelist both work according to the basic Neoplatonic view that the inanimate substratum of the material world is evil by default, as in "absent the good" – that is, the dark place from which all journeys toward enlightenment must begin (see Willis; Paiewonsky-Conde).

I would like to note three additional philological points regarding how we might now reposition El Greco and Cervantes in the history of Western thought, specifically with respect to the uses of Euclid in painting and narrative fiction. First, I think El Greco and Cervantes knew a mathematical version of the phrase *pons asinorum* that predates *The Flight to Egypt*. In particular, El Greco's Euclidean rendering of the Holy Family undercuts West and Thompson's hypothesis that the absence of the asinine phrase in Billingsley's 1570 edition of Euclid means that "its crossing into mathematics probably occurred at a later date" (88). Second, in 1791, English poet Thomas Campbell penned a comical poem, "The Pons Asinorum; or The Asses' Bridge," in which Mr. Miller's math students launch a metaphorical assault on Euclid's fifth proof. Poor Plumbano, "a comical man" who "soon found that his brains were wheeled round," is the sole casualty. Cervantes's textual, comical, and military framing of Euclid in both parts of *Don Quijote* suggests that the burlesque take on *Elements* I.5 as a transcendental battle that can be won only by an exceptional class of warriors predates Campbell's poem by at least two centuries. Third, although I would argue that Cervantes was familiar with El Greco (Graf, "The Devil's Perspective" and "The Politics of Salvation"), and that both men knew their Euclid, one might still claim that their axioms, triangles, squares, and circles in concert with biblical and Apuleian asses merely express a mildly esoteric or occultist sense of harmony. So one might reduce their Euclidean allusions to something along the lines of the perfunctory "topoi" amassed by Ernst Curtius. I think this would be too easy and arrogant on our part. Having studied the Cretan painter and the Spanish novelist for many years, and having experienced Euclidean logic first hand, I think it much more likely that El Greco and Cervantes imagined and structured their artistic and fictional universes in the more rigorous manner of Augustine or Dante (see Yates).

A final note on reason. The trajectory from *eros, curiositas,* and *polemos* toward *agape, caritas,* and *eirene* is not purely moral, social, and political. Euclid's presence in the Neoplatonic tradition signals that it's also a matter of questing after scientific knowledge (as the epigraph to this chapter suggests). Bacon pioneered empirical methods, Buridan paved the way for Copernicus and Newton, and their late-scholastic heirs at Salamanca were history's first economists. To borrow a term used by both Cervantes and Freud, such men "sublimated" their short-term instincts into technological pursuits. This helps us understand the meaning of the many machines of *Don Quixote*. Often our hero is a Luddite battling windmills, fulling mills, and waterwheels, but near the end of his life he comes to terms with sailing vessels, mechanical figures, and printing presses. Don Antonio Moreno's magical bronze head recalls the necromancy of Bacon, but it also alludes to the engineer Juanelo Turriano, whose clocks, automatons, and machines mesmerized the courts of Charles V and Philip II. El Greco's *Saint Martin and the Beggar* makes similar reference to these machines in the image of the squared circle, which is also a peculiar profile of Turriano's engine for raising water from the Tagus into the heart of Toledo. Beyond admiring technological innovation, Cervantes anticipated Montesquieu's vision of the civilizing effects of "doux commerce" and Adam Smith's notion of personal interest as the source of the unintended morality of the market economy (Quint; see Schwartz 103–32). The twentieth-century heir to these thinkers was Friedrich Hayek. On one hand, Hayek showed how capitalism is an essentially altruistic system, for to win one must serve and fulfil the needs of others (*Law*); on the other hand, he pointed out that the organic spontaneity of the market economy is not some mechanistic device that can be manipulated according to discernible laws (*The Fatal Conceit*). Cervantes's advantage over El Greco's painterly hagiographies is that his medium, the picaresque, delves deeply into such matters. Both the rationality of merchant morality and the irrationality of the market economy echo Apuleius's cult of Isis as the goddess of commerce at the end of *The Golden Ass*. In Hayekian and Apuleian fashion, Cervantes's relentless irony indicates a wondrous disorder. Progress requires liberty, not control. His is an anti-utopian utopia (see Maravall). Yes, thinking and calculation are essential. Technological betterment of human life goes hand in hand with market innovations. But the insights that make these innovations possible are not by design, nor are they intuitive. Thus, *Don Quixote* offers lessons about the time value of money, salaried labour's superior productivity over slave labour, and the dangers of a state monopoly on currency (Graf, "The Economy" and

"Juan de Mariana"). And Cervantes's major reference to the Pythagorean theorem in Part I, which gives way to the break between chapters 8 and 9 and then the winding quest through Toledo for a lost Arabic manuscript, indicates that the best resolution to the Morisco question is the marketplace – that is, a system of mutually beneficial exchange as opposed to mutually destructive rivalry. Although it might be difficult to perceive at first, the key to ending the injustice of Andrés's suffering, as well as that of the Africans of Micomicón or Moriscos such as Ricote, is a counterintuitive kind of calculus. More productive and more moral than irrational sentimentality, domination, and slavery are geometrical logic, respect, and pay for work.

NOTES

1 See the articles by Graf: "Cómo leer," "The Economy," "*Don Quijote* and Feminism," and "Cervantes es a Apuleyo."
2 See Graf's "La antropología subversiva," 23–7. Freud, too, drew on *Don Quijote* for his triads of human psychology.
3 See also Graf, "*Don Quijote* and Islam."
4 See Graf, "Cervantes es a Apuleyo" and "*Don Quijote* and Feminism."

REFERENCES

Apuleius. *The Golden Ass*. Translated by Jack Lindsay. Bloomington: Indiana University Press, 1960.

Augustine. *Confessions*. Translated by Henry Chadwick. Oxford: Oxford University Press, 2008.

Bacon, Fr. Rogeri. *Opus Tertium*. Vol. 1, *Opera Quaedam Hactenus Inedita*. Edited by J.S. Brewer. London: Longman, 1859.

Braudel, Fernand. *El Mediterráneo y el mundo mediterráneo en la época de Felipe II*. Vol. 2. Mexico City: Fondo de Cultura Económica, 1997.

Campbell, Thomas. *The Poetical Works of Thomas Campbell*. Boston: Little, Brown, 1864.

Caro Baroja, Julio. "Disertación sobre los molinos de viento." *Revista de dialectología y tradiciones populares* 8, no. 2 (1952): 212–366.

Cervantes, Miguel de. "The Dialogue of the Dogs." In *Miguel de Cervantes. Exemplary Novels*. Translated by Lesley Lipson. Oxford: Oxford University Press, 1992.

– *Don Quijote de la Mancha*. Edited by Francisco Rico. Barcelona: Crítica, 1998.

– *Don Quixote*. Translated by Edith Grossman. New York: HarperCollins, 2003.

– *El casamiento engañoso y El coloquio de los perros*. Edited by Agustín G. de Amezúa y Mayo. Madrid: Bailly, 1912.

Chaucer, Geoffrey. *Troilus and Criseyde*. http://quod.lib.umich.edu/c/cme/Troilus/.

Curtius, Ernst Robert. *European Literature and the Latin Middle Ages*. Translated by Willard R. Trask. Princeton, NJ: Princeton University Press, 1990.

Dante Alighieri. *Paradiso*. Vol. 3 of *The Divine Comedy*. Translated by Courtney Langdon. Cambridge, MA: Harvard University Press, 1921.

de Armas, Frederick A. *Don Quixote and the Saracens: A Clash of Civilizations and Literary Genres*. Toronto: University of Toronto Press, 2011.

de Secondat, Charles, Baron de Montesquieu. *The Spirit of the Laws*. London: J. Duncan and Son, 1793.

Dudley, Edward. "Don Quijote As Magus: The Rhetoric of Interpolation." *Bulletin of Hispanic Studies* 49 (192): 355–68.

El Saffar, Ruth. "In Marcela's Case." In *Quixotic Desire: Psychoanalytic Perspectives on Cervantes*, edited by Diana de Armas Wilson and Ruth El Saffar, 157–78. Ithaca, NY: Cornell University Press, 1993.

Euclid. *Elements*. Edited by Oliver Byrne. London: Pickering, 1847. www.math.ubc.ca/~cass/Euclid/byrne.html

– *Los seis libros primeros de la geometría de Euclides*. Translated by Rodrigo Zamorano. Seville: Alfonso de la Barrera, 1576.

– *The Thirteen Books of Euclid's Elements*. Vol. 1. Edited by Thomas L. Heath. Cambridge: Cambridge University Press, 1926.

Fajardo-Acosta, Fidel. "Don Quijote y las máquinas infernales: Vanidad del ejercicio de las armas." *Hispanic Journal* 10, no. 2 (1989): 15–25.

Flores, Robert M. "The Loss and Recovery of Sancho's Ass in *Don Quijote*, Part I." *Modern Language Review* 75 (1980): 301–10.

Freud, Sigmund. "Análisis de la fobia de un niño de cinco años." *Obras completas de Sigmund Freud*. Vol. 10. Translated by José Luis Etcheverry, 7–118. Buenos Aires: Amorrortu, 1976.

– "La novela familiar de los neuróticos." *Obras completas de Sigmund Freud*. Vol. 9. Translated by José Luis Etcheverry, 217–20. Buenos Aires: Amorrortu, 1976.

– "Moisés y la religión monoteísta." *Obras completas de Sigmund Freud*. Vol. 23. Translated by José Luis Etcheverry, 7–132. Buenos Aires: Amorrortu, 1976.

Gerli, E. Michael. *Refiguring Authority: Reading, Writing, and Rewriting in Cervantes*. Lexington: University Press of Kentucky, 1995.

Girard, René. *Deceit, Desire and the Novel: Self and Other in Literary Structure* [*Mensonge romantique et vérité romanesque*]. Translated by Yvonne Freccero. Baltimore. MD: Johns Hopkins University Press, 1976.

Graf, Eric Clifford. "Cervantes es a Apuleyo lo que Zoraida es a Isis: *Don Quijote* como apropiación cristiana de la trayectoria proto-feminista de la

novela pagana." In *Estas primicias del ingenio: Jóvenes cervantistas en Chicago*, edited by Francisco Caudet and Kerry Wilks, 99–112. Madrid: Castalia, 2003.
– "Cómo leer *Don Quijote* como un gran libro sobre el alma y la política: Primero, leer *El asno de oro* de Apuleyo y *La República* de Platón." *Destellos: Revista de pensamiento en español* 1, no. 1 (2014): 33–42.
– "The Devil's Perspective in El Greco's *Alegoría de la Liga Santa*, San Juan de la Cruz's *Cántico espiritual*, and Cervantes's *La Numancia*." *Romance Notes* 53, no. 1 (2013): 53–64.
– "*Don Quijote* and Feminism: Cervantes, Apuleius, Zoraida, and Isis." In *Cervantes and Modernity: Four Essays on Don Quijote*, 56–102. Lewisburg, PA: Bucknell University Press, 2007.
– "*Don Quijote* and Islam: When an Arab Laughs in Toledo." In *Cervantes and Modernity: Four Essays on Don Quijote*, 21–55. Lewisburg, PA: Bucknell University Press, 2007.
– "The Economy of Asses in *Don Quijote de la Mancha*: Metalepsis, Miscegenation, and Commerce in Cervantes's Picaresque." *eHumanista/Cervantes* 4 (2015): 255–88.
– "Juan de Mariana and the Modern American Politics of Money: Salamanca, Cervantes, Jefferson, and the Austrian School." *Quarterly Journal of Austrian Economics* 17, no. 4 (2014): 442–73.
– "La antropología subversiva de Freud y la alegoría cínica de Cervantes: *Moisés y la religión monoteísta* y *La novela y coloquio de los perros*." *Studi ispanici* 50 (2015): 23–41.
– "The Politics of Salvation in El Greco's Escorial Paintings and Cervantes's *Numantia*." In *Signs of Power in Habsburg Spain and the New World*, edited by Jason McCloskey and Ignacio López Almeny, 177–98. Lewisburg, PA: Bucknell University Press, 2013.
Hayek, Friedrich. *The Fatal Conceit*. Chicago: University of Chicago Press, 1988.
– *Law, Legislation, and Liberty*. London: Routledge, 1998.
Heilbron, J.L. *Geometry Civilized: History, Culture, and Technique*. Oxford: Oxford University Press, 1998.
Herrero, Javier. "The Beheading of the Giant: An Obscene Metaphor in *Don Quijote*." *Revista hispánica moderna* 39, no. 4 (1976–7): 141–9.
– "Sierra Morena as Labyrinth: From Wildness to Christian Knighthood." In *Critical Essays on Cervantes*, edited by Ruth El Saffar, 67–80. Boston: G.K. Hall, 1986.
Hobbes, Thomas. *Leviathan*. Edited by Richard Tuck. Cambridge: Cambridge University Press, 1996.
Lewis, Bernard. *Cultures in Conflict: Christians, Muslims, and Jews in the Age of Discovery*. Oxford: Oxford University Press, 1995.

López Baralt, Luce. "El cálamo supremo (Al-Qalam Al-'Alà) de Cide Hamete Benengeli." In *Mélanges María Soledad Carrasco Urgoiti*, edited by Abdeljelil Temimi, 343–61. Zaghouan, Tunisia: FTERSI, 1999.
Lynch, John. *Spain under the Habsburgs*. Vol. 2. Oxford: Alden Mowbray, 1969.
Maravall, José Antonio. *Utopía y contrautopía en El Quijote*. Santiago de Compostela: Pico Sacro, 1976.
Márquez Villanueva, Francisco. "El morisco Ricote, o la hispaña razón de estado." In *Personajes y temas del Quijote*, 229–85. Madrid: Taurus, 1975.
– "La cabra *manchada*." In *Personajes y temas del Quijote*, 72–92. Madrid: Taurus, 1975.
Mathews, Thomas F. *The Clash of Gods*. Princeton, NJ: Princeton University Press, 1993.
Murillo, Luis Andrés. "El Ur-Quijote: Nueva hipótesis." *Cervantes* 1, nos. 1–2 (1981): 43–50.
Pacheco, Francisco. *Arte de la pintura*. Edited by Bonaventura Bassegoda i Hugas. Madrid: Cátedra, 1990.
Paiewonsky-Conde, Edgar. "Cervantes y la teoría del deseo." *Anales cervantinos* 23 (1985): 71–81.
Plato. *The Republic*. Translated by Allan Bloom. New York: Basic, 1991.
– *Symposium*. Translated by Seth Benardete. Chicago: University of Chicago Press, 2001.
– *Timaeus*. Translated by Benjamin Jowett. *Project Gutenberg*. http://www.gutenberg.org/ebooks/1572.
Quint, David. *Cervantes's Novel of Modern Times: A New Reading of Don Quijote*. Princeton, NJ: Princeton University Press, 2003.
Schwartz Girón, Pedro. *En busca de Montesquieu: Democracia y mundialización*. Madrid: Real Academia de Ciencias Morales y Políticas, 2005.
Smith, Adam. *An Inquiry into the Nature and Causes of the Wealth of Nations*. Edited by Edwin Cannan. Chicago: University of Chicago Press, 1976.
Virgil. *The Aeneid*. Translated by John Dryden. New York: P.F. Collier and Son, 1909.
Wallis, Richard T. *Neoplatonism*. Indianapolis, IN: Duckworth, 1995.
West, A.F., and H.D. Thompson. "On Dulcarnon, Elefuga, and Pons Asinorum as Fanciful Names for Geometrical Propositions." *Princeton College Bulletin* 3, no. 4 (1891): 84–8.
Wilson, Diana de Armas. "'Passing the Love of Women': The Intertextuality of *El curioso impertinente*." *Cervantes* 7, no. 2 (1987): 9–28.
Yates, Frances A. *The Art of Memory*. Chicago: University of Chicago Press, 1966.

Chapter Four

Love and the Laws of Literature: The Ethics and Poetics of Affect in Cervantes's "The Little Gypsy Girl"

ELI COHEN

Cervantes's "The Little Gypsy Girl" ("La gitanilla"[1]) is full of emotion – or, rather, emotions. From awe, love, happiness, and desire to indignation, jealousy, envy, fear, shame, and repulsion, the story of Preciosa and Andrés Caballero is a veritable catalogue of feelings. While Andrés's impetuous love and ensuing jealousy are placed at the centre of the plot, along with the slow growth of Preciosa's own esteem and love over the course of the novella, the other emotions experienced at different times in the text play no less of a role in disentangling the various twists and turns the story takes as it proceeds to its resolution. As many scholars have noted, the presence and role of such emotions in determining the contours of plot structure can be seen as derived from similar patterns in the chivalrous romances and sentimental fiction that were so popular in Cervantes's day.[2] Joseph Ricapito, for example, describes with what seems to be a hint of distaste how Cervantes "resorts to the topos of jealousy" in "The Little Gypsy Girl," as if he could or should do otherwise (61). For such critics, the conventions of emotion go hand in hand with the other conventional aspects of both "The Little Gypsy Girl" and the *Novelas ejemplares* (*Exemplary Novels*) in general: plots of love and revenge, *engaños* and *desengaños*, mistaken identity and anagnorisis, or the use of binary opposites to set the plot in motion and endow it both with structure and with a sense of intrigue.[3] This last feature, the use of opposites, is in particular closely tied to the status of emotion in "The Little Gypsy Girl." Much has been said about the paired protagonists, who are simultaneously opposed and joined in parallel transformations, first through the noble Don Juan's apparently incongruous love for (what appears to be) a gypsy girl, however beautiful and talented, followed by his transformation into Andrés Caballero, and then through the mutual unveiling of both characters' true identities and conditions in the final pages. This pair of opposed figures is, moreover, marked by a radically dissimilar attitude toward love and emotion generally. Whereas Andrés falls emphatically in love with Preciosa at first sight, breaking all norms of social propriety in the process, Preciosa herself is characterized throughout most of the novel by a denial of emotion as a valid form of response to events and experiences of all sorts. Andrés and Preciosa thus present the reader with the apparently routine antithesis of *eros*, and the passions collectively, and reason, invigorated in this case by the irony that it is the very object (and cause) of affective response that repudiates the legitimacy of erotic love and maintains the superiority of reason. However, much like its protagonist, Cervantes's narrative presents what might be called an optics of *eros*, performing the appearance of romance in order to ultimately reveal itself as something quite different. Moreover, the particular relationship between affect and reason depicted by Cervantes in "The Little Gypsy Girl" enacts a transformation of the ethos of conventional love plots through its embodiment of contemporary philosophical and scientific considerations of the interplay between the emotions and the mind, in the process interrogating the role of affective response in shaping interpersonal behaviour, interpretation, and cognition in a broader context.

In claiming her position as the voice of reason in the early sequences of the novella, Preciosa goes so far as to chastise, on multiple occasions, Andrés and other characters in the text for being overly emotional. The first pages of the tale are indeed replete with examples of Preciosa's witty ripostes to and recriminations of what she views as the excessive affective attitudes of others. In one moment, Preciosa and her companions have been invited to dance for a group of gentlemen. One of the gypsy girls, Cristina, out of fear or a sense of shame, refuses to enter an enclosed space full of men: "If you want to go in, Preciosa ..., go right in; but I'm not going in to a place where there are so many men" (Si tu quieres entrar, Preciosa ..., entra enhorabuena; que yo no pienso entrar adonde hay tantos hombres [73]). Preciosa responds by suggesting that a woman's honour is more threatened by a single man alone than by a group of them:

> Look, Cristina ...: what you have to be careful of is one man alone and you by yourself, and not so many men all together; because their being so many removes the fear or suspicion that we might be insulted. Bear this in mind, Cristinica, and be sure of one thing: that the woman who decides to be virtuous can do so in the middle of an army. True, it is a good idea to run from occasions of sin, but they should be the secret ones, not the public. (73)

> (Mira, Cristina ...: de lo que has de guardar es de un hombre solo y a solas, y no de tantos juntos; porque antes el ser muchos quita el miedo y el

> recelo de ser ofendidas. Advierte, Cristinica, y está cierta de una cosa: que la mujer que se determina a ser honrada, entre un ejército de soldados lo puede ser. Verdad es que es bueno huir de las ocasiones; pero han de ser de las secretas, y no de las públicas. [73])

Preciosa's reply presents an unexpected logic, one that prompts Cristina to submit to her will: "Let's go in, Preciosa ...; for you know more than a wise man" (entremos, Preciosa ...; que tu sabes más que un sabio [73]). Preciosa counters Cristina's affective response to the scenario (marked here by a specific fear of *eros*) with her *sabiduría*, or knowledge, and, in this particular scene, rational discourse trumps emotion. Moreover, Preciosa's argument, in a move characteristic of Cervantes's narratives, forces a reconsideration of conventional thought regarding the dangers posed by the appearance of a potential physical and moral threat.[4] In this way, Preciosa establishes a fundamental link between reason and emotion, while at the same time outlining what will be a central component of Cervantes's poetics of the novel, in which conventions are engaged with and even deployed, but are ultimately subverted by the dialogue, architecture, and plot development of the *novelas* themselves. Thus, while Cervantes mobilizes both contemporary theories of the emotions and the thematic configurations of traditional love plots, novels like "The Little Gypsy Girl" manifest, to borrow Barthes's term,[5] "writerly" narrative performances that interrogate the ethics and poetics of affect as a component of both authorial and interpretive practice by disclosing and problematizing the operations of conventional structures of narration and reception on which they are grounded through their insertion into a context of social and rhetorical uncertainty in which adaptability and negotiation become fundamental ethical values.[6]

The articulation of affect and reason to which Preciosa gestures in the early passages of "The Little Gypsy Girl" has precedents in early modern work on the human condition by figures such as Juan Luis Vives and Huarte de San Juan, but it is echoed, and receives a more complex and complete expression, in modern affect theory, which can be employed effectually to understand the important manner in which Cervantes's text at once articulates and departs from the prevailing thought of his times.[7] In recent years, affect theory has gained a certain purchase among scholars of literature and culture in general as a means of stepping back from the cognitive abyss that separates us from our objects of study – whether they be contemporary or ancient – while simultaneously avoiding the historical bankruptcy of grand narrative theories. Though affect and emotion are no longer viewed as strictly opposed to cognition, as they have been by many thinkers even as far back as the Spanish Golden Age, they are still considered by many to be fundamentally distinct modes of experience.[8]

Researchers in neurobiology, sociology, and philosophy continue to explore the relationship between affect and emotion, on one hand, and cognition and rational thought, on the other. While reliable accounts remain elusive, scientists and philosophers insist upon the complexity of this relationship and at times have even suggested that affect and emotion themselves have a cognitive function, or at least play a role in determining the outcome of our rational mental processes (Kepecs 835). In conjunction with, or as a result of, this work, the past ten years or so have seen an explosion of renewed interest in affect and emotion in artistic productions of all kinds, leading to what has been called the Affective Turn.[9] This development is no less visible in studies of early modern culture. Articles, books, and conferences that focus on the presence and role of affect and emotion in early modern literature and visual art abound; the current volume is itself a testament to the increasing importance given to affect and emotion as potentially crucial sites of critical engagement with early modern culture and thought.

However, in spite of this surge in critical interest in affect, studies of early modern Spain and of Cervantes in particular generally remain focused on configurations of individual affects, emotions, humours, or passions, and are broadly rooted in what are thought to be historically accurate reconstructions of contemporary notions regarding the emotions.[10] There is a relative paucity of work that looks to explore in early modern literature what Juan Luis Vives called the field of affect (*ámbito afectivo*) (*De Anima* III.1–4).[11] That is, scholars have examined the contents of this "ámbito" but have not considered its function in its own right, therefore limiting its theoretical import and portraying it instead as a fundamentally thematic concern for early modern authors. Affect theory, on the other hand, privileges the singular over the plural, the category of affect as a form of experience over the experience of individual affects or emotions,[12] and therein lies its usefulness for scholars of the works and ideas of Cervantes and his contemporaries.

Texts such as "The Little Gypsy Girl" engage with and problematize affective experiences of all kinds, not merely as generic conventions, but as objects and forces of critical reflection whose significance is made manifest through their dramatic evocation in literary form. What is more, beyond the naming or description of any specific emotion in "The Little Gypsy Girl," it is affective experience itself that is explored and critiqued in the lines of the story. While love, and specifically passionate or erotic love, plays a pivotal role in Cervantes's *novela*, the text presents this passion as an index of emotional experience in general in order to probe the role of affect in determining cognitive and social processes. This emphasis on affect itself and, perhaps more importantly, on the outcome of this depiction of affect helps explain the story's position at the outset of the *Exemplary Novels* (*Novelas ejemplares*) as a sequence of texts, situating it as more than a merely conventional frame tale for the novellas that follow. For Cervantes's deployment of affect in "The Little Gypsy Girl" anticipates the role of affective response in the interpretive act, thus implicitly posing the question of the relationship between affect and cognition to the reader in the very first tale of the collection. This is done, as is often the case in Cervantes's texts, by inscribing instances of reception, affective or otherwise, within the work itself.

In a manner similar to that of her dialogue with Cristina, Preciosa's first encounters with Andrés are marked by her attempts to dissuade him from being carried away by his emotions. Her comments are clothed in almost comic or childish terms; as she herself notes, "they seemed to be a foolish trick" (parecían cosas de burla [97]). Yet they nonetheless stress the value of rational level-headedness. At one point she urges "easy, easy, excited little boy, and look before you leap" (sosiega, sosiega, alborotadito, y mira lo que haces primero que te cases [94]).[13] At another she sings a poem meant to "save you from heart attack and dizziness" (preservar el mal del corazón y los vaguidos de cabeza). The first lines read "Little head, little head, / keep it together, don't slip" (Cabecita, cabecita/tente en tí, no te resbales [97]). As Ruth El Saffar has pointed out, the emotional Andrés is viewed by Preciosa as worked up and impulsive and as suffering from some sort of malady – a sickness of the heart that is causing his mind to languish and slip into a dizzy, unsteady state (94–5). Andrés, in other words, is not thinking clearly and, moreover, presents what Robert Folger has identified as what were conceived in the period as "the disastrous emotional and physical effects of passionate love" (*Images* 13). This view of love has among its sources an adverse variant of Platonic love, described by Denis de Rougemont as "a transport, an infinite rapture away from reason and natural sense ... [I]t is 'a divine delirium'" (61). Andrés is in this way simultaneously removed and transfixed by *eros*, caught in an "amorous captivity" (Folger, *Images* 63).[14] Furthermore, Andrés feels unavoidably and uncontrollably propelled by the force of his emotion. As he says in his own words, "experience has shown me how far the powerful force of love extends, and the transformations it obliges in those it takes under its jurisdiction and rule" (la experiencia me ha mostrado adónde se estiende la poderosa fuerza de amor, y las transformaciones que hace hacer a los que coge debajo de su jurisdición y mando [112]). For Andrés, the experience of emotion can be overpowering and results in a disconcerting loss of agency. As with the other binary pairings already mentioned, this opposition between reason and emotion in the novella is likewise conventional in many respects and can be found in both the fiction and nonfiction of early modern Spain in the works of writers from Vives to Tirso de Molina.

Preciosa, on the other hand, is described as awing her interlocutors with her knowledgeable and rational discourse. In one instance, after telling Andrés what he must do in order to woo her, the old gypsy who has raised her exclaims, "You have Satan in your chest, child ... for you say things that not even a graduate from Salamanca would say! ... What is this? You're making me crazy, and I'm listening to you as if you were enchanted and could speak Latin without knowing it" (Satanás tienes en tu pecho, muchacha ... ¡mira que dices cosas que no las diría un colegial de Salamanca! ... ¿cómo es esto, que me tienes loca, y te estoy escuchando como a una persona espiritada, que habla latín sin saberlo? [87]). Ironically, Preciosa's rationalism produces the very thing it seeks to ward off: an overwrought emotional response. Preciosa is thus initially depicted as favouring reason over emotion, and the opposition of Preciosa and Andrés seems to be reinforced by their opposed attitudes toward affect: while Preciosa views emotion as something to be controlled by a clear head, mirroring "the Neoplatonist view that the mind could subdue sensual desire and thus enable man to attain some serenity" (Parker 48). Of special note in "The Little Gypsy Girl" is the inversion of the typically misogynistic configuration of this opposition, which identifies women with uncontrollable passion or emotion in a genetic perpetuation of the moment of original sin. Vives, in his *Education of a Christian Woman* (*Formación de la mujer cristiana*, 1524), affirms that women are particularly susceptible to being overcome by emotion:

> Some women, if they love a bit too impetuously, find themselves carried by force to break the harmony and, therefore, it is necessary to reactivate their prudence with the help of some simple precepts and to moderate their impulses. The most important thing of all is to restrain those impulses, that is, the passion and emotion which, like an immense whirlwind, snatch and carry away with them the pusillanimous spirits of women, since they can only resist with less vigor.
>
> ([A]lgunas mujeres, si aman un tanto atolondradamente, se ven arrastradas con fuerza a quebrantar la concordia y, entonces, habrá que reactivar su prudencia con la ayuda de unos breves preceptos y moderar sus impulsos. Lo más importante de todo es refrenar esos impulsos, es decir, la pasión y la emoción que, como un inmenso torbellino, arrebatan

> y arrastran consigo los espíritus pusilánimes de las mujeres, puesto que ellas pueden oponerse con menos vigor. [*La Formación* 3])[15]

While Cervantes is not the only writer to depict men experiencing overwhelming emotion, his proffering of Preciosa, a woman and a gypsy, as an icon of rational thought is nonetheless startling, though it may bring to mind other fictional women of the times (and especially of Cervantes's own fiction), such as Marcela of *Don Quixote*, among others.[16] Preciosa not only withstands the "enormous whirlwind" (*inmenso torbellino*) of passion, she appears to serve as a representative of what Christopher Tilmouth characterizes as the paradigm of "moral psychology during this time ... an austerely rationalist model of self-governance, one centred on ideas of psychomachia and a hostility to the passions" (1).

I will shortly address the importance of the fact that Preciosa is, or at least performs as, a gypsy woman. First, however, it is necessary to look at how Cervantes's novella disrupts these oppositions, which I have been insisting are merely apparent. In the first place, the story ends in familiar fashion: original social status is restored, enigmas are explained, and love triumphs. Through scenes of revelation and recognition, it is disclosed that Preciosa and Andrés are actually much more alike than was previously thought, thus enabling the happy resolution of their romance. An apparently conventional tale thus arrives at an apparently conventional termination. But in the context of this chapter, it is another collapsed opposition that proves more illuminating. The mechanism that brings about the favourable conclusion to the protagonists' stories is none other than the pathos of Preciosa's supplication to the representatives of justice, the *Corregidor* (chief magistrate) and his wife, who, it turns out, are also Preciosa's parents. Her explanation of Andrés's innocence and her appeals for his freedom are at once emotional and rational, and they move her interlocutors to action. We must suppose that Preciosa has little to say against the *Corregidora*'s tears of empathy and the *Corregidor*'s sympathy, which brings him to deliver Andrés to safety. This breakdown of the antinomy between reason and emotion stands in stark contrast to Preciosa's earlier criticism of emotion in others. Moreover, it represents a decisive departure from one view of early modern Neoplatonic and Christian thinking on the relationship between emotion and reason, as presented in the writings of Vives, who, as Carlos Noreña describes, suggests that "emotions could and should be controlled" (214). As Vives himself states:

> It is true that man experiences forceful and disturbing emotions ... but the author of our nature, in other animals, gave those emotions an absolute right, as it were, without appeal; the beast goes wherever it is carried by

fear, hope, love or hate, without the ability to resist, because the emotions reign completely over the beast. But in us, God, through a wide and graceful gift, separated all those emotions, like vile and evil slaves, from the ruling faculty of man: he made them subject to a noble spirit and he subjected them to a free and invincible will which, scorning the tumult and cries of the passions, indicate to man what is permitted of him. To this faculty he added, as the guide to his action, reason.

(Es cierto que el hombre experimenta emociones vehementes y perturbadoras ... pero el autor de nuestra naturaleza, en los demás animales, concedió a aquellas emociones un derecho absoluto y como si dijéramos, sin apelación; la bestia va arrebatada adonde la lleva el miedo, la esperanza, el amor, o el odio, sin poder dar marcha atrás, porque las emociones son dueñas de la bestia toda. Pero en nosotros, Dios, por una concesión amplísima y graciosa, segregó todas aquellas emociones, como esclavos viles y malos, de la facultad reguladora del hombre: las hizo súbditas de un espíritu noble y las sometió a una voluntad libre e invencible que, despreciando los tumultos y gritos de las pasiones, indicara al hombre lo que le está permitido. A esa voluntad le adjuntó, como directiva de su actividad, la razón. [*Concordia* 82–3])

Despite her previous attacks on affect, Preciosa appears to invert both her earlier position and that outlined by Vives. Without simply re-invoking the view of *eros* that is found in earlier sentimental fiction and that presented a decidedly pessimistic view of the possibility of taming the passions,[17] Preciosa nonetheless asserts a constructive role for affect in human affairs. How can these two attitudes be reconciled? What new relationship is Cervantes positing between affect and reason, assuming he is not merely reverting to convention at the close of his tale? Affect theory may provide us with a way of addressing these questions.

Current theories of affect such as that of the political philosopher Brian Massumi insist on the distinction between affect and emotion. According to Massumi, affect is equated to intensity – it is "a suspension of action-reaction circuits and linear temporality in a sink of what might be called 'passion.'" This intensity is qualified and concretized into specific and recognizable emotions. Massumi describes emotions as:

[a] subjective content, the sociolinguistic fixing of the quality of an experience which is from that point onward defined as personal. Emotion is qualified intensity, the conventional, consensual point of insertion of intensity into semantically and semiotically formed progressions, into narrativizable action-reaction circuits, into function and meaning. It is

> intensity owned and recognized ... [A]ffect is unqualified. As such, it is not ownable or recognizable, and is thus resistent to critique. (6)

To return to the example of Andrés's "fuerza de amor," the "fuerza," prior to being named and to taking shape as specifically the "fuerza de amor," is simply a force, an intensity of feeling. The materialization of this intensity through what Massumi calls "qualification" is what enables it to be identified and experienced as a concrete emotion. However, this process may be characterized by an extraordinary variation, which is precisely what happens in "The Little Gypsy Girl."

Marco Abel describes affect as a "force" and an "asignifying intensity." For Abel, "signaletic materials of any kind are not representations of something but, instead, constitute the reality of representations (or the real forces at work in what are often deemed representations)" (x). While I do not wish to discard so easily the representational aims of any aesthetic work, I do think Abel's assertions provide a particularly productive means of understanding what, in terms of affect and emotion, is going on in "The Little Gypsy Girl"; furthermore, it does so in a manner that allows us to move beyond consideration of these elements as mere topoi. According to Abel, if aesthetic objects and images are not essentially representational but rather configurations of affective forces, then the perceiver's interaction with those objects and images is shifted from an interpretive stance to an ethical stance. It is not a question of how one understands the aesthetic experience, but of how one responds to it, a view shared by early modern thinkers for whom "the capacity to experience affects is therefore a capacity to respond to the world" (James 201). Similarly, Charles Altieri considers the affective aspect of aesthetic works as requiring a fundamentally ethical rather than cognitive response, positing the critical need to "[attune] ourselves to their struggle for articulation" (12). Altieri makes the case that this is ultimately a wholly singular experience that cannot be subsumed under the categories of cognition and that must be treated as such (that is, as unique) if it is to be considered ethically. This is due in part to the phenomenological component of affect. Affect entails sensation and is itself a state of intensity instigated by specific sensations.

The emphasis of current theories on the physiology and phenomenology of affect interestingly situates them, if only distantly, within the intellectual tradition ranging from Aristotle to Huarte de San Juan that informed much of Cervantes's own thinking about affect and emotion. "The Little Gypsy Girl" exemplifies the scenario Parker envisions when he describes how "in Spanish literature of the late sixteenth century the idealization of love is confronted increasingly with the moral and social demands of everyday life" (107). In fact, "The Little Gypsy Girl" enacts a shift from the Neoplatonic ideal of *eros* governed by reason to a vision of the ethical function of affect in human affairs. In this way, Cervantes's text illustrates changing notions of what Susan James calls "the ethical dimension of the passions" in this period (200). James suggests that, in the sixteenth century, "the question of whether the passions are morally good or bad, and thus the extent to which virtuous people need to transcend or control them," was at the centre of debates on this aspect of emotional experience (ibid.). According to James, and as suggested by the early passages of Cervantes's text, "perhaps the most influential was the view that the passions can be controlled by reason"; however, although "the opposition between reason and passion dominated discussion throughout the early modern period, ... in the course of the seventeenth century it began to be comprehensively reexamined" (ibid.).

Similarly, Tilmouth writes that "a psychomachic view of the mind, and a dismissive view of the passions and the body, dominated ethical thinking (indeed, the moral imagination) in [the] late sixteenth century" (15). According to Tilmouth, "Aristotle's *Nicomachean Ethics* gives rise to a very different tradition of governance, one which emphasizes the cultivation (rather than suppression) of the passions" (20). He posits that the late sixteenth and early seventeenth centuries witnessed a revaluation of "the affections as controlled but morally constructive forces, qualities to be harnessed, not eliminated" (1). "The Little Gypsy Girl" narrativized this evolution in thinking on *eros* and affect more generally, moving from the double commonplace of *eros* represented as a kind of noble lovesickness that morally must be subjected to the constraints of reason to a more complex view according to which affective experience is reimagined as an ethical force in its own right.

The emphasis on the phenomenological aspect of affect also helps to explain the significance and highly visual presence of Preciosa as a gypsy. The majority of the affective states in the text occur in response to Preciosa as spectacle. The fact that Preciosa is a gypsy, or appears to be one, foregrounds her physical and auditory presence. Above all, she is seen dancing and heard singing or speaking. Paul Michael Johnson has elucidated the manner in which the presence of intradiegetic audiences in *Don Quijote* induces reflection on the ethical purport of the social conditions of affective experience, and a similar operation is at work in "The Little Gypsy Girl." The various responses to Preciosa as an affective force reflect very different ethical stances in relation to her presence in the text. It is to the divergent forms of response to the articulation of affect inscribed within "The Little Gypsy Girl" that I would now like to turn.

Two examples have already been indicated: that of Andrés and that of the *Corregidor* and his wife. There are many others, from those of Preciosa's several audiences to those of Clemente, the page-poet. Rather than looking at each one, I would simply like to outline what distinguishes those responses that earn Preciosa's contempt and those that do not. Andrés's expression of his affective response to Preciosa deploys generically conventional rhetoric and displays, at least in Preciosa's eyes, an absence of the critical self-reflection and subtlety that might characterize a truly ethical stance. Preciosa makes this clear when she replies to his claim that he appears before her "rendido a la discreción y belleza de Preciosa" (83) (overwhelmed by Preciosa's discretion and beauty). After Andrés expresses his desire to court her and his intention to "levantar a mi grandeza la humildad de Preciosa" (84) (raise Preciosa's humble status to my high rank), Preciosa admonishes him by warning him that, despite what her appearances might lead him to believe, she is not receptive to his rhetoric:

> [P]romises do not move me, gifts do not break down my will, submissiveness does not incline me, nor do loving compliments scare me; and though I am only fifteen years old (which, according to my grandmother's account, I'll turn this San Miguel day), I am already old in my thoughts and I understand more than my age suggests, more by my nature than by experience. But with the one and the other I know that passionate love in those who have recently fallen in love is like indiscrete forces that make the will exceed all proportion; which, trampling inconveniences, foolishly throws itself after what it desires, and thinking to attain its glory, attains only hell of its sorrows.
>
> (A mí ni me mueven promesas, ni me desmoronan dádivas, ni me inclinan sumisiones, ni me espantan finezas enamoradas; y aunque de quince años (que, según la cuenta de mi abuela, para este San Miguel los haré), soy ya vieja en los pensamientos y alcanzo más de aquello que mi edad promete, más por mi buen natural que por la experiencia. Pero con lo uno o con lo otro sé que las pasiones amorosas en los recién enamorados son como impetus indiscretos que hacen salir a la voluntad de sus quicios; la cual, atropellando inconvenientes, desatinadamente se arroja tras su deseo, y pensando dar con la gloria de sus ojos, da con el infierno de sus pesadumbres. [85])

Preciosa's critique of the "pasiones" that "hacen salir a la voluntad de sus quicios" is mirrored by the recurring depiction of the paralysis experienced by Andrés when he allows himself to be overcome by emotions as described above. As he himself says, with respect to

Preciosa, "with her my soul is wax, on which she can imprint whatever she wishes; and to save and keep it, it will not be as imprinted on wax, but rather sculpted in marble, whose hardness opposes the duration of time" (para con ella es de cera mi alma, donde podrá imprimir lo que quisiere; y para conservarlo y guardarlo no será como impreso en cera, sino como esculpido en mármoles, cuya dureza se opone a la duración de los tiempos [84]).

Andrés's experience of overwhelming emotion is not limited to his encounters with Preciosa; when Juana Carducha, the daughter of an innkeeper in whose inn Andrés as well as Preciosa and the other gypsies are staying and performing, accuses Andrés of stealing some of her property, Andrés is confident that her belongings will not be found among his effects. However, when the "the ministers of justice ... quickly found the stolen goods" (ministros de la justicia ... a pocas vueltas dieron con el hurto), Andrés "was left so frightened ..., and so absorbed, that he seemed like a statue, without a voice, of hard stone" (quedó tan espantado ..., y tan absorto, que no pareció sino estatua, sin voz, de piedra dura [143]). According to Vives, only excessive emotion poses such a threat.[18] Such emotions "are ... in truth, disturbances and excesses, as if the spirit was no longer in control of itself and passed into the hands of a strange force; they are so blinding that it can no longer perceive anything" (son ... en verdad, perturbaciones y desenfrenos, como si ya el espíritu no fuera dueño de sí y pasara a manos de un poder extraño; son cegueras por cuanto aquél no puede ya percibir nada) (*De Anima* III.10, introduction). Andrés is depicted in these scenes as ethically challenged: he is unable to exert his will and make rational judgments; he is instead a prisoner of affect.

Andrés's irresponsible acquiescence to his own affect is markedly unmitigated; he shows no signs of tempering his emotions with reason and is consistently reactive in his attitudes toward those around him. The *Corregidor* and his wife, on the other hand, while enacting a conventional denouement, are less rash in their articulation of the affective force Preciosa exerts on them. When Preciosa confronts Andrés regarding his love for her, Andrés's affective stance undergoes no change; on the contrary, his experience of being overwhelmed, and thus without comprehension or choice, seems reinforced by Preciosa's reasoning: "the young man froze upon hearing Preciosa's reasoning, and he became as if entranced, looking at the ground" (Pasmóse el mozo a las razones de Preciosa, y púsose como embelesado, mirando al suelo [86]). Andrés reveals himself to be among "those who are carried away by passion and do not guide themselves with the helm of reason and right judgment" (aquellos que se dejan arrastrar por la pasión y no se gobiernan por el timón de la razón y del justo juicio [3.7]). However, when Preciosa addresses first the *Corregidora*, and then the *Corregidor*, all three engage affect and reason in an ethical manner that makes possible the final outcome of the novella. Vives suggests that wisdom enables ethical action by proposing that a wise person "does not allow himself to be led by situations, rather he himself leads them being in control of himself by right and in practice with the aim of suppressing the passion that interrupts the force of nature with the restraint of reason and forces it to submit to right reason" (no se deja conducir por los asuntos, sino que él mismo los conduce siendo dueño de sí de derecho y de hecho a fin de que al irrumpir la pasión por la fuerza de la naturaleza, al punto la reprima con el freno de la razón y la obligue a plegarse al recto juicio [*De Anima* III.10]).

Andrés is among those of us who, "by not attending to the movement when it arises and not maintaining command over ourselves, ... give ourselves over to the thrust of the storm so it can take us not wherever we want, but rather where it wants" (al no atender al movimiento que surge y no conservar el dominio de nosotros mismos, nos entregamos al empuje de la misma tempestad para que nos lleve no adonde queremos nosotros, sino adonde le pluguiere a ella [*De Anima* III.13]). When Preciosa finds herself brought before Doña Guiomar de Meneses and Don Fernando de Azevedo, she explains the circumstances she and Andrés find themselves in and urges the *Corregidora*, "if you know what love is, and at some time you had it, and now you have it for your husband, feel for me, for I tenderly and honestly love mine" (si sabéis qué es amor, y algún tiempo le tuvisteis, y ahora le tenéis a vuestro esposo, doleos de mí, que amo tierno y honestamente al mío [126]). The coupling of *saber* and *amor* here reflects the complex relationship between reason and affect as presented by Vives (Noreña 146); the effects of affect can precede cognition and the acts of judgment, but affect itself can also be conditioned by reason. "There exist certain movements of the spirit or, better, natural impulses that arise from a condition of the body ... [T]hese impulses arise prior to judgment" (Existen ciertos movimientos del espíritu o, mejor, impulsos naturales que proceden de una afección del cuerpo ... Estos impulsos se anticipan al juicio [*De Anima* III.5]). However, "while the mind is instructed and educated in diverse ways, the emotions change, intensifying or diminishing; or they disappear totally and yield to the vigor and, so to say, to the law of others (a medida que la mente es instruida y educada de diversos modos, los afectos cambian, aumentando o disminuyendo; o bien desaparecen totalmente y ceden al vigor y, por así decirlo, al derecho de otros [*De Anima* III.5]). The Corregidor's response to Preciosa's pleas reflects this "intimate relationship" (Noreña 148) of affect and reason: "the Chief Magistrate was left once more in a state of suspense upon hearing the discrete reasoning of the little gypsy" (con nueva suspensión quedó el Corregidor de oír las discretas razones de la gitanilla [126]). Preciosa herself seems to recognize and value this complex interaction between reason and emotion, rather than to merely affirm the priority of reason over emotion or to fully condemn emotion and affect outright. Her own response to both Andrés and the *Corregidor* and his wife, affective forces in their own rights, reflects in this way a consistently ethical perspective, not only in terms of the attitude toward the affect it reveals, but also in terms of the concrete social action it makes possible.

Moreover, Preciosa recognizes the role affect plays in shaping her rational character, because she, as Jean-Raymond Fanlo points out, alludes to a "certain fantastic spirit" that she has "here within" and that is prior to reflection (95). In contrast to Andrés, whose emotions impede him from rational thought and ethical behaviour, Preciosa's social agility is marked precisely by her willingness to allow emotion and judgment to influence and transform one another in an economy of affect and reason. Crucial to both Vives's and Cervantes's portrayals of this ethical position is the notion of freedom. As Preciosa tells Andrés when he becomes jealous of another man's attentions, "jealousy never, as I imagine it ... leaves the understanding free to judge things as they are" (nunca los celos, a lo que imagino ... dejan el entendimiento libre para que pueda juzgar las cosas como ellas son [111]). Although the force of affect may impact and inform reason and judgment, it should never determine them. The otherwise conventional resolution of the novella's plot is belied by this complication of the mechanisms by which such plots were traditionally carried out.

Furthermore, Cervantes anticipates this scenario at the very outset of the novella. The first pages include a description of gypsies aimed at the reading audience, followed by the representation of an audience's reception of a group of gypsies that initiates the action of the tale in a manner that situates the extradiegetic reader of the text in a position parallel to that of the intradiegetic audiences described above. The text offers an image or appearance of a conventional narrative, and the narrator seems to tempt the reader to respond conventionally to a conventional depiction of gypsies, much as the audiences within the text, and particularly Andrés, respond to Preciosa; as Thomas Hart suggests, "the first sentence of 'The Little Gypsy Girl,' in which the word ladrón (thief) occurs five times, must have seemed to Cervantes' contemporaries merely a statement of an obvious truth" (29). The juxtaposition of this implied reception of a conventional narrative concerning gypsies to the explicit representation of the fictional crowd's reception of the gypsies should stand as an ironic warning to the reader, especially within the context of the critique of affective responsivity that occurs over the course of the novella. Karl-Ludwig Selig (and E. Michael Gerli following him) notes the importance of the very first word of the novella in establishing this ironic warning: "parece" (it seems). What is more, this implicit negative judgment of conventional readerly perspectives prepares the reader in this way for the experience of reading Cervantes's *Novelas ejemplares* as a whole. To return to Barthes in concluding, Cervantes's transformation of the poetics of affect realized through a fictional reflection on the ethical significance of one's attitude toward affect and reason, exhibits a writerly appeal to the reader to participate actively in the process of constructing meaning. In "The Little Gypsy Girl," Cervantes critiques the reader as a figure of passive reception of aesthetic and social convention, and establishes a paradigm for an ethically engaged audience for whom experience is made meaningful in the complex interplay of affect and reason in the singular event of reading.

NOTES

1 All translations are mine unless otherwise noted.

2 Concerning the generic nature of "La gitanilla," see, for example, Mancing and Lipson, who offer concise reviews of the literature on this topic.

3 The conventional romance aspects of the novella have been thoroughly explored by Casalduero, Forcione, El Saffar, and Pierce, among others, and will not be examined in depth here. On the influence of Ovid and the Italianate novel on Cervantes's *Novelas*, see Schevill.

4 Preciosa's admonition here seems to contradict a statement made in one of Cervantes's other *Novelas*: "An ounce of public shame is worse than a bushel of secret disgrace" (Más lastima una onza de deshonra pública que una arroba de infamia secreta [*La fuerza de la sangre*, 84]).

5 See Barthes, *S/Z*, 3–6. While the writerly text necessarily eludes being fixated by definition or by *a* definition (Barthes himself says "there may be nothing to say about writerly texts"), Barthes offers an outline of what it might look like: "the writerly text is a perpetual present, upon which no consequent language (which would inevitably make it past) can be superimposed; the writerly text is ourselves writing, before the infinite play of the world (the world as function) is traversed, intersected, stopped, plasticized by some singular system (Ideology, Genus, Criticism) which reduces the plurality of entrances, the opening of networks, the infinity of

languages" (5). The writerly text is constituted by a plurality rather than a singular meaning, and it stands in opposition to what Barthes calls the "readerly text," which he describes (in a manner that recalls Cervantes's own beginning of the *Quijote*) as a text that is consumed by a reader who is "plunged into a kind of idleness" (4).

6 Lipson has called this a "world of verbal instability" (35) and refers to "the various verbal intrigues that must be unravelled before such a happy ending is possible" (36). The position staked out here is not altogether dissimilar, but it rests on clarifying the economy of affect and reason, rather than of rhetoric, that underwrites and destabilizes the plot structure.

7 Athena Athanasiou, Pothiti Hantzaroula, and Kostas Yannakopoulos have pointed out that "the theoretical engagement with emotions and affectivity [that] Patricia Clough has identified as an 'affective turn' in the humanities and social sciences ... draw[s] on older genealogies of thought" that stretch back at least as far as the early modern period (5).

8 Both Juan Luis Vives and Huarte de San Juan describe this opposition in terms of a sort of power struggle, suggesting that the emotions, or passions, as the locus of irrationality, needed to be subjugated by reason for human virtue to impose itself on vice.

9 See, for example, Clough and O'Malley Halley; Leys; Athanasiou, Hantzaroula, and Yannakopoulos.

10 Recent work on emotion(s) in Cervantes includes that of Wagschal, Hutchinson, Wehrs, Bartra, Johnson, and others.

11 It should be noted that Vives himself, as Carlos Noreña has pointed out, devotes most of his discussion of the emotions to an "effort to define and classify [individual] emotions" (207). Nonetheless, Noreña proposes that this work "contrasts vividly with [Vives's] eagerness to probe and describe the complex interaction and intermeshing of our emotional reactions, motivations, and attitudes" in its dynamic entirety rather than as a collection of distinct experiences (207).

12 Despite this overall trend in affect theory, there have been important divergences in relation to the distinction between affect and the emotions; see, for example, Leys.

13 "Mira lo que hacer primero que te cases" is an idiomatic expression that could be translated literally as "think about what to do before you get married."

14 In other Cervantine texts, this captivity takes on different forms, including the similarly alienated (albeit importantly distinct) madnesses of lovers such as Don Quijote and Cardenio. See Feal for more on this.

15 Second book, on married women, chapters 5, on peace among the spouses.

16 It could be argued that, in the *Siglo de Oro*, this sort of representation had already become something of a convention; see the works of Lope de Vega

and Tirso de Molina (among others), for example. Folger makes a relevant statement regarding early modern sentimental fiction when he describes how, in Juan de Flores's *Grimalte y Gradissa* and Diego de San Pedro's *Cárcel de amor*, "only the shrewd women, Gradissa and Laureola, who have the strength to resist the power of passionate love and courtly persuasion, escape the cataclysm of love" (*Escape*, 18).

17 Parker suggests that "the poets of Courtly Love, Leone Ebreo and the Spanish mystics all knew that the senses and passions are not so easily subdued and pacified; and the great writers of the next century were to know it also" (109).

18 Noreña describes how "Vives uses the classic metaphors that Stoic philosophers applied to all the passions: the soul becomes the victim of an external blow, blinded, paralyzed, and irrational" (143).

REFERENCES

Abel, Marco. *Violent Affect: Literature, Cinema, and Critique after Representation*. Lincoln: University of Nebraska Press, 2007.

Altieri, Charles. *The Particulars of Rapture*. Ithaca, NY: Cornell University Press, 2003.

Athanasiou, Athena, Pothiti Hantzaroula, and Kostas Yannakopoulos. "Towards a New Epistemology: The 'Affective Turn.'" *Historein* 8 (2012): 5–16.

Barthes, Roland. *S/Z*. New York: Hill and Wang, 1974.

Bartra, Roger. *Melancholy and Culture*. Iberian and Latin American Studies. Cardiff: University of Wales Press, 2008.

Casalduero, Joaquín. *Sentido y forma de las "Novelas Ejemplares."* Madrid: Editorial Gredos, 1969.

Cervantes Saavedra, Miguel de. *Novelas ejemplares*. Madrid: Cátedra, 2001.

Clough, Patricia Ticineto, and Jean O'Malley Halley, eds. *The Affective Turn: Theorizing the Social*. Durham, NC: Duke University Press, 2007.

El Saffar, Ruth S. *Novel to Romance: A Study of Cervantes' Novelas Ejemplares*. Baltimore, MD: Johns Hopkins University Press, 1974.

Fanlo, Jean-Raymond. "Erudición y doctrina en Don Quijote y en las Novelas ejemplares." *Cervantes: Bulletin of the Cervantes Society of America* 30, no. 1 (2010): 87–98.

Feal, Carlos. "Against the Law: Mad Lovers in *Don Quixote*." In *Quixotic Desire: Psychoanalytic Perspectives on Cervantes*, edited by Ruth Anthony El Saffar and Diana de Armas Wilson, 179–99. Ithaca, NY: Cornell University Press, 1993.

Folger, Robert. *Escape from the Prison of Love*. Chapel Hill: University of North Carolina Press, 2009.

– *Images in Mind: Lovesickness, Spanish Sentimental Fiction and* Don Quijote. Chapel Hill: University of North Carolina Press, 2002.
Forcione, Alban K. *Cervantes and the Humanist Vision*. Princeton, NJ: Princeton University Press, 1982.
Gerli, E. Michael. "Romance and Novel: Idealism and Irony in La Gitanilla." *Cervantes: Bulletin of the Cervantes Society of America* 6, no. 1 (1986): 29–38.
Hart, Thomas R. *Cervantes' Exemplary Fictions: A Study of the Novelas Ejemplares*. Lexington: University Press of Kentucky, 1994.
Hutchinson, Steven. "Affective Dimensions in Don Quijote." *Cervantes: Bulletin of the Cervantes Society of America* 24, no. 2 (2004): 71–91.
James, Susan. "The Passions and the Good Life." In *The Cambridge Companion to Early Modern Philosophy*, edited by Donald Ruthersford. 198–220. Cambridge: Cambridge University Press, 2006.
Johnson, Paul Michael. "'Salido a la vergüenza': Inquisition, Penality, and a Cervantine View of Mediterranean 'Values.'" "Cervantes y el Mediterráneo/Cervantes and the Mediterranean." Special issue of *eHumanista/Cervantes* 2 (2013): 340–61.
Kepecs, Adam. "Decisions, Decisions ..." *Nature* 458, no. 7240 (2009): 835.
Leys, Ruth. "The Turn to Affect: A Critique." *Critical Inquiry* 37, no. 3 (2011): 434–72.
Lipson, Lesley. "La palabra hecha nada: Mendacious Discourse in La gitanilla." *Cervantes: Bulletin of the Cervantes Society of America* 9, no. 1 (1989): 35–53.
Mancing, Howard. "Prototypes of Genre in Cervantes' Novelas Ejemplares." *Cervantes: Bulletin of the Cervantes Society of America* 20, no. 2 (2000): 127–50.
Massumi, Brian. "The Autonomy of Affect." *Cultural Critique* 31 (1995): 83–109.
Noreña, Carlos G. *Juan Luis Vives and the Emotions*. Carbondale: Southern Illinois University Press, 1989.
Parker, Alexander A. *The Philosophy of Love in Spanish Literature, 1480–1680*. Edinburgh: Edinburgh University Press, 1985.
Pierce, Frank. "La Gitanilla : A Tale of High Romance." *Bulletin of Hispanic Studies* 54, no. 4 (1977): 283–95.
Ricapito, Joseph V. *Formalistic Aspects of Cervantes's* Novelas ejemplares. Lewiston, NY: Edwin Mellen Press, 1997.
Rougemont, Denis de. *Love in the Western World*. Translated by Montgomery Belgion. Princeton, NJ: Princeton University Press, 1983.
Schevill, Rudolph. *Ovid and the Renasance in Spain*. Berkeley: University of California Press, 1913.
Selig, Karl-Ludwig. "Concerning the Structure of Cervantes' La gitanilla." *Romantistisches Jahrbuch* 13 (1962): 273–6.
Tilmouth, Christopher. *Passion's Triumph over Reason: A History of the Moral Imagination from Spenser to Rochester*. Oxford: Oxford University Press, 2007.

Vives. Juan Luis. *Concordia y Discordia*. Preface by Laureano Sanchex Gallego. Mexico City: Seneca, 1940.

– *De Anima et Vita = El Alma y La Vida* [Texto Impreso] / *Juan Luis Vives;* [Introducción, Traducción Y Notas, Ismael Roca]. Valencia: Ajuntament de València, 1992. http://bivaldi.gva.es/corpus/unidad.cmd?idCorpus=1&idUnidad=9961&posicion=1.

– *La Formación de La Mujer Cristiana = De Institutione Feminae Christianae.* Traducción, Introducción y Notas por Joaquín Beltrán Serra. Valencia: Ajuntament de València, 1994. http://bivaldi.gva.es/i18n/corpus/unidad.cmd?idCorpus=1&idUnidad=10066.

Wagschal, Steven. "Digging up the Past: The Archeology of Emotion in Cervantes' 'Romance de Los Celos.'" *Cervantes: Bulletin of the Cervantes Society of America* 27, no. 2 (2007): 213–28.

– *The Literature of Jealousy in the Age of Cervantes*. Columbia: University of Missouri Press, 2006.

Wehrs, Donald R. "Affective Dissonance and Literary Mediation: Emotion Processing, Ethical Signification, and Aesthetic Autonomy in Cervantes's Art of the Novel." *Cervantes: Bulletin of the Cervantes Society of America* 32, no. 1 (2012): 1–30.

Chapter Five

Eros and *Ethos* in the Political and Religious Logos of *The Trials of Persiles and Sigismunda*: Anomic Characters in Cervantes

JESÚS MAESTRO

This chapter explores Cervantes's *The Trials of Persiles and Sigismunda* (*Los trabajos de Persiles y Sigismunda*) from an anomic perspective. "Anomie" may refer to a society that has been deprived of its liberties, as well as to a set of individuals who are unable to succeed in a politically and religiously repressive context. In the contemporary world, psychoanalysis finds its main path of enquiry in anomie; within literary studies, it is most frequently called on to analyse anomic characters. However, in what follows, I explore Cervantes's use of anomic characters from a narrative standpoint, as a literary device that allows the author to subvert the norms and expectations of Counter-Reformation orthodoxy. Although anomic characters are present in the majority of Cervantes's literary works, in *The Trials of Persiles and Sigismunda* these protagonists become especially significant. They seek freedom not as an act of overt resistance to power but rather as a means of avoiding the dominant social expectations imposed upon their behaviour. Anomic characters in this novel resist being deprived of their liberties but skirt those transgressions that are directly punishable by the political and religious systems of the time.

Cervantes's anomic protagonists assert their resistance through a careful exercise of *ethos, pathos* and *logos*, the three discursive dimensions distinguished by Aristotle: "Now the proofs furnished by speech are of three kinds. The first depends upon the moral character of the speaker [*ethos*], the second upon putting the hearer into a certain frame of mind [*pathos*], the third upon the speech itself, in so far as it proves or seems to prove [*logos*]" (I.2: 1356a). Philosophical materialism has reinterpreted these discursive categories by identifying *ethos* with the speaker's body, *pathos* with the speaker's psychology, and *logos* with the conceptual or scientific content of the speaker's argument (Maestro vols. 1–3).[1] All three are peculiarly interconnected in *The Trials of Persiles and Sigismunda;* Cervantes layers the contrasting opinions of characters, narrator, and author in competing vectors of persuasive speech. Using multiple voices to present the perspectives of desire, drive, and reason within his anomic characters' stories enables Cervantes to develop indirect critiques of Counter-Reformation social and relational norms: although no single character voices them, the accumulation of contrasting claims asserts them. Tales of sexual, social, and ideological anomie (of transgressive *eros* and *ethos*) thus introduce supposedly irrational, outsider practices in ways that end up demystifying not only *those* practices but also predominant rules governing virtue and devotional correctness.

For centuries, political organization, that is, the administration of freedom – and order – was deeply intertwined with religion in the administration of the state. Until the Enlightenment, this politico-religious connection determined the construction of anomic characters in literary works, characters who were marked by their deviant relationship with structures of political and religious power. The discourse through which anomic characters express themselves – discourse that makes up their *ethos*, and is made up from it – is the result of a dialectic between political and religious power, imposed on individuals as an unchanging moral order. When considering *eros* in literary representation, especially in the context of political and religious orthodoxy, the result of this dialectic is the widespread use of anomie as a governing quality of literary characters.

Freedom does not exist without power. As Gustavo Bueno has argued, the opposite of freedom is not slavery, but helplessness, or an absolute lack of power (*Sentido* 274). This should be kept in mind when citing Foucault uncritically, as some postmodern arguments about the function of power are out of touch with the reality from which they are developed. The lack of power is equivalent to the lack of freedom, but without some power it is not possible to exercise freedom. Thus, freedom is what others allow us to do, and, as such, freedom implies a struggle to act or express ourselves outside of external influence. While *ethos* in this medium allows characters to provide individual responses to authority, *eros* is the element or dimension that often pushes protagonists to issue those responses outside of their social milieu. In the case of Cervantes's characters, they tend to be cognizant of not only operations of these authority structures but also of the fractures of those operations. In his fiction, and despite this struggle, characters know very well how power is asserted and how it can be seduced, defeated, or mocked.

Anomic Characters in Cervantes's *The Trials of Persiles and Sigismunda*

Anomic characters live outside the normative systems of their societies, and their nonconformity is more pathological – or spontaneously subjective – than rational. Literature is full of anomic characters, and the Cervantine opus, in particular, provides extraordinary examples of anomie. Don Quixote is one such example. Other pivotal cases are Tomás Rodaja (the Glass Graduate Student), and the four characters committed to a mental asylum who appear at the close of "The Dogs' Conversation" (a poet, an alchemist, a mathematician, and an arbitrista); even the ensign Campuzano from this short novel is anomic. Numerous examples also exist in the Cervantine interludes, but *The Trials of Persiles and Sigismunda* is where Cervantes undoubtedly includes the highest number of anomic characters. In the following sections, I examine their anomic alienation by focusing on the persuasive responses they provide – through their *ethos*, *eros*, and *logos* – to structures of order, power, and orthodoxy.

Anomic characters behave in ways beyond the reach of power, even the most far- reaching and repressive power of the state, where such power is exerted religiously or secularly. As a result, such individuals are chronically marginalized by those systems and show little chance of overcoming their isolation. The struggle is not new; although not recognized by this name, anomic characters date back to ancient references in literature, as in the case of Lucio, the main character of Lucius Apuleius's *The Golden Ass* (*Asinus aureus*) and, before him, the highly renowned Aesop, of *Aesop's Life*, a short anonymous novella from the first century CE, whose paraenetic and cynical content has been considered a source for the *Quixote* (Rodríguez Adrados).

In those early depictions, anomie presents a social environment deprived of liberties, where individuals experience systemic and debilitating stress that often degenerates into deviant behaviour. In Cervantes's *The Trials of Persiles and Sigismunda*, a number of protagonists reflect this stress; these pages focus on seven of them who develop a non-conforming behaviour to the norms exerted by the political and religious logos. These characters represent tendencies and practices related to witchcraft and wizardry, intimidation through defamation, marginal forms of eroticism and sexuality, madness, pseudoscience (such as judicial astrology), misanthropy, and religious eccentricity. These traits are embodied in the characters Rutilio, Clodio, Renato, Cenotia, Soldino, a comic poet, and a *sui generis* pilgrim, all of whom I discuss below.

Rutilio: Witchcraft and Feminine Eroticism (I.8)

In this life story, Rutilio tells how he killed a witch who, in the context of an erotic relationship, transformed into a wolf; as a result he warns, "How this can be, I don't know, and as a Catholic Christian I don't believe it, but experience demonstrates just the opposite" (*Trials* I.8: 52) (Cómo esto pueda ser, yo lo ignoro y, como cristiano que soy católico, no lo creo; pero la esperiencia me muestra lo contrario [*Los trabajos* I.8: 189]). In this character's discourse, Cervantes deliberately pairs a religious imperative with a supernatural experience. Cervantes does not take the latter seriously, and maybe that is the reason why, with some very well-disguised Luddite allusions, he contrasts it with the seriousness of dogma, which he would otherwise not mock. What is true is that, in all of Cervantes's literary works, he demystifies behaviours and discourses that are not confirmed by experience. Magic, religious hypocrisy, individual and social vices, pseudoscience, and superstitions are subjected to frequent mockery and irony. These instances of playful criticism are particularly common in *The Trials of Persiles and Sigismunda*, a novel written against magic and other modes of superstition.

The narrator in *Persiles and Sigismunda* adopts a purely rational perspective in approaching any kind of fact or event. In many cases, this rational attitude coincides with that of the Catholic Reformation. In other cases, reason is not imposed from a secular, irreligious point of view, but always from the perspective of a politically advanced southern civilization set against a barbarian northern society. This is why, from the very beginning, the narrator adopts an *etic* perspective, condemning all activity that runs contrary to the scientific rationalism of Cervantes's contemporary world. The condemnatory example of the ritual at Barbara Isle does not leave any doubts: "the chief, wanting to get on with the test, the sooner to enjoy Periandro's companionship, ordered the youth sacrified immediately and his heart made into powder for the *ridiculous and fraudulent test*" (*Trials* I.4: 32; my italics) (El gobernador ... mandó que al momento se sacrificase aquel mancebo, de cuyo corazón se hiciesen los polvos de la *ridícula y engañosa prueba* [*Los trabajos* I.4: 41; my italics]).

While this episode does not censure witchcraft as an erotic instrument – as in the case of Cenotia, which will occur later – it does reveal a pathological *ethos* that leads to anomie. Here, Rutilio skirts the power of the Catholic Reformation *not* by eschewing reason (going directly against power) but by embracing a different *source* of reason (that is, avoiding power's direct influence). This is how Cervantine rationalism condemns magic, one of the four essential wisdoms of a barbarian culture. It will not be long before the rejection of *irrational myth* and *primary* or *numinous religion* are also present in the narrative. No specific statements about the idea of technique in barbarian cultures are noted in the novel, although the description of some of their procedures is present.

Clodio and Defamation (I.14)

The perspective of banished characters who speak from a Catholic point of view is frequently employed in the narration of *The Trials of Persiles and Sigismunda* to demystify reality. The narrator presents one such set of characters as evil, despicable, and vicious, yet they also manifest particularly authentic and essential human characteristics, such as revealing truth. Among all the characters that make up the retinue of pilgrims, four of them suspect a crucial truth – that is, the false siblinghood between Periandro and Auristela:[2] a nihilist (Clodio),[3] a witch (Cenotia),[4] a hermit (Soldino),[5] and a prostitute (Hipólita).[6] Cervantes deploys ironic dischord between the declarations of these characters and that of the narrator to establish the pilgrims' anomic position within the narrative – that is, their ability to perceive truth but not to assert it. Rosamunda, Clodio's alter ego expresses in her discourse, for instance, nothing but a mockery of the exemplary chastity that was expected from Renaissance heroines. Among such characters, the most striking is Clodio, who represents the prohibited truth through the irony of juxtaposed narrative perspectives.

The narrator of *Persiles and Sigismunda* creates Clodio with the objective of discovering what truth he is concealing. Such "truth," however, when spoken in a character of his temper, helps to qualify him as a slanderer, when in fact he is the only one who describes things by their names, names that decorum and faith prohibit. In this sense, the narrator is a sly cynic: he builds a character that he utilizes to assert what that narrator (or perhaps Cervantes) would otherwise never dare write. Clodio is an essential character, through whom the narrator states constant disagreements, and who at the same time voices and embodies the refutation of the moral and orthodox Counter-Reformist principles supposedly included (and exemplified) in the novel.

As an anomic character, Clodio serves as a safe vehicle of expression for critical truths that is skilfully exploited by the cynical narrator. The author, Cervantes, builds with this character – and his hostile relationship with the narrator – a medium able to reveal "truths" capable of challenging the fundamental ideological principles of his world. His unsympathetic *narrator* – who constantly accuses Clodio of being a slanderer without any proof or reason – provides the perfect protection for the author. Put in this impossible situation, the more Clodio defends himself from such accusations, the more he seems to reinforce them. His exchange with Rosamunda, for example, reveals him as an almost Shakespearian character, given his demystifying, and even nihilist, ontological perspective:

> Prisons didn't tie my tongue nor banishments quiet it nor threats frighten me nor punishment reform me ... [M]y conscience has never accused me of having told a single lie ... [If] they don't want me to speak or write they should cut off my tongue and my hands and even then I will put my mouth to the bowels of the earth and speak however I can ... [H]ow can someone who does wrong expect good things to be said of him? (*Trials* I.14: 72–3; 16: 78)

> (No me ataban la lengua prisiones, ni enmudecían destierros, ni atemorizaban amenazas, ni enmendaban castigos ... Jamás me ha acusado la conciencia de haber dicho alguna mentira ... Si quieren que no hable o escriba, córtenme la lengua y las manos, y aun entonces pondré la boca en las entrañas de la tierra, y daré voces como pudiere ... ¿Por qué ha de esperar el que obra mal que digan bien dél? ... ¿Por qué ha de esperar el que siembra cizaña y maldad, dé buen fruto su cosecha? [*Los trabajos* I.14: 99, 100, 101; 16: 110])

Freedom and truth are the true objectives of this speech. Few characters show comparable bravery in seeking them. The price Clodio pays for his pronouncements is to unfairly be considered a slanderer.

Cervantes, then, entrusts in Clodio all the subversive power of the truth, which is morally undermined on a continual basis by the narrator in order to disguise his authorial responsibility. Even when disguised, however, the authorial words entail the ultimate authority in the text, an authority that is ironically used to protect the author from external hegemonic accusations against the morality of the text. The narrator, to this end, acts and expresses himself as one more characters who pretend – or lie – when narrating their story; the discourse of this narrative voice is, then, that of a *pretender* – as he knows what he is concealing and the reasons why he is doing so.

Clodio's speech before Arnaldo, who takes him under his protection, far from being ridiculous and slanderous, represents one of the most brilliant and subversive interpretations of the praised *peregrinatio* of the characters:

> You, my Lord, love Auristela; not just "love," I should say "adore"; and to the best of my knowledge you know no more about her social position or

who she is than what she's been willing to tell you, which is nothing. She's been in your power for more than two years, during which time, according to what we're supposed to believe, you've made every possible effort to soften her firmness, tame her sternness, and subject her will to yours through the honorable and effective method of matrimony; yet she's just as firm in her resolve today as the first day you began to court her, from which fact I conclude that, just as you have too much patience, she shows too little gratitude; you need to consider that there must be some great mystery involved when a woman rejects a kingdom and a prince worthy of her love.

There's also something mysterious about a young vagabond woman wandering from land to land, from island to island, exposed to inclement weather from the sky as well as hazards on land, which are usually worse than those on the stormy sea. All this, while cautiously concealing her lineage and accompanied by a young man who, although she says he's her brother, may not in fact be so. Of the good things Heaven distributes among mortals, those having to do with honour should be the most esteemed, for honour should be placed before life itself; the wise measure their desires by the rule of reason and not by the desires themselves. (*Trials* II.2: 111–12)

(Tú, señor, amas a Auristela; mal dije amas, adoras, dijera mejor; y, según he sabido, no sabes más de su hacienda, ni de quién es, que aquello que ella ha querido decirte, que no te ha dicho nada. Hasla tenido en tu poder más de dos años, en los cuales has hecho, según se ha de creer, las diligencias posibles por enternecer su dureza, amansar su rigor y rendir su voluntad a la tuya por los medios honestísimos y eficaces del matrimonio, y en la misma entereza se está hoy que el primero día que la solicitaste, de donde arguyo que, cuanto a ti te sobra de paciencia, le falta a ella de conocimiento; y has de considerar que algún gran misterio encierra desechar una mujer un reino y un príncipe que merece ser amado. Misterio también encierra ver una doncella vagamunda, llena de recato de encubrir su linaje, acompañada de un mozo que, como dice que lo es, podría no ser su hermano, de tierra en tierra, de isla en isla, sujeta a las inclemencias del cielo y a las borrascas de la tierra, que suelen ser peores que las del mar alborotado. De los bienes que reparten los cielos entre los mortales, los que más se han de estimar son los de la honra, a quien se posponen los de la vida; los gustos de los discretos hanse de medir con la razón, y no con los mismos gustos. [*Los trabajos* II.2: 156–7])

Clodio is a rationalist of suspicion. He is a character whose discourse cannot prosper without punishment. His boldest Machiavellianism is manifest right before he is murdered by Antonio, in his dialogues with

Rutilio, when planning the absurd idea of seeking Auristela's hand (*Los trabajos* II.5: 307–10).

The nihilist Clodio and the blessed Sigismunda belong to two worlds that cannot plausibily coexist in a single universe. Sigismunda's virtue exists only verbally, as a fiction or myth. Clodio is the voice of real-life complexity and authenticity, with all the strength of his miseries and the qualities of his most immoral intelligence. He is one of the cracks in *The Trials of Persiles and Sigismunda*. As such, he cannot prosper, because his works and his words endanger the novel's integrity. From the very beginning, in fact, he is in the position of ruining the false identity farce regarding Periandro and Auristela. The author, Cervantes, creates Clodio while also creating a narrator who unjustifiably despises and condemns Clodio. Banned from England because he has revealed truths that power wished to hide, Clodio is also banished from *The Trials of Persiles and Sigismunda* with symbolic weight – through a hazardous and meaning-laden procedure – and given an unfair death, neither deserved nor solved. His character is thus an example of how political power transforms truth – and all possibility of announcing truth – into an anomic experience.

Cenotia: Witchcraft and Masculine Eroticism (II.8)

Cenotia is Rutilio's mirror image and counterpoint. I have already mentioned that, in *The Trials of Persiles and Sigismunda*, as in Cervantes's works as a whole, the value and power of magic is demystified. Cenotia's spells, so effective against Auristela's health, can do nothing against Antonio's rage: "Cenotia turned her head and saw the arrow's deadly blow. Fearing a second one, and taking no advantage of the many powers she claimed for her science but full of confusion and fear, she left the room stumbling here and falling there, resolved to take revenge on the cruel and cold-hearted youth" (*Trials* II.8: 140) (Volvió la Cenotia la cabeza, vio el mortal golpe que había hecho la flecha, temió la segunda y, sin aprovecharse de lo mucho que con su ciencia se prometía, llena de confusión y de miedo, tropezando aquí y cayendo allí, salió del aposento, con intención de vengarse del cruel y desamorado mozo [*Los trabajos* II.8: 335]). A similar process of demystification occurs when the narrator reveals Constanza's intentions as she meets the Pole Ortel's wife from Talavera de la Reina and pretends to know her identity through art and fortune telling: "But if I should tell you things already past of which I have no knowledge, nor indeed could have, what would you say then? Would you like to see that?" (*Trials* III.16: 280) (Si yo os dijese cosas pasadas, que no hubiesen llegado ni pudiesen llegar a mi noticia, ¿qué diríades? ¿Queréislo ver? [*Los trabajos* III.16: 585]).

Constanza is lying to her peers, but not to the reader, to whom the narrator reveals her secret: "No sooner had she said this than Constanza began to suspect she must be the Pole Ortel Banedre's wife, who'd been jailed in Madrid for adultery ... Then in a flash ideas came crowding into Constanza's mind and she came up with a plan that subsequently turned out to be almost exactly the way she'd imagined it would" (*Trials* III.16: 280) (A Constanza le vinieron barruntos de que debía de ser la esposa de Ortel Banedre el polaco, que, por adúltera, quedaba presa en Madrid ... Y en un instante fabricó en su imaginación un montón de cosas que, puestas en efecto, le sucedieron casi como las había pensado [*Los trabajos* III.16: 584]). Witchcraft and eroticism are frequently tied together in literature, and this is especially true in the Golden Age: Cenotia's actions with respect to Antonio represent a failed attempt at magic, in the same way that the deceit of the witch-turned-wolf failed with Rutilio. In both scenes, the use of witchcraft as an erotic instrument betrays and reveals anomie – that is, the pathological *ethos* of the character moved by a banned *eros*. Here, Cervantes seems to use both witches and the characters they affect (whether by desire or deception) to comment on structures of power, by showing an anomic character operating "outside" of established power structures.

Renato, Banished Hermit (II.18–21)

Renato's narration about his virginal married life with his wife, Eusebia[7] on the island of the Hermitages is placed in contrast to a speech by Mauricio, who demystifies the authenticity and legitimacy of hermitic life with evident subversion:

> But such considerations are applicable only to important people; we won't be all surprised to see a rustic shepherd withdraw into the solitude of the countryside, nor would we be amazed if someone who is starving to death in the city should seek solitary refuge where he won't lack for food. There are ways of living supported by idleness and sloth, and I'd be more than a little lazy if I were to leave the solution to my troubles in other hands, even if there were kind ones. (*Trials* II.19: 188)
>
> (Esas consideraciones han de caer sobre grandes sujetos; porque no nos ha de causar maravilla que un rústico pastor se retire a la soledad del campo, ni nos ha de admirar que un pobre, que en la ciudad muere de hambre, se recoja a la soledad donde no le ha de faltar el sustento. Modos hay de vivir

que los sustenta la ociosidad y la pereza, y no es pequeña pereza dejar yo el remedio de mis trabajos en las ajenas, aunque misericordiosas manos. [*Los trabajos* II.19: 259])

Even if it does not seem so, we are not that far from the aphorism that Nietzsche warns about in *Die fröhliche Wissenschaft* (1887), which states that it is easier to pray to a god than to build a bridge. Renato is the kind of poor devil who could belong to any historical period: an object of slander that he is unable to refute, he faces his rival in a duel and loses absolutely everything except his life. Ashamed and depressed, he flees until he reaches the northern lands, where he lives, accompanied by an unbelieving wife, as a desperate eunuch who is comforted by Catholic faith. Mauricio is right when he interprets Renato's hermitic life not as a virtue but, rather, as the consequence of vital failure.

Renato, then, is doubly anomic; the moral stature traditionally conferred on the hermit for his ascetic mode of living – for living outside the interests of an organized church – is diminished here, or negated altoghether, since his discourse portrays him simply as a rejected member of his social mileau.

Anomie and Poetry (III.2)

The demystification of poets, playwrights, and writers was a prevalent topic in Golden Age literature. These characters are subject to mockery, irony, and frequent parody. This can be seen at the beginning of Book III once the pilgrims arrive in Badajoz and find accommodations at an inn, where, at the same time, "a company of famous actors was staying" (*Trials* III.2: 203) (se alojaba una compañía de famosos recitantes [*Los trabajos* III.2: 441]). Among them is a poet "whom necessity had to obliged to exchange Mount Parnassus for roadhouses, and the springs of Castalia and Aganippes for the puddles and streams of the roads and inns" (*Trials* III.2: 204) (a quien la necesidad había hecho trocar los Parnasos con los mesones y las Castalias y las Aganipes con los charcos y arroyos de los caminos y ventas [*Los trabajos* III.2: 442]). This is the poet who thinks that Auristela would be a good "impostor." On this note, however, the narrator introduces a disparaging digression about poets and comedians: "Good Gracious! How easily a poet's wit runs away with him and tries a thousand roadblocks! How weak the foundations on which great fantasies are erected!" (*Trials* III.2: 204) (¡Válame Dios, y con cuánta facilidad discurre el ingenio de un poeta y se arroja a romper por mil imposibles! ¡Sobre cuán flacos cimientos levanta grandes quimeras! [*Los trabajos* III.2: 443]). The discourse of the "pilgrim poet" can be interpreted in a similar fashion (IV.6: 664 ff), when he appears with his extravagant story – and with "the Cross of Christ" – once the main retinue has arrived in Rome.

It should not be forgotten that, in this context, Rutilio is one of the first characters who is subject to mockery, because of his profession as a dancer: "He asked me if I knew some trade with which I could earn my keep while waiting for the time to return to my homeland. I told him I was a dancer, a very nimble fellow, and quite skillful at juggling and sleight-of-hand. He laughed heartily and told me those skills or occupations – or whatever I might want to call them – just weren't practiced in Norway or any of those parts" (*Trials* I.8: 53) (Preguntóme si tenía algún oficio en que ganar de comer, mientras llegaba el tiempo de volverme a mi tierra. Díjele que era bailarín y grande hombre de hacer cabriolas, y que sabía jugar de manos sutilísamente. Rióse de gana el hombre y me dijo que aquellos ejercicios, o oficios, o como llamarlos quisiese, no corrían en Noruega ni en todas aquellas partes [*Los trabajos* I.8: 190–1]). As Cervantes suggests with these characters, the supposedly marginal life of writers, poets, and actors explicitly nourished the world's social anomie before the Enlightenment.

The Idle Pilgrim: The Myth of the *Peregrinatio* (III.6)

One of the most intensively ironic moments in *Persiles*, because of its development and consequences, is the episode in which the pilgrims find themselves with a grotesque individual who introduces herself as a *peregrine*, or female pilgrim, and whose discourse is extremely subversive with respect to the ideas and purposes of any *peregrinatio*. Never before in the novel has anomie been so close to religion.

First, this pilgrim travels alone, which is unorthodox in itself, since it is customary to undertake pilgrimages in groups. Second, the character physically represents an overt demonstration of the grotesque, or at least that is how the narrator describes her:

> One side of her face ran into the other, and even someone with the eyesight of a lynx couldn't manage to see her nose, which was so flat and snub you couldn't have picked up a sliver of it with a pair of tweezers ... As they came up they greeted her, and she returned their greetings in the voice one would expect from the snubness of her nose, that is, more twangy than smooth. (*Trials* III.6: 228–9)

> ([P]orque la vista de un lince no alcanzara a verle las narices, porque no las tenía, sino tan chatas y llanas que con unas pinzas no le pudieran asir una

brizna de ellas; los ojos les hacían sombra, porque más salían fuera de la cara que ella ... Saludáronla en llegando y ella les volvió los saludos con la voz que podía prometer la chatedad de sus narices, que fue más gangosa que suave" [*Los trabajos* III.6: 484–6])

Third, the reader learns that she is a character discredited and mistreated, not only physically but also verbally, by the narrator: "She was totally worn out and looked every inch the penitent, and as became apparent later, was generally in a bad way" (*Trials* III.6: 228) (Toda ella era rota – leemos – , y toda penitente, y [como después se echó de ver] toda de mala condición [*Los trabajos* III.6: 484]).

Here, the narrator plays with a future that cannot be verified in the development of the novel; this character will not appear again, and even though she is labelled as having "a bad nature" (de mala condition), such evil never manifests itself against her. At the same time, when the narrator lets her talk, the pilgrim's speech ends up being particularly subversive, countering the very foundation of the fable of *Persiles and Sigismunda*: the *peregrinatio*. These are her words:

> Mine is a pilgrimage undertaken by a lot of pilgrims nowadays, by which I mean that they keep themselves busy in their idleness with whatever pilgrimage is closest and most convenient. And so I might as well tell you that right now I'm going to the great city of Toledo to visit the holy image of the Sagrario, and from there I'm going to the Niño de la Guardia; then veering off like a Norwegian falcon, I will entertain myself by going to see the Santa Verónica at Jaén, to spend time until the last Sunday in April rolls around, the day on which the festival of Nuestra Señora de la Cabeza is celebrated at the heart of the Sierra Morena mountains, three leagues from the city of Andújar. It is one of the festivals celebrated entirely in the out-of-doors, and from what I have heard, not even the earlier pagan festivals imitated by the Monda at Talavera could have oudone it. I wish I could, if only it were posible, pull it out of my imagination where it's imprinted in my mind's eye, paint it for you in words, and set it out for you to see, so taking it all in you might see just how very right I am to praise it to you ... It makes its home on this spacious, pleasant spot that's always green and peaceful thanks to the moisture reaching it from the waters of the Jándula river, which as though bowing in reverence kisses its skirts in passing. The place, the rock, the image, the miracles, the countless people who come from near and far, and the solemn day I told you about make it famous throughout the world and celebrated in Spain above all other places even the longest memories can recall ... I don't know which trip I'll take to pass the time and keep my idleness entertained the way many pilgrims do nowadays, as I've said. (*Trials* III.6: 228–9)

(Mi peregrinación es la que usan algunos peregrinos: quiero decir que siempre es la que más cerca les viene a cuento para disculpar su ociosidad; y así, me parece que será bien deciros que por ahora voy a la gran ciudad de Toledo, a visitar a la devota imagen del Sagrario, y desde allí me iré al Niño de la Guardia, y, dando una punta, como halcón noruego, me entretendré con la santa Verónica de Jaén, hasta hacer tiempo -fol. 141r- de que llegue el último domingo de abril, en cuyo día se celebra en las entrañas de Sierra Morena, tres leguas de la ciudad de Andújar, la fiesta de Nuestra Señora de la Cabeza, que es una de las fiestas que en todo lo descubierto de la tierra se celebra; tal es, según he oído decir, que ni las pasadas fiestas de la gentilidad, a quien imita la de la Monda de Talavera, no le han hecho ni le pueden hacer ventaja. Bien quisiera yo, si fuera posible, sacarla de la imaginación, donde la tengo fija, y pintárosla con palabras, y ponérosla delante de la vista, para que, comprehendiéndola, viérades la mucha razón que tengo de alabárosla ... En este espacioso y ameno sitio tiene su asiento, siempre verde y apacible, por el humor que le comunican las aguas del río Jándula, que de paso, como en reverencia, le besa las faldas. El lugar, la peña, la imagen, los milagros, la infinita gente que acude de cerca y lejos, el solemne día que he dicho, le hacen famoso en el mundo y célebre en España sobre cuantos lugares las más estendidas memorias se acuerdan ... Desde allí – prosiguió la peregrina – , no sé qué viaje será el mío, aunque sé que no me ha de faltar donde ocupe la ociosidad y entretenga el tiempo, como lo hacen, como ya he dicho, algunos peregrinos que se usan. [*Los trabajos* III.6: 311–12])

I do not think it is possible to read this speech without identifying the irony that was present in Cervantes's *intentio* when he wrote it. This is a statement that undermines the fundamentals of the Persilesque *peregrinatio* themselves. Even though the pilgrims in the retinue are acquainted with her words, it is Antonio, the father, who tells her, "It seems to me, pilgrim lady, you don't have the right idea about what a pilgrimage is" (*Trials* III.6: 229). (Paréceme, señora peregrina, que os da en el rostro la peregrinación [*Los trabajos* III.6: 311–12]). This statement allows the author to speak directly about the unethical side to the pilgrimage: "I know well enough they're pious, holy, and praiseworthy, and have always existed in the world and always will. But what I object to are bad pilgrims, the ones who make a profit out of holiness, and filthy gain from praiseworthy virtue; I mean the ones who rob alms from the truly poor. And I'll say no more although I could" (*Trials* III.6: 229) (Eso no – respondió ella – que bien sé que es justa, santa y loable, y que siempre la ha habido y la ha de haber en el mundo, pero estoy mal con los malos peregrinos, como son los que hacen granjería de la santidad, y ganancia infame de la virtud loable; con aquellos, digo, que saltean la limosna de los verdaderos pobres. Y no digo más, aunque pudiera [*Los trabajos* III.6: 312]). As usual, the silences in *The Trials of Persiles and Sigismunda* are telling (Egido). The silence of the retinue, which concludes this grotesque creature's speech, is more eloquent than the repeated words of the beautiful and fake Auristela and the brave but no less fake Periandro.

Soldino: Judicial Astrology as Pseudoscience (III.18)

Soldino is a grotesque character, a hermit vested with pseudo-sacerdotal garments and pretending to be a pilgrim or a religious man, who introduces himself as a judicial astrologer and is – in the narrator's words (*Trials* III.18: 289; *Los trabajos* III.18: 394) – neither one thing nor the other.[8] Astrology, despite being a pseudoscience, predicts a fire that actually takes place in the building – an inn – where the pilgrims of the *Persiles* are staying. Soldino then guides them toward his personal dwelling, which provides underground access to an arcadia that emblematizes the myth of an idyllic nature; following a recurrent literary convention, this beautiful meadow is associated with a disregard for the court and the worship of the village. The recurrent celebration of an ascetic life that leads to virtue, and the exaltation of an Edenic utopia that is presented as an earthly paradise – foreign or antagonistic to all human societies – is, however, intimately disrupted in the episode; Soldino's arcadia is heavily inflected by the *logos* of Counter-Reformist norms and those (political *logos*) of secular Spain, since it is in this idealized setting where he pronounces a striking speech – or conducts a master class – about the future military triumphs of the Duke of Alba and the death of King Sebastian of Portugal, following the convention of *post eventum* prophecies.

As a character, Soldino seems to embody a hybrid literary intertext that refers to the wide array of sorcerers, witches, judicial astrologers, fortune-tellers, prophets, shamans, and wizards that have inhabited literature since antiquity; similar figures can be found, in particular, in literary genres such as adventure novels, pastoral novels, and Greek tragedies. But Cervantes does not write *The Trials of Persiles and Sigismunda* to confirm the fixed and unchanging original nature of these literary genres; his intention is to subvert them. Cervantine characters are always a literary critique of the pre-existing models that inspire them and are used by the author to alter or deconstruct the meaning of these earlier eccentric and ridiculous figures.

Cervantes's anomic characters are carefully coated with secular, political, and religious *logos* that use the logic of this discourse against itself, as a narrative device possibly intended to elude censorship and inquisitorial intervention. Cervantes exposes the fractures of the political and religious society of his time, but with a critical and literary cynicism that is extraordinarily sophisticated. This analytical and censuring intent is the reason for the ambiguity of his entire oeuvre, and for the difficulty of classifying, even from an ironic Cervantine point of view, the critical and devastating power of his work.

Soldino himself, a grotesque and eccentric hermit, utters a speech that undermines any kind of virtue: "rarely does good reputation come out of a bad lie. It's not the coming but the going out that shows whether people are fortunate. When virtue has a vice as its goal, it's not virtue at all but simply vice" (*Trials* III.18: 289) (que tal vez la buena fama se engendra de la mala mentira. No la entrada, sino la salida, hace a los hombres venturosos. La virtud que tiene por remate el vicio, no es virtud, sino vicio [*Los trabajos* III.18: 394]). Again, the reader bumps into the moral deflation of virtue. In general terms, we may state that such deflation in *Persiles and Sigismunda* is built by specific hyperboles. Some of these hyperboles turn out to be comical,[9] not because of the way in which they are eventually enacted, but because of the way in which characters communicate them. For example, in the early tale that Taurisa tells Periandro about Auristela and her relationship with her suitor Arnaldo, there is an insistence on the main character's perpetual chastity vow: "But she herself resisted, saying it wasn't possible to break a vow she'd made to remain a virgin all her life, and she had no intention of breaking it any way even if they tried to convince her with promises or threaten her with death" (*Trials* I.2: 25) (Pero ella se defendía, diciendo no ser posible romper un voto que tenía hecho de guardar virginidad toda su vida, y que no pensaba quebrarle en ninguna manera, si bien la solicitasen promesas o la amenazasen muertes [*Los trabajos* I.2: 29]). Virtue, in this formulation, appears to exist only in conjuction with the threat to defeat it: in order not only to survive, but also to exist, it needs the circumstances that threaten it. That is why it is not surprising that the episode starring the fortune-teller Sordino is subject to some estrangement on the part of the silent and cynical narrator of the novel, who warns, "It has been said that things not very true to life or probable, even though they really happen, shouldn't be told in stories because if they aren't believed, they lose their value" (*Trials* III.18: 290) (Otra vez se ha dicho que no todas las acciones no verisímiles ni probables se han de contar en las historias, porque si no se les da crédito, pierden su valor; pero al historiador no le conviene más de decir la verdad, parézcalo o no lo parezca [*Los trabajos* III.18: 396]).

The narrator, a faithful Cervantine alter ego, wants to detach himself from the truth of the presented facts. We, Cervantes's readers, know that this author demystifies and criticizes everything that denies or argues against scientific truths: "for it is also clear that this monkey is not an astrologer, and neither he nor his master casts, or knows how to cast, the astrological charts used so widely now in Spain that there is not a fishwife, page, or old cobbler who does not presume to cast a chart as if it were the knave in the pack of cards lying on the floor, corrupting the marvelous truths of science with their lies and ignorance" (*Don Quixote* II.25: 626) (porque cierto está que este mono no es astrólogo, ni su amo ni él alzan ni saben alzar estas figuras que llaman "judiciarias," que tanto ahora se usan en España, que no hay mujercilla, ni paje, ni zapatero de viejo que no presuma de alzar una figura, como si fuera una sota de naipes del suelo, echando a perder con sus mentiras e ignorancias la verdad maravillosa de la ciencia [*Ingenioso hidalgo* II.25: 237]). The literary rationalism of these words against the fortune-teller Maese Pedro (*Don Quixote* II.25–7), the galley slave illegally freed by Don Quixote, reveals, along with episodes such as the charmed head (*Don Quixote* II.62–3), that the Cervantine attitude is contrary to pseudoscience, magic, numinous religious superstition, and techniques used by shamans, prophets, and haruspices.

Likewise, Leoncio's speech to Morandro in the tragedy *Numancia* makes the human spirit confront religious metaphysics and denies the value of transcendent destiny and its divine imperatives over the volitional faculties of human beings, which, from a Cervantine point of view, are always preceded by the exercise of freedom. Neither Oedipus, nor Electra, nor Orestes would ever dare to repeat these words about existence and the power of the transcendent moral order that guided their lives:

What are all these strange illusions?
Terrors grim and phantasies.
What are signs and witcheries?
Diabolical delusions.
Thinkest thou such things have worth?
Slender knowledge dost thou show;
Little care the dead below
For the living here on earth (*Numantia* II: ll.1097–1104)

(Que todas son ilusiones,
quimeras y fantasías
agüeros y hechicerías,
diabólicas invenciones.

No muestres que tienes poca
ciencia en creer desconciertos;
que poco cuidan los muertos
de lo que a los vivos toca. [*Numancia* II: ll. 1097–1104])

These are only a few of the many similar examples throughout Cervantes's literary works. Consider, finally, the episode about the grotesque witch Cañizares in "The Dialogue of the Dogs" ("El coloquio de los perros"). In this last exemplary novel, witchcraft is completely demystified. So Cipión states, "Camacha was a lying trickster, Cañizares a rascal, and Montiela a malicious and wicked fool" ("Dialogue" 293) (la Camacha fue burladora falsa, y la Cañizares embustera, y la Montiela tonta, maliciosa y bellaca ["El coloquio" 605]). In this manner, Cervantes's works are prime examples of critical literature because they embody four essential types of knowledge – science, philosophy, the demystification of unfounded beliefs, and the criticism of dogma. Moreover, further enriching the nuance of Cervantes's creation of critical literature, he creates singular and extraordinary anomic characters who rise up to subvert all four types.

NOTES

1 On ontological materialism, see Bueno, *Ensayos materialistas*. For materialist philosophy as a literary theory, see Maestro.

2 The motif of lovers pretending to be siblings is ancient, and even biblical, as illustrated by Abraham and Sara (Genesis 20), *Leucipe and Clitofonte, Teágenes and Cariclea*, and *Clareo and Florisea*. Other examples can be found in Boccaccio's *Decameron* (1353), and in Lope de Vega's *El peregrino de su patria* (*The Pilgrim in His Motherland*) (1604), among others.

3 "There's also something mysterious about a young vagabond woman wandering ... accompanied by a young man who, although she says he's her brother, may not in fact be so" (*Trials* II.2: 111) (Misterio también encierra ver una doncella vagabunda ... llena de recato de encubrir su linaje, acompañada de un mozo que, como dice que lo es, podría no ser su hermano [*Los trabajos* II.2: 290]).

4 "And why should she [Auristela] want to keep her word to return to take for her husband an old gentleman, which in fact you are, (the truths one recognizes about himself cannot be used to deceive him), when close at hand she has Periandro (who just might not be her brother)?" (*Trials* 2.11: 152) (Y ¿cómo querrá ella [Auristela] cumplir su palabra, volviendo a tomar por esposo a un varón anciano (que en efeto lo eres: que las verdades que uno conoce de sí mismo no nos pueden engañar), teniéndose ella de su mano a Periandro, que podría ser que no fuese su hermano? [*Los trabajos* II.11: 355]).

5 "And to you, Periandro, I give the assurance that your pilgrimage shall turn out well; your sister Auristela shall not be that for long – and not because she's soon going to lose her life" (*Trials* III.18: 291) (Y a ti, Periandro, te aseguro, buen suceso de tu peregrinación: tu hermana Auristela no lo será presto, y no porque ha de perder la vida con brevedad [*Los trabajos* III.18: 603]).

6 "Isn't it posible this young man has his heart set on someone else? Isn't it posible this Auristela isn't his sister?" (*Trials*IV.8: 333) (¿No sería posible que este mozo tuviese en otra parte ocupada el alma? ¿No sería posible que esta Auristela no fuese su hermana? [*Los trabajos* IV.8: 676]).

7 According to Renato,

> We gave each other our hands in lawful marriage, we buried fire in snow, and in peace and in love, like two mobile statues, we've lived in this place for almost ten years, during which not one year has gone by without my servants coming back to see me, supplying me with some of things that I need in this solitude. Sometimes they bring a priest with them to hear our confession, and in the hermitage we have sufficient vestments and vessels to celebrate the divine offices. We sleep apart, eat together, speak of Heaven, scorn life on this earth, and confident in God's mercy, await the eternal. (*Trials* 2.19: 187–8)
>
> Dímonos las manos de legítimos esposos, enterramos el fuego en la nieve, y en paz y en amor, como dos estatuas movibles, ha que vivimos en este lugar casi diez años, en los cuales no se ha pasado ninguno en que mis criados no vuelvan a verme, proveyéndome de algunas cosas que en esta soledad es forzoso que me falten. Traen alguna vez consigo algún religioso que nos confiese; tenemos en la ermita suficientes ornamentos para celebrar los divinos oficios; dormimos aparte, comemos juntos, hablamos del cielo, menospreciamos la tierra, y, confiados en la misericordia de Dios, esperamos la vida eterna (*Los trabajos* II.19: 258).

8 "He was dressed neither as a pilgrim nor as a member of a religious order" (*Trials* III.18: 288) (Venía vestido ni como peregrino, ni como religioso, puesto que lo uno y lo otro parecía [*Los trabajos* III.18: 394]).

9 Maybe Notter is right when he talks about the "hyperbole of tears" in *Persiles* (Cervantes, *Die Prüfungen* I, 5). He considers that Cervantes is ridiculing specific circumstances that reveal, or suggest, the characters' overtly sentimental nature. One example is Cloelia's death (I, 5).

REFERENCES

Aristotle. *Retórica*. Translated and annotated by Q. Racionero. Madrid: Gredos, 1990.

Bueno, Gustavo. *El sentido de la vida: Seis lecturas de filosofía moral*. Oviedo: Pentalfa, 1996.

– *Ensayos materialistas*. Madrid: Taurus, 1972.

Cervantes Saavedra, Miguel de. "The Dialogue of the Dogs." In *Miguel de Cervantes. Exemplary Novels.* Translated by Lesley Lipson. Oxford: Oxford University Press, 1992.

Die Prüfungen des Persiles und der Sigismunda: Eine nordische Geschichte. Translated by Friedrich Notter. 1617. Reprint. Stuttgart: Verlag der J.B. Mezlerschen Buchhandlung, 1839.

– *Don Quixote.* Translated by Edith Grossman. New York: HarperCollins, 2003.

– "El coloquio de los perros." In *Novelas ejemplares.* Edited by Jorge García López. Barcelona: Crítica, 2001.

– *El Ingenioso hidalgo Don Quijote de la Mancha.* Edited by Luis A. Murillo. Madrid: Castalia, 1978.

– *La Numancia.* Edited, introduced and annotated by F. Sevilla and A. Rey. Madrid: Alianza Editorial, 1996.

– *Los trabajos de Persiles y Sigismunda.* In *Obra Completa de Miguel de Cervantes.* Vol. 18. Edited, introduced and annotated by F. Sevilla and A. Rey. Madrid: Alianza Editorial, 1999.

– *Numantia: A Tragedy.* Translated by James Gibson. London: Kegan Paul, 1885.

– *The Trials of Persiles and Sigismunda.* Translated by Celia Richmond Weller and Clark A. Colahan. Indianapolis, IN: Hackett, 1989.

Egido, Aurora. "Los silencios del *Persiles.*" In *On Cervantes: Essays for L.A. Murillo,* edited by James A. Parr, 21–46. Newark, DE: Juan de la Cuesta, 1991.

Foucault, Michel. *Histoire de la folie à l'âge classique.* Paris: Gallimard, 1972.

Maestro, Jesús G. *Crítica de la razón literaria: El Materialismo Filosófico como Teoría de la Literatura.* 10 vols. Vigo: Editorial Academia del Hispanismo, 2004–15.

Rodríguez Adrados, Francisco. *El río de la literature: De Sumeria y Homero a Shakespeare y Cervantes.* Barcelona: Ariel, 2013.

PART III

Kissing between the Lines: Blurring Racial and Sexual Norms

Chapter Six

Sexy Beasts: Women and Lapdogs in Baroque Satirical Verse

ADRIENNE L. MARTÍN

Tucked away in a discreet corner of San Francisco's Presidio – the former military post overlooking the magnificent natural harbour where the Californian city was established in 1776 – an endearing pet cemetery houses the remains of beloved animal companions long gone: fish, birds, reptiles, rodents, cats, and dogs. Over 400 handmade headstones honouring the memory of pets[1] attest to the bond between humans and animals that was enjoyed by the military families stationed in the Presidio. Dating from the early 1950s, the Presidio Pet Cemetery is actually a late starter: the Hartsdale Canine Cemetery, founded in 1896 in Westchester County, New York, and the oldest pet cemetery in the United States, is more than half a century older.

Similar graveyards with equally appealing headstones, some simple and others surprisingly elaborate and engraved, can be found across Europe. For example, Lisbon's Cemitério de Animais is located in a serene corner of that city's zoo, and the art nouveau Cimetière des Chiens et Autres Animaux Domestiques in Asnières-sur-Seine, Paris (the oldest in Europe, founded in 1899) houses the remains of a lion, a monkey, and a racehorse besides more conventional pets. Because all of these places have been designated as historic sites, their preservation is assured. Many other animal resting places can be found across Europe, from London to Cologne and from Madrid to Milan, and they have several things in common: they contain sentimental, at times humorous, epitaphs to those companions; many of the epitaphs are written in verse; and the majority of the eulogized are canines.

One might assume that such testaments came about only after pet keeping surged in the nineteenth century. However, John Bradshaw's *The Animals among Us: The New Science of Anthrozoology* uses archaeological findings to date back to our distant ancestors the nature and profound depth of the emotional attachment people feel for their animal companions. Rather than being a modern phenomenon, Bradshaw affirms, "our ability to understand and feel affection for animals must be an ancient trait that most likely emerged as our brains evolved into their current form, about 50,000 to 30,000 years ago. If this is correct, pet keeping makes up an intrinsic part of what it is to be human" (23).

As we know, this notion of what it is to be human was a profound preoccupation for theologians and humanists during the Renaissance, a time of escalating pet culture and the discovery of unique species in the New World. Intellectuals were deeply engaged in establishing what it meant to be human, in determining what distinguished humans from the rest of the animal kingdom, in expressing moral concerns regarding the proper treatment of animals, and in empathetic writing such as eulogies, letters, and poems that showed great affection for their own individual animals. One of the most charming of these is the celebrated epistle written by Petrarch to his patron Cardinal Giovanni Colonna in 1347, in which he describes his life with the Spanish dog that Colonna had sent to him as a gift. The expressions of companionship and affection in the letter could easily have been written in the twenty-first century.[2]

Regarding early modern attitudes toward animals, particularly those held by Renaissance humanists, Benjamin Arbel has written that:

> the Renaissance period ... represents a significant new shift toward open empathy for animals and awareness of human responsibility for them in modes, contexts, and dimensions that had not existed in Europe since antiquity ... In various ways and forms, writers active between the age of Petrarch and that of Montaigne expressed a new sensitivity regarding animals, recognized their mental and emotional capacities, and also acknowledged a moral obligation toward them. (75)

Along with this renewed intellectual focus on animals, the increased traffic in exotic fauna from distant colonies expanded the possibilities for, and the popularity of, pet keeping, particularly among the wealthy. Moreover, as Juliana Schiesari points out, the increasing demand for pet dogs drove commercial markets in dog breeding to develop new, expensive, and specialized breeds of dogs, all in the service of the rising pet culture (9). This expanding awareness of the animal is manifested in many forms during the Renaissance: in the material culture of the time, in treatises on hunting, in philosophical tomes on ethics, and also in literature, especially poetry.

One particular modality of poetry that reflects the increased visibility of pets is the tradition of canine epitaphs or elegies (*epicedia*) that dates to Renaissance poets for whom classical writers such as Martial and his celebrated epigram on the hound Lydia served as models. In Book XI, epigram 69, Lydia ennobles herself from the tomb as follows:

Amphitheatrales inter nutrita magistros
venatrix, silvis aspera, blanda domi,
Lydia dicebar, domino fidissima Dextro,
qui non Erigones mallet habere canem,
nec qui Dictaea Cephalum de gente secutus
luciferae pariter venit ad astra deae.
non me longa dies nec inutilis abstulit aetas,
qualia Dulichio fata fuere cani:
fulmineo spumantis apri sum dente perempta,
quantus erat, Calydon, aut, Erymanthe, tuus.
nec queror infernas quamvis cito rapta sub umbras.
non potui fato nobiliore mori. (286–8)

(Reared among the trainers of the amphitheatre, a hunter, savage in the woods, gentle at home, I was called Lydia, most faithful to my master Dexter, who would not have prized Erigone's hound more than me, nor the one of Dicte's breed that followed Cephalus, and with him passed to the heaven of the goddess, the Bringer of Light. Not length of years nor fruitless age carried me off, as was the fate of the Dulichian hound: I was slain by the lightning tusk of a foaming boar, huge as was thine, Calydon, or, Erymanthus, thine. Yet I murmur not, albeit swiftly hurried to the Nether Shades: I could not die by nobler death. [287–9])

Martial's ur-text dignifies and elevates the hunting dog (especially the boar tracker) to epic hero among other mythical hounds, a tradition that continues with Renaissance and baroque poets from Italy and Spain. Cristiano Spila's *Cani di pietra, l'epicedio canino nella poesia del Rinascimiento* is a collection of similar verse epitaphs written in Latin and Italian by a highly respected roster of Renaissance poets such as Gasparo Visconti, Alessandro Guarini, Andrea Navagero, Anton Francesco Grazzini, Francesco Berni, Pietro Bembo, Ludovico Ariosto, Torquatto Tasso, Gian Battista Marino, and Giusto Lipsio. Several poems in this volume ventriloquize the dogs à la Martial, elevating them to Lydia's heroic heights in a highly learned style. In the introduction to his collection, Spila characterizes these animal epitaphs as both ludic (*giocoso*) and courtly in nature, encomiastic and celebratory, and states that they also attest to the existence of a current of cynophilia in the Italian Renaissance (xi–xii).[3]

Many of the Italian poets anthologized by Spila are renowned for their burlesque verse and all were models for Spanish Renaissance and baroque poets such as Garcilaso de la Vega, Luis de Góngora, and Francisco de Quevedo. Thus Quevedo, who typically confines dogs to satire, uses them to extol the virtues – by opposition – of the ferocious and courageous boar slain in 1625 by Maria Anna of Spain, queen of Hungary and Holy Roman empress (1603–45) in the *silva* "Al jabalí que mató con una bala la serenísima infanta doña María" (To the boar that the serene princess doña María killed with a bullet).[4] The poem begins by placing the boar into a position of scornful superiority with respect to its canine hunters – large *sabuesos* and *lebreles* (scent- and sight-hounds) – thus implicitly exalting the princess even more for her prowess:

Tú, blazon de los bosques
erizada amenaza de los cerros,
temeroso escarmiento de los perros,
que con las medias lunas espumosas
de marfil belicoso y delincuente,
más corto, sí, mas no menos valiente,
su latir porfiado despreciabas[5]

(You, blazon of the forests,
bristling menace of the mountains,
fearful chastiser of hounds,
who with your foaming crescents of belligerent, delinquent ivory,
shorter but no less valiant than the moon,
scorned their obstinate baying)

In contrast to the hunting hounds who often pose with their aristocratic and royal masters in baroque portraits and are treated respectfully, even reverently, in literature, lapdogs were considered to be of less inherent worth and thus do not enjoy the same admiration in early modern Spain and its literature. The accepted tasks of toy dogs in early modern Europe, besides being companions, were bosom, hand, lap, and bed warmers; flea attractors drawing fleas away from their mistresses; watchdogs within ladies' chambers; and colourful fashion accessories. Their main occupation was to provide diversion for and company to women, whose world revolved around the home and domesticity, hence their reduced "value." As the ultimate companion animal, they had access to the innermost private rooms where, then as now, they often slept on special cushions at the foot of the bed or in the bed with their mistresses.[6] And, as Schiesari notes, these intimate recesses

Fig. 6.1. Titian's *Federico Gonzaga, I Duke of Mantua*.
Source: Wikipedia Commons.

become places of potent sensuality in which everything – including the canine companions – becomes saturated with sexuality (27). Because of this close physical proximity between lapdogs and their female owners, both are treated ambivalently in literature and art, the pet being associated with women's supposedly aberrant or at least excessive sexuality.[7]

Given this gender specificity, Henry III of France's (r. 1574–89) excessive devotion to small lapdogs was considered to be not only extravagant but also unmanly. As Kathleen Walter-Meikle describes in *Medieval Pets*, the king apparently travelled with two hundred of the thousand pet dogs he was said to possess, along with their caretakers (governesses and servants) and the packhorses used to transport them, all at enormous expense (40–1). Given the foregoing, Titian's portrait of Federico Gonzaga, I Duke of Mantua (fig. 6.1) (a known animal lover), which is housed in the Prado museum, is unusual among aristocratic portraiture, specifically because it depicts the duke caressing a small dog.[8]

In the fifteenth century, the growing popularity of toy dogs such as spaniels, Brussels and Brabantine griffons, and the Maltese and Teneriffe led to the creation of new breeds such as the Bolognese, Pomeranian, bichon frise, papillon, King Charles spaniel, and pug, among others. Dogs of all of these breeds are commonly found in Renaissance and baroque painting. Schiesari points out that Bologna emerged early on as a major breeding and trading centre for them, followed by the other classic loci of high Renaissance culture, as evidenced by the very nomenclature of the breeds: northern Italy, Flanders, the Iberian Peninsula, and eventually France and the British Isles (19).

With respect to the gender-specific sexual symbology surrounding human-canine bonds, José Manuel Pedrosa has noted that the connections between animals, sexuality, and eroticism date from very far back in time and have been expressed through deeply entrenched and enduring clichés (125). As mentioned before, the very corporality and proximity to women of toy dogs, combined with the women's devotion to them, facilitated the supposition that they also functioned as sex partners.[9] Thus, one enduring cliché is interspecies sensuality, as manifested in poetry depicting erotic relations between women and their toy dogs, the topic I explore in the following pages – that is, I examine how sexual acts between women and lapdogs are imagined and articulated in representative satirical baroque poetry.

In a related masterful study of interspecies sensuality as depicted in eighteenth-century French painting, Jennifer Milam acknowledges that the lascivious function of lapdogs in both art and literature was a familiar trope long before the French artists she studies, such as Jean-Honoré Fragonard and François Boucher, put brush to canvas (199).[10] From the fifteenth century on, in fact, dogs were depicted as stand-ins for the absent male lover in works by Jan van Eyck, Lucas Cranach, and Jan Steen, while Venetian artists such as Titian and Veronese often represented courtesans and goddesses (especially Venus), with small dogs (Milam 208n55). Probably the best-known of these works is Titian's notorious *Venus of Urbino* (fig. 6.2) (held in the Uffizi Gallery in Florence), with the enigmatic toy dog who slumbers peacefully at the edge of his (or her) mistress's bed while she reclines, naked and alone, in a highly suggestive pose.[11]

Another prominent painting by Titian, *Venus and Music* (*Venus recreándose en la Música*) (fig. 6.3) dates from ca. 1550 and is held in the Prado. In this oil, an organist's gaze is directed toward the reclinimg woman's pubic area (nothing in the painting identifies her as Venus), while she contemplates a little dog, whom she caresses lovingly. This painting has been interpreted as an encomium of marriage since the woman clearly displays a wedding band and the dog is a common symbol of marital fidelity. Nonetheless, in *Venus and Music* the lapdog's tongue does stretch playfully and provocatively toward the woman's naked breast, suggesting other meanings.

Numerous other pictorial works from the time focus suggestively on women and their lapdogs, such as Veronese's *Ritratto di dama con un cane*; Giacomo Franco's portrait of a Venetian courtesan, *Habiti delle donne venetiane*; and Polidoro da Lanciano's *Dama con cane*. Milam

Fig. 6.2. Titian's *Venus of Urbino*.
Source: Wikipedia Commons.

Fig. 6.3. Titian's *Venus and Music*.
Source: Wikipedia Commons.

suggests for a subsequent period that this tendency to focus on women (rather than humankind) in zoophilic texts and images "has something to do with reading the lapdog in the bed of the woman as a highly sexualized space of intersubjective knowing" (205). I would suggest that precisely because pet dogs were welcomed into women's enigmatic and secluded sanctuary within the home, the sexualization of that space and its inhabitants by male writers and artists is far from surprising.

Such relations are also insinuated in several early modern Spanish poems. All of them are burlesque or satirical, and none communicate any affective relationship – only a sexual one – between the human and canine protagonists. For example, Quevedo's satirical ballad "A la jineta sentada" describes a prostitute – doña Tomasa – who sits alone lamenting her lack of paying customers and resulting poverty:

A la jineta sentada
sobre un bajo taburete
...
al un lado una guitarra,
al otro lado un bufete,
con un perrillo de falda,
que la lame y no la muerde (Quevedo, no. 730, ll. 1–2 and 13–16, p. 907)

(Sitting astride
a low stool
...
on one side a guitar
on the other a desk
with a little lapdog
who licks her but doesn't bite)

Although the poet does not specify the dog's actual location, it does say that the courtesan is sitting astride a low stool with her legs raised or spread. *A la jineta* is a style of riding with short stirrups, and the term is often associated with prostitutes, who are "ridden" in that manner. Hence even in today's Cuba, prostitutes are referred to as *jineteras*. The use of the present tense is also ambiguous: is the dog performing cunnilingus here, or is that one of his general functions?

Quevedo's ballad further exemplifies the commonplace association of toy dogs with prostitution in the early modern period – thus their routine appearance in paintings of brothel scenes or courtesans. In this regard, John Caius in his 1576 treatise *Of English Dogges* specifically mentions such an association and uses suggestive language to speak about popular Maltese-type dogs as follows:[12]

> These dogs are litle, pretty, proper and fyne, and sought for to satisfie the delicatenesse of dainty dames and wanton womens wills, instruments of folly for them to play and dally withall, to tryfle away the treasure of time, to withdraw their mindes from more commendable exercises, and to content their corrupted concupiscences with vaine disport ... These puppies the smaller they be, the more pleasure they prouoke, as more meete playfellowes for minsing mistrisses to beare in their bosoms, to keep company withal in their chambers, to succour with sleepe in bed. (27)

Notable in the quotation is Caius's naturalized dismissal of female sexuality as wanton folly, a way in which to trifle away time, vain disport for mincing mistresses. The implicit contrast with the necessarily asexual and noble sporting interactions between men and hunting hounds is significant.[13]

Another example of Spanish canine zoophilia that focuses on a lapdog (in this case a metaphorical one) is an anonymous *canción* published by José L. Labrador Herraiz and Ralph A. DiFranco in their "Florilegio de poesía erótica del Siglo de Oro."

El Perrito
¿Quién compra un perrito, damas,
que es muy barato y de falda?
Es muy bonito el perrillo,
que entre las faldas se mete,
todo amigo de juguete
por ser un juguetonçillo.
Tiene el petral amarillo
con cascabeles de plata,
que es muy barato y de falda.
Da contento y quita enojos
y es blanco como la nieve,
perlas con lágrima llueve
si se alegra por los ojos.
Es de los extremos rojos,
lanudo y de cola larga,
que es muy barato y de falda.
Hace una cosa de estima
no haciendo a todas parejas,
que huye de damas viejas

y a las moçuelas se arrima.
Amigo de andar ençima
y siempre escarbar la halda,
que es muy barato de de falda.
Es manchado, rubio y zarco,
brioso con ser chiquito,
que sabe tener pinito
y nada siempre en un charco.
Y salta por cualquier arco
sin ser por el rey de Françia,
que es muy barato y de falda. (*Florilegio* 136)

(The Little Dog
Ladies, who will buy this little pup,
he is very cheap and a lapdog.

The little dog who hides under women's skirts is very cute and fond of fun because he is very playful. He wears a yellow harness with silver bells, *he is very cheap and a lapdog.*

He pleases and dispels displeasure and is as white as snow, his eyes shed pearls of happiness when he is pleased. His points are red and he is fluffy and has a long tail, *he is very cheap and a lapdog.*

He does something splendid and doesn't treat all ladies the same, because he flees from old women and cuddles up to young girls. He likes being on top and digging into skirts, *he is very cheap and a lapdog.*

He is spotted, fair and blue-eyed, spirited even though he is small, he can stand on his hind legs and always swims in a puddle. He jumps through any hoop, not only for the King of France, *he is very cheap and a lapdog.*)

Equally pertinent to my discussion are the erotic allusions that characterize the talents the toy dog exercises beneath women's skirts: he is cute (*bonito*), small, and playful, a plaything (*amigo de juguete*), a ready and willing sex partner. *Juguetón* or *Juguetonçillo* is a common erotic term for randiness; for example, in Cervantes's novella "La gitanilla," the little gypsy girl, Preciosa, reads the lieutenant's wife's palm and denounces her husband as a corrupt fornicator: "que es juguetón el tiniente / y quiere arrimar la vara" (Cervantes 48) (the lieutenant is playful / and wants to bring his staff close). The dog in the *canción* wears a yellow harness (*petral amarillo*) adorned with silver bells (*cascabeles de plata*). Bells, given their shape, often signify testicles in erotic poetry, and here we have to ask whether they are canine or human.[14]

The fact that the dog's principal talent is to please and to dispel displeasure (*Da contento y quita enojos*) is another erotic double entendre for providing sexual satisfaction, since *enojos* in erotic poetry signifies unfulfilled sexual desire. When he is pleased, the "dog's" eyes shed pearls of happiness, that is, tears ... or is it? "[P]erlas con lágrima llueve / si se alegra por los ojos" refers to the happiness of the phallus in sexual culmination and is neither a surprising nor unknown allusion to ejaculation. A similar *seguidilla* is included in *Poesía erótica del Siglo de Oro*: "Lágrimas de aljófar llora mi Pedro, / blancas como nieve aunque es moreno" (131, p. 259) (My Peter sheds tears of pearls / white as snow although he is dark skinned). The little white dog in this poem is fluffy and has a long tail ("lanudo y de cola larga"). The *cola* (or *rabo*) is a common and transparent metaphor for penis in erotic poetry, for example in the "Elogio de la cola" attributed to Diego Hurtado de Mendoza and Gutierre de Cetina.[15] Thus this strophe continues the enigma introduced by the silver bells, of what, exactly, this dog symbolizes.[16] The riddle deepens when in strophe three we find that the dog flees from old women and sidles up, or cuddles up, to (*se arrima a*) young ones. He likes to be on top and always digs into skirts ("Amigo de andar ençima / y siempre escarbar la halda").

The puzzle is resolved in the final strophe, when the little dog is described as spotted, fair, and blue-eyed ("manchado, rubio y zarco"), and sexually aroused (*brioso*). As the text explains, he knows how to stand on his hind legs ("que sabe tener pinito"; from the verb *empinarse*), another apparent symbol of an erect phallus. Are we speaking here of a dog, a lover, a phallus, or all three? A being who swims in a puddle of vaginal fluid ("nada siempre en un charco") and jumps through a hoop on command, a typical dog trick, but also a reference to a hymen ("salta por cualquier arco").

The use of the term "dog" to mean phallus and/or testicles is by no means restricted to Spanish and is also common in English. Marjorie Garber reminds us that, in the seventeenth century, "dog" could mean penis, testicle (= dogstone), or dildo, and that a popular rhythm and blues song from the 1960s, "Walking the Dog," connotes the slang term for sex (142). In a similar metaphoric vein, a dog makes an anecdotal appearance in Diego Hurtado de Mendoza's infamous "Fábula del Cangrejo" (Fable of the Crab), one of the sixteenth century's most celebrated burlesque erotic poems. In it, the dog (although an *alano*, or mastiff, rather than a lapdog) functions metaphorically for the persistent little crab (the phallus) hidden away in the woman's sex, who refuses to be extricated:

> No de otra suerte el perro ardiente y fiero
> que presa de algún toro tiene hecha,
> ni puede desasirle el carnicero,
> ni el toro con sus cuernos le desecha,

antes la vida dejará primero
que deje aquella presa y lid estrecha;
el toro brama, el amo tira en vano
y no por eso afloja el fiero alano (389)

(Just like with the ardent and fierce dog
who has gripped a bull,
the butcher cannot make him release it
nor can the bull shake him off with his horns;
the dog will give up his life
rather than release the prey and surrender the fight.
The bull roars, the owner tugs in vain
but the fierce Alano refuses to loosen his grip.)

Returning to the anonymous erotic-burlesque poem, its cleverness lies precisely in its ambiguous allusiveness and the fact that it functions on several linguistic, nominal levels: the lapdog is a phallus and the phallus is a lapdog: a small, spirited, and skilled sex toy that provides low-cost (*barato*) pleasure to women. Consequently, this verse allegory that approximates the erotic enigmas popular at the time utilizes the cliché of the intimate bond between women and lapdogs and interspecies sensuality to foreground the phallus, the only "correct" sex partner for women, in this way displacing any real dog in the poem.

Considering the contextual intricacies I have described for these written and pictorical representations, the composition that best exemplifies my discussion of the allusive representation of sexual intimacy between women and their lapdogs in baroque satirical verse is a rarely anthologized and insufficiently annotated *décima* from 1622 by Góngora, which is included in Antonio Carreira's edition of Góngora's *Antología poética*:

De un perrillo que se le murió a una dama, estando ausente su marido
Yace aquí Flor, un perrillo
que fue, en un catarro grave
de ausencia, sin ser jarabe,
lamedor de culantrillo:
saldrá un clavel a decillo
la primavera que Amor,
natural legislador,
medicinal hace ley,
si en hierba hay lengua de buey,
que la haya de perro en flor. (no. 179)

(**About a lady's little dog who died during her husband's absence**
Here lies Flor, a little dog who,
in an absence due to a cold,
although he wasn't a syrup,
was a licker of *culantrillo*.
In spring a carnation will bloom
and say that according to Love,
the natural legislator
whose medicine is law,
if there is ox-tongue on the grass again,
so there will be hound's tongue on the flower.)

Although this is recognized as one of Góngora's most daring poems, only two commentaries have been dedicated to it so far, since most critics evidently prefer to leave well enough alone and not deal with a topic as sensitive as interspecies sex, even when it is cloaked in ironic allegory and penned by one of Spain's most justly celebrated baroque lyric poets.

Although many might find the subject matter of these poems discomforting and distinctly "unpoetic," we must acknowledge that, as Midas Dekkers points out in his study *Dearest Pet: On Bestiality*, "Bestiality is omnipresent – in art, in science, in history, in our dreams – but our gaze is averted, our giggles suppressed" (5). Indeed, from classical Greece and Rome on, literature, mythology, and folklore teem with human-beast couplings, combinations, meldings, and transformations; a few examples can suffice: Leda and the swan; Pasiphae and the bull and their offspring, the Minotaur; Pan; centaurs; Titania and Bottom in *A Midsummer Night's Dream*; and even the Virgin Mary and the Heavenly Dove of the Christian psalms. These and other examples are discussed in Dekkers's first chapter, departing from his view that "[t]he high regard in which love for animals is held is matched only by the fierceness of the taboo on having sex with them" (1).

A significant difference between Góngora's poem and the previous Spanish examples I have examined is that, as a canine epitaph, his refers back to all those who preceed him, from classical Greece to Renaissance Italy and possibly the poems anthologized by Spila. Góngora's poem deals with a specific woman (fictional or otherwise) and her deceased pet dog, an animal whose very proximity, whose domesticity, whose familiarity and foreshortened ontological distance from humans make hermenutic detachment more challenging. Robert Jammes has proposed that the poem's unnamed referent – the owner of the lapdog – could be María de Hurtado, who was left alone by her husband Gabriel

Zapata, and consoled by Góngora in 1620 (266–9). Such strictly biographical conjectures, however, do not help us to interpret the poem.

Because this and similar cultural expressions eulogize man's best friend, they automatically convert women's congress with a canine into an act of intimate betrayal and displacement of the human male in affairs of the heart (and body); in this sense the dog becomes a sexual rival. Hence a topos of classical and early modern poetry is the male lover's complaint of his beloved's greater affection for her pet.[17] As mentioned before, not only does the pet dog have access to the woman's private chamber, but also to her bed and body (the erogenous zones of lap and breast), thus usurping the lover's rightful place. Nonetheless, this very domesticity and the topic's raw sensuality do not negate the erudite, aesthetic nature of Góngora's poem, in terms of its use of tropes, allegory, witticisms, wordplay, *culteranismo*, and *conceptismo*.

Carreira affirms that the poet uses allegory precisely to elegantly conceal the coarseness of the sexual theme (Góngora 629) – a common, if transparent, practice in erotic poetry and one at which Góngora is an expert.[18] In this regard, in her article that explores the diverse properties of the word *flor* in Góngora's poetry, Ly concludes that this poem "si bien es un acertado y agudo juego, atrevido, impudente y jocoso, no deja sin embargo de transfigurar la crudeza del tema sexual en logro estético por medio de la flor, literal y metafórica, que corona el diminuto edificio conceptista" (91) (even though the poem is a daring, brazen, and playful game, it still transfigures the crudeness of the sexual theme into an aesthetic achievement through the literal and metaphorical flower that crowns the diminutive conceptist structure). If one were needed, this is the rationalization for studying erotic compositions such as "Yace aquí Flor": their intrinsic value as skilful achievements within the genre of satirical poetry.

In this particular poetic game of an epitaph to a lapdog, Góngora employs puns and double entendres based on the word *flor* and other botanical and medicinal terms that contain secondary erotic signifiers whose very designation – as we have seen – indicates the animal's function as close companion and sex toy. As Garber notes in *Dog Love*, the term "lapdog" "described not only their privileged place, but sometimes their imagined function" and that "[i]t should not escape our attention that a lot of these poetic fantasies are male fantasies about the insatiable sexuality (and sexual duplicity) of women" (143).[19]

The poem's first verse, with the opening line "Yace aquí Flor, un perrillo," establishes that the poem is, first of all, an epitaph reminiscent of other burlesque epitaphs of the "Al túmulo" (to the tomb) type. These were written by Greek, Latin, Renaissance, and baroque poets such as Quevedo, and many of them begin or conclude with forms of the expression "yace aquí" (here lies). Here the term refers not only to the sepulchre but also to the poetic edifice; in other words, it is, paradoxically, in the very poem (and probably only there) that Flor exists and becomes embodied. Furthermore, the name "Flor" is neither innocent nor gratuitous. As Ly has pointed out, the allegorical veil consists of a witticism that puts into play *flor* (flower), the dog's name, as well as the *clavel* (carnation) that will sprout from the earth covering Flor's body in spring. It should be noted that the *clavel* emerges systematically in Golden Age poetry as the preferred erotic metaphor for women's sensual lips and mouth, as well as her sex.[20]

In the first four verses, a series of conceits that juxtaposes the meanings and sounds of botanics and medicinals with erotic signifiers establish Flor's function during the husband's absence due to a cold ("un catarro grave / de ausencia"), an absence that is likely performative rather than physical. In other words, Flor substitutes for a man who lacks interest or virility and whose impotence leaves an erotic space that Flor willingly fills. Double entendres, paronyms, and suggestive, witty homonyms combine semantic fields in the typical manner of erotic poetry. First the little dog is described as a "lamedor de culantrillo." A *lamedor* is an expectorant with a consistency somewhere between syrup (*jarabe*) and jam that slides slowly down the throat to the chest. *Culantrillo* is the common Venus maidenhair fern (*Adiantum capillus-veneris*) from which the *lamedor* is made. This medicinal's appearance, as with any dense, curly plant, combined with its soil and moisture preferences – it grows in warm, moist environments – also suggests pubic hair (*capillus veneris*) and what this conceals.[21] At the same time, *culantrillo* is a highly suggestive paronym of *culo* or anus (and often vagina) and the root of *lamedor* is the verb *lamer* (to lick). This lexicon combined with the plant's botanical name *capillus-veneris*, leaves no doubt regarding Flor's utility as sexual consolation.

The final six verses of this compact poem jump from Flor's death to the future, when the *clavel* will bloom once again and *Amor* (Love), the natural legislator whose medicine is law, will dictate that if *lengua de buey* (*Buglossa*, ox-tongue) will grow in the grass again, so there will be *lengua de perro en flor* (*Cynoglossum*, hound's tongue, a type of comfrey). In other words, as Poggi (198) explains, it is natural that if oxen lick grass as they graze (and *buey* also alludes to the absent husband), then there will be hound's tongue (both the botanic and the literal lapdog's tongue) on the flower (both literally and figuratively, pubis). Clearly, this complex allegory sidesteps any explicit mention of interspecies sex. Instead, it alludes to it through the type of intricately constructed framework of linguistic levels and semantic fields based on puns and witticisms that typifies

Góngora's mature work. Flor is simultaneously a flower, a lapdog, a pubis, and, above all else, an astonishing poetic edifice that illustrates how a brilliant poet can transform a cliché into a diminutive work of art.

My particular exploration into poetic representations of sexual intimacy between women and lapdogs reveals a set of telling underlying assumptions, one of which is that women's relationships with their pets are put to literary use by sexualizing them. Another one is that the bonds between women and their pets in the seventeenth century are based on love and companionship, just as they are in the twenty-first. In this regard, in her philosophical exploration of the implosion of nature and culture, *The Companion Species Manifesto*, Donna Haraway notes regarding our relationships with dogs that "*we are, constitutively, companion species. We make each other up, in the flesh. Significantly other to each other, in specific difference, we signify in the flesh a nasty developmental infection called love. This love is an historical aberration and a natural cultural legacy*" (2–3; emphasis in original).

To conclude, these early modern Spanish texts and others like them enhance the ability to apply recent findings from the fields of gender, sexuality, animal, and cultural studies to a unique set of erotic images to whose complexities the term "bestiality" cannot do full justice. Moreover, although Haraway writes about an economy of affection in which the dog relies upon the its engagement with humans, literature can reveal how humans rely on the affection of dogs, even when done satirically, as in the poems examined here. The enigmatic scene depicted in *Venus and Music* can reveal the rationale for sexualizing women and beasts: a beautiful nude interacts with her little canine companion, seemingly unaware of or uninterested in the male creator while he – musician, poet, or artist – gazes on for stimulation and inspiration.

NOTES

1 In the recent past, the term "pet," designating domestic animals who share our homes and whose primary role is not utilitarian, such as guarding or vermin control, has fallen into political disfavour in some animal studies circles. In this essay, I use the term interchangeably with "companion" to refer to those non-human animals who are highly regarded as friends or family, whether today or in early modern Europe.

2 See the letter in Petrarch, *Selected Sonnets* (127–30); it is excerpted in Arbel (66).

3 I thank my colleague Jesús Ponce Cárdenas for bringing this book to my attention. I have been unable to consult M. Fava's 1969 study, "I cagnolini nell'epigrammatario colocciano." Nonetheless, in a note, Spila

acknowledges that Fava speaks of a "'curiosa corrente cinofila' caratterizzata da un lato 'humoristico e leggermente sdolcinato'" (a curious cynophilic current characterized by a humorous and slightly corny side [xxv n2]).

4 All translations from the original Spanish into English are my own; in translating I have tried to convey the meaning, rather than the style, of the original.

5 Quevedo, *Poesía original completa*, no. 204, ll. 1–7, p. 218.

6 But human nature always interfered, and this bed-sharing could lead to tragic misunderstandings in thirteenth-century *exempla* that relate tales of mistaken identity in which knights kill their wives or mistresses when they see shapes (which turn out to be dogs) under the sheets with them (Walter-Meikle 60).

7 Giulia Poggi writes about how the change in focus from the dog's courage and strength to its affective relations with the female owner follows on the change in perspective from the public to the private sphere, a development that refers back to classical epicedic poetry on one hand and Latin elegiac poetry on the other (192).

8 See the discussion and reproductions of Velázquez's portraits of aristocrats with their hounds in my "Zoopoética quijotesca," 449–51. Small fluffy pet spaniels are also commonly portrayed in baroque portraiture, although practically always in scenes of domestic life in palaces or stately homes, along with women and children.

9 Pedrosa quotes some *seguidillas* that insist on women's preference for toy dogs, while men prefer cats because that animal is identified with the female sex organ: "De perrillos de falda / gustan las damas, / yo de gatos rellenos / dentro del arca" (While ladies fancy lapdogs, I enjoy pussies stuffed in a vault [131]).

10 Milam's article includes provocative zoophilic illustrations, including Fragonard's *Young Girl in Her Bed, Making Her Dog Dance* and *Young Girl with Puppies*, as well as Boucher's intensely erotic depiction *Leda and the Swan*.

11 Schiesari analyses this painting in her psychoanalytic reading of the relationship between pet ownership and female sexuality as an example of the sexually charged underpinnings of the domestic sphere and as an illustration of how toy dogs came to be linked not only with courtly and affluent women of high social standing but also with women of ill repute, as shown by countless paintings of naked courtesans with their lapdog (28).

12 According to Schiesari (27), Caius's treatise was written for inclusion by Conrad Gesner in the first volume of his *Historiae animalium* (1551) and subsequently appeared in Topsell's abridged translation of Gesner's *The Historie of Foure-Footed Beastes* (1607).

13 It should be acknowledged, however, that the Kinsey Reports from the twentieth century reveal that the dog was a more popular partner for

women than men who engaged in a variety of zoophilic acts (Garber 151), which suggests that these cultural manifestations of bestiality can reflect reality to some degree, and within that framework can be "sexy." Thus, in the last century, Rafael Alberti's sonnet "Rubios, pulidos senos de Amaranta, / por una lengua de lebrel limados" (*Cal y canto*) (Amaranta's pale, polished breasts / burnished by a greyhound's tongue) could hardly surprise readers.

14 See Kornelis Visscher's sketch (ca. 1650) of a "butterfly dog" (papillon) wearing a belled collar in Bradshaw (47). Although bells were perhaps a useful and popular adornment for dog collars and harnesses at the time, this does not belie their erotic connotations. See examples of *cascabeles* meaning testes in Labrador Herraiz and DiFranco; as a corollary, *sin cascabeles* is used to signify eunuchs.

15 See the explanation of this encomium of the *cola* in Díez Fernández, 310–12 and in general the entire chapter on burlesque poetry in praise of the phallus.

16 See discussion of the multivalent signifiers of *rabo* and *cola* in my *An Erotic Philology of Golden Age Spain*, 44–73; examples in *Poesía erótica del Siglo de Oro*, and especially Díez Fernández 310–12.

17 See, for example, Sir Philip Sidney's sonnet 59 from the *Astrophel and Stella* sequence (1581–3), which describes the poet's sexual envy for his lady's dog because of its place in her lap (Garber 143). See other examples in Poggi, particularly Marino's sonnet "Al cagnolino della sua donna" (To his lady's little dog): "Ond'è che, del mio ben fatto beato, / invido can, nemico a' desir miei, / volgi con occhi a me sì torvi e rei, / qual geloso custode, il dente irato?" (Against whom, creature of my beloved / invidious canine, enemy of my desires, / do you direct with such a livid and threatening glance, / like a jealous guard, your irate fang? [194]).

18 In his edition, Carreira includes two other *décimas* with a similar sexual content, "Con Marfisa en la estocada" and "Casado el otro se halla." Poggi notes that "se trata en efecto de un *microcorpus* que...se caracteriza por dos elementos solo aparentemente en contradicción: un mensaje acentuadamente obsceno, por un lado y, por otro, su enunciación a través de un estilo refinado" (in effect we are dealing with a microcorpus characterized by two elements that are contradictory only in appearance: a decidedly obscene message on one hand, and on the other its enunciation in a refined style [109]).

19 While examining how the sexual involvement of humans and animals is represented in art and popular culture (with a wealth of illustrations), in chapter 8 of *Dearest Pet*, Dekkers includes data from the Kinsey Reports and European court proceedings that reveal that interspecies sexuality involving women and dogs is not always just a male fantasy. See also the chapter "Sex and the Single Dog" in Garber.

20 See discussion of *flor* and *clavel* in chapter 2, "La abeja y la flor: Paradigma para un pequeño escorzo" of Ponce Cárdenas's *El tapiz narrativo del Polifemo* and Alonso, "El clavel como motivo poético."

21 It is used in this sense in the anonymous *letra* " – Perejil y culantro seco. / –Dóminos teco" (Labrador Herraiz and DiFranco, 138–41).

REFERENCES

Alberti, Rafael. *Cal y canto.* Madrid: Alianza, 1926–7.

Alonso Miguel, Álvaro. "El clavel como motivo poético." In *I canzonieri di Lucrezia: Los cancioneros de Lucrecia. Atti del convegno internazionale sulle raccolte poetiche iberiche dei secoli XV–XVII,* edited by Andrea Baldissera and Giuseppe Mazzocchi, 193–205. Padua: Unipress, 2005.

Arbel, Benjamin. "The Renaissance Transformation of Animal Meaning: From Petrarch to Montaigne." In *Making Animal Meaning,* edited by Linda Kalof and Georgina M. Montgomery, 59–80. East Lansing: Michigan State University Press, 2011.

Bradshaw, John. *The Animals among Us: The New Science of Anthrozoology.* London: Penguin Random House, 2017.

Caius, John. *Of English Dogges, the Diversities, the Names, the Natures and the Properties.* Translated from Latin by Abraham Fleming. London, 1576.

Cervantes, Miguel de. *Novelas ejemplares.* Edited by Jorge García López. Barcelona: Cátedra, 2001.

Dekkers, Midas. *Dearest Pet: On Bestiality.* Translated by Paul Vincent. London: Verso, 1994.

Díez Fernández, J. Ignacio. *La poesía erótica de los Siglos de Oro.* Madrid: Laberinto, 2003.

Fava, M. "I cagnolini nell'epigrammatario colocciano." In *Atti del Convegno di Studi su Angelo Colocci* (Jesi, 13–14 settembre 1969), 231–42. Città di Castello: Amministrazione Comunale di Jesi, 1972.

Garber, Marjorie. *Dog Love.* New York: Touchstone, 1997.

Góngora, Luis de. *Antología poética.* Edited by Antonio Carreira. Barcelona: Crítica, 2009.

Haraway, Donna. *The Companion Species Manifesto: Dogs, People and Significant Otherness.* Chicago: Prickly Paradigm Press, 2003.

Hurtado de Mendoza, Diego. *Poesía completa.* Edited by J. Ignacio Díez Fernández. Seville: Fundación José Manuel Lara, 2007.

Jammes, Robert. *La obra poética de Luis de Góngora.* Translated by Manuel Moya. Madrid: Castalia, 1987.

Labrador Herraiz, José J., and Ralph A. DiFranco, eds. *Florilegio de poesía erótica del siglo de oro. Calíope* 12, no. 2 (2006): 119–67.

Ly, Nadine. "Entre flor y flor (De unas propiedades de la palabra *flor* en la poesía de Góngora." *Creneida* 1 (2013): 81–133.
Martial. *Epigrams*. Translated by Walter C.A. Ker. Vol. 2. London: Heinemann; Cambridge, MA: Harvard University Press, 1968.
Martín, Adrienne L. *An Erotic Philology of Golden Age Spain*. Nashville, TN: Vanderbilt University Press, 2008.
– "Zoopoética quijotesca: Cervantes y los Estudios de Animales." *eHumanista/Cervantes* 1 (2012): 448–64.
Milam, Jennifer. "Rococo Representations of Interspecies Sensuality and the Pursuit of *Volupté*." *Art Bulletin* 97, no. 2 (June 2015): 192–209. Published online 26 May 2015.
Pedrosa, José Manuel. *Bestiario: Antropología y simbolismo animal*. Madrid: Medusa, 2002.
Petrarch. *Selected Sonnets, Odes and Letters*. Edited by Thomas G. Bergin. New York: Appleton-Century-Crofts, 1966.
Poesía erótica del Siglo de Oro. Edited by Pierre Alzieu, Robert Jammes, and Yvan Lissorgues. Barcelona: Crítica, 1984.
Poggi, Giulia. "Entre eros y botánica (la décima 'Yace aquí Flor, un perrillo')." In *Góngora y el epigrama: Estudios sobre las décimas*, edited by Juan Matas Caballero, José María Micó, and Jesús Ponce Cárdenas, 189–205. Pamplona: Universidad de Navarra; Iberoamericana/Vervuert, 2013.
Ponce Cárdenas, Jesús. *El tapiz narrativo del Polifemo: Eros y elipsis*. Barcelona: Universitat Pompeu Fabra, 2010.
Quevedo, Francisco de. *Poesía original completa*. Edited by José Manuel Blecua. Barcelona: Planeta, 1990.
Schiesari, Juliana. *Beasts and Beauties: Animals, Gender, and Domestication in the Italian Renaissance*. Toronto: University of Toronto Press, 2010.
Spila, Cristiano. *Cani di pietra: L'epicedio canino nella poesia del Rinascimento*. Edited by Cristiano Spila. Translated by Maria Gabriella Critelli. Rome: Quiritta, 2002.
Walter-Meikle, Kathleen. *Medieval Pets*. Woodbridge, UK: Boydell Press, 2012.

Chapter Seven

Sexual Deviance and Morisco Marginality in Cervantes's *The Trials of Persiles and Sigismunda*

CHRISTINA LEE

I'm telling you, my clever barbarian, that persecution in Spain by those known as Inquisitors tore me from my homeland, for when one is forced to leave it, one doesn't simply leave but feels torn away.

Dígote, en fin, bárbaro discreto, que la persecución de los que llaman inquisidores en España, me arrancó de mi patria; que, cuando se sale por fuerza della, antes se puede llamar arrancada que salida.

– Miguel de Cervantes, *The Trials of Persiles and Sigismunda*[1]

Cervantes's fictionalization of the Morisco problem in *Don Quijote de la Mancha* and in *The Trials of Persiles and Sigismunda* shows a profound understanding of the fact that Moriscos were faced with a dire predicament, regardless of the sincerity of their faith. From 1609 through 1614, Philip III passed a series of expulsion edicts against all the Moriscos in the Spanish kingdoms. In his first edict targeting the Moriscos in Valencia, he declared: "I have been convinced that I punish them by taking hold of their lives and property without any scruples, because they have proven with their crimes to be heretic apostates and guilty of high treason" ([a]ssigurandome que podia sin ningun escrupulo castigarlos en las vidas y haziendas, porque la continuacion de sus delitos los tenia conuencidos de hereges apostatas, y proditores de lesa Magestad diuina y humana) (qtd. in García-Arenal 252). There was an effort to save "good" Christians from banishment, but, due to the large number of people claiming to fit under that category, Crown officials decided in 1611 that all Moriscos had to be expelled.[2]

An abundant number of studies speak to Cervantes's criticism of the implications of the expulsion decree for even the most exemplary Moriscos.[3] Although the loyalty of the character of Ricote in *Don Quijote* continues to be a subject of heated debate, there is general agreement in scholarship that Cervantes positions Ricote's daughter, Ana Félix, and Rafala and her uncle Jarife from *The Trials of Persiles and Sigismunda* as blameless victims of the Crown's draconian policy regarding its Morisco subjects. Criticism has concurred, more vehemently, on Cervantes's hostile treatment of the Morisca Cenotia, from *The Trials of Persiles and Sigismunda*, and her deserved demise. That Cenotia is as unidimensional as Cervantine characters could be is evident. And readers could be quite dismayed at her open and unabashed perversity. The aging Cenotia is indeed presented consistently in the novel as the embodiment of religious and sexual deviance. Yet, while studies on Ana Félix and Rafala have been generally linked to the context of the expulsion, I am not aware of any work that has explicitly connected the development of Cenotia's character to her experiences as a Morisca in Spain.[4] I propose that a sustained analysis of her sexual deviance and its connection to her subaltern status as a Morisca in Spain can shed light on her curious behaviour.[5] More specifically, I argue that Cenotia's obsessive fascination with the adolescent Antonio might be read as a metonymical gesture that seeks to counter her rejection from the Spanish body politic.[6]

Cenotia's episode takes place in the second book of *The Trials of Persiles and Sigismunda* (chapters 8–17). A group of pilgrims – Auristela, Periandro, Rutilio, the satirist Clodio, the elder Antonio, the Barbarian Ricla, and their children (and namesakes) Antonio and Ricla – arrives on an island ruled by King Policarpo. Policarpo's closest adviser is Cenotia, a self-proclaimed magician of advanced age and of Spanish Moorish origins. Readers first encounter Cenotia as she irrupts into the bedchamber of the young Antonio and offers herself to the teenager as his love slave. When Cenotia attempts to embrace him, the young Antonio is so frightened that he shoots her with his arrow, which accidently kills Clodio instead. The Morisca continues to pursue her sexual interest by trying to apply a poison that nearly kills him and then by planning the kidnapping of the boy. As the plan for the abduction of the boy (and of Auristela, of whom Policarpo is enamored) goes awry, the inhabitants of the island depose Policarpo and hang Cenotia from a pole. The pilgrims (now reunited with Mauricio, Transila, and Ladislao) escape unscathed on a ship and continue their journey.

The Morisca Cenotia's most problematic quality, perhaps, is her intense desire to transgress her "natural" limitations and her refusal to conform to the social expectations associated with her ethnicity in Spain.[7] Her overreaching tendencies are reflected immediately in her physical appearance. She attempts to fashion herself as a young woman, something that the narrator derides. She is a woman that "seemed about forty years old, though her energy and grace probably hid ten more. She wasn't dressed in the style of that country but rather after the Spanish fashion" (*Trials* II.8: 137) (de hasta cuarenta años de edad, que, con el brío y donaire, debía de encubrir otros diez, vestida, no al uso de aquella tierra, sino al de España [*Los trabajos* II.8: 329]). She also overreaches in her proud assertion of Moorish heritage. José-Ignacio Díez Fernández and Luisa Fernanda Aguirre de Cárcer have insightfully pointed out that Cenotia refers to herself as a Spaniard of Agarene lineage and not as a Morisca.[8] The use of the euphemism "Agarene" – literally, a descendant of Hagar – reflects a contrived effort on the part of the Morisca to be associated with the nobler Iberian Muslims of the pre-Reconquest (detached from *limpieza de sangre*) rather than with the vanquished and debased Moriscos of her time. It reflects a desire to produce a discourse of selfhood that opposes the marginalizing one that was imposed on her in Spain.

Cenotia, furthermore, overreaches when she claims to possess supernatural powers. She presents herself as an enchantress of a renowned lineage of magicians and insists on not being confused with a lowly sorcerer. "You should know," she tells Antonio, that:

> [I]n the city of Alhama there has always been a certain woman with my name, who along with the name Cenotia inherits the knowledge teaching us not to be witches, as some people call us, but enchantresses or sorcerers – words that describe us more accurately ... [W]e, who are known as sorcerers and enchantresses, are people of distinction; we deal with the stars, we contemplate the motion of the heavens, we know the power of herbs, of plants, or stones, of words, and by the joining of the active to the passive we seem to perform miracles. We dare things so wondrous that they astonish people. (*Trials* II.8: 138–9)

> ([E]n aquella ciudad de Alhama siempre ha habido alguna mujer de mi nombre, la cual, con el apellido de Cenotia, hereda esta ciencia, que no nos enseña a ser hechiceras, como algunos nos llaman, sino a ser encantadoras y magas, nombres que nos vienen más al propio ... [L]as que tenemos nombre de magas y de encantadoras, somos gente de mayor cuantía; tratamos con las estrellas, contemplamos el movimiento de los cielos, sabemos la virtud de las yerbas, de las plantas, de las piedras, de las palabras, y, juntando lo activo a lo pasivo, parece que hacemos milagros, y nos atrevemos a hacer cosas tan estupendas que causan admiración a las gentes. [*Los trabajos* II.8: 331])

Cenotia's self-aggrandizing description comes to a head with the figure readers actually see in the text. She accomplishes nothing that could be described as supernatural.

Cenotia is, in essence, neither enchantress nor magician, not even a "lowly" sorcerer, as the elder Antonio and the narrator would have it (*Los trabajos* II.8: 338 and 395). She is simply an isolated aging woman who has been uprooted forcefully from Granada due to her Moorish ancestry and heterodox cultural practices, and who seeks to sustain herself on Policarpo's island by pursuing the magic arts she deems to run in her lineage. On the island, freed from the persecution of Spanish authorities, she deceives herself and Policarpo into believing that she has unencumbered access to her inherited powers. She asserts that she can read the stars, contemplate the motions of the heavens, and manipulate otherwise ordinary substances for the purpose of seemingly changing the course of nature.But her only viable expertise proves to be the concoction of poison, which, if we were to follow the definition in the *Diccionario de Autoridades* does not even qualify as an *hechizo* (sorcery).

Hechizo is defined in *Autoridades* as "a spell performed by magic or charm" (encanto, maleficio que se hace a alguno, por arte mágica or por sortilegio), and it does not include the use of poison. As an example, it quotes from Inca Garcilaso's usage of the term, "they cast spells that had the same effects as poison" (hacían con los hechizos los mismos efectos que con el veneno).[9] In effect, Díez Fernández and Aguirre de Cárcer show that Cenotia's expertise lies in medicine practices commonly used in Morisco communities (52–3). Policarpo, however, takes her at face value, as he is devoid of a critical capacity to evaluate the individuals he meets. The narrator ridicules his gullibility when he mentions the king's lack of questioning of Cenotia's actions. His comment that "Policarpo believed her as though her words had been spoken by an oracle" (*Trials* II.9: 142) (Creyóla Policarpo como se se lo dijera un oráculo [*Los trabajos* II.9: 338]) is manifestly uttered tongue-in-cheek. Cenotia's self-aggrandizing behaviour leads to her downfall, which begins in Spain and ends on Policarpo's island. The image we see of her prior to her execution is of literal physical diminishment: "gnawing on her hands, cursing her deceitful science and the promises of her damned teachers" (*Trials* II.17: 176) (mordíase las manos Cenotia y maldecía su engañadora ciencia y las promesas de sus malditos maestros [*Los trabajos* II.17: 394]).

Cenotia's sexual longing for the young Antonio might be interpreted as a depraved manifestation of her overreaching tendencies and of her urge to subvert dominant ethnic and gender hierarchies.[10] Her desire may be read as an expression of her fantasy to be welcomed by the body of the Spanish male who, like herself, embodies cultural hybridity, but who, unlike her, is allowed to pass on to dominant spheres of Christian society. Antonio may be identified as an allegory for Spain, as Rachel

Schmidt perceptively noted. His mixed heritage – half Barbarian, half Spanish – and his characteristic bow and arrows evoke the zodiac sign of Sagittarius, which was a figure widely used in anti-Morisco official discourses to represent Spain (31–2). Grace Magnier reminds us, for instance, that Pedro Aznar Cardona, in his explanation of the divinely predetermined expulsion of Moriscos writes, "in my judgment, our sovereign God himself, in his sacred scripture, promises his most Christian majesty and his Sagittarians, that is, we Spaniards, the glory of this much-desire victory of victories, with the acquisition of all the riches, prosperity, honours, assets, positions, kingdoms and provinces possessed by tyrants and barbarian kings" (qtd. in Magnier, 131) (a mi juycio, el mismo soberano Dios en su escriptura santa, promete a la christiandad de su magestad con sus sagitarios, que somos los españoles, la gloria desta tan desseada victoria de victorias, con adquisione de todas las riquezas, prosperidades, honras, patrimonios, dignidades, reynos y prouincias poseydos de tyranos y reyes barbarous [Aznar Cardona, 144r–5r]). Marcos de Guadalajara, in another retrospective interpretation of the expulsion, references the work by a supposed Muslim astrologer and pronounces: "The crocodiles of the Nile will die; and the Sagittarians are stronger than the Elephants ... Cry Hagar and weep Nile, because you will not see the millennium end. This is the payment for your cruelties and the reward for your sodomies ... I already hear the trumpets of the Sagittarians (this is of the Spaniards, who are under the sign of Sagittarius)" (qtd. in Magnier, 133) ([Y] morirán los Cocodrilos del Nilo: y son más fuertes los Sagitarios que los Elephantes ... Llora Agar, y lamenta Nilo, que no veras cumplido el milenario. Este es el pago de tus crueldades, y el premio de tus Sodomias ... Ya me parece que siento las trompetas de los Sagitarios (esto es los Españoles, a quien predomina el signo de Sagitario) [Guadalajara, 161v–2r]). It is fitting that Sagittarius was iconographically depicted as an archer with the upper body of a male human and with the lower body of a horse (Schmidt 27). Schmidt has also shown that the young Antonio's personality fits the astrologer Jerónimo Cortés's description of males born under the sign of Sagittarius. In the most widely read work of Spanish astrology, *Lunario y pronostico perpetuo* (Lunary and Perpetual Prediction) (1594), Cortés deems Sagittarians to be "shy, affable, honest, and adventurous" as well as "inclined to journey by sea" (Schmidt 20).[11] The young Antonio, nonetheless, does not represent an outright "vision of the monster that is Spain" (una visión del monstruo que es España) (qtd. in Schmidt 32).

For Cenotia, the young Antonio's initial demeanour toward her, courteous and unsuspecting, represents her ideal Spaniard, someone who has not yet been corrupted by culturally constructed prejudices. Unlike his Spanish father, he has not been trained in classifying Spaniards according to their social standing and has yet to learn what Michael Armstrong-Roche calls "the religion of honour."[12] Let us remember that his father was forced to leave his hometown in Spain because he injured another man for refusing to address him with the honorific "vuesa merced." It is, however, ironic that the resentful Cenotia, just like the Spaniards who had persecuted her, is unwilling to see beyond the stereotype of the Spaniard in the character of the elder Antonio and perceive his desire to overcome the hubris and violent tendencies that precipitated his past downfall.[13]

The autobiography Cenotia narrates prior to thrusting herself onto the young Antonio serves as a compelling case in point that illustrates her anguish at having been forcefully ejected from her community. It is the story of a social misfit who was forced into exile from her homeland in order to avoid death or, even worse, unbearable humiliation by unjust Spaniards who persecuted her and whom she associates with savage dogs:

> I'm telling you, my clever barbarian, that persecution in Spain by those known as Inquisitors tore me from my homeland, for when one is forced to leave it, one doesn't simply leave but feels torn away. I came to this land by strange roundabout ways, through countless dangers, and since I almost always felt as if they were nearby I kept turning my head around, thinking those dogs – which I fear to these days – were nipping at my skirt. (*Trials* II.8: 139)
>
> (Dígote ... bárbaro discreto, que la persecución de los que llaman inquisidores en España me arrancó de mi patria; que, cuando se sale por fuerza della, antes se puede llamar arrancada que salida. Vine a esta isla por estraños rodeos, por infinitos peligros, casi siempre como si estuvieran cerca, volviendo la cabeza atrás, pensando que me mordían las faldas los perros, que aun hasta aquí temo. [*Los trabajos* II.8: 332])[14]

It is significant that, given her personal history, Cenotia appears on the island of Policarpo dressed "not in the fashion of that land, but rather in the Spanish way" (no al uso de aquella tierra, sino al de España).[15] We could read this move as her response to the Inquisition authorities' attempt to symbolically disrobe her (by extension, robe her in a *sambenito* garment). It reflects her profound desire to physically look like a dominant Spaniard, even if the latter had rejected her.

Cenotia reassures the young Antonio that she is far from the dehumanized subject depicted in anti-Morisco discourses. She is not "a monster" but rather a person who shares his cultural heritage, as she speaks the same language he does.[16] For Cenotia, the young Antonio functions as a kind of potential antidote to her traumatic experience of rejection. This becomes evident when she tells him that she has been merely surviving dispassionately in Policarpo's island, "not seeking any further pleasure, nor would I have sought any now had my fortune, good or bad, not brought you to this land, for it's in your hands to give me whatever fate you may wish" (*Trials* II.8: 139) (sin procurar otro algún deleite, ni le procurara si mi buena o mala fortuna no te hubieran traído a esta tierra, que en tu mano está darme la suerte que quisieres [*Los trabajos* II.8: 333]). The opportunity (*suerte*) to be loved, however, must come voluntarily, because, as Cenotia had stated earlier, desire cannot be manipulated. The antidote to her marginality, Cenotia implies, can be effective if she is erotically desired by the uncorrupted Antonio out of his own free will.[17]

It is possible to further unravel the hidden script in Cenotia's longing for the young Antonio – without downplaying her perversity – by considering how terrified she is of his father, who serves as a foil to his unprejudiced and ingenuous son. While Cenotia sees the young Antonio as representing a potentially tolerant version of the figure of the Spaniard, she perceives the father as the stereotype of the honour-obsessed and anti-Morisco dominant male. Cenotia recoils when the elder Antonio launches at her, dagger in hand, "full of Spanish fury and blind rage" (*Trials* II.11: 150) (con cólera española, y discurso ciego [*Los trabajos* II.11: 352]), possibly because it triggers memories of cruel treatment by men who resembled him physically and spoke with the same violence. It is particularly revealing that, even though it is the young Antonio who aims his arrow at Cenotia, it is his father who becomes the primary bearer of her desire for retaliation. Cenotia might be appropriating the dominant notion of contamination when she suggests that young Antonio's heritage is problematic, just as hers is problematic in the Spanish context. She poisons the young Antonio, but with the goal of weakening him mentally and physically, not with the intention of killing him.[18] The narrator tells us that Cenotia "removed from a door hinge all the spells she'd prepared to consume bit by bit the life of the cruel youth that had conquered her with the magic of his grace and charm" (*Trials* II.11: 151) (sacó del quicio de una puerta los hechizos que había preparado para consumir la vida poco a poco del riguroso mozo que con los de su donaire y gentileza la tenía rendida [*Los trabajos* II.11: 353]). I interpret "consume" (*consumir*) in this context to mean wear down (*gastar*) and not extinguish (*extinguir*).[19]

Readers might recall, in addition, that when Policarpo asks Cenotia to save the young Antonio, she assures him that he would not die from the illness.[20] Cenotia's retort to the elder Antonio's demand for his son's health first addresses the young Antonio's scorn toward her, but her subsequent statement is incongruous with the son's behaviour. She tells the father: "Advise him to act in the future with more humane compassion for those who surrender to him and not to show contempt for those who beg him for mercy" (*Trials* II.11: 150–1) (aconséjale que se humane de aquí adelante con los rendidos y no menosprecie a los que piedad le pidieren [*Los trabajos* II.11: 353]). These words are not directed specifically to the young Antonio, who continues to be the object of Cenotia's affection.[21] Rather, they are directed at the father and the persecutory authorities he represents in his fury. They evoke the excessive punishments even the most unthreatening Moriscos had to endure, such as the forceful relocation of Granadan Moriscos in the aftermath of the Alpujarras revolts of 1569–71 and the mass expulsion of all Moriscos.

Cenotia's justification for abducting Antonio (and Auristela) borrows from the rhetoric utilized by expulsion apologists. She states, "The offenses committed by a man in love to satisfy his desires aren't really offenses, because the desires aren't his, nor is he the one who commits them, since it's love that really commands his will" (*Trials* II.13: 159) (Las culpas que comete el enamorado en razón de cumplir su deseo no lo son, en razón de que no es suyo, ni es él el que las comete, sino el amor, que manda su voluntad [*Los trabajos* II.13: 365]). Cenotia and Policarpo's purported god, Eros, may be analogized to the Christian god to whom the demise of the Moorish Spaniards was attributed. Cenotia evokes the primary justification for the expulsion by the leading expulsion apologists Marcos de Guadalajara, Pedro Aznar Cardona, and Damián Fonseca who published their works during Cervantes's lifetime. Their discourses repeatedly emphasize that the suffering of the Morisco people at the hands of Christians should not be questioned because such was the will of God.[22] Cenotia's attempt to abduct Antonio may be further read as a form of retaliation against the specter of the anti-Morisco Spanish official she projects onto Antonio's father. It could be interpreted as Cenotia's way of avenging the Spanish Crown's scheme for breaking up families and abducting the young children of banished Moriscos during the expulsion.

The Crown's initial plan for the expulsion was to keep young Morisco children in Spain under the care of Christian families and priests.[23] Georgina Dopico-Black found an unpublished letter that Philip III sent in 1609 to the archbishop of Valencia, Juan de Ribera, with orders detailing the procedure for taking children younger than ten years old away from their banished parents for the purpose of proselytism. The letter mandates that these children be assigned (*encomendados*) to priests or other trustworthy people; it dictates that, if the parents show "repugnance" (*repugnancia*) at the idea of being separated from children who are older than five, expulsion ministers "behead" (*degollar*) the parents; it finally rules that children who show repugnance at the idea of being separated from their parents be imprisoned until the expulsion of their parents is fulfilled (Dopico Black 93). Some dominant Spaniards seem to have taken the responsibility of removing Morisco children from their parents into their own hands. In his account of the expulsion in Valencia, Fonseca speaks of noblewomen, such as Isabel de Velasco, who snatched young children from their Morisco parents for the purpose of converting them and raising them in servitude for the sake of the Catholic religion (Fonseca, 233). While Fonseca portrays Velasco in a heroic light for her initiative to rescue the souls of Morisco children, Cervantes interrogates such zealotry. Is not Velasco's conversion scheme analogous to Cenotia's plan to "convert" the teenage Antonio to her personal depraved variant of Eros worship? It is quite feasible that, in drawing attention to Cenotia's extreme measures to satisfy her sexual craving for Antonio, Cervantes encourages us to problematize religious discourses that advocate the devastation of the family unit for the sake of religious conversion.

Moriscos were blamed because of their unwillingness to truly convert to Catholicism by completely abandoning the cultural practices dominant Spaniards consider to be non-Christian. For the large majority of Moriscos, it was not feasible to suddenly forget their dialects, to abandon the way in which they celebrated births or honoured their dead, to silence the music that played in their minds, or to give up their dietary habits. And even the Moriscos who did manage to disengage themselves from their inherited culture continued to be ostracized, as seen in the fictionalized cases of Ana Félix and Rafala. Both of these exemplary Cervantine women publicly disavow their cultural differences and uproot themselves from their lineages. Ana Félix never acknowledges her father, Ricote, even after he risks his life to save hers, and Rafala denounces hers to the Christian pilgrims.

Cenotia is the antithesis of these self-sacrificing and virginal Moorish women we see in Ana Félix and Rafala. She is the ostensible heretic, the sexual predator.[24] While her Moorish counterparts respond to social stigmatization by striving to be the best, the most exemplary of their kind, she strives to be the worst. Cenotia's execution thus could be justified, but the uncertainty of the futures of Ana Félix and Rafala in spite of their sacrifices is unsettling. I suggest that by reading these cases of humanized and dehumanized Moriscas in juxtaposition, we might be able to better appreciate Cervantes's representation of the complexity of the Morisco condition and his criticism of the Crown's devastating policies for all Spaniards.

NOTES

1 I use Carlos Romero Muñoz's edition of *Los trabajos de Persiles y Sigismunda*, and Celia Richmond Weller and Clark A. Colahan's translation of *The Trials of the Persiles and Sigismunda*.

2 Lee discusses he Morisco expulsion in *The Anxiety of Sameness*, 153–68. The Moriscos of Murcia, most of whom were descendants of *mudéjares* who had lived peacefully in the region since the thirteenth century, were exempt from the order of expulsion until the end of 1613 (Lea 356). The order also made exceptions for Morisco priests, monks, nuns, and the Morisco wives of Old Christians and their children (Lea 352).

3 There are too many relevant studies, but the following are among the ones that have been referred to frequently in the past thirty years: Francisco Márquez Villanueva, *Personajes y temas del Quijote* and *El problema morisco desde otras laderas*; Stanislav Zimic, "El drama de Ricote el morisco"; René Querillac, "Los moriscos de Cervantes"; Julio Baena, "Sintaxis de la ética del texto"; Michael Gerli, *Refiguring Authority*, 40–60; and William Childers, *Transnational Cervantes*, 171–93. I have also discussed the subject in *The Anxiety of Sameness*, 199–207, and "Don Antonio Moreno y el 'Discreto' negocio de los moriscos ricote y Ana Félix."

4 Although Barbara Fuchs does not investigate Cenotia's connection to her history in Spain, she does point out that Cenotia and her fraught interactions with the young Antonio and his father should be read as a commentary on the racialized persecution of Spain's others (96–7).

5 Following Spivak (28), I define "subaltern" as a person "without lines of social mobility."

6 In this essay, I will refer to the character of Antonio, the archer, as "the young Antonio" and to his father as "the elder Antonio."

7 As I discuss in *The Anxiety of Sameness*, Moriscos are considered non-problematic minorities as long as they accept the dominant cultural norms of speaking, eating, dressing, and worshipping and do not overstep their social boundaries by camouflaging their religious origins or by striving to be socially analogous to, or better than, their Old Christian counterparts (167–8).

8 See also Isabel Lozano-Renieblas, *Cervantes y el mundo del Persiles*, 145.

9 "Hechizo," Real Academia Española, *Autoridades* (1734), http://web.frl.es/DA.html, accessed 10 April 2016.

10 Mary Elizabeth Perry observes that the "practice of witchcraft not only gave women power over men and thus inverted gender power positions but also threatened to take from men control over their own sexuality" (190).

11 According to Cortés, "el varón que naciere debajo del ascendente de este signo será vergonzoso, afable, honesto y venturoso: señala, que será inclunado á ir por el mar" (the man born under this sign will be shameful, friendly, honest,

and prosperous: it is a sign that he should will be inclined to travel by sea [Cortés, 155]). Cortés's *Lunario* appeared in the Inquisition's 1632 *Index*.

12 Michael Armstrong-Roche states, "Indeed, throughout the novel and especially in the South the real rival to Catholic orthodoxy – however defined – is not a Christian counter-orthodoxy or even an heterodoxy, but the religion of honour" (157).

13 The elder Antonio, in fact, chastises his son for shooting at Cenotia and advises him to avoid violence against "those who love and desire you" (*Trials* II.9: 141) (a los que te aman y te quieren [*Los trabajos* II.9: 336]).

14 *Autoridades* defines "discreto" in the following terms: "Wise and with good judgement, who knows how to weigh and discern issues, and assign them the right importance" (Cuerdo y de buen juicio, que sabe ponderar y discernir las cosas, y darle a cada una su lugar, http://web.frl.es/DA.html, accessed 10 April 2016).

15 While Cenotia is described as "dressed ... after the Spanish fashion" (*Trials* II.8: 137) (vestida a la española [*Los trabajos* II.8: 200]), Rafala is "dressed in Morisco clothing" (*Trials* III.11: 258) (vestida en traje morisco [*Los trabajos* III.11: 545]). Cervantes disassociates appearance and Christianity, as the first Cenotia is a heretic and Rafala is the most devout Christian.

16 "[Y]ou aren't talking to some monster or anyone who'd try to tell you or advise you to do anything against human nature. Notice I'm speaking Spanish to you, the language you understand" (*Trials* II.8: 138) (no está hablando contigo algún mostruo ni persona que quiera decirte ni aconsejarte cosas que vayan fuera de la naturaleza humana. Mira que te hablo español, que es la lengua que tú sabes [*Persiles* II.8: 330]).

17 According to Cenotia, "changing people's minds and judgment violates the principle of free will, no science can do it nor are the herbs powerful enough to bring it about" (*Trials* II.8: 139) (mudar las voluntades, sacarlas de su quicio, como esto es ir contra el libre albedrío, no hay ciencia que lo pueda, ni virtud de yerbas que lo alcancen [*Los trabajos* II.8: 332]).

18 Rudolph Schevill and Adolfo Bonilla think that Cervantes might have been inspired by Inca Garcilaso, who writes about men and women who used poison to kill, to drive a person insane, to disfigure, or to weaken the mental state of a person who is the object of one's affection (xxviii).

19 To "consume" (*consumir*) is defined as to "undo, spend, extinguish, obliterate, or consum something" (deshacer, gastar, extinguir, o reducir a nada alguna cosa," Real Academia Española, *Autoridades* [1729], http://web.frl.es/DA.html, accessed 10 April 2016).

20 "She was encouraging, assuring him the disease wouldn't be fatal but recommending a delay in treatment for awhile [*sic*]" (*Trials* II.9: 142) (Ella le dio buenas esperanzas, asegurándole que de aquella enfermedad no moriría, pero que convenía dilatar algún tanto la cura [*Los trabajos* II.9: 338]).

21 According to the narrator, Cenotia continues to be smitten with the "cruel youth who had conquered her with the magic of his grace and charm" (*Trials* II.11: 151) (riguroso mozo que con los de su donaire y gentileza la tenía rendida [*Los trabajos* II.11: 353]).

22 Pedro Aznar Cardona states: "Because these mandates and dispositions are ordered by the incomprehensible divine will: We shall obey them, then, point by point, aided by his Grace" (Porque, de las ordenanças y disposiciones de la absoluta incomprehensible, voluntad de Dios: Lo hacedero es cumplirla con todo afecto y efecto, en todo lo posible, ayudados de la diurna gracia) [51r]). Damián Fonseca believes that "God's judgement is a Deep abysm, but is God's will" (los juyzios de Dios son vn abismo profundo, antes pensemos muy á menudo, que es voluntad de dios [76]), And Marcos de Guadalajara argues that "I see this issue ruled by the hand of Our Lord, as he has ... indicated His Will to his Majesty, instructing him in the proper justification of this cause, sent with paternal wishes for the spiritual and worldy prosperity of his Highness and that of this Spanish provence" (veo que anda en este negocio la mano de Dios nuestro Señor, y que ha querido ... decir a V. Magestad su voluntad, y apercebirle para mayor justificación de su causa, con deseo paternal del bien y prosperidad espiritual y temporal de V. Magestad y desta Prouincia de España [93v]).

23 The plan was only partly successful, due to Morisco refusal to give up their children (although some willingly left their children with the hope that they would at least survive) and to the lack of resources, and it became unfeasible to uphold (see Mercedes García-Arenal, *Los moriscos*).

24 As Adrienne Martin observes, "heresy, witchcraft, and sexuality are tightly interwoven in the early modern European mind and ... sexual and religious deviants commonly transgress together" (58).

REFERENCES

Armstrong-Roche, Michael. *Cervantes' Epic Novel: Empire, Religion, and the Dream Life of Heroes in* Persiles. Toronto: University of Toronto Press, 2009.

Aznar Cardona, Pedro. *Expulsion justificada de los moriscos españoles.* Huesca, ES: Pedro Cabarte, 1612.

Baena, Julio. "Sintaxis de la ética del texto: Ricote en el Quijote II, la lengua de las mariposas." *Bulletin of Spanish Studies* 83, no. 4 (2006): 506–22.

Cervantes Saavedra, Miguel de. *Los trabajos de Persiles y Sigismunda.* Edited by Carlos Romero Muñoz. Madrid: Cátedra, 2002.

– *The Trials of Persiles and Sigismunda.* Translated by Celia Richmond Weller and Clark A. Colahan. Indianapolis: Hackett, 1989.

Childers, William. *Transnational Cervantes*. Toronto: University of Toronto Press, 2006.
Cortés, Jerónimo. *El non plus ultra del lunario y pronóstico perpétuo, general y particular*. Barcelona: Valero Sierra y Martí, 1823.
Díez Fernández, José-Ignacio, and Luisa Fernanda Aguirre de Cárcer. "Contexto histórico y tratamiento literario de la 'hechicería' morisca y judía en el Persiles." *Cervantes: Bulletin of the Cervantes Society of America* 12, no. 2 (1992): 33–62.
Dopico Black, Georgina. "Ghostly Remains: Valencia, 1609." *Arizona Journal of Hispanic Cultural Studies* 7 (2003): 91–100.
Fonseca, Damián. *Iusta expulsion de los moriscos de España*. Rome: Jacomo Mascardo, 1612.
Fuchs, Barbara. *Passing for Spain: Cervantes and the Fictions of Identity*. Champaign: University of Illinois Press, 2003.
García-Arenal, Mercedes. *Los moriscos*. Madrid: Editora Nacional, 1975.
Gerli, Michael. *Refiguring Authority: Reading, Writing, and Rewriting in Cervantes*. Lexington: University Press of Kentucky, 1995.
Guadalajara, Marcos de. *Memorable expulsión y justísimo destierro de los Moriscos de España*. Pamplona: Nicolás de Assiayn, 1613.
Harris, A. Katie. *From Muslim to Christian Granada*. Baltimore, MD: Johns Hopkins University Presss, 2007.
Lea, Charles. *The Moriscos of Spain*. Vol. 3. London: Bernard Quaritch, 1901.
Lee, Christina. *The Anxiety of Sameness in Early Modern Spain*. Manchester: Manchester University Press, 2016.
– "Don Antonio Moreno y el 'Discreto' negocio de los moriscos ricote y Ana Félix." *Hispania* 88, no. 1 (2005): 32–40.
Lozano-Renieblas, Isabel. *Cervantes y el mundo del Persiles*. Alcalá de Henares, ES: Centro de Estudios Cervantinos, 1998.
Magnier, Grace. *Pedro de Valencia and the Catholic Apologists of the Expulsion of the Moriscos: Visions of Christianity and Kingship*. Leiden, NL: Brill, 2010.
Márquez Villanueva, Francisco. *El problema morisco desde otras laderas*. Madrid: Ediciones Libertarias, 1998.
– *Personajes y temas del Quijote*. Madrid: Taurus, 1975.
Martín, Adrienne. *An Erotic Philology of Golden Age Spain*. Nashville, TN: Vanderbilt University Press, 2008.
Núñez Muley, Francisco. *Memorandum for the President of the Royal Audiencia and Chancery Court*. Translation by Vincent Barletta. Chicago: University of Chicago Press, 2007.
– "The Original Memorial of Don Francisco Núñez Muley." Edited by K. Garrad. *Atlante* 2, no. 4 (1954): 199–226.
Perry, Mary Elizabeth. "Between Muslim and Christian Worlds: Moriscas and Identity in Early Modern Spain." In *Beyond the Harem: Women in the Empires*

of Islam, 1453–1798, edited by Bindu Malieckal and Nabil Matar. *Muslim World* 95, no. 2 (2005): 177–98.

Querillac, René. "Los moriscos de Cervantes." *Anales Cervantinos* 30 (1992): 77–98.

Schevill, Rodolfo, and Adolfo Bonilla. "Introducción." *Persiles y Sigismunda*. 2 vols. Madrid: Imprenta Bernardo Rodríguez, 1914.

Schmidt, Rachel. "La maga Cenotia y el arquero Antonio: el encuentro en clave alegórica en el *Persiles*." *eHumanista/Cervantes* 2 (2013): 19–38.

Spivak, Gayatri Chakravorty. *Toward a History of the Vanishing Present*. Cambridge, MA: Harvard University Press, 1999.

Valencia, Pedro de. *Tratado acerca de los moriscos de España*. Edited by Joaquín Gil Sanjuán. Málaga: Algazara, 1997.

Zimic, Stanislav. "El drama de Ricote el morisco." In *Literature, Culture and Ethnicity: Studies on Medieval, Renaissance and Modern Literatures: A Festschrift for Janez Stanonik*, edited by Mirko Jurak, 297–302. Ljubljana, SI: Znanstveni inštitut, 1992.

Chapter Eight

The Black Madonna Icon: Race, Rape, and the Virgin of Montserrat in *The Confession with the Devil* by Francisco de Torre y Sevil

JOHN BEUSTERIEN

Have not religious icons been emptied by aesthetic judgment,
absorbed by art history, made routine by conventional piety,
to the point of being dead forever?
On the contrary ... religious images
are still the ones that attract the fiercest passions.

Bruno Latour, "What Is Iconoclash?"

Men oftentimes invest female shoes with an erotic charge. For Iberian men in the early modern period, footwear represented everything they loved to not love. By regulating footwear, males perpetuated heterosexual normativity through the fantasy of the vaginal quality of the shoe: it was dirty and base, in that it held the part of the female body that touched the ground. The masculinist legal system interdicted certain types of female shoes; prohibiting an object implicitly linked to sexuality paradoxically elevated the shoe into a spiritual realm, endowing it with an erotic and even a religious aura.

The status of the female shoe as prohibited object made it fervently desired and cherished. Another finely crafted object, the Marian icon, also formed part of the kernel in the fantasy of early modern Iberian masculine desire. Like the shoe, the Marian icon is aura-filled and connected to lust. Religious icons, though, were not prohibited, like some types of female shoes, and, in fact, were copied and disseminated throughout the seventeenth-century Spanish world. Moreover, men coded the Madonna icon in the opposite way from that of the shoe: the starting point of the vector of erotic desire did not begin in the nether female region, which pointed upward toward a celestial realm. In the case of the Madonna icon, the starting point of the ocular vector of masculine erotic desire began with the visualization of the icon as heavenly and, in an opposite trajectory from the gaze of the shoe, the optical vector pointed toward the ground. The Madonna ostensibly did not touch the ground, in that it was an exemplary object of chastity and pure cleanliness – the woman who had never been penetrated. But, with its status as a premier unattainable object of desire, men inadvertently converted the icon into a sought-after object of erotic desire.

A study on the shoe in the early modern Iberian world, edited by Noelia Cirnigliaro and myself, examines the shoe as both a low and high object of masculine desire. But the double erotic meaning of the Madonna icon as celestial and also sexualized in the Iberian masculinist sexual fantasy needs more scholarly work, especially when the icon is a black Madonna.[1] In this chapter, I attempt to spark that scholarship by examining the play *The Confession with the Devil* (*La confesión con el demonio*) by Francisco de la Torre y Sevil (1625–81), which dramatizes masculine erotic desire with regard to the black Madonna icon.[2]

I divide the essay into three parts. The first contextualizes how the colour of the Madonna icon is associated with feminine beauty and ugliness. The second examines how Saint Vincent Ferrer's view of the religious outsider informs the notion of dark skin colour as overtly associated with ugliness in the Iberian social conscious. It focuses on the plot based on a rape commited by a black man in Act 3 of *The Confession with the Devil*, arguing that this theme is a radically different, but complementary, transformation of Ferrer's notion of sex and religious exogamy. Finally, the third section shows how the representation of the blackness of the Virgin of Montserrat icon in *The Confession with the Devil* connects to the rape scene in the play. Ultimately, the representation of *eros* in the play perpetuates a notion of race based on colour with regards to the Montserrat Madonna icon, demonstrating how theatre constructs supposedly proper sexual norms tied to skin colour.

Plays can teach people *how* to see, and *The Confession with the Devil* in particular teaches how to see race, and, in so doing, it propagates racism. The meaning of the black Madonna icon in a Spanish play from the seventeenth century – as a sign of both promiscuousness and unblemished sexual purity – illuminates the calculus of a dominant and imperial perspective with respect to race as it relates to the history of visual perception. This play reflects masculine social norms about gender and race when visualizing the Madonna icon and serves as a model and guide for how society constructs the optics for perceiving these norms.

Calling attention to the presence of skin colour in Spanish theatre better enables the dis-assembling of the racial calculus that pervades optical perception. In an effort to eliminate unproductive, masculinist visualizations of the icon, then, this chapter shows how anti-black racism functions in the genealogy of the black Marian image. In the following sections, I expose the masculinist visual perception of blackness that informed seeing the Madonna icon as it guided a history of oppression. My goal is not to dismiss the importance of the icon but to value it, like the author Sandra Cisneros and historian Mary Elizabeth Perry, who productively see the Madonna icon as a way to reach toward motherhood and maternal caring.[3] This chapter shares Cisneros's and Perry's perspectives, proposing that the critical exposure of a masculinist vision will aid scholarship to better embrace the neglected everyday lives and voices of Afro-Hispanic women.[4]

A Brief History of the Visual Perception of the Black Madonna in Early Modern Spain

Because the primary female character of the play is Vincente Ferrer's sister, the religious charge of the Madonna icon in *The Confession with the Devil* is found in the theme of religious exclusion and sexual paranoia taken from the sermons of this fourteenth-century sermonizer. Ferrer's main problem was that Jews and Muslims had become invisible. They were hated as religious outsiders, but were indistinguishable from Christians, since they lived among them, dressed like them, and even adopted Christian names. In seventeenth-century Spain, preachers did not forget the tenor of Ferrer's stance toward Jews. They sometimes invested religious icons, particularly the bleeding Christs that artists and icon artisans produced ad nauseam during the Counter-Reformation, with Ferrer's vehement anti-Jewish spirit.[5]

But Catholic icons in the Iberian world were not only connected with attacks on an unseen religious other. Society also charged religious icons with a racial logic based on black skin. Iberian men who conquered and won campaigns did not return to the hometown or regional chapel. They felt it necessary to pay respects to the Madonna at shrines in Montserrat and Guadalupe in Estremadura, Spain. In the hierarchical logic of religious sanctuaries, icons in shrines as opposed to common chapels serve a higher and more permanent level of Marian advocacy, and, in the sixteenth century, the Montserrat shrine was to Aragon what Guadalupe was to Castile: each was the respective kingdom's most important shrine (Christian 121).

Two Iberian Madonnas are the highest-ranked images of Mary in the empire, and each of these is black. Why did the most powerful men of the period make their most significant petitions to black Madonnas? Like the figure of Santiago, for medieval and early modern Spanish men of war, the Madonna was a royal battle patron.[6] Men gave thanks to her for healing war wounds, for victory, and for aid in granting a safe journey home from conquered lands. Columbus and Cortez returned from American expeditions and made pilgrimages to the Madonna in Guadalupe, Spain. Cortez was so enraptured and fanatically devoted to the Madonna in Guadalupe that he copied her image and carried it on his banner as he conquered American territory. In the case of the black Madonna in Montserrat, the emperor Charles V visited her, and the great imperial leaders Juan de Austria, the duke of Alba, and Philip II made numerous visits to the the site after military victories. Juan de Austria brought to the shrine trophies from his victory over the Turks at Lepanto, including a lantern from a Turkish ship, which became famous as the Lamp of the Moorish King (Perry 114).

Aside from its war iconicity, something about the icon that absorbed the male viewer was not accessible in language. The linguistic inability to define the power of the black Madonna is directly related to the radically altered meaning of skin colour within the geopolitical scope of the Iberian world system that initiated black slavery and sought to eliminate the Moorish presence in Iberia. Early sixteenth-century Spain marked the first time that the blackness of the icon connected to nascent modern identity categories related to race, region, and religion. In the sixteenth century, well before the fully realized nineteenth-century exploration of the racial valence of the icon, early Spanish masculine desire for and repulsion from dark skin colour already shaped *votos* to black virgins. The violence that lay as the foundation of Iberian imperial trauma *created* the aura that made the black Madonna special, because her skin colour became increasingly symptomatic of Spain's violence directed at recently conquered Moorish people, especially unheard captive women, and the thousands of newly enslaved sub-Saharan Africans, especially women, taken to the peninsula and its territories.

In the sixteenth and seventeenth century, a slew of male and female religious icons were produced, and black skin on the icon connected it to divinity and beauty.[7] Stephen Benko explains that the pan-European phenomenon of black Madonnas was part of the Christian transformation of earlier traditions of representing goddesses associated with earth as black, including in statues and paintings of Demeter (210–12). But geopolitical events in the sixteenth-century Iberian world gave new significance to the dark Madonna. Monique Scheer underscores the need to establish when and why society first visualized the icon's skin colour (when she *became* black in modern terms), in order to improve the historical understanding of perception. Elisa Foster repeats Scheer's point in her study of the black Madonna of Montserrat when she points out that scholars need to identify exactly when people perceived the blackness of the icon and when that colour emerged as an important identifying factor (45).

The first commentaries on the dark skin of the icon occur in the early decades of the sixteenth century, just after the defeat of the Moors at Granada and as Iberia began shipping Africans as chattel to the Americas. In a manuscript that scholars think was written about 1515, Pedro de Burgos writes that the Virgin at Montserrat is *morena* and "very well shaped and made" (qtd. in Foster 39). Published in subsequent editions in the sixteenth and seventeenth century, Burgos's words are a landmark in the history of perception (Foster 20n5, 39n66). Prior to Burgos, people may have seen the icon's skin colour, shade, or tones, but they did not remark on them. In this sense, skin colour was not *regarded*: it was neither observed nor remarked upon. In terms of the history of representing the Montserrat icon, regardless of whatever may have been its *real* colour, prior to the sixteenth century, colour was largely irrelevant, as artists depicted the icon sometimes as black and other times as white.[8]

In the sixteenth century, with the advent of the Iberian system of slavery, in which dark skin colour acquired a demeaned status, the skin tone on the Madonna icon was, ironically, a sign of beauty. Following Burgos, the Madonna as *morena* entered into the Iberian mindset, acquiring significance across the Iberian world and in Europe. By the end of the sixteenth century, accounts describe the Virgin in Guadalupe (in Spain) in ways similar to the Montserrat Madonna: she is beautiful, *but* dark. In a widely circulating chronicle about the monastery of Guadalupe, Gabriel de Talavera describes the Virgin of Guadalupe with a specific reference to the bride in the Song of Songs: "The color is dark (*moreno*) because of her great antiquity, the face very beautiful, so serious and perfect as to reveal the majesty of Her Lady; and it corresponds to the letter which mentions the bride: Although her color is somewhat burnt (*tostado*), her face is lovely" (qtd. in Peterson 35).

While early references visualized the Madonna's darkness with reference to the beauty of the biblical bride from the Song of Songs, by the beginning of the seventeenth century, texts shifted the visualization of blackness away from the textual authority of the Bible to a visibility based on connecting the skin colour of the icon with that of African peoples. Alonso de Sandoval (1577–1652), a Jesuit and an early critic of slavery, was born in Seville, a city with a significant Afro-Hispanic population, and died in the Americas (Cartagena de Indies). In his work entitled *The Nature, Sacred and Profane Practices, Customs and Rituals, Discipline and Evangelical Catechism of All Ethiopians*, published in Seville in 1627, Sandoval wrote that the Montserrat Virgin was black and that, because of her skin colour, she favoured the regions where dark people originate.[9] He claimed that the Montserrat Virgin was "known to love the color black," which was proven by the fact that "many of the oldest and most miraculous images of the Virgin are colored black" (qtd. in Harpster 87). For Sandoval, Montserrat and other black Marian shrine images, including Guadalupe, connected the image to a group of people or *nación*, and he wrote that the icon showed a fondness for the black "color and nation" (Que muestra bien la mucha afición que esta divina Senora tenía a este color y nación [qtd. in Harpster 87]).

In the early seventeenth century, Diego de Ocaña also visualized the black Madonna as beautiful and noted that her skin colour connected her to a people – in his case not Africans, but people in the Americas. Ocaña was a Jeronymite friar who spent much of the first decade of the seventeenth century in the Americas. In Potosí, Bolivia, he created his version of the Guadalupe Madonna and wrote a short play about her, in which he extolled that "greater than the sun is her celestial beauty" (qtd. in Peterson 60). He also explained that he painted her with a skin colour that imitates that of the indigenous population. He noted that, because of her skin tone, the Indians stated that his image of the Madonna was more beautiful than the other icons and that they loved her best "because she was of their color" (qtd. in Peterson 59).

The colour of the icon mattered in the sense it was associated with specific people from a region. Colour also mattered in the sense that the materiality of the colour of the paint on the icon took on relevance for the first time. One main character from the seventeenth-century picaresque novel *Alonso, Servant Boy of Many Masters* (*Alonso, mozo de muchos amos*), by Jerónimo de Alcalá (contemporary to Torre's *The Confession with the Devil*) observes that darker Madonna icons must actually be white and not black:

> Because one could not imagine that any painter would use such a dark shade as appears on some virgins such as ... on Guadalupe, or Montserrat, or other such ones ... it is her right that she be white because of who she is: she is the most chaste; the most honest; and the most holy of all women; she is purer and cleaner than heaven.
>
> (Porque no se puede entender que pintor alguno diese tal matiz, tan moreno como algunas tienen, como la imagen de ... Guadalupe, de Montserrate y otras semejantes ... Y ser blanca la santísima Virgen le viene de derecho, por ser como es, la más casta, la más honesta y más santa de las mujeres; más pura y limpia que los cielos. [948])

These words show that not all agree with Sandoval's comments that the Madonna truly has dark skin. But the mere existence of a debate about her skin colour proves that suddenly people were perceiving the materiality of the colour of the paint when visualizing the icon. The affirmation that "it is her right that she be white" indicates that, for this commentator, the representation of dark skin pigmentation was worrisome. Fundamentally, the issue is not whether the Madonna is or is not black, but that a seventeenth-century author felt the need to answer the question about what skin colour the icon supposedly *really* had.[10]

Jerónimo de Alcalá's insistence that the icon was white demonstrates the relationship between beauty and skin colour. The question of whether the Virgin was really white shows how an essentializing racial category developing in the sixteenth century after the Spanish arrival in the Americas informed notions of race on the peninsula in the seventeenth century. With the emergence of skin colour as a sign that differentiates people, a conscious masculine erotic fantasy emerged in which the truly beautiful Iberian woman (the one whom a man is *supposed* to reproduce with) was white. As opposed to the Burgos description of the black Madonna as beautiful (pure, chaste, "very well shaped and made"), authors begin to dehumanize and objectify black women by making them speak in a non-standard way and by portraying them as physically ugly, immoral, and promiscuous characters. The linking of beauty with the white skin of women in the Spanish-American context initiated a complicated, but constantly repeating and predictable, paradox across the Iberian world: white skin is a sign of beauty, and black skin is overtly an arch-sign of ugliness in the social consciousness – even as blackness is the sign of beauty in the social unconscious.

Saint Vincent Ferrer, Sex, and Racial Mixing

I have traced a few of the attitudes toward skin colour and Madonnas in the sixteenth and seventeenth century that inform their representation in Torre's play. To further explain the masculine attitude toward the black Madonna icon with respect to sexuality and race in *The Confession with the Devil*, one also has to look to the medieval period and examine the religious and historic context of the Ferrer name. Although the peak of the action of *Confession* centres on Act 3, when a black man rapes the main female character, the author, nonetheless, is most concerned with dramatizing a moment from Spanish history in order to celebrate the life of Saint Vincent Ferrer (1350–1419), the most notorious figure in Spanish history associated with anti-Jewish sermonizing.

Torre uses one significant source text for the basic plot structure of *The Confession with the Devil*: Francisco Redón's *The Best Prodigy and An Exemplary Case: The Origin of the Masses of Saint Vincent Ferrer* (1634) (*El mayor prodigio y caso exemplar: Origen de las missas de San Vicente Ferrer*). This work, a hagiographic prose narrative, underscores the life of Saint Vincent even though its actual storyline concerns an episode in the life of his sister and other events tangential to the life of the saint. *The Best Prodigy* is a novel, rather than a play, and includes poems in which the religious faithful sing about their white souls while looking upon the beauty of the black Madonna icon. It also describes the same version of a black man's rape of Ferrer's sister as found in *The Confession with the Devil* (the name of the black man changes). In Redón's version, Francesca describes her rapist as "terribly ugly" (*horrible aspecto* [128]) and includes details of the rape, as well as Francesca's subsequent killing of the black man and her self-induced abortion. It also describes the striking scene found later in Torre's play: Francesca's husband discovers her tomb, where he finds the black man devouring her aborted fetus.

Most significantly, the source text for the Torre play – Redón's novel – frames the story as one that belongs as part of a litany of stories that prove Vincent's hagiographic worth. These stories, both the source text and the publication of the Torre play, coincide with other publications and plays, most notably Antonio Enríquez Gómez's play *The Masses of Saint Vincent Ferrer* (*Las misas de Vincente San Ferrer*), which rode a wave of Catholic stories that provided ideological fodder for Ferrer's 200th anniversary of sainthood, celebrated in Valencia.

Despite its unusual plot twists and patently artificial story of a black man's violation of Saint Vincent's sister, Torre's play was read by the censors and deemed to be in line with Catholic dogma. The scene of the black man eating the aborted fetus and other references to blackness did not bother the Inquisitorial censors.[11] In his approval for the publication of the plays in the book in which the play appears, Francisco de Avellaneda wrote that he found nothing in the plays that "opposes the Catholic purity of our sacred observations that are exemplary" (se oponga a la católica pureza de la verdad de nuestras sagradas observaciones, antes por ejemplares [Torre y Sevil n.p.]). Avellaneda's approval of this play as in line with Catholic doctrine suggests that its version of Ferrer's sainthood and the depiction of the Madonna in the play conform to a racial logic based on skin colour compatible with Spain's sense of religious purity.

The end of *The Confession with the Devil* is the first moment in which Saint Vincent Ferrer appears, and then only as a reference. The play concludes with a striking image: Saint Vincent's dead sister appears on stage with the dead black rapist, Tucapel, at her feet. Tucapel is eating their son, whom Francesca has aborted. Consistent with the seventeenth-century context, the woman, not the man, takes responsibility for the rape. The ghost of Francesca pronounces that she has sinned by having had adulterous relations with Tucapel. She has confessed her sin, but the priest to whom she made her confession was the devil, who took the form of a father confessor. For this reason, her brother Vincent needs to intercede on her behalf. Through his intercession, Francesca is able to leave purgatory and be saved. The dead Francesca, surrounded by flames, states:

> I confessed and then after a few days
> I die, and I go in front
> Of God where he measures my fate
> With severe judgment
> So that until judgment day
> He condemns me to the suffering
> Of Purgatory, from where
> Today through the intercession
> Of my brother Friar Vincent,
> The Saint Gregory Masses
> Are saving me with happy eternity.
>
> (Confesé, y a pocos días
> muero, y paso a la presencia
> de Dios, donde de mi vida
> se mira la cuenta estrecha;
> y hasta la del postrer día,
> a las penas me condena
> de Purgatorio, de donde
> hoy para la dicha eterna
> las Misas de San Gregorio
> me sacan, por diligencias
> de mi hermano Fray Vicente. [35])

Aside from this reference, Saint Vincent does not appear as character, and nothing related to his life or sermons directly forms part of the story in the play. Even though the saint is not a protagonist or even a character, Torre's play formed part of the vast fictional seventeenth-century narrative inventions typically embellishing the lives of saints, and especially that of Vincent, who was celebrated in a propaganda campaign at the time that Torre wrote the play.

Despite his absence from the plot, Ferrer's anti-Jewish ideas indirectly influence the treatment of race in the play. The fabricated narrative about Saint Vincent's life finds its climax in the third act, in which Torre radically recasts Vincent's vehement hatred of Jews upon the black body. As historian David Nirenberg has noted, Ferrer's sermons in the late fourteenth century revolutionized the art of sermonizing. The sermons lambasted Jews and those Jews who had recently converted to Christianity. Ferrer wanted to see converted Jews segregated, and he provided the founding logic of anti-Semitism on the Iberian Peninsula. Nirenberg explains that Vincent Ferrer lived through a crisis of identification. It suddenly became difficult to establish the religious classification of individuals; to put more bluntly, the real ambiguities of identity "were allowing Jews (and Muslims) to have sex with Christians more often than in the past" (145–6). According to Nirenberg, so powerful was Ferrer's "reasoning that it mobilized one of the most extensive attempts at segregation before the modern era" (144). Largely as a result of Ferrer, Jewish ghettos were set up throughout Castile, Aragón, and across Iberia.

Underpinning Ferrer's notion of segregation was paranoia about exogamic procreation. In other words, as Nirenberg argues, Ferrer feared increased sexual mixing between those of different religious faiths, even though such fears were historically unfounded. Because of his anger at the prospect of sexual contamination of faiths, a fundamental linchpin of Ferrer's sermons was the fortification of ideological walls of sexual prohibition to bar different religious groups from co-mingling. *The Confession with the Devil* recalibrates and redirects Saint Vincent's paranoia into a different optic frame by rewriting the saint's story as one in which the chief protagonist of sexual pollution is not the Jew, who was invisible to the public at large, but the black man, who was visible at a glance.[12]

The Madonna Icon and Race in *The Confession with the Devil*

With a knowledge of the vehemence of Vincent Ferrer's position on sexuality and early modern Iberian attitudes toward the black Madonna in mind, we can now turn to the representation of the Madonna icon in *The Confession with the Devil*. Many Spanish literary works depict icons or paintings of sacred images. Often when an image of Mary appears in literary works, her body acquires the quality of whiteness through a contrast with black characters. In a poem by Góngora, the Madonna icon is assumed to be white so that, when the black character Juana looks at it, she thinks that she is white like Mary because her soul is white, even though she has black skin.[13]

In another play from the period, *The Comic Interlude Featuring Blacks* (*Entremés de los negros*), the Madonna icon is also coded as white in a racial sense. The character Dominga looks at the Madonna icon and distinguishes herself from its skin colour, but associates herself with the black tunic that clothes the image: "I am the tunic of the Virgin of Solitude" (samo tunica de la Soledad [qtd. in Beusterien, *Eye* 137]). Plays such as this demonstrate the complex materiality that whiteness – the meaning of white paint or, in this case, the Virgin's black tunic – achieved as it relates to questions of race and religion. Dominga adds that, even though her skin is not the colour of the white paint on the icon and her skin tone is more closely related to the black tunic, she nonetheless is not at all like the Jew who carries the image: "[A]t least I am not the Jew that carries her" (no samo a lo meno de lo judio que yeba lo paso [qtd. in ibid.]).

Through its contradistinction with the representation of Afro-Iberians, whiteness, then, is not an abstract allegorical concept, but a material reality. Lope de Vega's play *La limpieza no manchada* also depicts an image of a Madonna. The title of this play resonates with important abstract notions of whiteness from religious discourse from the period, most especially, the Spanish support for the doctrine of the Immaculate Conception, a Counter-Reformation theological tenet that Mary was free of sin when conceived. The title of Lope's play echoes the Immaculate Conception doctrine by using the words *limpieza* (purity) and *no manchada* (free from stain) to suggest that Mary was free from the stain of original sin. The title also resonates with racial preoccupations associated with religion during this period – the same type of attitude that is found in Dominga's spiteful comment about the Jew – since it evokes paranoia about the *limpieza* of the hidden religious other and the notion of pure Christian blood not *manchada* by Jewish or Moorish ancestry.

But, as the finale of *La limpieza no manchada* makes manifest, the play ultimately dramatizes skin colour – just as *The Confession with the Devil* does – as an overriding visual signal of identity difference for the audience. The allegorical character Ethiopia in *La limpieza no manchada* speaks a non-standard black Spanish dialect and most probably is a man that appears in blackface.[14] The play concludes with a scene in which Spain asks Ethiopia (and the other allegorical characters in the play) to observe a Marian image – that is, a large painting of the Immaculate Conception. The final stage directions of the play indicate that a curtain is to be pulled open to observe the "Immaculate Conception of Our Lady" (limpia concepción de Nuestra Señora [qtd. in Pérez 36]).

The final curtain-opening moment in *La limpieza no manchada* is a meta-theatrical moment that illuminates the complex role of race in general in seventeenth-century Spanish drama. After the curtain opens on an image of the Immaculate Conception, the stage directions indicate that a group of black characters dance and sing around the Madonna. Such final dances are typical of the interludes that form a part of dramatic productions from the period. Although the dancers are not necessarily black characters, the final dancing scene of the interlude nearly always has African connotations, since wild dancing, such as the *chacona*, was associated with Africa. Lope's *La limpieza no manchada* shows a Marian image on stage that directly references the Immaculate Conception and indirectly references Spain's Jewish and Moorish past. But the play's final scene – black characters dancing around the Marian image – visually makes manifest an emerging racialization based on skin colour: Mary's purity and Spain's invisible past religious impurity intimately connect with the presence of a notion of whiteness that contrasts with the dark skin colour of Afro-Iberians.

La limpieza no manchada embodies the contradictory conscious and unconscious social valence of racialized sexuality with respect to the skin colour of the Madonna: the virginal sacred body acquires material significance in the context of a visual spectacle of the ludic celebration of black dance. Its final scene is emblematic of how drama depicted the Madonna icon as painted white within a discourse of whiteness associated with chastity but inextricably linked with erotic movement – Mary is a celestial icon observed on stage inseparable from an eroticized dance celebration of black bodies. If one conceives of the final scene of the play as a single image or a single portrait – as opposed to visualizing only the Immaculate Conception portrait – then the play depicts a final scene in which the Madonna is coded as sexually pure while in the presence of the libidinous sexuality of ludic African dancers; through the contrast of characters coded as black on stage, the audience visualized the skin colour on the icon as white.

When art critics look at paintings of the Immaculate Conception from the period, they generally ignore the question of skin colour. Likewise, when scholars of Spanish drama look at Marian images in plays, they do not mention skin colour either. Francisco de la Torre y Sevil, the author of *The Confession with the Devil*, also co-authored a play with José Arnal de Bolea. That play, *The Lily from Ethiopia* (*La Azucena de Etiopia*), is an allegorical drama that celebrates the Immaculate Conception. Giovanni Cara, the scholar who edited the play, virtually ignores its treatment of skin colour. Rather, he sees the two allegories in this play – the whiteness of the lily and the blackness of Ethiopia – as forming part of a conceptual baroque play on meaning that embellishes a system of religious truth celebrating the Immaculate Conception within the context of the abstraction of baroque allegory.

But a closer study of Torre's work more broadly reveals that he is interested not only in the colours white and black as baroque embellishments but in the question of blackness as it relates to skin colour. Torre was concerned with the representation of the anxiety of the mixed-race child, as the title *The Lily from Ethiopia* invokes Heliodorus's Chariclea, a character from a work that had been become popularized in sixteenth-century Spanish literature. Chariclea is white even though her parents are Ethiopian, and her mother abandons her because she fears she will be accused of adultery when the father sees the child.

In other works, Torre defiles women for being black. For instance, in one poem, "For a Black Woman with Makeup" (A una muger negra y afeitada), he repeats a common jab at the ugliness of black women when he writes: "Clori puts on her makeup / trying something new / but it is not something new / to put makeup on one's ink" (Con polvos Clori se pinta / y ser cosa nueva prueba/pero no son cosa nueva / los polvos sobre la tinta [Alvar 226]). Torre suggests the ugliness of a black woman who is unable to doll herself up because she is already the colour of ink.

As opposed to the more common representation of white Madonna icons in plays and paintings, Torre's play *The Confession with the Devil* represents a black Madonna with erotic connotations. The comic character in the play, Colchón, jokingly states: "I also want to praise the Virgin / of Montserrat: she is black after all" (También quiero a la Virgen / de Monserrate alabarla: es morena [240]). He calls her the *morena* a second time and comments on her brown or toasted colour: "She is the black one / and she will also be the one of a toasted colour" (es la morena, / también será la tostada [240]). Colchón is the *gracioso* and tells lewd jokes during the course of play. He appears on stage without any clothes and with a sheet on his head, and makes a pun with his name when he states that his naked body is the mattress (*colchón*). When he describes the icon as *morena* and *tostada*, his purpose is radically different from that of Gabriel de Talavera's sober description of the Guadalupe Madonna, which uses the same adjectives to describe that black Madonna. In contrast to Talavera's association with the Biblical *nigra sed formosa*, Colchón's interest in the black woman is sexual, in keeping with other jokes that degrade black skin.

Contrasting with Madonna images and, indeed, women protagonists in plays in general, the image of the vast majority of black female characters in drama from the period is not one of chastity and purity. Black female characters perform lewd, oftentimes prohibited, dances.

They have a hungry sexual appetite. Mari López, the *negra* referred as the Ethiopian in the anonymous long-form sixteenth-century poem *Carajicomedia* (Prick Comedy) is referred to as "having an insatiable cunt" (de coño veloce). Playwright Lope de Rueda represents black women as libidinous, and he himself took on the role of a black woman in which he cross-dressed and exaggerated the character's comic sexuality and ridiculousness (Beusterien, *Eye* 159). Authors also depict the *negra* as talking continuously, unable to shut her mouth, such as in *The Black Woman Reader* (ibid. 147). In the prose novella, María de Zayas describes a *negra* as having "thick lips" and a "big snout" (ibid. 190n3). Aside from her mouth, she is linked to sexuality through an ample body. In Lope de Vega's *The Gentleman from Olmedo* (*El caballero de Olmedo*), the character Tello is promised a *negra* size extra large (*talle estremado*) as a recompense for his duties to the hag character Fabia.

Madonna icons are by definition never signs of venery, but of virginity. But Colchón's joke about the icon suggests a connection between the *morena* and multiple dramatic references to the sexuality of the black female in drama from the period. In doing so, his joke also invokes Montserrat as a place of concupiscence: the cave and its forests connect with hidden sexuality. Indeed, popular cults connected the Montserrat Madonna location to a Venus cult, and sources referred to it as *crines pubis* – that is, a place of luring and sexual temptation (Beusterien, *Eye* 149; Greer 411n26).[15]

Beyond the lewd connotation of Colchón's joke, the blackness of the Madonna relates to sexuality in a more profound and direct way. *The Confession with the Devil* dramatizes a pilgrimage to Montserrat, and the journey to see the Madonna icon enables the venery of the play, which results in the devil literally appearing in the body of a priest, the black body of the male protagonist, and the black body of his child. In this way, the *gracioso* Colchón's joke about the *morena* Madonna evokes the polluting potential in black sexualized stereotypes. The joke alludes to the pivotal action of the play: Tucapel's rape of Francesca. In the play, the pilgrimage to the Montserrat icon provides the time and space for the rape to occur; at the same time, the rape provides a lens for perceiving dark skin as symptomatic of libidinousness and for the patriarchal fear of the darkness of sexuality. *The Confession with the Devil* echos Saint Vincent Ferrer's attitude toward sex with the religious other, but transfers that attitude to black Africans. The Montserrat icon signals both virginity and promiscuity, since the pilgrimage to it permits the act of forbidden sexual penetration that destroys a marriage and the lives of the adulterers.

Some literary examples of pilgrimages to Madonna icons from Miguel de Cervantes echo parts of the story of promiscuity and rape found in

The Confession with the Devil. In Miguel de Cervantes's "The Deceitful Marriage" (El casamiento engañoso), sexual deceit in a duplicitous marriage is made possible by a pilgrimage to the Virgin of Guadalupe. In this case, a woman falsely states that the house where she works as a maid is her own. She is able to pretend that the house is hers since the owners are away on the pilgrimage to Guadalupe, and she uses that fact to deceive and seduce her lover.

In "The Illustrious Kitchen Maid" (La ilustre fregona), a novella from the same collection as "The Deceitful Marriage," Cervantes provides another literary precedent for the representation of the Madonna icon in Torre's play. "The Illustrious Kitchen Maid" is about Constanza, whose mother was raped. After being raped, Constanza's mother takes on the persona of the Pilgrim Madonna, a version of Mary and exemplar of Christian virtue (Lee). Upon learning that she has conceived the child of her rapist, Constanza's mother in the role of the Pilgrim Madonna sets off to visit the shrine of the Virgin of Guadalupe to find refuge and guidance. In Cervantes's version of the story, the raped woman gives birth to Constanza following a peaceful, painless delivery in keeping with those in popular Marian narratives, and she then makes a pilgrimage to the Madonna shrine.

Like Constanza's mother in Cervantes, Francesca in *The Confession with the Devil* is a Madonna-type character, a human reflection of the Mary icon and iconic female saints. She has waited three years for her husband to return from his pilgrimage; she has physical beauty, noble birth, spiritual devotion; and she concludes the play confessing her sin of lust. But, in contrast to Constanza's mother, Francesca's husband goes to the Madonna icon *prior* to the rape, and his absence during his pilgrimage to the Madonna provides the opportunity for the rape. After the rape, and, again, in contrast to Constanza's mother, Francesca feels she will never be chaste in her soul. She does not turn to a female icon but repents to her brother, a symbol of the religious patriarchy. In radical distinction to the Cervantes tale, in *The Confession with the Devil* the raped woman does not deliver but aborts her baby and then dies.

Whenever actresses appear on stage, even when they play Marian or chaste female characters (to whom Francesca aspires), audiences might still connect them with sexuality because of the link at the time between the life of an actress and prostitution (Fernández 66). But, in a permutation on the paradox of the promiscuous actress who plays the virtuous female protagonist, the dramatic portrayal of a material icon in *The Confession with the Devil* is also of a female character embodying simultaneous lust and spiritual love. In an act of devotion, Francesca's husband, Bartolomé, dismisses any connection between the Madonna icon and skin colour. He looks to the Virgin and asks her to dismiss

Colchón's *morena* joke: "forgive my Lady / such ridiculous words" (perdonad Señora / tan ridículas palabras [240]). Nonetheless, even as this character dismisses the connection, the play connects the icon to skin colour and lust. Bartolomé's visit to Montserrat makes manifest skin colour since his pilgrimage to the icon ignites the story of a black man's rape of his wife.

When Bartolomé goes to Montserrat, he tells his black friend Tucapel to deliver his wife a letter telling her that he cannot make it home. Bartolomé says to Tucapel:

> I am giving you a letter
> To take to my house
> I cannot go there
> Since I must go visit the
> Divine sanctuary at Monserrat
> With a faithful vow of thanks
> For having saved us from the storm.
> Meanwhile you will let my wife know
> Of my imminent arrival.
>
> (Te remitiré a mi casa
> con una carta
> Dejaré allí, que yo
> no puedo, aunque me avezino
> llegar a mi casa antes
> de visitar el divino
> santuario de Monserrate
> fiel voto que en el peligro
> de la tormenta ofrecí
> darás tu entretanto aviso
> de mi venida a mi esposa. [224])

Bartolomé grants Tucapel entrance to his house and access to his wife so that he can visit the Madonna. Through symbolic phallic transfer, Bartolomé opens his home to a black man. After the explanation of his need to go to the Virgin at Montserrat, Bartolomé gives Tucapel his sword, saying, "since you are a Christian, I grant you this sword" (como a cristiano, esa espada te permito [224]). His visit to the Virgin then serves as his moment of chastity (the pilgrimage takes three years), a sign of self-willed sexual control that passes on sexual potency to Tucapel, who is granted access to his house and to his wife.

When Bartolomé finally returns home with Colchón after visiting Montserrat, the playwright has each character mention skin colour.

When they enter the house, Colchón tells the joke about the Montserrat icon being the *morena*. Then, moments later, Bartolomé is mortified to realize that "the black lives in my house" (el negro en mi casa vive [241]). At this moment in the play, he sees his wife's tomb, out of which a group of people surface in a striking pose. Stage directions indicate that "[a] woman comes out of a tomb among flames. A black man at her feet eating a child of the same colour" (Sale de la tumba entre llamas una mujer, a sus plantas un hombre negro, comiéndose un niño del mismo colour [241]). Torre creates an image – what we might call a dramatic icon – in which a dead woman stands in flames with her black rapist at her feet, eating their child.

The image of the black man eating his son evokes medieval iconography in which the gates of hell are depicted as a large mouth of a devil who devours sinners. It also evokes American cannibalism, showing how Spanish letters transformed the demonization of the invisible religious outsider onto a visible black body. Of the three versions of this story of rape by a black man that existed in the seventeenth century, Torre is the only author to use the name "Tucapel." In his play, Tucapel is a Moor who converts to Christianity and who then rapes Francesca. But Torre, by using the name Tucapel, imprints the black Spanish-American experience onto the story: Tucapel was a famed war site where the Spanish lost a battle on American soil and is also the name of the indigenous American rebel who served as a foil in Pedro de Oña's epic poem *First Part of the Araucan Conquest* (*Arauco domado*, 1596) and in other plays from the period.[16]

Like Tucapel in Torre's play, the experience of the Spanish black Madonna icon was a visual experience of Spain's demonization of Africa and America. The scene in the play that shows Francesca's ghost with Tucapel at her feet is a dramatic icon that radically transforms the iconic heavenly image of the *morena* Madonna at Montserrat that Bartolomé just visited. The black Madonna icon transforms into a new image of a mixed-race couple and child. The play's symbolic icon, then, is not the Madonna, but the scene of Francesca with Tucapel at her feet, eating their aborted son – a symbol of Francesca's sin and racial pollution.

Torre makes reference to the sin of adultery and the loss of family honour that resulted from Francesca's having been violated by Tucapel. The play concentrates less on the ubiquitous trope of honour found in Spanish Golden Age plays and more on the question of race and the racial pollution of a mixed-race child. When pregnant, aside from calling the child a black image, Francesca calls the child within a "black shadow" (negra sombra [238]). Francesca's labelling of her offspring as shadow recalls an earlier speech by Tucapel in which he describes himself in a self-deprecating way with a catalogue of black things, concluding: "I am black ... a black shadow of that light" (Sombra soy ... sombra oscura de esa luz [231]).

In this play, the black Madonna icon as the votive to virginity transforms into a myth in which the white man's alter ego, the black man, becomes the icon of promiscuity. When she finds out that she is pregnant, Francesca states that Tucapel "printed this black image in my entrails" (en mis entrañas / imprimió esta imagen negra [234]). Soon after, the devil possesses the body of the child and appears on stage. Stage directions indicate the child should appear in blackface: "a boy comes out, his face black" (sale un niño, negra la cara [236]). This boy then informs Francesca: "I am the result of your destroyed birth of your tyranny / before arriving to be born (soy el que fui infausto / parto de tu tiranía / antes que llegue a ser parto [236]).[17]

The play connects Francesca's religious pollution to that of racial pollution through her description of her self-induced abortion using the rhetoric of a dirty stain: "because he was a storm, a chain / because he was a slave / I destroyed him before letting him stain / the clean and clear glass / of baptism" (por ser tormento / cadena, por ser esclavo; / le rompí antes de teñirle / en el cristal limpio, y claro / del bautismo [235]). Francesca not only indicates her shame in terms of her reason for her abortion – that is, preventing the child from being born out of wedlock – but she also codes her shame in terms of skin colour, using typical lexical associations with the word "black" like *teñir* (staining). *Teñir* is the most common word found in plays to describe the action when actors put on makeup to perform in blackface, and it thereby connects skin colour to the material practice of stage makeup (Beusterien *Eye,* 103).

Evoking the black skin on the Madonna icon, in her mind Francesca makes a direct connection between religious purity ("the clean and clear glass of baptism") and racial impurity by implying that she broke the glass rather than staining it with the son of a black slave. Prior to Francesca's racial connection between her offspring and baptism, the play has already directly associated Tucapel's slave status with tropes of blackness, ugliness, and monstrousness. When she sees Tucapel, Francesca tells him that he has a deformed shape and face (*forma disforme* [226]; *cara disforme* [227]). Another female character pronounces Tucapel "a black man, a monster / a deformed Ethiopian" (un negro, un monstruo / un Etiope disforme [226]) and exclaims "dear Jesus, what an ugly man!" (qué hombre tan feo, Jesús [227]). After the rape scene, Francesca is not so horrified that she has been violated by a man as that she has been violated by a slave and a monster: "[W]hat a sad horror! How can I breathe? / With a monster. How can I continue? / With a slave. How can I see?" (triste horror! ¿cómo aliento? / a un monstruo! Como discurro? / a un esclavo! ¿cómo veo? [225]).

The first act of the play appears to praise the Tucapel. It does not describe his ugliness, but rather his heroism, how he suffered in Africa, and his Christianity and faithfulness to Bartolomé. Based on the first act, the play begins by seeming like it might fit into the genre of the black saint play, the most common play about Afro-Iberian male chararcters in seventeenth-century drama.[18] By the third act, however, we find that Torre's primary goal is to celebrate Vincent Ferrer, not Tucapel, as saint. When the Madonna enters into the plot, the black man changes from saint to sinner. Bartolomé's visit to the icon brings the devil to his family in the shape of Tucapel, a black man who rapes his wife and returns in the shape of the devil and as a ghost who literally eats a fetus.

During the Counter-Reformation, with the surging cult of the Virgin of the Immaculate Conception, Marian icons were sculpted to represent the sexually untouched woman, an eternal feminine spirit unsullied by human time, the human body, and the weight of sin. Moreover, images of the Virgin as mother or pregnant mother give way to those of the Immaculate Conception as a nubile girl-woman, familiar and yet pure and untouched, looking down from her portraits at the viewer.[19] Such Marian icons played a role in shaping masculine fantasy by projecting a type of heteronormative masculine desire toward this type of idealized woman.

The typical Mary of the Immaculate Conception was white, and *The Confession with the Devil* adds a racial dimension to visualization of the Madonna icon because it dramatizes how the blackness of the icon points downward from divine beauty to racial exclusion. The play both inverts and joins the logic of the new Mary icons that ignore Mary's pregnancy. Tucapel, a black man, is father to a son who is black, and the play ignores any aspect of Francesca's role in motherhood. No suggestion is made that the child might belong to Francesca: a black father begets a black child and both burn in flames in limbo. In a perfect inversion of the male Godhead who creates Christ, the play does not consider that the two black male characters might ever, or could ever, leave the flames. Only the white woman is saved: the play has the woman, Francesca, call forth her brother, Saint Vincent, to release her from purgatory, which, in turn, naturalizes the black body in eternal flames. Even though Tucapel is called a Christian, the play never considers the question of whether Ferrer might also save Tucapel and the child. Ferrer's exclusive interest is the salvation of Francesca.

The thirteenth-century *Cantigas de Santa María* provides source material for the final scene in *The Confession with the Devil*. In the *Cantiga*, the

Madonna saves a wife dishonoured by a Moorish servant with African features. The Moorish servant is consumed by flames.[20] In contrast to the *Cantigas de Santa María*, Saint Vincent Ferrer, not Mary, saves the dishonoured woman. The play, ostensibly about a Catholic saint, turns out to be much more closely akin to a perverse modern telenovela with a preposterous and melodramatic plot of rape and the devil's possession of a child's body.

The contradiction related to skin colour is a constricting duality in Tucapel's story – a black saint character in Act 1 and a sinner in Act 3. This is the same duality found in the Madonna icon: she is the holy Marian figure and also a sexualized *morena*. Within that duality, the play sides with the representation of black skin as connected to pollution, and it transforms the social fear of sexuality from the Jew to the black body. While adultery, religion (through Ferrer's family name), and honour are important in this play, the appearance of the *morena* Madonna and Francesca's subsequent horror over the black child and its black father ultimately connect the action of the play to race.

Conclusion

The Confession with the Devil provides an ideal Petri dish in which to study the history of perception of a religious icon. Torre's seventeenth-century play marks the beginning of an important chapter in eighteenth-century formulations of race, since it portrays the Madonna as *morena* in the context of a black sex crime described in terms of pollution and race. The dramatization of Tucapel as a rapist and the joke that connects the Montserrat Virgin with the *morena* are manifestations of the incipient workings of a forming white ideology. Everyday lives of Afro-Iberians are not represented, but instead the drama depicts a stock character type and a black religious icon. Rather than a representation of an authentic woman, the Madonna icon in this play is symptomatic of and perpetuates a patriarchal fear of sexuality based on race, a fear that morphed into a generalized racial fear in Europe and America in the centuries that follow.

In Torre's play, race is inextricably linked to the question of fear and attraction. The black Madonna icon is the hidden object of desire that organizes the plot of the play, a sign that forms part of a religious and social structure that organizes the complicity between the contradiction of idealizing and denigrating darker-skinned women. The virgin icon captures the workings of the imperialist and masculinist attraction to and repulsion from dark skin colour.[21] Linked to the racializing vectors of desire with respect to women, the play explicitly connects the worship of the dark Madonna icon with the perpetuation of staged aberrant black sexuality. The play displaces the black skin colour on the icon into a new story – that of the cliché of the male rapist – a sexual fantasy that pervades the logic of modern racist narratives.

A basic assumption of this chapter is that it's necessary to study the Madonna icon from a male point of view in order to have the vocabulary for dismantling the optics behind the racial logic of whiteness that causes literary scholars to ignore plays like this one and that causes historians to ignore the plight of Afro-Iberians. Ultimately, I hope that the type of scholarship presented here helps overcome and even ridicule the painful spectacle of race, with the goal of envisioning a racial landscape devoid of the suffering caused by the operative category of whiteness present in the world system.

One Spanish play, *El prodigio de Etiopia*, a black saint play from the seventeenth century, suggests that the greatest roadblock in overcoming the pain of racism is the persistence of a type of vision that accompanies racist thinking. One character in this play states that what has affected him the most has been the pain of how he has seen the world:

Since the best of the senses
Is sight, the cause of my pain,
Of my torment
Of my hurt,
Are my eyes.

(Siendo el sentido mejor
La vista, en el mal que siento
Los ojos son mi tormento,
Los ojos son mi dolor. [123])

The lament of this character from the seventeenth century has not lost its potency. In an uncanny echo, the best-selling African-American author Ta-Nehisi Coates writes a letter to his son in which he wants to explain the workings of race in North America. In *Between the World and Me* (2015), Coates observes: "[O]h, my eyes. When I was a boy, no portion of my body suffered more than my eyes" (116).

NOTES

1 Mary Elizabeth Perry provides an explanation for the simultaneous and paradoxical coding of holy chasity and sexual desire on the black Madonna. Influenced by the anthropologist Mary Douglass's ideas about rituals, Perry explains that people worship the Montserrat Madonna icon

in order to deal with a fear of difference and convert the nefarious quality of blackness on the Montserrat icon into a sign of the sacred (117).

2 This chapter is the first study in English of Torre's *The Confession with the Devil*. Although the earliest published version of the play is 1678, Torre wrote the play around 1655 (see Beusterien, "La discriminación"). The appearance of the play coincided with the increased interest in Saint Vincent Ferrer in Valencia surrounding the celebration of the 200th anniversary of his canonization. For the plot Torre adapted, see *El mayor prodigio* (1698), a novel written by Francisco Redón.

3 Cisneros writes: "When I see la Virgen de Guadalupe I want to lift her dress as I did my dolls and look to see if she comes with *cones*, and does her *panocha* look like mine, and does she have dark nipples too? ... She is not neuter like Barbie. She gave birth. She has a womb" (51). In turn, Mary Elizabeth Perry comments: "[The Montserrat Madonna] can teach everyone to be a mother, not biologically, of course, but figuratively – to remind men and women alike of the caring quality that we human beings all hold in common" (117). Perry examines the Montserrat Madonna as ordinary, everyday, and empowering, illuminating the lives of oppressed peoples. My essay works in concert with studies that seek to encourage caring and also those that seek to find how literary texts reveal the authenticity of black lives. As a complementary study, the work of Nick Jones illuminates the beauty of lives of Afro-Iberian peoples in representations from early modern Iberia. Jones elucidates expressions from black women and how Luis de Góngora celebrates beauty through recuperating vestiges of her speech, her dance, her self-confident beauty and her "stylin' out," vitalizing an appreciation for the language and lives of often unnamed black women from history.

4 Tamar Herzog notes that much of the historical work on Afro-Iberians has been done, but the reasons for historiographic neglect are still in need of further exploration: "We already have sufficient evidence that slavery existed in Spain, that it was an important phenomenon, and that during the early-modern period most slaves were of African descent. What we need perhaps are not additional studies but an evaluation of why memory of them disappeared and what it will take to awaken it" (7).

5 In the twelfth century, a shift in the focus of Christian veneration brought Jews to the fore as preachers, and artists began to dwell in vivid detail on Christ's pain and emphasize the cruelty of Jewish tormentors (Lipton). Seventeenth-century icons revitalized medieval anti-Semitism. Sermons sometimes asked those who viewed bloody Christ icons to see Jews as responsible for the blood. The priest Martin Caballero de Isla (1659) saw a narrative when he looked on a bloody icon of Christ: "I see some fierce-looking men, some idolatrous Jews throw it down on the ground ... I see them spilling the blood of the dead image as if it were alive" (Veo,

que unos hombres fieras, unos judíos idolatras, arrojándola en el suelo ... veo derrmamar sangre a aquella imagen muerta, como si estuviera viva [qtd. in Beusterien, *Eye*, 74]). Francisco Quevedo describes the icon of the Patient Christ in his prose piece *Execration against Jews*. He writes that, when the parishioners arrived to the icon "of the Holy Christ to worship, it spoke to them and bled signaling those Hebrews that had committed the sacrilege against it" (para venerarle, adonde subcedió aquel sacrilegio del Santo Cristo que aquellos hebreos hicieron con su imagen que les habló y virtió sangre [qtd. in Beusterien, *Eye*, 74]).

6 For the historical precedent to the Marian association with war, see Remensnyder.

7 For the black Magus, see Brewer Garcia. For a black Jesus, saints, and others, see Beusterien, *Eye*, and Rowe.

8 For a series of artist renderings of images of the icon of the Montserrat Madonna that vary between white and darker shades (for instance, the *Libro rojo* of the Abbey of Montserrat depicts the Madonna with light skin), see Albareda.

9 The original title of this work by Alonso de Sandoval is *Naturaleza, policia sagrada y profana, costumbres y ritos, disciplina y catecismo evangélico de todos etíopes* (Sevilla, 1627). It was later titled *De Instauranda: Aethiopum Salute*. See Harpster.

10 Scholars and the popular media have continued to debate the authenticity of the colour of the icon. The English newspaper the *Telegraph* reported in 2001 that the Montserrat black Virgin "was white originally," and it quotes a priest who says, "[I]n Montserrat we have assumed for some time that the statue is not black" (Wilkinson, "Montserrat Black Virgin," *Telegraph*, 3 April 2001, http://www.telegraph.co.uk/news/worldnews/europe/spain/1316133/Montserrat-Black-Virgin-was-white-originally.html). More scholarly work needs to be done on the historiography of the black Madonna with regards to racism and the perception of race and whiteness in contemporary Europe and Spain.

11 For a history of the Inquisitional censorship of the Enríquez Gómez play that has the same plot, see Domínguez de Paz; Den Boer.

12 For further exploration of how anti-Semitism and black racism simultaneously operate in the context of a white regime of vision in theatre in the early modern Iberian world, see my *Eye on Race*. With respect to race studies and Iberia, the Islamic presence is the most important identity node against which a sense of Hispanic national self emerges, since it is based simultaneously on the religious and dark-skinned outsider that shapes the white vision regime. See Beusterien, *Eye*, 16.

13 Black characters who describe themselves as white are found in many plays from the period (see chapter 3 in Beusterien, *Eye*). This phenomenon

is not limited to literature, but can also be found in the historical record. One particularly relevant case is the that of María Blanca. Inquisitional records list María Blanca, a name that literally means Mary the White, as Congolese, a slave, and black (see McKnight).

14 For the practice of blackface, see Beusterien, *Eye*, 101–4.

15 For the Madonna of Guadalupe as a palimpsest for a pagan landscape, see Schmidt.

16 The character Tucapel appeared in Pedro de Oña's epic poem *Arauco domado* and also in plays from the period, such as *Algunas hazañas de las muchas de Don García Hurtado de Mendoza, Marqués de Cañete* (1622). In the same way that Torre celebrates Tucapel's heroism and then disparages him, so Tucapel in *Arauco domado* is an apparent hero figure: he is feisty and has the capacity to convert to Christianity. Yet, like Tucapel at the end of the play, Tucapel in *Arauco domado* is portrayed as lustful and not a true Spanish Christian. It should be noted that Afro-Hispanics in Chile were represented as both the oppressor and the oppressed. For example, Juan Valiente, who was black, was an important soldier in the conquest of Chile (Restall). But black people are also characterized as lesser individuals. The cacique in Ercilla's epic disparages his executioner because he is a *negro*. For more on Tucapel in Golden Age drama, see Castillo. Thanks also to Miguel Martínez.

17 For more on medieval and early modern abortions, see Muller; and Van De Walle.

18 Especially since the title of Lope's black saint play called *El prodigio de Etiopía* is an echo of the title of the source text *El mayor prodigio*, which also features a black man in a narrative identical to the one told in *The Confession with the Devil*. For the genre of black saint plays, see Beusterien, *Eye*.

19 Pregnant virgins were taken off altars, especially in western Iberia (Portugal and Galicia), as a result of the Counter-Reformation (Warner 134). One reason for this was, as Maria Aline Seabra Ferreira writes, "the Virgin's pregnancy can be equated with a positive vision of feminine autonomy from men" (176). The church implicitly plays a fundamental role in denying the power of the fertility of women by eliminating pregnant virgins – commonly called "O" virgins or *vírgenes de la O*, in a reference to their rounded pregnant midsection – from the catalogue of sacred sculptures and paintings. For a general overview of how traditional cultural icons have degraded and suppressed women, see Radford Ruether. In contrast to Sandra Cisnero's portrayal, the seventeenth-century portrayal of the icon is unsexed and never pregnant.

20 The *cantiga* by Alfonso X is 186 (*Cantigas* [Madrid: Cátedra, 1988]). Thanks to Nick Jones for this reference.

21 Seventeenth-century England also adopted the trope of female dark skin as exemplary of the patriarchal fear of the darkness of female sexuality

(see Boose; Habib; and Hall). Othello is a case in point, since Shakespeare's play is structured around the pairs of opposition that give the black Madonna meaning, like beauty and ugliness, and virginity and motherhood (Hopkins). A study of the black Madonna in *The Confession with the Devil* complicates the English imperial model (the Spanish experience was unique, as Spain witnessed an explosion of icons as England abandoned them). More important, the study of Spain enriches scholarly understanding of the history of the perception of race, since representations of blackness in the early modern imperial arena were not just of unrepresentability, as is commonly suggested in the case of England, but also of representability, as in the case of theatre from Spain.

REFERENCES

Albareda, Anselm. *Història de Montserrat*. Barcelona: Publicacions de l'Abadia de Montserrat. 1972.

Alcalá, Jerónimo de. *Alonso, mozo de muchos amos*, II. In *La novela picaresca española*. Edited by Florencio Sevilla, 914–62. Madrid: Castalia. 1989.

Alvar, Manuel. *Edición y estudio del Entretenimiento de las Musas de Don Francisco de la Torre y Sevil*. Valencia: Universitat de València, 1987.

Benko, Stephen. *The Virgin Goddess: Studies in the Pagan and Christian Roots of Mariology*. Leiden, NL: Brill, 1993.

Beusterien, John. *An Eye on Race: Perspectives from Theater in Imperial Spain*. Lewisburg, PA: Bucknell University Press, 2006.

– "La discriminación contra los afro-hispanos en una obra teatral del siglo XVII: Una escena grotesca de *La confesión con el demonio* de Francisco de la Torre y Sevil." In "Lo abyecto, lo grotesco y lo sublime en la literatura áurea hispánica." Special issue of *Hispania felix: Revista rumano-española de cultura y civilización de los Siglos de Oro*, edited by Robert Lauer. 7 (2016): 97–118.

Beusterien, John, and Noelia Cirnigliaro, eds. "Touching the Ground: Female Footwear in the Early Modern Hispanic World." Special issue of *Journal of Spanish Cultural Studies* 14, no. 2. (2013).

Boose, Lynda E. "'The Getting of a Lawful Race': Racial Discourse in Early Modern England and the Unrepresentable Black Woman." In *Women, "Race," and Writing in Early Modern England*, edited by Margo Hendricks and Patricia Parker, 35–54. New York: Routledge, 1994.

Brewer-García, Larissa. "Imagined Transformations: Color, Beauty, and the Black Christian Conversion in Seventeenth-Century America." In Patton, *Envisioning Others*, 111–41.

Castillo, Moises R. *Indios en escena: La representación del amerindio en el teatro del Siglo de Oro*. West Lafayette, IN: Purdue University Press, 2009.

Catlos, Brian A. *Muslims of Medieval Latin Christendom, c. 1050–1614.* Cambridge: Cambridge University Press, 2014.

Christian, William A. *Local Religion in Sixteenth Century Spain.* Princeton, NJ: Princeton University Press, 1981.

Cisneros, Sandra. "Guadalupe, the Sex Goddess." In *La Diosa de las Americas: Writings on the Virgin of Guadalupe*, edited by Ana Castillo, 46–51. New York: Riverhead Books, 1996.

Coates, Ta-Nehisi. *Between the World and Me.* New York: Speigel & Grau, 2015.

Den Boer, Harm. "¿Católico Zárate, judío Muley? Nueva lectura de Las misas de San Vicente Ferrer." In *Antonio Enríquez Gómez: Un poeta entre santos y judaizantes*, edited by J. Ignacio Díez and Carsten Wilke, 15–34. Kassel, DE: Reichenberger, 2015.

Domínguez de Paz, Elisa. "*Las misas de San Vicente Ferrer*, una controvertida comedia de Zárate censurada por la Inquisición (siglos XVII y XVIII)." *Anagnórisis: Revista de investigación teatral* 6 (2012): 6–39.

Fernández, Esther. *Eros en escena: Eroticismo en el teatro del Siglo de Oro.* Newark: Juan de la Cuesta, 2009.

Foster, Elisa. "The Black Madonna of Montserrat." In Patton, , 18–50.

Greer, Margaret. *María de Zayas Tells Baroque Tales of Love and the Cruelty of Men.* University Park: Pennsylvania State University Press, 2000.

Habib, Imtiaz. *Shakespeare and Race: Postcolonial Praxis in the Early Modern Period.* Lanham, MD: University Press of America, 2000.

Hall, Kim. *Things of Darkness: Economies of Race and Gender in Early Modern England.* Ithaca, NY: Cornell University Press, 1995.

Harpster, Grace. "The Color of Salvation: The Materiality of Blackness in Alonso de Sandoval's *De instauranda Aethiopum salute.*" In Patton, *Envisioning Others*, 83–110.

Herzog, Tamar. "How Did Early Modern Slaves in Spain Disappear? The Antecedents." *Republic of Letters: A Journal for the Study of Knowledge, Politics, and the Arts* 3, no. 1 (2012): 1–7.

Hopkins, Lisa. "'Black Is Beautiful': Othello and the Cult of the Black Madonna." In *Marian Moments in Early Modern British Drama*, edited by Regina Buccola and Lisa Hopkins, 75–86. Aldershot, UK: Ashgate, 2007.

Jones, Nick. "Cosmetic Ontologies, Cosmetic Subversions: Articulating Black Beauty and Humanity in Luis de Góngora's 'En la fiesta del Santísimo Sacramento.'" *Journal for Early Modern Cultural Studies* 15, no. 1 (2015): 26–54.

Latour, Bruno. "What Is Iconoclash? Or Is There a World beyond the Image Wars?" In *Iconoclash: Beyond the Image Wars in Science, Religion, and Art*, edited by Bruno Latour and Peter Weibel, 14–37. Cambridge, MA: MIT Press, 2002.

Lee, Christina H. "La Señora Peregrina as mediatrix in 'La ilustre fregona.'" *Cervantes* 25, no. 1 (2005): 45–68.

Lipton, Sara. *Dark Mirror: The Medieval Origins of Anti-Jewish Iconography*. New York: Metropolitan, 2014.

McKnight, Kathryn Joy. "Blasphemy as Resistance: An African Slave Woman before the Inquisition." In *Women in the Inquisition: Spain and the New World*, edited by Mary E. Giles, 229–53. Baltimore, MD: Johns Hopkins University Press, 1998.

Michael D. McGaha, "Entre el 'Noble Moor' y el 'Negro Perro Moro': *Ótelo* y *Las misas de San Vicente Ferrer*." In *Vidas paralelas: El teatro español y el teatro isabelino, 1580–1680*, edited by Anita K. Stoll, 37–44. Boston: Tamesis, 1993.

Muller, Wolfgang P. *The Criminalization of Abortion in the West: Its Origins in Medieval Law*. Ithaca, NY: Cornell University Press, 2012.

Nirenberg, David. "Enmity and Assimilation: Jews, Christians, and Converts in Medieval Spain." *Common Knowledge* 9, no. 1 (2003): 137–55.

Patton, Pamela A., ed. *Envisioning Others: Race, Color, and the Visual in Iberia and Latin America*. Leiden, NL: Brill, 2015.

Pérez, Mirzam C. *The Comedia of Virginity: Mary and the Politics of Seventeenth-Century Spanish Theatre*. Waco, TX: Baylor University Press, 2012.

Perry, Mary Elizabeth. "The Black Madonna of Montserrat: Legend, Ritual, and Iconography." In *Views of Women's Lives in Western Tradition*, edited by Frances Richardson Keller, 110–28. Lewiston, NY: Edwin Mellen Press, 1989.

Peterson, Jeanette Favrot. *Visualizing Guadalupe: From Black Madonna to Queen of the Americas*. Austin: University of Texas Press, 2014.

Radford Ruether, Rosemary, ed. *Religion and Sexism: Images of Woman in the Jewish and Christian Traditions*. New York: Simon and Schuster, 1974.

Redón, Francisco. *El mayor prodigio y caso exemplar: Origen de las missas de San Vicente Ferrer*. Valencia: Jaime de Bordazar, 1698.

Remensnyder, Amy G. *La Conquistadora: The Virgin Mary at War and Peace in the Old and New Worlds*. Oxford: Oxford University Press, 2014.

Restall, Matthew. "Black Conquistadors: Armed Africans in Early Spanish America." *Americas* 57, no. 2 (2000): 171–205.

Rowe, Erin Kathleen. "Visualizing Black Sanctity in Early Modern Spanish Polychrome Sculpture." In Patton, *Envisioning Others*, 51–82.

Scheer, Monique. "From Majesty to Mystery: Change in the Meanings of Black Madonnas from the Sixteenth to Nineteenth Centuries." *American Historical Review* 107 (2002): 1379–1411.

Schmidt, Rachel. "The Stained and the Unstained: Feliciana de la Voz's *Hymn to Mary* in the Context of the Inmaculist Movement." Paper presented at the Sixth Texas Cervantes Symposium, 21 October 2016.

Seabra Ferreira, Maria Aline. "Paula Rego's (Her)ethical Visions." In *The Sacred and the Feminine: Imagination and Sexual Difference*, edited by Griselda Pollock and Victoria Turvey-Sauron, 166–77. London: I.B. Taurus, 2007.

Torre y Sevil, Francisco de la. *La confesión con el demonio.* In *Parte quarenta y quatro de comedias nuevas, nunca empresas, escogidas de los mejores ingenios de España*, 197–242. Madrid: Roque Rico de Miranda. 1678.

Torre y Sevil, Francisco de la, and José Arnal de Bolea. *La Azucena de Etiopía: Comedia de fiesta.* Edited by Giovanni Cara. Alinea, ES: Florence, 2006.

Van de Walle, Etienne. "'Marvellous Secrets': Birth Control in European Short Fiction, 1150–1650." *Population Studies* 54, no. 3 (2000): 321–30.

Vega, Lope de. *El prodigio de Etiopia.* Edited by John Beusterien. Vilagarcía de Arousa, ES: Mirabel. 2005.

Warner, Marina. *Alone of All Her Sex: The Myth and the Cult of the Virgin Mary.* New York: Knopf, 1976.

Wilke, Carsten Lorenz. *Jüdisch-christiches Poppeleben Im Barock: Zur Biographie des Kaufmanns und Dichters Antonio Enríquez Gómez.* Frankfurt am Main: Peter Lang, 1994.

PART IV

Recasting Epic and Heroic Moulds

Chapter Nine

For Love of the White Sea: The Curious Identity of Uludj Ali

DIANA DE ARMAS WILSON

The story of Uludj Ali, the illiterate renegade whose love of the Mediterranean – known to Ottoman Turks as the *Bahr-i Sefid* or "Pure White Sea" – spurred his rise to grand admiral of the Ottoman navy, continues to captivate Western scholars. His spectacular evolution from disenfranchised Christian origins to the Ottoman military elite demonstrates the broad range of opportunity afforded by the fluid Mediterranean world to adopt and revise religious and cultural identities. Uludj Ali's years as a galley slave, his impromptu conversion to Islam, and his canny decisions at sea made him an almost undefeatable enemy, vulnerable in the end only to *eros*.

This chapter traces Uludj Ali's path to extraordinary prominence as a commander whose passions, oriented toward the White Sea and its commercial riches, dovetailed with his major loyalties: to Islam, the Ottoman Empire, and his mentor Turgut Reis, known to the West as Dragut. Uludj Ali's self-reinvention was striking: he crafted a complex personal identity that reflected the early modern Mediterranean in both its diversity and conflicts. Reading his story through the lens of "love" means not only noting his eventual defeat in the arms of *eros* but also considering the motivating forces and contradictions that emerged from his change of identity. Given the expanding demand for information about Islam – and the aim of this volume to reassess love in early modern literature – this chapter will flesh out the composite identity of Uludj Ali, an illiterate self-made man with a disfiguring disease. What follows addresses his Italian Christian origins, his years as a galley slave, his impulsive turn to Islam, his career as a pirate/privateer, his rise to grand admiral of the Ottoman navy, and his death in the arms of Eros.

Turning Turk

Uludj Ali was a renegade, one of the flood of Christian men and women who "turned Turk" during the sixteenth century, inviting accusations of treachery or even of formal treason: "If Turks were the epitome of evil" in Christian Europe, Tobias Graf asks, "How much worse was a Christian who had chosen to become one of them?" (31, 34). In the classic French study *Christians for Allah* (*Les chrétiens d'Allah*), Bartolomé and Lucile Bennassar broadly describe the phenomenon of early modern Christians who apostatized to gain freedom and, often, financial security. Because the Grand Turk needed artisans, weavers of silks and damask, shipbuilders, seamen, ironmongers, and so on, "men flocked from Christendom to Islam, which tempted them with visions of adventure and profit – and paid them to stay"; this flock became a tidal wave, with "no comparable flow in the other direction" (Braudel, 2:799–800). Habsburg *presidios* or garrisons in North Africa, such as that in Oran, suffered epidemics of desertion. Christian soldiers quartered there would sometimes defect to Islamic lands to escape the general rigours of military life, including debt, isolation, and even hunger. This kind of defection was not the case, as what follows will show, with Uludj Ali. My quest for his many-pronged identity begins with early modern Spanish texts by Antonio de Sosa and Miguel de Cervantes. Being aware, however, that much "European research bears the mark of the Christian perspective" (Kologlu 513), I have also turned to various Turkish sources to help me trace Uludj Ali's amazing climb from fisherman to galley slave to lord high admiral.

Beyond any ethnic nationalism, the complex mechanism of identity may also be shaped by race, religion, nation, tribe, language, gender, social class, education, profession, disability, and so on. Identities can of course be shared – leading to identity politics – and some, as in the case of Uludj Ali, can also be unmade or remade in the course of a lifetime. For those in our age who might fear that their national identity has been collapsing, it is instructive to look back at the early modern Mediterranean during the age of Uludj Ali. The *Mare Nostrum* or White Sea was a shared geography of ethno-religiously diverse character, of multiple denominations, both sincere *and* sanctimonious. A theatre of both conflict and coexistence, it was also a region where issues of identity were often shifting, blurred, or ambiguous.

The Renegade

Nowhere was a crisis of identity more theatrically portrayed than in the person of Uludj Ali (1518?–87), whose very nickname in Arabic signifies a shift: it literally means "the renegade Ali" – that is, a new Muslim, a convert to Islam. He was born Giovanni Dionigi Galeni to impoverished Christian parents in the Kingdom of Naples, in Licasteli, a small village in the province of Calabria near Cape Colonna. Because his parents were fishers, Giovanni took on fishing or boating jobs as a youth. At some unknown date he was snatched in a raid by the Greek renegade Ali Ahmed Reis and became a galley slave, a Christian consigned to rowing the oars of a Turkish ship for years.

Legend has it that one day Uludj Ali was insulted by a fellow oarsman and, because as a Christian he could not wreak vengeance on his attacker, at that point he apostasized. In Dr. Sosa's explanation of this conversion scene, "having been punched one day by a lewend (that is, a corsair soldier), [Uludj Ali] turned Turk and renegade intending to avenge this blow, which he could not do as a Christian" (dándole un día un levante (esto es, un soldado cosario) un bofetón, se hizo turco y renegado con intención de vengarse dél, pues siendo christiano no lo podía hacer) ["Epítome" 347]).[1] As a captive clergyman, Dr. Sosa generally displayed an ideological ferocity toward converts to Islam. His writings often contribute to the stock tropes of cruelty and sensuality in Christian-European writings about renegades, who were envisioned as evil people who had abandoned Christian values. Readers may be amazed, however, at Dr. Sosa's remarkably tame chapter on the renegade Uludj Ali, where he is painted as a superb sailor, able to arm a frigate or brigantine for his corsair activities across the high seas (*Reyes*, 346–61). Poised as he was between two warring empires and religions, Uludj Ali curiously defected in a moment of revenge, after which he never looked back. Wright, Spence, and Lemons rightly see him as a Turkish challenge "to European identity" (xiv).

Uludj Ali's conversion is colourfully fictionalized in Cervantes's "Captive's Tale," a three-chapter inset story in Part I of *Don Quijote* (I.39–41). The figure of Uludj Ali there – Cervantes uses the Spanish corruptions Ochalí or Uchalí – spends fourteen years rowing in the galleys. He becomes a renegade when he is over thirty years old in order to wreak vengeance on a corsair who, in keeping with Dr. Sosa's claims, had punched him in the face. María Antonia Garcés, author of the prize-winning study *Cervantes in Algiers*, notes that readers can find across the Cervantine *obra* "a complete typological panorama of renegades, from the virulent defector, the indecisive convert, the opportunistic turncoat, to the repentant apostate" ["Captivity," n.p.]. I would add to this catalogue the figure of Uludj Ali as an *impulsive* convert, a man with a curiously nested religious identity.

From these marginal beginnings as a Christian captive fisherman – an origin found in all the sources – Uludj Ali rose to become a pirate-entrepreneur and, in time, grand admiral of the Ottoman navy in a meritocratic Muslim world. This rise was not unusual. Because the

Turks "did not recognize the idea of nobility through birth," fully one-third of the top level of the Ottoman ruling class was held by men "of non-Turkish origin" (Kologlu 518, 523).

Pre-Lepanto Career

In 1548, Uludj Ali joined forces with Turgut Reis (Dragut), a great lord in Barbary who would become his mentor and sponsor. Uludj Ali's official career was launched several years later, in 1551 in Constantinople, where he received a salary and the right to carry one lantern (*fener*) on his ship as a sign of imperial service to the reigning sultan, Süleyman the Magnificent. Another decade would follow before Uludj Ali distinguished himself as a Turkish warrior.

When the Spanish occupied Djerba in 1560, Uludj Ali was influential in putting together a relief fleet that attacked the island, one of the greatest disasters of Philip II's reign. Over half of the nearly fifty ships of the Christian armada were lost, and close to 10,000 Spaniards surrendered. On 1 October 1560, the Turks made a triumphal entry into Constantinople harbour amid the salvoes and festivities of the crowds: a green-painted flagship was followed by fifteen bright red galleys. Long processions of Christian captives were led in triumph through the streets of the city, in chains and with their armour worn backwards. A leading captive, Álvaro de Sande – who years later would become commander in Naples of Cervantes's regiment – was ransomed after two years by Ogier Ghiselin de Busbecq, the imperial ambassador at Constantinople from 1554 to 1562. Busbecq movingly discusses the "Jerba" disaster in the fourth of his *Turkish Letters* (169–243). This Spanish loss was a notable gain for Uludj Ali's reputation across the Mediterranean.

After Djerba, Uludj Ali participated in the Siege of Malta. To visit Malta is to hear, again and again, that Saint Paul was a castaway there. But in Uludj Ali's day the island was home to the Knights of the Hospital of Saint John of Jerusalem, an order of military monks founded in the eleventh century. After the Knights Hospitallers were expelled from Jerusalem, they reestablished themselves in Rhodes until the Turks drove them out in 1522. The Knights resettled in Malta in 1530, when Carlos V granted them the island for the annual tribute of one Maltese falcon to be sent, on All Saints' Day, to him or his viceroy in Sicily. The Knights of Malta, who became "defenders of the faith" in the Mediterranean, were also, as Howard Mancing reminds us, "the most prominent Christian pirates of the sixteenth century" (529). Operating, as is well known, on both Christian and Muslim sides, pirates were regarded by the age as entrepreneurial corsairs or privateers – that is, as businessmen. From the Turkish point of view, Malta was regarded as "a Christian corsair den" (Gürkan 125).

In 1565, the residents of Malta had to defend their island against a huge Turkish fleet whose arrival on their shores "hit Europe like a hurricane" (Braudel, 2: 1014). Attached to this fleet was Uludj Ali, who fought for the Muslims during Malta's legendary five-month siege. Unlike the losses at Djerba, Malta was a victory for some 10,000 Christian defenders, who held off an Ottoman force double that size or more. Uludj Ali fought in the company of his aged sponsor Dragut, who was killed by a blow from a stone dislodged by a bullet that fell from the fortress of Saint Elmo. After the five-month siege, the Turks finally retired to Constantinople, where their Muslim countrymen were "universally in mourning," even hurling stones at Christians in the streets (Braudel, 2: 1020).

Upon leaving Malta, Uludj Ali headed directly for Tripoli, which he governed for three and a half years (1565–68) in place of the dead Dragut, whose great wealth he inherited – including ships, munitions, clothing, monies, slaves, and properties. During this period, Uludj Ali became an extremely wealthy man, thanks to both Dragut's legacy and his own corsair activities around the coasts of Sicily, Calabria, and Naples. Soon after these years in Tripoli, the sultan appointed Uludj Ali to be *beylerbeyi* of Algiers, a term translated as governor or viceroy – or, as Dr. Sosa puts it, as king – the nineteenth of the thirty "Reyes de Argel" who feature in his *Epítome* (346–61).

Battle of Lepanto

While ruling Algiers, Uludj Ali took part in the epic and bloody sea Battle of Lepanto (7 October 1571), fighting against the Holy League Alliance of Spain, the Papacy (Pius V), and Venice, headed by Philip II's twenty-four-year-old half-brother Don Juan of Austria. Uludj Ali commanded the left flank of the Ottoman fleet, sailing in a galley that resembled a sea dragon. Cervantes would be wounded at that battle, which he would later call, in the prologue to his *Exemplary Novels*, "the most memorable and noblest occasion that past centuries have seen, and that future ones cannot hope to see" (la más memorable y alta ocasión que vieron los pasados siglos, ni esperan ver los venideros) [63]).

Lepanto was a battle of unimaginable carnage. Spanish reports note that the Ottoman admiral Ali Pasha (the sultan's brother-in-law) died in blood combat aboard his flagship *Sultana*, his severed head displayed atop a pike as a Christian trophy, his two adolescent sons taken captive. Due in large part to the Venetian galleasses or "floating fortresses" at this battle – merchant ships retrofitted for warfare by the Christian League – Sultan

Selim II lost at Lepanto some 20,000–30,000 men, dead or wounded, plus some 15,000 Christian galley slaves who were liberated (Braudel 2: 1112). Uludj Ali was the only member of the Ottoman high command to escape the carnage. He managed to outmanoeuvre Giovanni Andrea Doria, to capture the flagship (*la capitana*) of the Knights of Malta, and to escape with thirty galleys intact and the flag of the Maltese ship. He was received as a hero in Constantinople and promoted to *kapudan pasha* (lord high admiral), a position he held until his death sixteen years later.

In a description of the Battle of Lepanto in "The Captive's Tale," Cervantes paints his Uchalí as a "bold and daring corsair" (atrevido y venturoso cosario), a Muslim who captures the Christian flagship just before it is rescued by a ship carrying Cervantes's fictional hero Captain Ruy Pérez de Viedma (*Ingenioso hidalgo* I.42). Forced to retreat from battle, Uchalí manages to carry to Constantinople the Maltese flag, a historical fact. But he also brings back that fictional Spanish captain as a slave, captured when Pérez dutifully leaps unto the enemy ship and, separated from all his fellow soldiers, is left wounded and surrounded by Turks: "And as you've heard, gentlemen, Uchalí and all his squadron managed to escape, with me as his captive and in his power, the only sad man among so many happy souls, the only prisoner among so many free men" (Y como ya habréis, señores, oído decir que el Uchalí se salvó con toda su escuadra, vine yo a quedar cautivo en su poder, y solo fui el triste entre tantos alegres y el cautivo entre tantos libres [*Ingenioso hidalgo* I.39: 478]). Despite being enslaved, however, Cervantes's fictional captive will eulogize Uchalí, his owner, as "a man of goodness [un hombre de bien]" who treated his 3,000 slaves "with great humanity" (con mucha humanidad [*Ingenioso hidalgo* I.40: 484]). Writing on the day of Uludj Ali's death in 1587, the *bailo* or Venetian ambassador to Turkey, Lorenzo Bernardo, claimed that Uludj Ali had over 2,000 slaves who were "very well treated by him" (qtd. by Sola, *Uchali*, 29).

Cervantes's strongly autobiographical inset story "The Captive's Tale" contains various sly departures from his own life. Although he did fight and was badly wounded at Lepanto, Cervantes never went to Constantinople. Nor was he ever a captive of the humane slave-owner Uludj Ali. Cervantes was instead purchased, in real life, by a one-time slave of Uludj Ali, Hasan Pasha the Venetian, whose extravagant savagery is chronicled in *Don Quijote*. Cervantes portrays him there as "the cruelest renegade ever seen" (el más cruel renegado que jamás se ha visto) and, a page later, as a "murderer of the whole human race" (homicida de todo el género humano [*Ingenioso hidalgo* I.40: 485]). Uludj Ali's humane treatment of his slaves seems to have had no impact on the homicidal character of his own one-time slave Hasan Pasha.

In *The Battle of Lepanto*, a collection elegantly edited and translated by Elizabeth Wright, Sarah Spence, and Andrew Lemons, a clutch of Latin poets predictably take the Christian-European side of this battle, hurling verbal abuse at Uludj Ali. Pompeo Arnolfini sneers at his "infamous flight" (180–1), and an anonymous poet stresses his treachery (*tua perfida* [106–7]). But perhaps the Latin poet who best illustrates this negative attitude is Giovanni Baptista Arcucci: "For wild Uluj Ali, who was born, they say, in the Calabrian Mountains and was baptized in the purifying spring, but soon embraced the false doctrines of the Arab priests; who, the story goes, though once all of Libya and Asia and even the great part of our Europe honoured him, foreswore the true God, and swerved from the righteous path of his parents" (221). In a major Latin epic titled *The Song of John of Austria* (*Austrias Carmen*), the black poet Juan Latino, an ex-slave teaching Latin in Granada, scolds Uludj Ali for having renounced Christianity for the "Muhammadan plague" (Mahumeti peste [360–1]). All these attacks are mildly redeemed by the Latin poet Giovanni Antonio Taglietti, who paints Uludj Ali in his *Ecloga Nautica* as being "mighty in war, no stranger to the sea, and unyielding in suffering" (*Battle*, 140–1).

Disfigurement and Death

Let me close this profile with several items that shed light on both the suffering and the unyielding identity of Uludj Ali. As regards the former, he was disfigured and ridiculed for it: both Cervantes and Sosa stress that Uludj Ali's fellow oarsmen called him *fartax*, which in Turkish means "scabby." He suffered from a condition known as *tiña*, the result of a parasite that produces ulcerations, scabs (*costras*), and loss of hair on the scalp. Dr. Sosa explains how Uludj Ali was bullied for this: "he would receive a thousand insults from the other Christians, who sometimes refused to eat with him, or even to pull oars on the same bench" (recibía mil afrentas de los otros christianos, que no querían a veces comer con él ni bogar en su bancada) (347). Emilio Sola has written a splendid book in Spanish about Uludj Ali, whose very subtitle – *El Calabrés Tiñoso* – announces this disfigurement.

In yet another misery to consider, Uludj Ali appears to have suffered from bouts of melancholy after his retirement. In the wake of a military excursion across the Black Sea beyond Trabzon that proved a failure and cost the lives of many Turks, he returned to Constantinople "very discontented" (muy descontento). According to Dr. Sosa: "He had this custom: that on the day on which he felt somewhat melancholic or did not wish to speak about business matters, he would dress in black; and when he would dress in colours, that was a sign that anyone could approach him and happily do business with him" (Tenía una costumbre: que el día en que estaba algún tanto melancólico o no quería que hablasen en negocios, se vestía de negro; y cuando de colores se vestía, era señal que cada uno pudiese llegar a él y negociar a placer [360]). Thanks to Uludj Ali's high status as an Ottoman grandee, he could select and even signal these periods of withdrawal from human company.

A third and last marker of identity to ponder was the amazing constancy of Uludj Ali after his apostasy from Christianity. Whether or not he severed ties with his kinspeople, Spanish envoys would try to exploit his former connections in Christian Calabria. These envoys would often entice high-level renegades in Ottoman lands with financial rewards, offering them land grants or dukedoms to betray their rulers and return to Christianity. Based on dozens of documents in the Spanish archives at Simancas, the Turkish Hispanist Emra Safa Gürkan exposes the clandestine measures and covert operations employed by Habsburg secret service agents to remind Uludj Ali of his Christian origins and obligations to the Spanish king. When all these missions failed, the Habsburgs even considered assassination, but these plots came to nothing (Gürkan, 135–7). Despite offers of fiefdoms and aristocratic titles – of count, duke, and marquis – Uludj Ali could not be bought. Claiming that the Sultan "gave him everything he wanted," not only did he refuse all offers of defection, but also he "never denounced the Habsburg agents who offered them" (Gürkan, 139, 142). Tobias Graf also discusses the resistance of Uludj Ali to Spanish secret diplomacy as well as the attempts to assassinate him: "Realizing the danger that the Ottoman fleet and corsairs created for their defenses, the Habsburg secret service dispatched a number of go-betweens in order to remind Uluc Ali of his Christian past and obligations to his true monarch" (abstract). Uludj Ali, in short, could never be bribed by the envoys of Spain to give up his sense of allegiance to Islam. He remained constant, at least in orthopraxy, to the love of Allah.

Uludj Ali did not die by assassination but by an untimely act of Eros. His sudden death on 21 June 1587 is described by the American historian Bruce Ware Allen as "the result of overexertion in the arms of a slave girl (against the express advice of his doctor)" (261). A Turkish source seconds this kind of death: "while playing with a young girl, his soul flew from his body to the other world" (Kologlu, 531). The Venetian *bailo* or resident ambassador to Constantinople, Lorenzo Bernardo, describes Uludj Ali's death more decorously, claiming that it was caused by "committing a certain intolerable disorder at his advanced age" (a causa de haber hecho cierto desorden que no soportaba su edad) [qtd. by Sola, 483]). Although Uludj Ali may never have enjoyed a family life – the sources mention that he left no children – he managed to die by Eros.

NOTE

1 All translations are mine.

REFERENCES

Allen, Bruce Ware. *The Great Siege of Malta: The Epic Battle between the Ottoman Empire and the Knights of Malta*. Lebanon, NH: University Press of New England, 2015.

Bennassar, Bartolomé, and Lucile Bennassar. *Les chrétiens d'Allah: L'histoire extraordinaire des renégats (XVIe et XVIIe siècles)*. Paris: Perrin, 1989.

Braudel, Fernand. *The Mediterranean and the Mediterranean World in the Age of Philip*. Vol. 2. Translated by Siân Reynolds. New York: Harper and Row, 1972.

Busbecq, Ogier Ghiselin de. *The Turkish Letters of Ogier Ghiselin de Busbecq*. Translated by Edward Seymour Forster. Baton Rouge: Louisiana State University Press, 2005.

Cervantes, Miguel de. *El ingenioso hidalgo Don Quijote de la Mancha*. Vol. 1. Edited by Luis Andrés Murillo. Madrid: Clásicos Castalia, 1973.

– *Novelas ejemplares*. Vol. 1. Edited by Juan Bautista Avalle-Arce. Madrid: Editoria Castalia, 1982.

Garcés, María Antonia. "Captivity in Cervantes." In *The Oxford Handbook of Cervantes*, edited by Aaron Kahn. Oxford: Oxford University Press, forthcoming.

– *Cervantes in Algiers: A Captive's Tale*. 2nd ed. Nashville, TN: Vanderbilt University Press, 2005.

Graf, Tobias. *The Sultan's Renegades*. Oxford: Oxford University Press, 2017.

Gürkan, Emrah Safa. "My Money or Your Life: The Habsburg Hunt for Uluc Ali." *Studies of History* 36 (2014): 121–45.

Haedo, Fray Diego de, ed. *Topografía e historia general de Argel de Antonio de Sosa*. Vol. 1. Madrid: Sociedad de Bibliófilos Españoles, 1927.

Koluglu, Orhan. "Renegades and the Case Uluç/Kiliç Ali." http://www.storiamediterranea.it/public/md1_dir/b699.pdf. Accessed August 2017.

Mancing, Howard. *The Cervantes Encyclopedia*. Vol. 2. Westport, CT: Greenwood Press, 2004.

Sola Castaño, Emilio. *Uchalí, el Calabrés Tiñoso o el mito del corsario muladí en la frontera*. Barcelona: Edicions Bellaterra, 2010.

Sosa, Antonio de. "Epítome de los reyes de Argel." In Haedo, 213–426.

Wright, Elizabeth, Sarah Spence, and Andrew Lemons, eds. *The Battle of Lepanto*. Cambridge, MA: Harvard University Press, 2014.

Chapter Ten

Writing a Tragic Image: *Eros* and *Eris* in Lope de Vega's *Jerusalem Conquered*

JASON McCLOSKEY

The unapologetic *eros* of the mythological paintings Titian created for Philip II of Spain, known as the *poesie*, forces observers of the canvases to consider the relationship between desire, visual art, and poetry.[1] For Thomas Puttfarken, the paintings exhibit the essential tenets of tragedy, and their seductiveness produces the *maraviglia* that captures the attention of viewers and pulls them into the pictorial plot.[2] The works of Lope de Vega reflect his fascination with Titian's paintings, and his familiarity with and imitation of the *poesie* has been adduced to explain his debated conception of "tragedy" in his drama *Adonis y Venus* (1597–1603). In his interpretation of this *comedia,* Frederick de Armas follows Puttfarken arguing, "The Venetian painter used the technique of hiding the tragic through the erotic. I would say that Lope, following the painter, hides and displaces the tragedy to emphasize the erotic" (El pintor veneciano usaba la técnica de esconder lo trágico a través de lo erótico. Yo diría que Lope, siguiendo al pintor, esconde y desplaza la tragedia para recalcar la pasión amorosa).[3] This chapter argues that Lope also imitated Titian's mythological *poesie* in a series of fictional artwork that appears in his so-called tragic epic *Jerusalem Conquered* (*Jerusalén conquistada*, 1609). Yet in his ekphrasis, Lope changes the myths, and, rather than obscuring tragedy behind the erotic content, he subdues *eros* and subordinates it to the *eris* of tragedy. This strategy reflects the conventional rejection of love in the epic genre and supports Lope's eristic imitation of Torquato Tasso's *Gerusalemme liberata* (1593). However, his emphasis on tragedy may also call into question the epic *ethos* of his poem.

In the prologue to his poem, Lope de Vega introduces *Jerusalem Conquered* as a bold, patriotic rival to Torquato Tasso's epic. He presents this epic as an attempt to redress Tasso's omissions of Spanish heroism in the First Crusade with his own version of the Third Crusade. His account includes the exploits of Richard the Lionheart of England and Philip II of France, who really did take part in the campaign to regain Jerusalem from Saladin, as well as those of the Spanish knights and their king, Alfonso VIII of Castile, who never actually participated in the enterprise. Lope likewise portrays *Gerusalemme liberata* as merely the first part of the story ("la primera parte de esta historia ha sido cantada del Tasso"),[4] thereby presenting *Jerusalem Conquered* as its sequel. As Elizabeth Davis writes, "Lope's poem is, thus, a pro-Castilian revision of Tasso's *Gerusalemme Liberata* (*Jerusalem Delivered*), and indeed, of history itself."[5] Yet instead of an unequivocally triumphant epic, Lope calls his poem a "tragic epic" (epopeya trágica), and defends his subtitle by invoking Aristotle's authoritative support of the tragic genre.

Lope's association of his epic with tragedy has generally been criticized as perplexing and illogical, but some have sought to clarify the sense in which the poem is tragic.[6] Florence D'Artois, for example, has most recently argued that *Jerusalem Conquered* is tragic in its eliciting of fear and pity, the emotions proper to Aristotelian tragedy. This, she proposes, is achieved in the poem through memorable and vivid descriptions of physical pain and suffering, borrowed from the classical tradition of the *imago agens*. She writes: "In effect, when it came time to compose a tragic poem, that is, a text that elicits tragic passions rather than responding to Aristotelian rules of *compositio*, the Post-Tridentine poets could do little more than apply the method that they had been taught at school: place before the eyes of the reader, as in theater, horrific and moving images properly conceived" (Efectivamente, a la hora de redactar un poema trágico, es decir, un texto que suscite las pasiones trágicas antes de responder a las reglas aristotélicas de la *compositio*, los poetas tridentinos no podían más que aplicar el método que se les había enseñado en los colegios: poner ante los ojos de sus lectores, como en un teatro, imágenes horrendas y patéticas, debidamente concebidas).[7] D'Artois's work marks a welcome reorientation in the approach to what Lope means by "tragedy" in *Jerusalem Conquered*, by moving beyond a definition of "tragic" that is merely synonymous with "sad" and "unfortunate," as maintained by some previous interpretations.[8] It also contributes to the study of the many notional ekphrases, or the descriptions of fictional artwork, in the poem that have been largely neglected.[9] The mythological paintings described in Book 5 of the epic provide one such example.

By Book 5, everything is beginning to unravel for the crusaders, who are riven with internal strife and beset by loss. The legitimacy of King Guy of Jerusalem comes into dispute when his wife, Queen Sibylla, and children die during Saladin's siege of Tyre. As a result, Sibylla's sister,

Isabella, becomes a political pawn as the last surviving descendant of Godfrey of Bouillon. In an attempt to seize power, Conrad of Montferrat abducts Isabella and forces her into marriage. Meanwhile, Emperor Frederick Barbarossa slowly makes his way from Europe toward Jerusalem, and Saladin retreats at the news of his approach. Yet the emperor never arrives, because he drowns in the Saleph River in Turkey, leaving the crusaders divided and leaderless. In this ominous context, and, specifically, on the dome of the palace where Conrad's forced marriage takes place, a group of mythological paintings appears. The artwork depicts the tales of 1) the Giants' storming of Mount Olympus; 2) Phoebus and Phaëthon; 3) Icarus and Daedalus; 4) Boreas and Orithyia; 5) Zetes, Calais, and the Harpies; and 6) Jupiter and Ganymede. The ekphrastic description spans eight stanzas[10] and begins by detailing the colours, such as "blues and golds" (azules y dorados);[11] the intricate architectural designs, including "coffers" (artesones") and "moldings" (molduras);[12] and the varied geometrical patterns, like "ovals and squares" (óvalos y cuadros) and "hexagons and circles" (hexágonos y círculos)[13] that frame the paintings. Significantly, and despite the decidedly downcast subjects of the paintings, their inspiration is attributed to the "Typhis of Love,"[14] Ovid's self-appellation in his *Ars amatoria,* and are said to lend "elegance, richness, splendor and ornament" (gracia, riqueza, resplandor y adorno)[15] to the ceiling.

In Habsburg Spain, paintings of Phaëthon, Ganymede, and Icarus appeared in a variety of places, such as Juan de Arguijo's library in Seville, to name one notable example.[16] As a complete set, however, Lope's artwork invites comparison specifically with Titian's *poesie,* whose six erotic mythological paintings were based on Ovid and intended to adorn the *camerino* of Philip II. As mentioned above, Lope knew these paintings well, alluding to and imitating certain ones in his texts. Like Titian's *poesie,* Lope's series consists of six paintings depicting mythological subjects that appear in a palace. Furthermore, their attribution to Ovid, the "Typhis of love," recalls the striking eroticism of Titian's paintings, condemned by some for their perceived lasciviousness.[17] Finally, Lope's paintings appear tragic, not merely for their depiction of failure and misfortune, but in the ways in which Puttfarken has interpreted the *poesie* as painted tragedies. Puttfarken summarizes own his interpretation of the *poesie* by rephrasing Philip Fehl's words: "It is the daring presence of his [Titian's] nudes in human actions, evoking passion, marvel, pity and fear, and involving a reversal of fortune leading either to inevitable suffering or even death, or to salvation, that characterizes Titian's choice of themes from Ovid in the 1550s and '60s."[18] None of the myths from Titian's series (Danae, Venus and Adonis, Perseus and

Andromeda, Europa, Diana and, and Diana and Callisto) appear on the ceiling of the Tyrian palace in *Jerusalem Conquered*; rather, Lope creates his own original *poesie* that operate in much the same way as Titian's. Only two of his ekphrastic myths (Boreas and Orithyia and Jupiter and Ganymede) deal overtly with *eros*. These myths describe the passion felt by Boreas and Jupiter for their would-be lovers, whom they abduct. However, all of the myths involve *eris*, or conflict, the common subject of epic poetry. The myth of the giants, for example, concerns conflicts between rival gods, while the tales of Icarus and Phaëthon depict disobedient sons. Zetes and Calais battle the harpies, and Orithyia and Ganymede struggle against their abductors.

As I have discussed, D'Artois's work demonstrates that Lope's conception of tragedy was Aristotelian in its concern for the rhetorical production of fear and pity through vivid descriptions. Now, following Puttfarken's interpretation of Titian's *poesie*, I read Lope's ekphrases as also reflecting Aristotelian concepts, such as catharsis, *peripeteia*, and *anagnorisis*. In Renaissance Spain, the eliciting of fear and pity was tied directly to the production of a catharsis, which was, according to Seneca and Horace, associated with a morally edifying lesson.[19] The tragic situations of reversal, or *peripeteia* ("a complete swing in the direction of the action"), and recognition, or *anagnorisis* ("a change from ignorance to knowledge"), served to intensify the central tragic emotional responses through irony and paradox.[20] Lope could have identified these ideas at work in the paintings of Titian, but he was also aware of the basic tenets of Aristotle's theory through Latin commentaries, which he famously defied in his *comedias* and acknowledged in his *Arte nuevo de hacer comedias*.[21] Below, I quote all or some of the significant lines of the ekphrases to identify these characteristics.

The Giants

There, so that the earth-born giants can oppress them with their own weight, Mount Ossa, on top of Mount Pelion, raises its face to the heavens, which they conquer. But later with thunderous lightning bolts they bore the harsh mountain on top of them where Typhus groans under Aetna, Lipari, and Inarime.

(Allí por los terrígenas gigantes
el Osa en Pelión la frente arrima
al cielo que conquistan arrogantes
porque su mismo peso los oprima;
mas luego con relámpagos tronantes

el duro monte tolerando encima
estaban donde agora Tifón gime
debajo de Etna, Lípar e Inarime.)[22]

By the early seventeenth century, the myth of the Giants' siege of Olympus had secured a reputation in painting as a terrifying subject. For example, the sight of the Sala dei Giganti, painted by Giulio Romano in the Palazzo del Te, struck Giogrio Vasari with fear, as he famously writes: "[L]et no one ever imagine seeing a work from the brush that is more horrible or frightening or more realistic than this one."[23] In Lope's painting, the Giants and the massive rocks they pile up in their war against Olympus are described thus: "Allí, por los terrígenas gigantes / el Osa en Pelión la frente arrima / al cielo que conquistan arrogantes / porque su mismo peso los oprima."[24] The rebels are so strong that they can literally move mountains like Ossa and Pelion, stacking them to heaven. At first, their mass weighs down the boulders in their prideful ascent until they suffer a crushing *peripeteia*. Jupiter, invoked metonymically through a synesthetic reference to his "thunderous lightning," repels the rebels, and the huge chunks of earth that once served as the stepping-stones for the Giants bear down on top of them ("el duro monte tolerando encima/estaban ...").[25] The reversal, occurring over two lines, is complete and emphasized by the end rhymes of the words that relate their change of position. At first, the mountains, piled high so that the Giants' own bulk might oppress them ("oprima"), end up on top ("encima") of the Giants. Their recognition of the futility of their efforts is communicated only by the groans emitted by Typhus, buried under the earth, and the cathartic moral for readers is conveyed in the characterization of the Giants' actions. They have displayed an excess of pride and ambition, which led them hubristically to conquer ("conquistan arrogantes") heaven, and, if the tale serves as a warning, then readers might not only see the giants as frightful monsters. The stanza could suggest that, in as much as any human can similarly be ensnared by the traps of pride, the fate of the Giants should be feared as the consequence of divine justice. In this way, these creatures can elicit both terror as well as sympathy.

Phaëthon

[A]nd then in a triangle the fierce horses of the Sun, falling; a thousand pieces of clouds torn by the kicking hooves of Pyrois, Eous, and Phlegon, and throughout diverse lands and horizons, the cores of the hills burning. In another part, Phaëthon (his hair overturned like roots, his soles to the sun) was showing himself to be son of the beautiful rays of the bright Phoebus, although in great misfortune.

([Y] luego en un triángulo feroces
los caballos del Sol precipitados;
mil pedazos de nubes a las coces
de Pirois, Eos y Flegón rasgados,
y por diversas tierras y horizontes
ardiendo las entrañas a los montes.

Mostraba en otra parte (los cabellos
vueltos como raíz, y al sol las plantas)
Faetónser hijo de los rayos bellos
del claro Febo, aunque en desdichas tantas.)[26]

These represent the last of the twenty-eight lines (the longest ekphrasis of the set) devoted to the tale of Phaëthon, whose corresponding images are distributed over distinct adjoining spaces on the ceiling. This is the moment of Phaëthon's reversal, as his horses plummet downward with the clouds at their hooves. Their falling recalls the etymological derivation of *peripeteia* from the verb "to fall," and the destructive conflagration caused by the falling chariot contrasts with the life-sustaining water described in the preceding octave. Through his crash, Phaëthon "mostraba ... / ... ser hijo de los rayos bellos / del claro Febo, aunque en desdichas tantas,"[27] and this revelation of his true identity as the son of Phoebus constitutes a moment of ironic recognition. The rash youth effectively dispels the doubts concerning his parentage that instigate his story and provides the evidence for all to see that he is, indeed, descended from the sun god. Yet, this unmistakable proof comes at the price of Phaëthon's life, and the contrast between what would be expected to produce a happy, positive result in Phaëthon and the actual, unfortunate ending is conveyed in the concluding concessive clause: "aunque en desdichas tantas." Despite his success in proving that the sun god is his father, Phaëthon's unhappy ending illustrated the kind of paradox that often characterizes reversal and recognition.[28] It also enables a sympathetic response toward the fate of Phaëthon consistent with the reaction of the Naiads, his sisters, who weep profusely until transforming into willow trees.[29]

Icarus

In another part, everything was burning; for wanting to reach the holy lights, the Phoenix man with foolish feathers gave a name to the unknown foam.

(En otra parte estaba todo ardiendo en ellos;
por querer alcanzar sus luces santas
el hombre Féniz que, con locas plumas
dio nombre a las incógnitas espumas.)[30]

The flames from the paintings of Phaëthon appear to spill over into the picture of Icarus, just as the poem transitions from one story to another within the same stanza. Icarus does not burn, but the heat is enough to bring about the tragic *peripeteia* of the human Phoenix ("el hombre Féniz"). According to the well-known tradition, the heat of the sun melts the wax that glues together the feathers of his fabricated wings. The fall of the boy, as a tragic reversal, further underscores his similarities with the rash son of Phoebus, but the *anagnorisis* is unique. Daedalus's daring son gives his name to the body of water that was once unknown ("incógnitas espumas"), and it thus passes from anonymity to universal recognition as the Icarian Sea. The ekphrasis does not suggest, however, that the fame of the sea likewise grants Icarus a kind of vicarious immortality. Rather, the delicacy and lightness of the newly named metonymical "espuma" suggest the vanity of his actions.

Boreas and Orithyia

In another picture, holding Orithyia in his arms in sweet war, Boreas showed that in his realm love subdues and defeats air, water and land with its impious force.

(Bóreas en otro cuadro, en dulce guerra,
por su región en brazos a Oritía,
mostraba que el amor, aire, agua y tierra
sujeta y vence con su fuerza impía.)[31]

This painting depicts Boreas, frigid god of the North Wind, engaged in "sweet war," resulting from the reversal in his approach to wooing Orithyia, daughter of Athenian king Pandion. Ovid relates that, when Boreas's impassioned pleas failed to win the princess, he returned to tactics more accustomed to him. Indignant and frustrated, he defiantly protests: "Force is my fit instrument. By force I drive on the gloomy clouds, by force I shake the sea, I overturn the gnarled oaks, pack hard the snow, and pelt the earth with hail" (apta mihi vis est: vi tristia nubila pello, / vi freta concutio nodosaque robora verto/induroque nives et terras grandine pulso).[32] In these lines, his force ("vi") is emphasized through anaphora, and he unleashes all this chilling power upon Orithyia, who reacts with fear when the "thief" and "frozen tyrant" descends on wing from his icy climes and abducts her.[33] His tactical reversal from rhetoric to violence parallels her change from liberty to captivity. Lope writes that Boreas's love conquers and subjects air, land, and sea to its rule through "fuerza," and this recalls Virgil's famous line "omnia vincit Amor."[34] Yet his force is *impía*, literally "pitiless," and Boreas's indifference to the suffering he causes the young woman elicits compassion and sympathy for her, even if details of her fearful resistance are left unrecorded. The use of the verb "to show" ("mostraba") connotes both "to make visible," as in the imagined painting, as well "to make known." In this latter sense, the verb communicates an *anagnorisis*, much like it does in the preceding ekphrasis of Phaëthon; the spectacle conveys the potential despotism of lust but also, more broadly, the vulnerability of the weak to the powerful and unjust. Along with the revelation comes a cathartic moral condemnation of the abuse of power.

Zetes, Calais, and the Harpies

> [A]nd then in the same way Zetes banishes the bird woman, the fierce Harpy, with help from Calais, and both of them fierce sons of Boreas, and like him swift.
>
> ([Y] luego de la suerte que destierra
> Zeto el ave mujer, la fiera Arpía,
> de Calais ayudado, y los dos fieros
> hijos de Aquilón, como él ligeros.)[35]

Here, the sequence of the paintings in *Jerusalem Conquered* follows the *Metamorphoses*, in which the story of Boreas and Orithyia closes Book 6 and the adventure of Zetes and Calais opens Book 7. Ovid devotes only four lines to the sons of Boreas, or the Boreads, and their chasing away of the harpies from the blind prophet Phineus as the Argonauts journeyed towards Colchis. Lope's equally brief ekphrasis of Zetes and Calais also directly follows his account of the Boreas painting, and it is the least detailed of all his pictorial descriptions. Yet, in a marginal note, he directs readers to a much more extensive treatment of the myth in Book 4 of Valerius Flaccus's epic *Argonautica*, and it invites readers to understand the meaning of the painting in conjunction with this classical text.

In the *Argonautica*, the harpies perpetually stole Phineus's food as a punishment unjustly levied by Jupiter. When the adventurous sailors come upon him, Phineus pleads for their help with a graphic description of his suffering that is "clearly intended to horrify his listeners,"[36] the Argonauts. His speech, which relies on the mental visuality of hypotyposis, moves Zetes and Calais to pursue the harpies and expel them forever from Phineus's table.[37] Thus, much like the tapestries of Book 1 and Saladino's reaction to them, this episode from the *Argonautica* could be seen as allegorizing the effects for which Lope was striving with his mythological ekphrasis.[38] Just as Phineus sought to move his audience to fear and pity, so too does Lope with the paintings in *Jerusalem Conquered*.

Lope's brief ekphrasis of the Zetes and Calais painting focuses on the *peripeteia* and related catharsis without mentioning Phineus. The Boreads successfully banish (*destierra*) the fearsome harpy, thereby enacting a reversal in Phineus's condition. This is the only instance in all of the paintings where a change from bad to good fortune is depicted, and, although it is less common, such a *peripeteia* was considered acceptable both by Aristotle and Renaissance theorists.[39] Quite unlike their father, Boreas, they are avengers of the unfairly persecuted. Zetes and Calais thus represent heroic restorers of justice to those who suffer undeservedly, just as they are portrayed by the Spanish mythographer Juan Pérez de Moya, who maintains that their names etymologically mean "el que busca el bien" (he who seeks the good).[40]

Jupiter and Ganymede

> Another picture honoured tearful Ganymede (throwing the rich cloak to the air), the hound with its raised snout barked menacingly at the eagle: she applied her curved beak to his rosy lips to soothe him, and in the distance how Juno resented seeing the child serve nectar at the table.
>
> (Ganimedes lloroso [dando el rico
> manto a los aires] otro cuadro honraba,
> por el lebrel que con alzado hocico
> el águila ladrando amenazaba:
> ella por aplacarle el corvo pico
> a los rosados labios aplicaba,
> y en lejos cómo a Juno ver le pesa
> que sirva el niño el néctar a la mesa.)[41]

The first two words of this ekphrasis dictate the interpretation of the last mythological painting. Despite all the catastrophes suffered by pitiable victims in the preceding paintings, this is the only one in which the subject is said to cry. According to Renaissance thought, the painted image of someone crying would provoke the same reaction in onlookers. As the early art theorist Leon Battista Alberti said in his examination of a classical painting of the tragedy of Iphigenia, "we weep with the weeping."[42] The tearful Ganymede is being carried aloft by Jupiter transformed into an eagle, while the boy's greyhound snarls at the bird. For this detail, Lope departs from Ovid, who mentions no dogs, and opts for Virgil's version of the myth instead. In the *Aeneid*, the myth of Ganymede also appears as an ekphrasis of an intricately woven cloak, and the fabric shows the story of the handsome youth in the midst of hunting with dogs and companions when he is suddenly seized by an eagle.[43] Including the dog in the painting highlights the *peripeteia* of the myth, as Ganymede goes from undaunted hunter chasing down stags to the helpless prey of the eagle. In the painting, once the raptor is in flight, it makes a futile effort to assuage the fear of the young Trojan, which Lope describes in a virtuosic display of poetics. Lines 5 and 6 of the stanza chiastically link corresponding nouns ("pico" and "labios") that refer to the mouths of the bird and boy, and verbs whose infinitives differ in only one vowel ("aplacar" and "aplicaba") and denote the desired effect of the eagle's action on the boy. Yet rather than calming Ganymede, surely the feeling of the eagle's curved beak pressing into his rosy lips would only intensify the horror experienced by the helpless youth. This description retains some of the erotism of Ovid and later Renaissance poets and artists, but it remains relatively weak.[44] His lips are the only body part described, and though undeniably erotic, other depictions of Ganymede are much more explicitly sensual. Michelangelo's influential drawing, for example, renders the completely nude youth intertwined with his abductor and with an entranced look on his face.[45] Ganymede's tearful reaction is indicative of his unwillingness to go with Jupiter and diminishes potential Neoplatonic characteristics.[46] Rather, the painting casts the myth as a tragedy, evoking pity in readers with the image of Ganymede crying and the sudden reversal of his status from hunter to prey.

~

In sum, these paintings invite a rather conventional admonitory interpretation of the destructive consequences of ambition, envy, pride, and lust. They signal their resemblance to the *poesie* in source, subject, and number, and, like Titian's paintings, they reflect a conception consistent with Aristotle's definition of tragedy. The eroticism of Titian's paintings, however, appears in only a subdued form in the paintings of Boreas and Orithyia and Jupiter and Ganymede. Unlike Titian's *poesie*, these paintings are not, as a whole, seductive and salacious, but their lack of eroticism may paradoxically account for the misapprehension of their moralizing catharsis by the characters in the poem. Had the paintings been more sexually alluring, they may have drawn the attention of Conrad, but he appears not to notice the images. Instead, the crusaders fail to heed the lessons of the myths, and they repeat and fall victim to the same kind of mistakes depicted in the paintings. That is, their portrayal functions as a kind of typological narrative ekphrasis of the tragic mythological artwork.[47] Beginning in Book 5 and continuing throughout the epic, the crusaders fail to control their passions, and they bicker with, abandon, and attack each other in a manner similar to interactions in the myths. This internal strife, sometimes explicitly alluded to as "discordia," divides the Christians and dooms their campaign.[48] Thus, in typical epic fashion, the ekphrases function symbolically, serving as "microcosms ... as they prophesy, summarize, or interpret the meaning of the action."[49] And it is in this capacity as microcosm that the paintings elucidate the decidedly eristic, or emulative, relation of *Jerusalem Conquered* to Tasso's *Gerusalemme liberata*.[50]

Immediately after describing the mythological paintings overhead, the narrator of *Jerusalem Conquered* focuses on another series of tapestries, which line the walls below the vault:

> In sum, such stories adorned the rich ceiling, and the wall was clad in tapestries that related the wars and victories of the divine Godfrey; there the inscriptions and records between the high borders were seen in verses that conserved such immortal deeds despite oblivion.
>
> (Adornaban, en fin, tales historias
> el rico techo, y la pared vestían
> tapices que las guerras y victorias
> del divino Gofredo referían;
> allí las inscripciones y memorias
> entre las altas márgenes se vían
> en versos que conservan inmortales,
> a pesar del olvido hazañas tales.)[51]

If the mythological paintings symbolize the actions of *Jerusalem Conquered*, then these fabrics do much the same for Tasso's *Gerusalemme liberata*. Like these woven pictures and accompanying inscriptions, which are said to rescue from oblivion the deeds of the "divine" Godfrey, Tasso's poem preserves, for future memory, the triumph of the Frankish king and the First Crusade. Following Aristotle, Tasso conceived of the epic genre as closely related to tragedy, but with certain fundamental distinctions. As explained above, Aristotle allowed for two types of *peripeteia* in tragedies; one kind of reversal went from adversity to prosperity, while the other reversed that process. Tasso advocated the first kind for epic poems, and thus, in keeping with his own theories, there occurs a *peripeteia* in canto 13 of *Gerusalemme liberata,* as the narrative shifts and the prospects of the crusaders decisively improve.[52] Therefore, in Tasso's epic, the crusaders experience difficulties and internal conflicts, but these differences are resolved by what ultimately constitutes a happy ending, from the perspective of the crusaders. Taking this happy ending as its professed starting point and concluding in misfortune, the reversal in Lope's epic operates in the opposite direction, which Tasso prescribes for tragedy. In this sense, the whole of *Jerusalem Conquered* might be interpreted as the reversal of Tasso's epic, as the Christians go from controlling Jerusalem to losing the city, and this outcome is inexorably set into motion by the events of Book 5 of Lope's epic.

Lope's tragic reversal of Tasso's poem represents a change in strategy for him, and it entails several advantages and disadvantages. As de Armas has argued, Lope hides the tragedy of *Adonis y Venus* behind erotic passion, but in *Jerusalem Conquered,* he foregrounds the *eris* of tragedy against a muted background of *eros.*[53] The difference in genre could help explain this change. Lope's presentation of the mythological paintings is consistent with the conventional epic distrust of *eros* and the surprisingly common sad endings of epics. For example, Alonso de Ercilla's *La Araucana,* an even more influential text for the Spanish conception of epic poetry than Tasso's *Gerusalemme,* famously rejects amorous subjects in the opening stanza: "Not women, love or gallantries / of enamored knights do I sing / nor the displays, gifts or tenderness / of amorous affects and cares" (No las damas, amor, no gentilezas / de caballeros canto enamorados, / ni las muestras, regalos y ternezas / de amorosos afectos y cuidados).[54] Like many other epics since antiquity, Ercilla's poem ends in tears, which Felipe Valencia considers befitting the poet's adoption of the lyric mode.[55] But unlike the subversive effect that Valencia attributes to the lyric in *La Araucana,* the adoption of a tragic perspective in *Jerusalem Conquered* could be interpreted as preserving traditional heroic ideology.[56] The moralizing catharsis provided by the paintings serves to warn the crusaders of the repercussions of the disobedience, arrogance, and disunity that threaten the epic *ethos* from within the Christian alliance. This admonition goes unheeded, but the tragic portrayal of the Third Crusade still allows for a perception of the subsequent military defeat of the Christians as self-inflicted rather than as a loss to a superior foe. And, as I have discussed, adopting the tragic framework also allows Lope to defeat Tasso's poem by sabotaging its ending. However, Lope's own competitive strategy is itself reminiscent of the actions taken by the same mythological characters that his poem implicitly criticizes, and this recalls the moral objections to the concept of *eristic* imitation or emulation.[57] Perhaps more importantly, in foreshadowing the self-destructive failures of the crusade, the paintings suggest a collapse of the triumphant epic *ethos*. This undercutting effect very likely accounts for why Tasso advocated a reversal from misfortune to success, and it reveals the ambivalent relation that tragedy has to epic ideology in *Jerusalem Conquered*.

Jerusalem Conquered may thus be tragic in both a specific and general sense. The "sad" ending of Lope's poem can be understood as tragic in its inverse relation to the ending of Tasso's poem and to the production of pity and fear through *peripeteia* and *anagnorisis*. The tragic reversal of *Jerusalem Conquered* begins with Titian's erotic paintings reimagined through notional ekphrasis with different myths and ends in the eristic dismantling of the crusade and of Tasso's *Gerusalemme*. This use of *eros* for eristic ends, which foreground the poet's artistry and his nationality, places Lope in a rich Spanish tradition that begins with Garcilaso and continues among his contemporaries.[58] But the "tragic" ending also suggests that, in some conflicts, such as the Third Crusade, there are only symbolic, poetic victories, with few or no real triumphs, especially when internal disunity undermines the common cause. And even these poetic victories can be morally ambiguous, as in the case of Lope's triumph over Tasso. Finally, Lope's poem has been read in the context of Philip III's new policies of peace toward Spain's uneasy allies in *Jerusalén conquistada* (France and England), and this sobering suggestion about the futility of war might help to justify the *Pax hispanica* to the monarch's critics.[59]

NOTES

1 I would like to thank Steven Wagschal for his help with the early version of this essay, which appeared in substantially different form as a chapter in my doctoral dissertation.

2 Puttfarken, *Titian and Tragic Painting*, 155–81.

3 de Armas, "*Adonis*," 100. For more on Lope and Titian see also de Armas's now classic study, "Lope de Vega and Titian."

4 Lope de Vega, *Jerusalén conquistada*, 20.

5 Davis, *Myth and Identity in the Epic of Imperial Spain*, 172.
6 For example, editors of the poem, Joaquín de Entrambasaguas (*Jerusalén conquistada*, 3 vols. [Madrid: CSIC, 1951], 3:225) and Antonio Carreño (Vega, *Poesía, III*, xvi), criticize Lope's choice of subtitle.
7 D'Artois, "Las 'imagines agentes' y lo trágico en la *Jerusalén conquistada*," 28.
8 Ibid., 20, 32.
9 On notional ekphrasis see de Armas, *Quixotic Frescoes*, 9–10. Felisa Guillén ("Ekphrasis e imitación en la *Jerusalén conquistada*") and Elizabeth Wright ("A New Beginning, chap. 3) are among the few who study ekphrasis in the poem.
10 Lope de Vega, *Jerusalén conquistada*, V.23.1–V.31.8. All subsequent citations of the epic refer to the book with Roman numeral and stanza and verse with Arabic numerals.
11 Ibid., V.23.2.
12 Ibid., V.23.2 and V.23.7.
13 Ibid., V.23.3 and V.23.4.
14 Ibid., V.23.5.
15 Ibid., V.23.8.
16 Mary E. Barnard, in "Inscribing Transgression, Siting Identity," discusses the paintings of Ganymede and Phaëthon in Arguijo's library, while de Armas, in "Deflecting Desire," focuses on Ganymede.
17 Cruz, "Titian, Philip II, and Pagan Iconography," i7.
18 Puttfarken, *Titian and Tragic Painting*, 155–6.
19 Hermenegildo, *La tragedia en el Renacimiento español*, 41, 45; Puttfarken, *Titian and Tragic Painting*, 63–4.
20 Aristotle, *The* Poetics *of Aristotle*, 42, 43, 116.
21 Ley, "Lope de Vega y los conceptos teatrales de Aristóteles," 2: 584.
22 Vega, *Jerusalén conquistada*, V.29.1–8.
23 Vasari, *The Lives of the Artists*, 372.
24 Vega, *Jerusalén conquistada*, 5.24.1–4.
25 Ibid., 5.24.6–7.
26 Ibid., V.27.3–28.4.
27 Ibid., V.28.1, 3–4.
28 Aristotle, *The* Poetics *of Aristotle*, 116.
29 Ovid, *Metamorphoses*, 2.340–66.
30 Vega, *Jerusalén conquistada*, V.28.5–8.
31 Ibid., V.29.1–4.
32 Ovid, *Metamorphoses*, 6.690–2.
33 Ibid., 6.710. 6.711, 6.707–10.
34 Virgil, "Eclogue X" in *Eclogues*, v. 69.
35 Vega, *Jerusalén conquistada*, V.29.5–8.
36 Murgatroyd, *A Commentary on Book 4 of Valerius Flaccus'* Argonautica, 225.

37 Gaius Valerius Flaccus, *Argonautica*, vv. 4.450–9.
38 D'Artois, "Las 'imagines agentes,'" 30–2.
39 Puttfarken, *Titian and Tragic Painting*, 65.
40 Juan Pérez de Moya, *Philosofía secreta*, 451.
41 Vega, *Jerusalén conquistada*, V.30.1–8.
42 Alberti, *On Painting*, 77.
43 Virgil, "Aeneid V" in *Eclogues*, vv. 244–57.
44 See de Armas, "Deflecting Desire," and Barnard, "Inscribing Transgression," on the homoeroticism of the myth.
45 Barnard, "Inscribing Transgression," 118–20.
46 For typical Neoplatonic readings of the myth, see Barnard, "Inscribing Transgression," 121, and de Armas, "Deflecting Desire," 236.
47 On narrative ekphrasis, see de Armas, *Quixotic Frescoes*, 9–10.
48 For example, *discordia*, Latin for *eris*, appears in Vega, *Jerusalén conquistada*, VII.49.4, VIII.56.6, and XVIII.76.2. See Davis, *Myth and Identity*, 175, 181.
49 Bergman, "The Painting's Observer in the Epic Canvas," 272. Guillén emphasizes the symbolism inherent to ekphrasis in "Ekphrasis e imitación en la *Jerusalén conquistada*."
50 On eristic emulation, see Pigman, "Versions of Imitation in the Renaissance."
51 Vega, *Jerusalén conquistada*, V.31.1–8.
52 Tasso, *Discourses on the Heroic Poem*, 79; Unglaub, *Poussin and the Poetics of Painting*, 183, 193–7.
53 de Armas, "*Adonis y Venus*," 100.
54 Alonso de Ercilla, *La Araucana*, I.1.1–4.
55 Valencia, "Las 'muchas (aunque bárbaras)' voces líricas de *La Araucana*,'" 166–7.
56 See Valencia, who writes, for example, that "Al igual que en el soneto de Garcilaso, en la epopeya de Ercilla se produce una oposición entre la voz masculina, el género épico y la temática imperial, por un lado, frente a la voz feminina, el género lírico y la temática introspectiva, por otro" (as in Garcilaso's sonnet, Ercilla's epic poem establishes an opposition between the male voice, the epic genre, and an imperial theme, on one side, and the female voice, lyric poetry, and an intimate themes, on the other) ibid., 162.
57 Pigman, "Versions of Imitation," 23–4.
58 See Torres, *Love Poetry in the Spanish Golden Age*.
59 On Spain's new peace with England and France and the implications for the *Jerusalén*, see Davis, *Myth and Identity*, 181, 184–5; Wright, "A New Beginning," 90, 100–1; and Sánchez Jiménez, "Quevedo y Lope (poesía y teatro) en 1609," 32.

REFERENCES

Alberti, Leon Battista. *On Painting*. Translated and edited by John R. Spencer. New Haven, CT: Yale University Press, 1956.

Aristotle. *The* Poetics *of Aristotle*. Translated and edited by Stephen Halliwell. Chapel Hill: University of North Carolina Press, 1987.

Barnard, Mary E. "Inscribing Transgression, Siting Identity: Arguijo's Phaëthon and Ganymede in Painting and Text." In *Writing for the Eyes in the Spanish Golden Age*, edited by Frederick A. de Armas, 109–29. Lewisburg, PA: Bucknell University Press, 2004.

Bergman, Emile. "The Painting's Observer in the Epic Canvas: *La hermosura de Angélica*." *Comparative Literature* 38, no. 3 (1986): 270–88.

D'Artois, Florence. "Las 'imagines agentes' y lo trágico en la *Jerusalén conquistada*." *Anuario Lope de Vega* 12 (2006): 19–34.

Davis, Elizabeth B. *Myth and Identity in the Epic of Imperial Spain*. Columbia: University of Missouri Press, 2000.

de Armas, Frederick A. "*Adonis y Venus*: Hacia la tragedia en Tiziano y Lope de Vega." In *Hacia la tragedia áurea: Lecturas para un nuevo milenio*, edited by Frederick A. de Armas, Luciano García Lorenzo, and Enrique García Santo-Tomás, 97–115. Madrid: Iberoamericana, 2008.

– "Deflecting Desire: The Portryal of Ganymede in Arguijo's Art and Poetry." In *Lesbianism and Homosexuality in Early Modern Spain: Literature and Theater in Context*, edited by María José Delgado and Alain Saint-Saëns, 235–56. New Orleans: University Press of the South, 2000.

– "Lope de Vega and Titian." *Comparative Literature* 30, no. 4 (1978): 338–52.

– "Lope's Speaking Pictures: Tantalizing Titians and Forbidden Michelangelos in *La quinta de Florencia*." in *A Companion to Lope de Vega*, edited by Alexander Samson and Jonathan Thacker, 171–82. Woodbridge, UK: Tamesis, 2008.

– *Quixotic Frescoes: Cervantes and Italian Renaissance Art*. Toronto: University of Toronto Press, 2006.

Ercilla, Alonso de. *La Araucana*. Edited by Isaías Lerner. Madrid: Cátedra, 2005.

Guillén, Felisa. "Ekphrasis e imitación en la *Jerusalén conquistada*." *Hispania* 78, no. 2 (May 1995): 231–9.

Hermenegildo, Alfredo. *La tragedia en el Renacimiento español*. Barcelona: Planeta, 1973.

Ley, Charles David. "Lope de Vega y los conceptos teatrales de Aristóteles." In *Actas del Quinto Congreso Internacional de Hispanistas*, edited by Maxime Chevalier, François López, Joseph Pérez, and Nöel Salomón, 2: 579–85. Bordeaux: Université de Bordeaux III, 1977.

Murgatroyd, Paul. *A Commentary on Book 4 of Valerius Flaccus'* Argonautica. Boston: Brill, 2009.

Ovid. *Metamorphoses*. Translated by F.J. Miller. 3rd ed. 2 vols. Cambridge, MA: Harvard University Press, 1984.

Pérez de Moya, Juan. *Philosofía secreta*. Edited by Carlos Clavería. Madrid: Cátedra, 1995.

Pigman III, G.W. "Versions of Imitation in the Renaissance." *Renaissance Quarterly* 33, no. 1 (Spring 1980): 1–32.

Puttfarken, Thomas. *Titian and Tragic Painting*. New Haven, CT: Yale University Press, 2005.

Quint, David. *Epic and Empire: Politics and Generic Form from Virgil to Milton*. Princeton, NJ: Princeton University Press, 1993.

Sánchez Jiménez, Antonio. "Quevedo y Lope (poesía y teatro) en 1609: Patriotismo y construcción nacional en la *España defendida* y la *Jerusalén conquistada*." *Perinola* 17 (2013): 27–56.

Tasso, Torquato. *Discourses on the Heroic Poem*. Translated and edited by Mariella Cavalchini and Irene Samuel. Oxford: Clarendon, 1973.

Torres, Isabel. *Love Poetry in the Spanish Golden Age: Eros, Eris and Empire*. Woodbridge, UK: Tamesis, 2013.

Unglaub, Jonathan. *Poussin and the Poetics of Painting: Pictorial Narrative and the Legacy of Tasso*. Cambridge: Cambridge University Press, 2006.

Valencia, Felipe. "Las 'muchas (aunque bárbaras)' voces líricas de *La Araucana* y la índole poética de una 'historia verdadera.'" *Revista Estudios Hispánicos* 49, no. 1 (2015): 147–71.

Valerius Flaccus, Gaius. *Argonautica*. Translated by J.H. Mozley. Cambridge, MA: Harvard University Press, 1972.

Vasari, Giorgio. *The Lives of the Artists*. Translated by Julia Conaway Bondanella and Peter Bondanella. Oxford: Oxford University Press, 1998.

Vega, Lope de. *Jerusalén conquistada*. In *Obras completas de Lope de Vega. Poesía III*. Edited by Antonio Carreño. Madrid: Fundación José Antonio de Castro, 2003.

Virgil. *Eclogues, Georgics, Aeneid 1–6*. Translated by H.R. Fairclough and revised by G.P. Goold. Cambridge, MA: Harvard University Press, 1999.

Wright, Elizabeth R. *Pilgrimage to Patronage: Lope de Vega and the Court of Philip III, 1598–1621*. Lewisburg, PA: Bucknell University Press, 2001.

Chapter Eleven

The Unromantic Approach to *Don Quixote*: Cervantine Love in the Spanish Post-War Age

ANA MARÍA LAGUNA

In her acceptance speech of the 1988 Cervantes Award, María Zambrano (1904–91) surprised her audience by contending that the "lack of a [real] beloved" in *Don Quixote* was ultimately "symptomatic of an underlying lack of love" in the narrative (la inexistencia del amor [andaba representada] en forma de una mujer inexistente).[1] By describing Cervantes's classic as essentially devoid of love, Zambrano contravened a long critical school that read the novel not only as an elegy of love but as the expression of its "most elevated" and "cosmic" variety.[2] The contradiction would not surprise those well versed in Cervantine ambiguity, since *Don Quixote* – as criticism has amply noted – praises the amorous pursuits of its protagonist as often as it ridicules them; for every critic who believes, with Roberto González Echevarría, that *Don Quixote* "is about love" even more than about "[c]hivalry or any other subject,"[3] there is another like Diana de Armas, who regards the theme as "dead-ended" as the street where Dulcinea is supposed to reside at El Toboso.[4]

Intrigued perhaps by this interpretive discrepancy, a group of writers associated with the Generation of 1927, who had superbly treated the theme of *eros* in their own work, decided to tackle the question in Cervantes.[5] For them, a serious literary exploration of the wide-ranging "mutations of the theme of love" that transcended the narrow attention to "Petrarchism" constituted an embarrassing oversight that they were determined to remedy.[6] While few literary authors deserve this critical enquiry more than Cervantes, the group soon realized that the writer's relationship with the emotion (and its literary tradition) was almost as unique as Don Quixote's affair with his beloved.

It early on became apparent, as Max Aub (1903–72) noted, that, despite being "deeply entrenched in the literary passions of his time" (metido hasta el cogollo en las pasiones literarias de su época), Cervantes did not seem interested in making love the central subject of his writing.[7]

Vicente Gaos (1919–80) attributed that reticence to the author's overarching emotional "bleakness" (sequedad) and "intellectualism" (intelectualidad),[8] while Samuel Gili Gaya (1892–1976) believed that this general negative attitude was tied to his incursions on genres like the pastoral, probably the most prone to erotic and sentimental excess. There, Cervantes, a master in conceptual constructions, seems to lead shepherds like Elicio "to define [love] rather than singing it" (sus pastores, y singularmente Elicio, definen más que cantan [el amor]).[9] Such a contrived amorous treatment could apply to almost all Cervantine exercises in all genres, including chivalric fiction (probably the only narrative more open to sexual exploits than the pastoral), since *Don Quixote* disrupts the chivalric fluid relationship of the heroic and the erotic by presenting a knight who, rather than enjoying the fruits of love with his lady, spends most of his time ruminating over her existence.

Only Pedro Salinas (1891–1951) would infer what most of his contemporaries couldn't, a Cervantine theory of love, precisely by doubling down on the writer's bleak and cerebral approach to the sentiment. The insight led Salinas to conclude that, in *Don Quixote*, Cervantes had, in fact, written "[t]he most beautiful love letter of Spanish literature," a perplexing indictment that will be the focus of this chapter.[10] In order to explore Salinas's views on Cervantine love, however, we must also examine the critical manoeuvring in which the poet was forced to engage. Like other writers of the '27 group, Salinas did have to contend not only with the extreme rationality of Cervantes, and the misjudgments of his protagonists, but also with the apparently misguided interpretations left behind by a powerful group of critical predecessors: the Generation of 1898. As this chapter details, when progressive writers such as Salinas and Aub looked for love in Cervantes, they would have to confront the overtly symbolic interpretations of critics such as Ramiro de Maeztu (1874–1936), Miguel de Unamuno (1864–1936), and Ramiro de Ledesma (1905–36), whose assessments of Cervantes's (and Quixote's) views on heroism and love became particularly problematic in the Spanish political context of the 1930s and 1940s.

The transgenerational disagreement among these luminary thinkers produced one of the most fascinating and little-explored controversies of twentieth-century Spanish criticism. The lapse, although greatly determined by the canonic status of both groups – more conducive to reinforcing than to challenging established critical views – reveals the lingering misunderstandings and under-recognition of the contributions of the Spanish diaspora.[11] Exiled writers (after 1939) associated with the '27 group are, for example, still assumed to have "regarded the Generation of '98 as a landmark in the recuperation of a [national] consciousness, given how that generation had looked at the past, seeking to recover its popular essence" (consideraban a la Generación del 98 un hito en la recuperación de esta conciencia por dirigir su mirada hacia atrás y buscar su pueblo);[12] yet, as this chapter will show, most of those younger writers were far from agreeing with their predecessors on the terms of that consciousness, and even less inclined to consider them as a landmark critical reference.

Rather than expressing deference to or inspiration from the ultra-symbolic criticism of the '98 critics, younger writers such as José Enrique Rebolledo (1911–?) lamented the effect that this critical outlook had infused in the 1940s understanding of Cervantes's work. To Rebolledo, the '98 group had

> [D]isintegrated Don Quixote by mocking the hero and by dissociating us from him ... The Generation of 98 offers reliable proof [of this dissociating process] ... By wondering what Spain is, they found in the tormented figure of Quixote a faithful justification for their angst and pessimism. Their interpretation of Quixote offers a *lyric* and *demonic* tirade [representing] that battered Spanish way of thinking.[13]

> ([D]esintegrado a Don Quijote porque hemos burlado y disociado al héroe ... ahí está la Generación del 98 como testimonio fiel ... Preguntándose por España, encontraban en la atormentada figura de Don Quijote verónica fiel para su desazón y pesimismo. Su interpretación del Quijote es una escapada *delírica* y *luciferina* del abatido pensamiento español.)[14]

As Rebolledo's protestations imply, the '98 group, heavily affected by the 1898 colonial disaster and deeply influenced by Romantic philosophy, used *Don Quixote* nostalgically to express their longing for the long-lost Spanish imperial glory. For Rebolledo, this projected imperial nostalgia only alienated Cervantes's protagonist from its text, and contemporary readers from the novel. Writers such as Luis Cernuda (1902–63) shared this criticism, believing the '98 symbolic and Romantic lens had seriously – and recklessly – jeopardized a true understanding of the author. "For 1898 critics," Cernuda writes, "Don Quixote was a symbol, a mythical and mystic incarnation of Spain. But turning things into symbols is quite dangerous, and whoever does it must do it on his own, without putting the destiny of somebody else's work at risk" (Para la gente de 1898 ... Don Quijote es un símbolo: encarnación mítica y mística de lo español. Pero convertir las cosas en símbolos es un tanto peligroso y quien tal haga, hágalo a su cuenta y razón, pero no debe arriesgar el destino de la obra ajena).[15] Exiles like them, profoundly afflicted by the aftermath of the Civil War, and well-versed in New Critical methodology, would be much more interested in exposing Cervantes's emotional or political disaffection through the nuanced complexities of his texts.[16]

While authors of both generations reflected differently on the empire question, intellectuals of the '98 group showed little interest in themes such as *eros*, instead concentrating almost exclusively on broader historical or philosophical concerns, such as the idea of Spanish destiny or national identity.[17] The group of '98's attention to Cervantes and *Don Quixote* had been, in fact, propelled largely by the above-mentioned interest in resurrecting a "heroic" imperial past, since they believed that, just as Quixote attempted to recuperate the Golden Age of chivalry, modern Spaniards could bring back the country's past splendour by emulating the Quixotic thrust.[18] The Quixote that emerged in this context became, as Christopher Britt Arredondo has shown, "an icon for the defense of a Hispanic cultural empire with Castile as its center ... and all of Latin America at its grasp" (16); such a mindset would nurture the idea of a Spanish moral and colonial superiority that paved the way for the formulation of Spanish fascism and the outbreak of the Civil War.[19]

In contrast, the idea of an imperial and colonial age was abhorrent to most '27 writers. For them, the erotic and chivalric follies of *Don Quixote* mocked rather than extolled the "doomed" ambitions of the empire, a political entity they considered morally reprehensible and politically unsustainable. In their view, the Spanish colonial past – and the mindset that defended it – had always stood in the way of true modernization of the country, a position that aligned them politically with a Republican ideology.[20] When the thinkers associated with this younger generation turned to Cervantes, they approached him not as a myth but as a perceptive writer who, in the 1600s, had faced an earlier version of the challenges that Spain was experiencing in the 1940s (religious extremism, autocracy, and bigotry) and who had reflected on these pressing issues with grace, irony, and depth. "Spain," as Aub passionately argues, "at the peak of its glory, is also headed for internal collapse" (en el colmo de su gloria, está interiormente vertida hacia la ruina), and if anyone can see this destructive paradox, it is Cervantes: "scabs cover the apparent glowing shell of the empire," Aub continues, "and whoever has a good ear can hear the woodworms. Many writers had such insight, but nobody like Cervantes" (crecen oscuras costras en la aparentemente formidable coraza del imperio, quien tiene buen oido oye la carcoma, pero nadie como Cervantes).[21] It was this profoundly critical dimension of the author that made a novel like *Don Quixote* – in Ramón J. Sender's (1901–82) opinion – ultimately "irreconcilable with any fascist and/or imperialist strictures" (proscrita del imperio de la España Fascista).[22]

Aware that their perspective was widely ignored and obviously annoyed by this disregard, exiled thinkers such as Isidoro Enríquez Calleja (1900–71) lamented, in the late 1940s, the lingering influence of the Generation of '98: "In what we have seen of this century," he notes, "Spanish life has unfolded, full of twists and turns, at an accelerated pace ... What took place in Spain should have filled the bookstores with suggestive, deep novels that defined our times in a different way. But what happened was quite the opposite. The writers who keep setting the tone ... are the novelists of the Generation of '98" (En lo que va de siglo la vida española se ha desenvuelto a un ritmo acelerado de visicitud, y en los últimos años ... han pasado cosas como para abarrotar las librerías de novelas sugestivas y profundas que hubieran definido nuestro tiempo de modo definitivo. Pues no, continúan partiendo el bacalao ... los novelistas de la Generación del 98).[23]

British Cervantist Anthony Close's seminal study *The Romantic Approach to "Don Quixote,"* first published in 1978, is perhaps the clearest illustration of the reasons for Enríquez Calleja's frustration. While it shares his rejection of the '98's nationalist and symbolic approach, it also completely neglects diasporic voices like Calleja's own when it flatly resolves that twentieth-century Spanish scholarship "did not produce any Quixotic criticism which could be regarded as a really significant landmark."[24]

Close's "Romantic approach" explored the interpretative praxes of Romantic German critics such as Georg Friedrich Hegel (1770–1831), Karl Friedrich Schlegel (1772–1829), and Arthur Schopenhauer (1788–1860) that had arrived in Spain via writers such as Unamuno, Maeztu, Ledesma, Angel Ganivet (1865–98), José Martínez Ruiz "Azorín" (1873–1965), and José Ortega y Gasset (1883–1955). The Romantic-inflected view of this group, which was almost exclusively composed of '98 writers, produced some of what Close considered the most influential – also incredibly "simplifying and philistine" – interpretations of *Don Quixote*.[25] As Close would bitterly make clear, these problematic views were overwhelmingly anachronistic, since they reflected philosophical and national preoccupations of the present day rather than seventeenth-century realities. For Close, this anachronism moved '98 authors to ignore "the novel's artistic texture – perhaps precisely because this is something difficult to analyze." For him, it was this systemic disregard of the text that allowed '98 authors to use the novel as a mere "vessel" for their historical and philosophical preoccupations.[26]

Close's assessment of this critical school was hard and direct, but what made it absolutely demolishing was the extrapolation of the Hispanist's conclusions that conflated *all* Spanish criticism produced over nearly two centuries; he claimed that "[f]rom the end of the Spanish Civil War to 1965, Spanish Quixote criticism of the 1940s and 1965 period resembles its counterpart between 1833 and 1859."[27] Completely unaware of the friction between the '27 and '98 sensibilities, Close categorically denied any form of evolution or dissention in Spanish critical culture.

While Close's assumptions have remained largely (and perplexingly) unchallenged in the past forty years, they cannot be sustained when confronting the critical contributions of the diaspora.[28] Had Close been aware of the refined critique of '98 thought issued by writers associated with the Generation of '27 – a critique that preceded his own by many decades – he might have produced a more nuanced assessment of the Romantic reach in Spanish letters. As these pages demonstrate, the heated transgenerational debate on the role of erotic and heroic themes in *Don Quixote*, against the backdrop of Francisco Franco's newly installed dictatorship (1939–75), becomes an indispensable reference for understanding how Cervantes's text was read in the complex ideological and critical context of the Spanish twentieth century, a context that would forge rich Cervantine developments on both sides of the Atlantic.

Cervantes, Chivalric *Eros*, and Spanish Post-War Criticism

A sympathetic reader and critic of *Don Quixote* can have little trouble in forgiving the obvious shortcomings of its protagonist as lover. After all, it is Quixote's devotion to Dulcinea – even when she does not exist – that allows him to justify his existence as a knight in accordance with his fictional models. Love, in chivalric fiction, constitutes a "sort of professional obligation" that determines all other heroic premises, and nobody better than the Manchegan knight exemplifies that principle by illustrating the dependence of one concept – heroism – on the other – love. As Quixote famously retorts:[29]

> There cannot be a knight errant without a lady, because it is as fitting and natural for them to be in love as for the sky to have stars, and, just as certainly, you have never seen a history in which you find a knight errant without love, for if he had none, he would not be deemed a legitimate knight, but a bastard who had entered the fortress of chivalry not through the door but over the walls, like a robber and a thief.

> ([N]o puede ser que haya caballero andante sin dama, porque tan propio y tan natural le es a los tales ser enamorados como al cielo tener estrellas, y a buen seguro que no se haya visto historia donde se halle caballero andante sin amores ... sin ellos, no sería tenido por legítimo caballero, sino por bastardo, y que entró en la fortaleza por la caballería dicha, no por la puerta, sino por las bardas, como salteador y ladrón.)[30]

When examined in detail, the implications of this erotic mandate are puzzling, since a knight should act heroically for the sake of moral imperatives, not out of erotic aspirations.[31] And yet chivalric protagonists seem uniquely concerned with the narrowly defined role of honouring the love of a specific person through their fight, an *eros/ethos* ambivalence that is not always amicable or loving. As Henry Higuera reminds us, "running parallel to their doctrines of love, the Books of Chivalry contain elements that correspond to this [violence] and inflame ...warlike [and thus not very amorous] passions."[32] In the name of love, the knight can exhibit an idea of justice dangerously close to that of personal revenge, and his desire to assist the afflicted and the weak can easily translate into a draconian thirst for power and recognition.[33]

Complicating this ambiguity further is the fact that the inherent erotic/heroic permutations of *Don Quixote* could not have been more disparately interpreted than in the first part of the Spanish twentieth century, one of the most ideologically controversial and literarily productive periods in the country's history.[34] As seen, unlike the Generation of '98, whose interpretations of love and heroism rang as nostalgic cries for the lost empire, the '27 writers identified in Cervantes a more critical – dissenting – perspective on his imperial culture. Even the gentle Salinas could not help censuring his '98 predecessors for their inability to appreciate a fresher perspective of Cervantes, noting that "like other quixotic knights errant, the '98 men set off to look for the ideal Spain of Dulcinea, giving up on the other, more material Spain, Aldonza's" (los hombres del 98 parten como tantos otros caballeros andantes aquijoteados en busca de España – Dulcinea, la ideal, desdeñosos de España – Aldonza, la material).[35] In the conflicted, heavily politicized context in which the members of both generations operated, the '27 group would consistently warn about the dangers of an unchecked idealization of a mythical chivalric world. Long before Close, then, writers of the Generation of '27 had both softly and passionately critiqued the '98 critics' inability to read "*Don Quixote* in abstract of 'the problem of Spain,'"[36] and independently from their own political context.

The Heroic without the Erotic – A '98 Trap

The critical debate about how to best read *Don Quixote* to serve Spain's future found rich fodder in the question of whether love and the figure of the beloved should motivate the hero's military accomplishments. Thus, demonstrating that there could be a knight errant without a lady, Unamuno, Azorín, Ortega, and Maeztu would progressively identify (and ultimately substitute) abstractions such as glory, beauty, and faith for the role of Quixote's beloved, Dulcinea. Unamuno specifically claims that the knight would learn to love without the help or model of his lady, as it was ultimately his affection for Sancho that had taught him how to love humanity at large, "since it is in the face of your fellow companion that you love everyone else" (pues [es] en cabeza de un prójimo y en la comunidad donde se ama a todos los demás).[37]

When forced to speak precisely about Quixote's mandate to have a beloved, Unamuno first admits that "all forms of heroism sprout out of a woman's love. The love of a woman has inspired the most profound ideals, the best philosophical formulations" (del amor a mujer brota todo heroísmo. Del amor a mujer han brotado los más fecundos y nobles ideales, del amor a mujer las más soberbias fábricas filosóficas).[38] However, he warns later that "the care for a woman ties up the wings of a hero" (el cuidado a la mujer ata las alas a otros heroes), adding – to reinforce the domestic connotations of the warning – that "women hinder [heroes] tremendously!" (¡cómo embaraza la mujer!).[39] Ultimately, Unamuno believes that Don Quixote avoided falling prey to such feminine "entrapments" (or, literally, "pregnancies" [embarazos]) precisely because he "wisely" pursued glory more than – or instead of – a beloved. At one point, the philosopher cannot avoid fusing both ideas, heroism and womanhood, into a unified abstraction, declaring that Quixote ultimately "loved the idea of Glory embodied in a woman" (amó a la Gloria encarnada en mujer).[40]

Operating within an obvious regenerationist mindset, Unamuno cancels out Quixote's intrinsic erotic drive, replacing it instead with a purely chivalric (bellicose) inclination to be a "real" hero, the type that would allow Spain to recuperate its true, dominating essence and past glory. He traces this return to glory in his "Sepulcro del Quijote," a piece that he published separately in 1905 and later included in his 1908 version of the *Vida de Don Quijote y Sancho* only to have it removed from the 1914 edition.[41] In this meditation, Unamuno's profound "nostalgia" for the Middle Ages invites his contemporaries to embark on a new holy crusade that would liberate Don Quijote from the old guardians who had cancelled out his ennobling message:

You will witness how, as soon as the sacred squadron gets on its way, a star appears in the sky, a star visible only to crusaders, a shiny and resounding star that will sing a new song in this night that surrounds us all. The star advances as soon as the crusaders advance, and once they win their fight, or once they all have died – which is the only way to win – the star will fall from the sky, indicating the place where the sepulchre is located. The sepulchre lies where the squadron dies.

(Verás cómo así que el sagrado escuadrón se ponga en marcha aparecerá en el cielo una estrella nueva, sólo visible para los cruzados, una estrella refulgente y sonora, que cantará un canto nuevo en esta larga noche que nos envuelve, y la estrella se pondrá en marcha en cuanto se ponga en marcha el escuadrón de los cruzados, y cuando hayan vencido en su cruzada, o cuando hayan sucumbido todos – que es acaso la manera única de vencer de veras –, la estrella caerá del cielo, y en el sitio en donde caiga allí está el sepulcro. El sepulcro está donde muera el escuadrón.)[42]

Unamuno, here, associates Quixote with an imperialist-crusader ethos; it is almost impossible to miss the parallel between Quixote's sepulchre and Santiago's, the discovery of which set off the Reconquista in Spain in the ninth century.[43] This origin – and the troubling parallel that Unamuno later establishes between Quixote and the best-known Spanish conquistadors – characterizes Quixote's heroic pursuits as essentially imperialistic: "What led to Don Quijote, Colón, Cortés o Pizarro, and Magallanes's actions, and [those of] all the other members of the lasting race of heroes? A generous and big dream: the dream of glory" (¿Qué llevó a la acción a Don Quijote, y a Colón, y a Cortés y Pizarro y Magallanes y a toda la perdurable raza de los heroes? Un sueño generoso y grande: el sueño de Gloria).[44] Unamuno goes on to associate this panegyric with other proto-fascist ideas, such as a distrust for knowledge,[45] the blind exaltation of faith,[46] and the justification of violence as a course of action:

What are we are going to do while we are on our way? What? Fight! Fight! And how? What if you encounter a liar along the way? Shout at the man in his face, "Lie!" and keep going! What if you find a man who steals? Shout, "Thief!" and keep going! What if you find one talking nonsense, who is listened to by a jaw-dropped crowd? Scream at all of them, "Stupid!" and keep going. Always, keep going!

(Qué vamos a hacer en el camino mientras marchamos? ¿Qué? ¡Luchar! ¡Luchar!, y ¿cómo? ¿Cómo? ¿Tropezáis con uno que miente?, gritarle a la cara: ¡mentira!, y ¡adelante! ¿Tropezáis con uno que roba?, gritarle:

¡ladrón!, y ¡adelante! ¿Tropezáis con uno que dice tonterías, a quien oye toda una muchedumbre con la boca abierta?, gritarles: ¡estúpidos!, y ¡adelante! ¡Adelante siempre!)[47]

Invocations such as these clearly detach the knight from Quixote's fictional framework, stripping him of any erotic or amorous aspiration, and detaching him, too, from the humanist context in which the novel heavily invests. The main emphases of Unamuno's (and his fellow Romantic critics') readings are the chivalric ethos of the character and the supposedly direct ties linking this ideal to the Spanish Empire, an association that Francoist ideologues such as Ramiro de Ledesma would promptly celebrate. In his *Conquista del estado* (1931), in fact, Ledesma explicitly commends Unamuno's Cervantism for having given "the war tone" to young *falangistas*:[48] "[Unamuno], who imagined a crusade to rescue Don Quixote's grave, in 1908 produced some of the most energetic pages that the universal [Spanish] spirit has seen lately, urging us to mobilize with our bayonets under the imperial cry to dominate" ([Unamuno] que imaginó una cruzada para rescatar el sepulcro de Don Quijote, lanzó a los aires hacia 1908 las páginas más vigorosas de que el espíritu universal de estos años últimos – movilizado con bayonetas al grito imperial de predominio).[49]

Ledesma's perspective obviously misrepresents that of Unamuno, who in other texts came to symbolize a brave opposition to fascism – as epitomized in his famous "you will win but will not convince" (Venceréis pero no convenceréis).[50] Nevertheless, Ledesma's use of Unamuno's words testifies to the eagerness (and ease) with which Falangist and Francoist thinkers took advantage of the rich and suggestive imaginary left behind by the Generation of '98.

Demonstrating a strikingly different sensibility, Cernuda gives a voice to his own literary generation, the '27 writers, when he judges Unamuno's apology for the crusaders to be a "strange confusion" (extraña confusión) and "articulate rant" (elocuente tirada).[51] Cernuda censures Unamuno's secular pilgrimage for "locating in Don Quixote's grave the cure to all national evils and tragedies, even when Unamuno himself was not convinced that such a thing was possible" (como si al encontrar al fin aquel tan deseado sepulcro, aunque Unamuno mismo no está convencido de que tal cosa sea posible, todos los males y desgracias nacionales se curarían casi por ensalmo).[52] By reminding his reader that "behind Quixote lies his author, Cervantes" (tras don Quijote está su autor),[53] Cernuda encourages a more ideologically neutral reader to remember the eternity of Cervantes rather than the mortality of Don Quixote, thus deflecting Romantic – and Francoist – desires to pin nationalist hopes on the image of the knight's tomb, and to embrace a vision of *Don Quixote* from which *eros* had been evacuated in favour of force.

For writers of the Generation of '27, works like *Don Quixote*, rather than providing Spain with a political or literary gospel, constituted a masterful and largely misunderstood *tour de force*. Thus, just as Ledesma's understanding of Unamuno's metaphoric reading came to define the Fascist approach to Cervantes and his protagonist in the late 1930s and beyond, Cernuda's, Rebolledo's, and Aub's readings of *Don Quixote* would characterize the corrective logic of the post–Generation of '27 group that inherited their politics. Rather than celebrating the military thrust and aims – victory or glory – of a chivalric hero like Don Quixote, critics and poets such as Cernuda concentrated on the gentler motivation of the knight's quest, love. For them, the sentiment constituted the "most important, humanly accessible ... mirror of eternity," a delusion that Cervantes had masterfully exploited in his novel.[54] Thus, the '27 focus on love not only in *Don Quixote* but also in Cervantes would revolve around the illusionary dimension of this emotional experience, rather than on the celebration of the disastrous epic undertakings it produced.

The Erotic without the Heroic: Cervantes on Love

It is hardly surprising that, out of the many literary explorations on *eros* prompted by the '27's attention to the theme, Salinas's would be one of the most successful. The so-called poet of love had masterfully reflected on the emotion in his own poetry, which uniquely reflects polychronic "influences from the totality of the Spanish Lyric."[55] In fact, as Enric Bou has reminded us, Salinas's accomplishments as a poet have sometimes distracted us from his achievements as a critic, which "is a disservice to his reputation."[56] The critic-poet's fine irony and sensibility shine in his suggestive study entitled "The Best Love Letter of Spanish Literature" (La mejor carta de amores de la literatura española), dedicated to *Don Quixote*; using a thematic approach, Salinas focuses on a specific cluster of episodes (chapters 23–6) from the first part, where Quixote composes an intimate love letter to Dulcinea that Sancho must impossibly "hand deliver." In the many stages and accidents of this fictional composition, Salinas wittily infers Cervantes's critique of the artificiality of the Petrarchan and courtly paradigms of love, the two literary models chiefly responsible for Quixote's misguided attempt to live as a knight errant.

Salinas opens his essay by reminding us that it is Cardenio's diary (*libro de memorias*) – the book full of love poems and letters that Quixote and Sancho find accidentally – that first gives the knight the idea of writing his own missive. It is thus Cardenio's plight – not Dulcinea's absence – that first stimulates Quixote's poetic and erotic imagination. As the knight glances over the pages of that diary looking for the identity of the owner, he is increasingly inspired by its perfectly crafted poems deeply imbued in courtly and Petrarchan convention.[57] Salinas reminds us how Cervantes cleverly juxtaposes the effects that this stigmatized code has on knight and squire: while Quixote feels intimately enticed to produce a similar declaration of love, Sancho grows increasingly irritated by what he perceives to be the author's nonsensical speech.

This impasse is underscored by the commonly shared goal of finding out of the identity of the diary's author; after reading a sonnet cryptically dedicated to "Fili" – the generic name that many poets conventionally used to address the beloved – Sancho promptly concludes that "[f]rom this poem ... you can't learn anything" about the author or his lady (Por esa trova ... no se puede saber nada).[58] Forced to agree with him, Quixote then moves on from poetry to the more accessible love letters, only to quickly realize that they are hardly any clearer or more useful, since one could infer even "less ... than from the verses about the man who wrote it" ([m]enos por ésta que por los versos se puede sacar más de que quien [sic] la escribió).[59] Everywhere Quixote and Sancho turn to, they find – to Sancho's now full-fledged annoyance – the same customary "complaints, laments, suspicions, joys and sorrows" (quejas, lamentos, desconfianzas, favores, y desdenes).[60]

The experience cleverly exposes the alienating force of Petrarchism, a literary tradition that so obviously dissolved the ontological specificity of its practitioners. There is nobody better than Sancho to comically illustrate the tragic consequences of this loss of reference, as he does in chapter 25, when he hilariously figures out the real identity of Dulcinea. In understanding that Quixote's lady is no other than "Lorenzo Corchuelo's daughter, also known as Aldonza Lorenzo, is the lady of Dulcinea of Toboso" (la hija de Lorenzo Corhuelo es la señora Dulcinea del Toboso llamada por otro nombre Aldonza Lorenzo),[61] Sancho not only comprehends that this princess or empress of la Mancha is in reality one of his own hair-on-her-chest fellow peasants, but also, and more importantly, finally grasps the delusional impasse between the idealized, literary-constructed reference of his master and the material reference of the world they both share.

Salinas calls attention to how the materiality of Quixote's troubled letter brilliantly underscores this material divide; every corporeal detail of the knight's missive draws a starker contrast between the real circumstances of the Manchegans and the insubstantiality of the amatory discourse that produced Dulcinea in the first place. Salinas reminds us that

Quixote's love letter, in fact, stands in "humiliating proximity" (proximidad humillante) to the "donkey's bond" (célula de pollinos) that the astute Sancho has forced his master to write as payment for his services.[62] The comic, textual juxtaposition (of Quixote's love letter and Sancho's donkey contract) advances the full-fledged association between Dulcinea and the humble animal that will take place during the "enchantment" that Sancho will cast on the lady in the second part of the novel.[63]

In a classic Cervantine move, the letter serves a multitude of purposes. For Salinas, one of the most obvious is exposing the clash of literary and experiential perspectives of the two main protagonists of the novel, a clash that allows them to engage in one of the most sincere and in-depth conversations about the use and sense of literary "[a]rtifice, verbal ostentation, and detachment from reality" (artificio, encumbramiento verbal, su apartamiento de toda naturalidad) ever seen in Spanish literature.[64] It is in such conversation where we are able to see, with Sancho, how lost Quixote really is in his ardent defence of an empty literary convention, an attitude that declares him an expert in the "the logic of the absurd" (maestría en la lógica del absurdo), the fallacious (amatory) rationale that sustains the heroic edifice of chivalry.[65]

Salinas brilliantly guides his readers to understand that the novel ultimately declares all heroic and erotic pursuits involved in Quixote's chivalric quest, so heavily dependent on courtly and Petrarchan ideals, thin as air. Quixote's journey, rather than the bold guidance toward individual and collective glory that the '98 critics had made it out to be, constituted for Salinas a deep and far-reaching critique of the "masterful" but "delusional logic" that ruled Golden Age literature. Quixote's "lack of love" and of a "beloved" in this absurd quest – exactly what Zambrano would identify more than forty years later – far from indicating Cervantes's belief in the "cosmic" reach of the emotion, conveyed Cervantes's demolishing critique of the empty amatory and heroic patterns that defined some of the most reputed literary developments of this time.

Salinas's reading manages to detach Cervantes from the heavy symbolic excess and political manipulation that had defined a previous critical generation. The poet's keen critical sensibility and textually bound perspective demonstrates, furthermore, how '27 writers enriched Spanish Cervantism in a period that Close had so provocatively but inaccurately assessed in the late 1970s. Interpretations like Salinas's, Aub's, and Cernuda's, though unknown to Close, re-energized a particularly difficult moment of Spanish history with a refreshing dose of literary and critical apostasy. In (re)examining a theme like love in Cervantes, exiled authors ultimately sought to understand the literary prowess of the author, not the validity of their own preconceived opinions, and, whether Close knew or not, their contributions made us all better lovers of Cervantes's art.

NOTES

1 María Zambrano, "Discurso de María Zambrano," *Televisión española*, 10 October 2014, http://www.rtve.es/rtve/20141021/discurso-maria-zambrano-premio-cervantes-1988/1033544.shtml. Zambrano's view of love is often complex and paradoxical. In *La razón en la sombra*, for example, she claims that love is an emotion that allows any being to transcend its limits by gaining full awareness of its needs and fractures; love is, then, "a transcending force" (el amor trasciende siempre) that unravels and enhances the nature of whoever or whatever it touches (634).
2 Maeztu (1875–1936) *Don Quijote o el amor*, 153. Unless otherwise noted, all translations are mine.
3 The full quotation reads: "Más que la caballería, o cualquier otro tema, *Don Quijote de la Mancha* trata del amor" (More than chivalry or any other theme, *Don Quixote* is mostly concerned with love). Echevarría, "El prisionero del sexo," 15.
4 Diana de Armas's argument is that it is the expression of desire, not an obtuse idea of love, that rules most Cervantine fiction. "From its pastoral romance beginning to its Greek romance endings," she argues, "Cervantes's literary project focused on one recurrent question: how does one articulate the concept of desire?" (*Allegories of Love*, 92). Edward Dudley believes that, while "the role of love in ... *Quijote* is often overlooked in favor of more abstract considerations ... love, that is, the relationship between the sexes, is the basic concern of the entire book" ("The Wild Man Goes Baroque," 119). Henry Higuera similarly believes that love is explicitly invoked by Quixote is his famous Golden Age speech as the ultimate reason for the foundation of knight-errantry, since the order "is not instituted (as we might expect from the first sentence of the speech) to protect what is left of communism in the Golden Age, but what is left of the modest yet free love that characterized the maidens of that age ... 'for whose safety, as the ages passed and malice grew, the order of knight errant was established.'" (*Eros and Empire*, 113). However, other scholars, such as Cesário Bandera, continue to question not only Cervantes's willingness to capture a fulfilling romantic story but also his interest in understanding (or validating) the sentiment. Even in a case in which lovers have obviously risked their lives to escape literal and societal entrapments (e.g., Zoraida and Ruy Pérez de Viedma), Bandera wonders if the motivating factor Cervantes describes can really be called true love:

> [A]re they [Zoraida and Ruy Pérez de Viedma] really in love? The question has been asked occasionally of these two exemplary betrotheds. It seems to be a logical question. After all, if their story is supposed to stand in contrast to the other love stories, it seems logical to make sure that we are comparing apples with apples. But one must be careful, for the question sounds a little like the one every adolescent (at least in our modern Western culture) has asked of his or her own feelings: Is it really, really love? What if it is not? What if it is only infatuation, or only friendship, or maybe only a feeling of compassion, or something else? What are the signs of true love? How can I know for sure? (Bandera, *The Humble Story of Don Quixote*, 272)

As Bandera notes, the text does provide sufficient cues about this love story: the captive attention to Zoraida, her beauty, and so on. However, we are also given enough hints to equate this very peculiar affair with other romantic ventures from the novel – those of Grisóstomo and Marcela, or Cardenio and Luscinda, to name just two. In every case, Bandera argues, "Cervantes is not in the business of analyzing and categorizing feelings," since, for this critic, the author does not tackle some of the obvious questions about the main love stories he presents: "Is Don Quixote in love with Dulcinea in the same way that he is in love with Aldonza? Does it matter to him, or to Cervantes, whether or not a real Aldonza exists somewhere beyond fantastic Dulcinea? And what about Grisóstomo? Is he really in love with Marcela when he kills himself 'for love'? What of Cardenio? Does he go crazy out of love for Luscinda? Does Don Fernando love Dorotea, or Dorotea Fernando, or could it be something else here too?" (273). Bandera concludes: "Frankly, I do not think that Cervantes the novelist, the author of *Don Quixote*, ever worried about those questions" (ibid.).

5 By "the Generation of 1927," I refer to a group of writers and artists that includes, among others, Rafael Alberti (1902–99), Manuel Altolaguirre (1905–59), José Ramón Araña (1905–73), Max Aub (1903–72), Francisco Ayala (1906–2009), Luis Cernuda (1902–63), José Gaos (1900–69), Federico García Lorca (1898–1936), Pedro Salinas (1891–1951), Ramón J. Sender (1901–82), José María Luelmo (1904–91), Manuel Andújar (1913–94), Ramón J. Sender (1901–82), José Bergamín (1895–1983), and María Zambrano (1904–91), as well as painters José Caballero (1915–91), Eugenio Granell (1912–2001), Alfonso Ponce de León (1906–36), Maruja Mayo (1902–95), and Gregorio Prieto (1924–96). General but essential references for the study of this group include José Carlos Mainer, *Edad de Plata*; Anthony L. Geist, *La poética de la generación del 27 y las revistas literarias*; Francisco Javier Díez de Revenga, *Panorama crítico de la generación del 27*; and Antonio Martín Ezpeleta, *Las historias literarias de los escritores de la generación del 27*.

By recovering the forgotten female members of the generation, Tània Balló's multimedia project *Las sinsombrero* (Barcelona: Planeta, 2016) provides an idea of the foundational dimensions of the group that still await serious consideration.

6 "At most," Cernuda had complained, "we study 'Petrarchism' ... and that is about it" (the whole quote in Spanish reads: "a lo más se habla de 'petrarquismo' al referirse al amor entre los poetas renacentistas y eso es todo"). Luis Cernuda, *Estudios sobre la poesía española contemporánea*, 77–8.

7 Aub, *Manual de historia de literatura Española*, 303. All translations, unless otherwise noted, are my own.

8 Gaos, *Cervantes Novelista, dramaturgo, poeta*, 184.

9 Gili Gaya, Galatea *o el perfecto y verdadero amor*, 3.

10 Salinas, "La mejor carta de amores," 39–55.

11 Scholarship of the last twenty to thirty years has been working to correct this oversight, although these contributions too are taking some time to be completely registered in current critical discussions. See, for example, José Luis Abellán, *El exilio español de 1939*; Estaban Luis de Llera, *El último exilio español en América*; José María Balcés and José Antonio Pérez Bowie, *El exilio cultural de la Guerra Civil*; Francisco J. Caudet, *Hipótesis sobre el exilio republicano de 1939*; and Michael Ugarte, *Shifting Ground*.

12 Pulido, "El Quijote y el pensamiento teórico-literario en los exiliados del 39," 448. It should be noted that Pulido focuses on Salinas's case, the gentlest critic of '98 figures such as Unamuno. Her work is certainly full of insightful contributions. See "El Quijote y el pensamiento" and "El Quijote de Pedro Salinas en su contexto."

13 Salinas alludes tangentially to this tendency, establishing that this form of criticism "easily forgets, from the stilts of critical arrogance, that a poem has been written to be read and lived by the reader. The critic's only role is bringing the poet closer to the reader, rather than using him as a bell to announce his glory" (olvida muy fácilmente desde los zancos de la pedantería profesorial que el poema has sido escrito para ser leído y vivido por el lector.... la función del crítico es aproximar el poeta al lector y no encaramarse sobre ellos y que les sirvan de escabel para su gloria) *Quijote y lectura*, 20.

14 Rebolledo, "Sobre el quijotismo de Sancho Panza," 8; my emphasis.

15 Cernuda, "Cervantes" [1940] in *Obras Completas*, 671–2.

16 I am here identifying general, not uniform, trends. Within the '27 group, writers such as Gerardo Diego did not share these political ideas or the experience of exile. The philosopher Zambrano, who did have to leave the country, approached Cervantine fiction with a philosophical, often extra-textual, logic. Yet most of the members of her generation were exiled after the Civil War and ended up working as literature professors – a good number of them were professors of literature before the war – including

Salinas (Seville, Johns Hopkins, Wellesley), Cernuda (Glasgow, Cambridge, Mount Holyoke), Amado Alonso (Centro de Estudios Históricos, Instituto de Filología in Buenos Aires, Harvard), and Francisco Ayala (Princeton, Rutgers, New York University), among others. The peak of their critical activity coincided with that of the New Criticism movement in the 1940s and 1950s. Adopting a text-bound New Critic praxis would infuse formidable strength into their arguments, making their critical method diametrically opposed to that of the '98 critics. For more specific information on the academic careers of these diasporic figures, see Jose María Naharro, "Calderón Twentieth-century Literature in Exile."

17 For more on the national focus – and latent imperialism – of the '98 group's view of *Don Quixote*, see Christopher Britt Arredondo, *Quixotism* and Dagmar Vanderbosch, "Quixotism as a Poetic and National Project." For a general introduction to the political views of the group, see Joseph Harrison and Alan Hoyle's *Spain's 1898 Crisis*.

18 Britt Arredondo, *Quixotism*, 13.

19 See especially ibid., 8, 16, 69, 142, 173.

20 Like Bergamín, the national director of Agrarian Society, a good number of these intellectuals occupied prominent positions in the Republican government. Domenchina, for example, headed the Spanish Information Service of the Republican government, and Zambrano and Cernuda participated in the Pedagogical Missions, the well-known Republican educational initiative. Zambrano would later lead the Propaganda Department, while Salinas would be appointed as a researcher at the Centro de Estudios Históricos. Many others, like Alberti, Altolaguirre, and (León) Felipe, would be even more militant in the defence of the Republican government: Felipe and Altolaguirre enlisted and fought in the Republican army, and Alberti became the poetic voice of the Republican resistance in Madrid. For a detailed retrospective on the subject, see D. Moss's first chapter, "Intellectuals and the Second Republic," in *Political Poetry in the Wake of the Second Spanish Republic*. For more on the political inclinations of the generation, see Juan Cano Ballesta, *Voces airadas* and Manuel Aznar Soler, *República literaria y revolución (1920–1939)*.

21 Aub, *Manual* 291; Sénder. "Hace cuatro siglos que nació Cervantes," 169.

22 Aub, *Manual* 291.

23 Enríquez Calleja, "Emilia Pardo Bazán," 9.

24 Close, *The Romantic Approach to "Don Quixote,"* 256.

25 Ibid., 28. Many Cervantists have considered Close's evaluation of the Romantic approach a painful but necessary exercise: "[t]his is a book that needed to be written," observed Frank Pierce in a review soon after its publication in 1977 (477). In another review, Richard L. Predmore objected that a "partisan rhetoric" obsessed with denouncing the "perverse" errors

of the Romantic tradition dominated Close's work (258). Most scholars shared Close's objections to the Romantic detachment of Cervantes's text, agreeing that it had produced readings at best symbolic and at worst esoteric. Fellow Cervantists also concurred with Close's objection to the excessive weight Romantic critics gave to the historical circumstances of the Spanish turn of the century.

26 Close, *The Romantic Approach*, 28, 136.

27 Ibid., 257.

28 It seems that the greatest pushback that Close's "romantic" ideas received was right after the publication of the book, and that his general thesis has remined since then largely uncontested. Perhaps one of the most effective arguments against it was Ruth El Saffar's brilliant reminder that a novel like *Don Quixote* always gets "the last laugh," often being able to transcend the literal, symbolic, or historic awareness – and limitations – of its readers and critics (whether contemporary with Cervantes or not) (404). 404. Rachel Schmidt has more recently re-evaluated the critical Romantic addressed by Close in a more positive way. See her *Forms of Modernity*.

29 The quote is by Close, from a separate study on love: "Don Quixote's Love for Dulcinea," 246.

30 Cervantes, *El Ingenioso higalgo*, I.13: 175; *Don Quixote*, I.13: 90. All quotes from *El Ingenioso idalgo* are from Murillo's edition, and all translations – unless otherwise noted – are from Edith Grossman's *Don Quixote*.

31 Higuera, *Eros*, 9. As Lina Bolzoni points out, in the knight-errant tradition, "[l]ove implies overturning relationships of power ... [I]t is the power that undermines the epic code from within." "An Epic Poem of Peace," 272.

32 Higuera, *Eros*, 18.

33 See, for example, Bandera, *The Humble Story*, 160–2; Close's "The Liberation of the Galley Slaves and the *Ethos* of *Don Quijote* Part I"; Fuchs, "Dismantling Heroism"; and Rupp, *Heroic Forms*, 198–200.

34 In historical terms, its first fifty years were dominated by a series of failed governments: the Restoration first, the dictatorship of General Primo de Rivera later (in 1923), then the Second Republic in 1931, followed by Franco's regime in 1939.

35 Salinas, "La Generación del 98," in *Ensayos de la literatura hispánica*, 279.

36 Close, *The Romantic Approach*, 142.

37 Unamuno, *Vida de Don Quijote y Sancho*, 74.

38 Ibid., 104.

39 Ibid., 105.

40 Ibid., 109.

41 All quotations from this work are from the 1908 edition.

42 Unamuno, *Vida*, 27.

43 Britt Arredondo, *Quixotism*, 13.

44 Unamuno, *Obras completas*, 3: 957.

45 "[D]esconfía del arte, desconfía de la ciencia, por lo menos de eso que llaman arte y ciencia y no son sino mezquinos remedos del arte y de la ciencia verdaderos" (distrust art, distrust knowledge, because that which they are calling art and science are only miserable traces of the true art and science). Unamuno, *Vida*, 23.

46 "Que te baste tu fe. Tu fe será tu arte, tu fe será tu ciencia" (your faith should be enough. Your faith will be your science). Ibid., 24.

47 Ibid., 19.

48 To expand on the fascist appropriation of the Cervantine opus – and to see its ideological coincidences with and departures from Francoism – see Ferrán Gallego and Francisco Morente Valero's *Fascismo en España* and Jacques Lezra, "Filología y falange," expanded in 2016 in "*Contra todos los fueros de la muerte.*"

49 Ledesma, "Grandezas de Unamuno."

50 Kevin M. Cahill, in *To Bear Witness*, describes the famous scene when Salamanca had fallen to Franco's forces and Unamuno, as the provost of the university, defied the Falangist general who entered the academic space crying "Muerte a la inteligencia" (death to the intellectuals). Unamuno, as Cahill describes, "waited in vain for quiet and then slowly responded, 'Venceréis pero no convenceréis ... you will win but you will not convince.' You will win because you possess more than enough brute force, but you will not convince since to convince means to persuade. And in order to persuade you would need what you lack, reason, and right in the struggle. I consider it futile to exhort you to think of Spain. I have finished" (92).

51 Cernuda, "Cervantes" in *Obras Completas*, 673. Critics such as Aub, unlike Close, recognized the positive contributions of the Romantic school, which had been responsible for bringing "Cervantes back to the light" (Aub, "La Numancia de Cervantes," 55), after rescuing him "out of the contempt where certain Spanish [Restoration] authors had placed [him], (comically) believing [such Restauration authors] to be better than him" (Aub, "Algunos Quijotes," 42). Cernuda believed that Cervantes had been very inaccurately read by some of the critics of the '98 school, especially by Unamuno. The poet seems to be speaking from one generation to another when he posits: "Y si a Unamuno le molesta Cervantes, y pretende dejarle a un lado, *no pueden movernos* las mismas razones *a quienes sólo afecto, admiración y respeto sentimos hacia él*" (If Cervantes bothers Unamuno to the point of putting aside the author, *we cannot be moved by the same motive, since we only feel affection, admiration, and respect for him*) (*Obras Completas*, 673; emphasis added).

52 Cernuda, *Obras*, 673.

53 Ibid., 673.

54 Cernuda, *Estudios*, 91.
55 Barnstone, *My Voice Because of You*, xiv.
56 Bou, "Aafterword," 199. In full, Bou states that "[t]o read Pedro Salinas's work under the limited light of twentieth-century love poetry, no matter the depth and sophistication of his achievements, is a disservice to his reputation" (199).
57 The allusion to Fili reads:

> If I say you, Phyllis, then I am wrong,
> for evil has no place in so much good
> nor does my woe rain down on me from heav'n.
> Soon I must die, of that I can be sure;
> when the cause of the sickness is unknown
> only a miracle can find the cure. (*Don Quixote* I.23: 175–6)
> Si digo que sois vos, Fili, no acierto,
> que tanto mal en tanto bien no cabe,
> ni me viene del cielo esta rüina.
> Presto sabré de morir, que es lo más cierto;
> que al mal de quien la causa no se sabe
> milagro es acertar la medicina. (*Ingenioso Hidalgo* I.23: 282)

58 *Don Quixote* I.23: 176; *Ingenioso Hidalgo* I.23: 282.
59 *Don Quixote* I.23: 177; *Ingenioso Hidalgo* I.23: 283.
60 *Don Quixote* I.23: 177; *Ingenioso Hidalgo* I.23: 284.
61 *Don Quixote* 1.25: 199; *Ingenioso Hidalgo* I.25: 311.
62 Salinas, *La mejor carta*, 114–15.
63 The supposed "enchantment" takes place in *Don Quixote* II.10: 516–20. See Laguna's article "Eroticism in Unexpected Places."
64 Salinas, *La mejor carta*, 117.
65 Ibid.

REFERENCES

Abellán, José Luis. *El exilio español de 1939*. Madrid: Fundación universitaria, 1997.

Armas, Diana de. *Allegories of Love*. Oxford: Oxford University Press, 1991.

Aub, Max. "Algunos Quijotes." In *España y la Paz*. Mexico City: n.p., 1955. Reprinted in Aznar Soler, *De Max Aub a Cervantes*, 41–7.

– "La Numancia de Cervantes." *La Torre*, 14 April 1956. Reprinted in Aznar Soler, *De Max Aub a Cervantes*, 49–70.

– *Manual de historia de la literatura española: De los orígenes a Cervantes*. Vol. 1. Mexico City: Pormaca, 1960.

Aznar Soler, Manuel, ed. *De Max Aub a Cervantes*, Djelfa, Algeria: Segorbe, 1999.

– *República literaria y revolución (1920–1939).* Madrid: Renacimiento, 2010.
Balló, Tània. *Las sinsombrero.* Barcelona: Planeta, 2016.
Balcés, José María, and José Antonio Pérez Bowie. *El exilio cultural de la Guerra Civil (1936–1939).* Salamanca, ES: Ediciones Universidad, 2001.
Bandera, Cesáreo. *The Humble Story of Don Quixote: Reflections on the Birth of the Modern Novel.* Washington, DC: Catholic University of America Press, 2006.
Barnstone, Willis, *My Voice Because of You, by Pedro Salinas.* New York: SUNY University Press, 1976.
Bolzoni, Lina. "An Epic Poem of Peace: The Paradox of Representation of War in the Italian Chivalric Poetry of the Renaissance." In *War in Words: Transformations of War from Antiquity to Clausewitz,* edited by Marco Formisano and Hartmut Böhme, 271–90. Berlin and New York: DeGruyer, 2010.
Bou, Enric. "Afterword." In to *Love Poems by Pedro Salinas: My Voice Because of You and Letter Poems to Katherine.* Chicago: University of Chicago Press, 2010.
Britt Arredondo, Christopher. *Quixotism: The Imaginative Denial of Spain's Loss of Empire.* Albany, NY: SUNY Press, 2004.
Cahill, Kevin M. *To Bear Witness: A Journey of Healing and Solidarity.* Oxford: Oxford University Press, 2013.
Cano Ballesta, Juan. *Voces airadas.* Madrid: Cátedra, 2013.
Caudet, J. Francisco. *Hipótesis sobre el exilio republicano de 1939.* Madrid: Fundación Universitaria Española 1997.
Cernuda, Luis. *Estudios sobre la poesía española contemporánea.* Madrid: Guadarrama, 1957.
– *Obras Completas.* Edited by Derek Harris and Luis Maristany. Vol. 2. Madrid: Siruela, 1994.
– *Poesía y literatura,* vol. 2. Barcelona: Barral, 1975.
Cervantes, Miguel de Saavedra. *Don Quixote.* Translated by Edith Grossman. New York: HarperCollins, 2003.
– *El ingenioso hidalgo Don Quijote de la Mancha.* Edited by Luis A. Murillo. Madrid: Castalia, 1978.
Close, Anthony. "Don Quixote's Love for Dulcinea: A Study of Cervantine Irony." *Bulletin of Hispanic Studies* 50 (1973): 237–56.
– "The Liberation of the Galley Slaves and the *Ethos* of *Don Quijote* Part I." *Cervantes: Bulletin of the Cervantes Society of América* 27, no. 1 (2007): 11–30.
– *The Romantic Approach to "Don Quixote": A Critical History of the Romantic Tradition in "Quixote" Criticism.* Cambridge: Cambridge University Press, 1978.
Díez de Revenga, Francisco Javier. *Panorama crítico de la generación del 27.* Madrid: Castalia, 1987.
Dudley, Edward. "The Wild Man Goes Baroque." In *The Wild Man Within: An Image in Western Thought from the Renaissance to Romanticism,* edited by Edward Dudley and Maximillian E. Novak, 115–40. Pittsburgh, PA: University of Pittsburgh Press, 1972.

Echevarría, Roberto González. "El prisionero del sexo: El amor y la ley en Cervantes." *Temas* 32 (2003): 15–45.

El Saffar, Ruth. Review of *The Romantic Approach to "Don Quixote": A Critical History of the Romantic Tradition in "Quixote" Criticism*, by Anthony Close. *MLN* 94, no. 2 (1979): 399–405.

Enríquez Calleja, Isidoro. "Emilia Pardo Bazán." *Las Españas* 2 (1946): 9.

Fuchs, Barbara. "Dismantling Heroism: The Exhaustion of War in Don Quixote." *PMLA* 124, no. 5 (October 2009): 1842–6.

Gallego, Ferrán, and Francisco Morente Valero, eds. *Fascismo en España: Ensayos sobre los orígenes sociales y culturales del franquismo*. Barcelona: El Viejo Topo, 2005.

Gaos, Vicente. *Cervantes Novelista, dramaturgo, poeta*. Barcelona: Planeta, 1977.

Geist, Anthony L. *La poética de la generación del 27 y las revistas literarias: De la vanguardia al compromiso (1918–1936)*. Guadarrama, ES: Punto Omega, 1980.

Gili Gaya, Samuel. Galatea *o el perfecto y verdadero amor*. Madrid: n.p., 1948.

Harrison, Joseph, and Alan Hoyle. *Spain's 1898 Crisis: Regenerationism, Modernism, Postcolonialism*. Manchester: Manchester University Press, 2000.

Higuera, Henry. *Eros and Empire: Politics and Christianity in Don Quixote*. Lanham, MD: Rowman & Littlefield, 1995.

Laguna, Ana Maria. "Eroticism in Unexpected Places: Equine Love in *Don Quixote*." In *Sex and Gender in Cervantes / Sexo y género en Cervantes: Ensayos en honor de Adrienne Laskier Martin*, edited by Esther Fernández Rodríguez and Mercedes Alcalá Galán, 113–32. Kassel, DE: Reichenberger, 2019.

Ledesma, Ramiro de. "Grandezas de Unamuno." *La conquista del estado* 2 (March 1931), 1. http://filosofia.org/hem/193/lce/lce021a.htm. Accessed 1 January 2018.

Lezra, Jacques. *"Contra todos los fueros de la muerte": El suceso cervantino*. Buenos Aires: La Cebra, 2016.

– "Filología y falange." In *USA Cervantes: 39 cervantistas en Estados Unidos*, edited by Georgina Dopico Black and Francisco Layna, 761–90. Madrid: Polifemo, 2009.

Llera, Estaban Luis de. *El último exilio español en América, grandeza y miseria de una formidable aventura*. Madrid: Mafre, 1996.

Maeztu, Ramiro de. *Don Quijote o el amor, ensayos en simpatía*. Edited by Alberto Sánchez. Salamanca: Anaya, 1964.

Mainer, José Carlos. *Edad de Plata (1902–1932)*. Madrid: Cátedra, 1981.

Martín Ezpeleta, Antonio. *Las historias literarias de los escritores de la generación del 27*. Madrid: Arco, 2008.

Moss, D. "Intellectuals and the Second Republic." In *Political Poetry in the Wake of the Second Spanish Republic*, 1–32. London: Lexington, 2018.

Naharro, Jose María. "Calderón Twentieth-century Literature in Exile." In *The Cambridge History of Spanish Literature*, edited by David T. Gies, 620–7. Cambridge: Cambridge University Press, 2009.

Pierce, Frank. Review of *The Romantic Approach to "Don Quixote": A Critical History of the Romantic Tradition in "Quixote" Criticism*, by Anthony Close. *Modern Language Review* 74, no. 2 (1979): 477–8.
Predmore, Richard. L. Review of *The Romantic Approach to* Don Quixote: *A Critical History of the Romantic Tradition in Quixote Criticism*, by Anthony Close. *Modern Philology* 77, no. 2 (1979): 257–60.
Pulido Tellado, Genara. "El Quijote de Pedro Salinas en su contexto." In "Cervantes, política nacional y estética nacionalista 1920–1975." Special issue of *Ehumanista* 3 (2014): 1–19. http://www.ehumanista.ucsb.edu/cervantes/volumes/3. Accessed 1 June 2016.
– "El Quijote y el pensamiento teórico-literario en los exiliados del 39." In *El Quijote y el pensamiento teórico-literario: actas del Congreso Internacional celebrado en Madrid los días del 20 al 24 de junio de 2005*, edited by Miguel Angel Garrido Gallardo and Luis Alburquerque, 447–68. Madrid: Consejo Superior de Investigaciones Científicas, 2008.
Rebolledo, José Enrique. "Sobre el quijotismo de Sancho Panza." *Las Españas* 5 (1947): 8.
Rozas, Juan Manuel, *La generación del 27 desde dentro*. Madrid: Ediciones Itsmo, 1986.
Rupp, Stephen. *Heroic Forms: Cervantes and the Literature of War.* Toronto: University of Toronto Press, 2014.
Salinas, Pedro. *Ensayos de la literatura hispánica. Del "Cantar del Mío Cid," a García Lorca.* Madrid: Aguilar, 1961.
– "La mejor carta de amores de la literatura española" (1952). Reprinted in *La generación del 27 visita a Don Quijote*, 39–55. Madrid: Visor, 2005.
– *Quijote y lectura: Defensas y fragmentos*. Edited by Enric Bou. Madrid: ELR, 2005.
Schmidt, Rachel. *Forms of Modernity: "Don Quixote" and Modern Theories of the Novel.* Toronto: University of Toronto Press, 2011.
Sénder, Ramón J. "Hace cuatro siglos que nació Cervantes" in *La literaturas del exilio republicano de 1939*, edited by Manuel Aznar Soler, 167–70. Seville: Renacimiento, 2000.
Ugarte, Michael. *Shifting Ground: Spanish Civil War Exile Literature.* Durham, NC: Duke University Press, 1989.
Unamuno, Miguel de. *Obras completas*. 9 vols. Edited by M. García Blanco. Madrid: Escelicier, 1966–71.
– *Vida de Don Quijote y Sancho*. Madrid: Austral, 1908.
Vanderbosch, Dagmar. "Quixotism as a Poetic and National Project in the Early Twentieth-Century Spanish Essay." In *International Don Quixote*, edited by Theo D'haen and Reindert Dhondt, 15–32. Amsterdam: Rodopi, 2009.
Zambrano, María. *La razón en la sombra.* Madrid: Siruela, 2004.

Contributors

Mercedes Alcalá Galán (associate professor in the Department of Spanish and Portuguese, University of Wisconsin, Madison) explores poignant questions of early modern poetics, gender construction, and visual culture. She has published a book on Cervantes, entitled *Escritura desatada: poéticas de la representación en Cervantes* (Centro de Estudios Cervantinos, 2009), and another volume entitled *La silva curiosa de Julián de Medrano* (Peter Lang, 1998). She is the co-editor – with Antonio Cortijo-Ocaña and Francisco Layna Ranz – of the special issue "Si ya por atrevido no sale con las manos en la cabeza: el legado poético del Persiles cuatrocientos años después" *Ehumanista* 5 (2016), and with Esther Fernández Rodríguez, of the volume *Sex and Gender in Cervantes / Sexo y género en Cervantes: Ensayos en honor de Adrienne Laskier Martín* (Reichenberger, 2019). She is the author of more than sixty articles on early modern and contemporary Spanish literature and is the vice-president of the Cervantes Society of America.

Diana de Armas Wilson (professor emerita of Renaissance studies at Denver University) is the author of *Allegories of Love: Cervantes's* Persiles and Sigismunda (Princeton University Press, 1991) and *The Novel and the New World* (Oxford University Press, 2000). She has edited two volumes: *Quixotic Desire: Psychoanalytic Perspectives on Cervantes*, with Ruth El Saffar (Cornell University Press, 1993), and the latest Norton Critical Edition of *Don Quixote* (1999). She has also translated a Spanish chronicle of captivity in Ottoman Algiers in a volume titled *An Early Modern Dialogue with Islam* (Notre Dame University Press, 2011).

John Beusterien (professor, Texas Tech University) is author of *Canines in Cervantes and Velázquez: An Animal Studies Reading of Early Modern

Spain (Routledge, 2013) and *An Eye on Race: Perspectives from Theater in Imperial Spain* (Bucknell University Press, 2006). He has also co-edited *Death and Afterlife: The Case of the Early Modern Hispanic World* (University of Minnesota Press), *Sustaining Ecocriticism: Comparative Perspectives* (Pennsylvania State Press, 2013); and *Touching the Ground: Female Footwear in the Early Modern Hispanic World* (Routledge, 2013), which won the Collaborative Project Award, Society for the Study of Early Modern Women.

Joan Cammarata (professor of modern languages and literature at Manhattan College) has published widely on early modern Spanish literature, specifically on comparative approaches to early modern Spanish and British drama, women's discourse, and the socio-historical implications of Cervantes's *Don Quixote* and has more than thirty articles on these subjects. She has authored a book entitled the *Mythological Themes in the Works of Garcilaso de la Vega* (Porrúa, 1983) and edited the collection *Women in the Discourse of Early Modern Spain* (University Press of Florida, 2003).

Eli Cohen (visiting assistant professor of Spanish, Swarthmore College) specializes in early modern fiction, especially the origins of the novel in Spain and England. His current research focuses on the development of prose fiction in early modern Spain, with a particular emphasis on the writings of Cervantes and on the relationship between literature, perception, and knowledge in early modern Spanish fiction. He has published work on Cervantes's *Novelas ejemplares* and *Don Quijote.*

Eric Clifford Graf (Universidad Francisco Marroquin) has written numerous articles and essays on the *Poema de Mio Cid,* Garcilaso de la Vega, San Juan de la Cruz, El Greco, Miguel de Cervantes, José Cadalso, Sigmund Freud, Vicente Aleixandre, and Julio Cortázar, appearing on sites and in journals such as *PMLA, Modern Language Notes,* the *Bulletin of the Cervantes Society of America,* the *Journal of Spanish Cultural Studies, Hispanic Review,* and *Ehumanista.* He is also the author of *Cervantes and Modernity: Four Essays on* Don Quijote (Bucknell University Press, 2007); *De reyes a lobos: Seis ensayos sobre Cervantes* (Juan de la Cuesta, 2019); and *Anatomy of Liberty in* Don Quijote de la Mancha: *Religion, Feminism, Slavery, Politics and Economics in the First Modern Novel* (Lexington Books, forthcoming). In 2011, he received the Cervantes Society of America's Luis Murillo Award for best essay in the field.

Ana María Laguna (associate professor at Rutgers University–Camden) explores the relationship between literature, politics, and the visual arts, focusing on how literature reflects prominent artistic and socio-political anxieties. She is the author of *Cervantes and the Pictorial imagination* (Bucknell University Press, 2009) and various chapters and articles appearing in such venues as *MLN, Hispanic Review, Hispanófila,* and the *Bulletin of Comediantes.* She is currently a member of the executive and editorial board of the Cervantes Society of America.

Christina Lee (tenured research fellow in the Department of Spanish and Portuguese, Princeton University) has published *The Anxiety of Sameness in Early Modern Spain* (Manchester University Press, 2015), *Western Visions of Far East in a Transpacific Age* (Routledge, 2012), *Reading and Writing Subjects in Medieval and Golden Age Spain: Essays in Honor of Ronald E. Surtz* (Juan de la Cuesta, 2016), and the Spanish edition of Lope de Vega's *Los mártires del Japón* (Juan de la Cuesta, 2006). She is also the co-editor of the global history book series Connected Histories in Early Modern Europe, published by Arc Humanities Press. She is currently a member of the executive board of the Cervantes Society of America.

Jesús Maestro (professor in the Department of Spanish Literature and Literary Theory, University of Vigo, Spain) is the author of more than eighty articles on Golden Age literature. He is also the founding editorial member of two journals, the *Revista de poética de teatro* and the *Anuario de estudios cervantinos.* He has published thirteen volumes as the main editor of Editorial Academia del Hispanismo, including *Crítica de la Razón Literaria. El Materialismo Filosófico como Teoría, Crítica, y Dialéctica de la Literatura,* 3 vols. (Hispanismo, 2017), *Cervantes y la filosofía* (Hispanismo, 2017), and *Cervantes y los géneros literarios* (Hispanismo, 2016).

Adrienne L. Martín (professor at University of California, Santa Cruz) has published dozens of articles in Spain, Latin America, and the United States on a variety of topics and genres of Golden Age literature, including Cervantes, Góngora, humour, sexuality, eroticism, and women's lyrics. She is the author of the following monographs: *An Erotic Philology of Golden Age Spain* (Vanderbilt University Press, 2008), *Venus venerada II: Literatura erótica y modernidad en España* (Universidad Complutense, 2007), *Venus venerada: Tradiciones eróticas de la literatura española* (Universidad Complutense, 2006), *La poesía erótica de Fray Melchor de la Serna* (2003), and *Cervantes and the*

Burlesque Sonnet (University of California Press, 1991). She was the editor of a special issue of *Calíope: Journal of the Society for Renaissance and Baroque Hispanic Poetry* on Golden Age erotic poetry (12, no. 2 [2006]) and the co-editor of a collected volume titled *Spain's Multicultural Legacies: Studies in Honor of Samuel G. Armistead* (Juan de la Cuesta, 2008). She is a former president of the Cervantes Society of America.

Jason McCloskey (associate professor of Spanish, Bucknell University) has published numerous articles in such venues as *Hispanic Review* and *Revista de Estudios Hispánicos*. He is the co-editor of *Signs of Power in Habsburg Spain and the New World* (Bucknell University Press, 2013).

Index

TORONTO IBERIC

1 Anthony J. Cascardi, *Cervantes, Literature, and the Discourse of Politics*
2 Jessica A. Boon, *The Mystical Science of the Soul: Medieval Cognition in Bernardino de Laredo's Recollection Method*
3 Susan Byrne, *Law and History in Cervantes' Don Quixote*
4 Mary E. Barnard and Frederick A. de Armas (eds), *Objects of Culture in the Literature of Imperial Spain*
5 Nil Santiáñez, *Topographies of Fascism: Habitus, Space, and Writing in Twentieth-Century Spain*
6 Nelson Orringer, *Lorca in Tune with Falla: Literary and Musical Interludes*
7 Ana M. Gómez-Bravo, *Textual Agency: Writing Culture and Social Networks in Fifteenth-Century Spain*
8 Javier Irigoyen-García, *The Spanish Arcadia: Sheep Herding, Pastoral Discourse, and Ethnicity in Early Modern Spain*
9 Stephanie Sieburth, *Survival Songs: Conchita Piquer's* Coplas *and Franco's Regime of Terror*
10 Christine Arkinstall, *Spanish Female Writers and the Freethinking Press, 1879–1926*
11 Margaret Boyle, *Unruly Women: Performance, Penitence, and Punishment in Early Modern Spain*

12 Evelina Gužauskytė, *Christopher Columbus's Naming in the* diarios *of the Four Voyages (1492–1504): A Discourse of Negotiation*
13 Mary E. Barnard, *Garcilaso de la Vega and the Material Culture of Renaissance Europe*
14 William Viestenz, *By the Grace of God: Francoist Spain and the Sacred Roots of Political Imagination*
15 Michael Scham, Lector Ludens: *The Representation of Games and Play in Cervantes*
16 Stephen Rupp, *Heroic Forms: Cervantes and the Literature of War*
17 Enrique Fernandez, *Anxieties of Interiority and Dissection in Early Modern Spain*
18 Susan Byrne, *Ficino in Spain*
19 Patricia M. Keller, *Ghostly Landscapes: Film, Photography, and the Aesthetics of Haunting in Contemporary Spanish Culture*
20 Carolyn A. Nadeau, *Food Matters: Alonso Quijano's Diet and the Discourse of Food in Early Modern Spain*
21 Cristian Berco, *From Body to Community: Venereal Disease and Society in Baroque Spain*
22 Elizabeth R. Wright, *The Epic of Juan Latino: Dilemmas of Race and Religion in Renaissance Spain*
23 Ryan D. Giles, *Inscribed Power: Amulets and Magic in Early Spanish Literature*
24 Jorge Pérez, *Confessional Cinema: Religion, Film, and Modernity in Spain's Development Years (1960–1975)*
25 Joan Ramon Resina, *Josep Pla: Seeing the World in the Form of Articles*
26 Javier Irigoyen-García, *"Moors Dressed as Moors": Clothing, Social Distinction, and Ethnicity in Early Modern Iberia*
27 Jean Dangler, *Edging toward Iberia*
28 Ryan D. Giles and Steven Wagschal (eds), *Beyond Sight: Engaging the Senses in Iberian Literatures and Cultures, 1200–1750*
29 Silvia Bermúdez, *Rocking the Boat: Migration and Race in Contemporary Spanish Music*
30 Hilaire Kallendorf, *Ambiguous Antidotes: Virtue as Vaccine for Vice in Early Modern Spain*
31 Leslie Harkema, *Spanish Modernism and the Poetics of Youth: From Miguel de Unamuno to* La Joven Literatura
32 Benjamin Fraser, *Cognitive Disability Aesthetics: Visual Culture, Disability Representations, and the (In)Visibility of Cognitive Difference*
33 Robert Patrick Newcomb, *Iberianism and Crisis: Spain and Portugal at the Turn of the Twentieth Century*
34 Sara J. Brenneis, *Spaniards in Mauthausen: Representations of a Nazi Concentration Camp, 1940–2015*

35 Silvia Bermúdez and Roberta Johnson (eds), *A New History of Iberian Feminisms*
36 Steven Wagschal, *Minding Animals In the Old and New Worlds: A Cognitive Historical Analysis*
37 Heather Bamford, *Cultures of the Fragment: Uses of the Iberian Manuscript, 1100–1600*
38 Enrique Garcia Santo-Tomás (ed), *Science on Stage in Early Modern Spain*
39 Marina Brownlee (ed), *Cervantes'* Persiles *and the Travails of Romance*
40 Sarah Thomas, *Inhabiting the In-Between: Childhood and Cinema in Spain's Long Transition*
41 David A. Wacks, *Medieval Iberian Crusade Fiction and the Mediterranean World*
42 Rosilie Hernández, *Immaculate Conceptions: The Power of the Religious Imagination in Early Modern Spain*
43 Mary Coffey and Margot Versteeg (eds), *Imagined Truths: Realism in Modern Spanish Literature and Culture*
44 Diana Aramburu, *Resisting Invisibility: Detecting the Female Body in Spanish Crime Fiction*
45 Samuel Amago and Matthew J. Marr (eds), *Consequential Art: Comics Culture in Contemporary Spain*
46 Richard P. Kinkade, *Dawn of a Dynasty: The Life and Times of Infante Manuel of Castile*
47 Jill Robbins, *Poetry and Crisis: Cultural Politics and Citizenship in the Wake of the Madrid Bombings*
48 Ana María Laguna and John Beusterien (eds), *Goodbye Eros: Recasting Forms and Norms of Love in the Age of Cervantes*